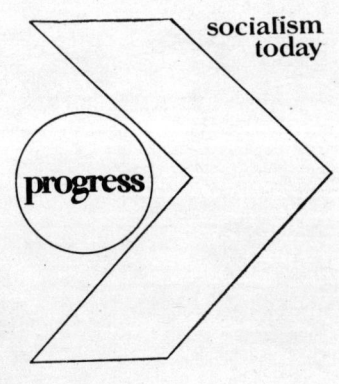

A. KH. MAKHNENKO

The State Law of the Socialist Countries

Edited by Candidate of Juridical Sciences, Docent *B. A. Strashun*

PROGRESS PUBLISHERS
MOSCOW

Translated from the Russian by *Denis Ogden*

А. Х. МАХНЕНКО

ГОСУДАРСТВЕННОЕ ПРАВО СОЦИАЛИСТИЧЕСКИХ СТРАН

На английском языке

First printing 1976

© Издательство «Прогресс», 1976

© Translation into English. Progress Publishers 1976
Printed in the Union of Soviet Socialist Republics

CONTENTS

Introduction 9

Chapter I. STATE LAW AS A BRANCH OF LAW AND SCIENCE. METHOD OF EXPOSITION 18

1. Introductory Remarks 18
2. Fundamental Elements in the Definition of State Law . . 19
3. The Subject-Matter of State Law. State-Legal Relationships and Their Subjects 21
4. The Definition of State Law. The Place of State Law in the System of Socialist Law 26
5. The Sources of the State Law of the Socialist Countries 34
6. The Science of the State Law of the Socialist Countries, Its System and Party Spirit 39

Chapter II. THE CONSTITUTIONS OF THE SOCIALIST COUNTRIES. 49

1. The Essence of the Constitutions of the Socialist Countries 49
2. Fundamental Features of the Constitutions of the Socialist Countries 55
3. Distinctive Features of the Constitutions of the Socialist Countries 59
4. The Juridical Nature of the Constitutions of the Socialist Countries 62
5. The Democratic Procedure of the Drafting, Adoption and Amendment of the Constitutions of the Socialist Countries 65

Chapter III. THE CONSTITUTIONAL FOUNDATIONS OF THE SOCIAL STRUCTURE OF THE SOCIALIST COUNTRIES 69

1. Introductory Remarks 69
2. The Class Nature, Purposes and Functions of the State in the Socialist Countries 73
3. Representative Organs as the Foundations of the State Apparatus of the Socialist Countries 91
4. The Economic Foundation and Structure of the Socialist Countries 99
5. The Class Structure of Society in the Socialist Countries 114
6. State Planning of Economic and Cultural Development 124
7. Labour—a Duty and Matter of Honour for Every Citizen. The Socialist Principle of Distribution According to Work Done 128

Chapter IV. THE ROLE OF THE COMMUNIST AND ASSOCIATED DEMOCRATIC PARTIES AND MASS ORGANISATIONS IN THE POLITICAL STRUCTURE OF SOCIETY IN THE SOCIALIST COUNTRIES 131

1. The Communist (Workers') Parties—the Leading and Guiding Force in the Socialist State and Society 131
2. The Role of Mass Organisations in the Political Structure of the Society; Their Participation in the Implementation of the Functions and Tasks of the Socialist State . . . 144
3. The Place and Role of Non-Communist Democratic Parties in the Political Structure of the Society and Forms of Their Co-operation with the Communist (Workers') Parties . . 162
4. The People's (National) Front 174

Chapter V. CITIZENSHIP AND THE CONSTITUTIONAL FOUNDATIONS OF THE LEGAL STATUS OF CITIZENS IN THE SOCIALIST COUNTRIES 185

1. Introductory Remarks 185
2. Citizenship 186
3. The Socialist Democratic Character of the Constitutional Rights and Duties of Citizens of Socialist Countries . . 190
4. The Equality of Citizens Irrespective of Sex, Race, Nationality or Religious Persuasion 193
5. Constitutional Rights in the Socialist Countries 196
6. The Constitutional Duties of Citizens of the Socialist Countries 202

Chapter VI. THE NATIONAL-TERRITORIAL STRUCTURE OF THE MULTI-NATIONAL SOCIALIST STATES . . 206

1. Introductory Remarks 206
2. Socialist Federalism 207
3. National-Territorial Autonomy 221

Chapter VII. THE SYSTEM OF STATE ORGANS IN THE SOCIALIST COUNTRIES 232

1. Introductory Remarks 232
2. The Basic Types of State Organs in the Socialist Countries 232
3. Distinctive Structure of Organs of Control in Some Socialist Countries 239
4. Special Organs of Constitutional Control in Certain Socialist Countries 242

Chapter VIII. THE CONSTITUTIONAL PRINCIPLES GOVERNING THE ORGANISATION AND FUNCTIONING OF STATE ORGANS IN THE SOCIALIST COUNTRIES 247

1. Introductory Remarks 247
2. The Constitutional Foundations (Principles) Underlying the Organisation and Functioning of the Organs of the Socialist State 248
3. The Active Participation of the Mass of the Working People in the Organisation and Functioning of the Organs of the Socialist State 251
4. Democratic Centralism 257
5. Proletarian (Socialist) Internationalism 260
6. Socialist Legality 264

Chapter IX. THE PRINCIPLES AND PROCEDURE GOVERNING THE FORMATION OF REPRESENTATIVE ORGANS OF STATE POWER IN THE SOCIALIST COUNTRIES 268

1. The Concept of an Electoral System 268
2. The Fundamental Principles of the Electoral Systems of the Socialist Countries 270
3. The Organisation and Conduct of Elections 288

Chapter X. THE SUPREME REPRESENTATIVE ORGANS OF STATE POWER OF THE SOCIALIST COUNTRIES 298

1. General Description of the Status and Role of Supreme Organs of State Power 298
2. The Internal Structure of the Supreme Representative Organs of State Power 309
3. The Term of Office and Procedure of the Supreme Organs of State Power 330
4. Legislation 341
5. Control Over the Work of Other State Bodies 354

Chapter XI. HIGHER ORGANS OF STATE POWER ELECTED BY SUPREME REPRESENTATIVE BODIES 365

Chapter XII. THE CONSTITUTIONAL FOUNDATIONS OF THE ORGANISATION AND FUNCTIONING OF THE HIGHER ORGANS OF STATE ADMINISTRATION IN THE SOCIALIST COUNTRIES 391

1. Title and Methods of Formation of Governments . . . 391
2. Composition and Term of Office 393
3. Powers and Procedure 396
4. Higher Departmental Organs of State Administration . . 399
5. Responsibility and Accountability to Supreme Organs of Popular Representation 402

Chapter XIII. THE LOCAL ORGANS OF STATE POWER OF THE SOCIALIST COUNTRIES 403

1. The Administrative-Territorial Division and the System of Local Organs of State Power 403
2. The Representative Character of Local Organs of State Power and the Legal Status of Their Members 408
3. The Powers of Local Organs of State Power 412
4. The Organisational Forms of Work of Local Organs of State Power 418
5. Popular Participation in the Work of Local Organs of Power 430
6. The Direction, Control and Supervision of the Work of Local Organs of Power and Administration 435

INTRODUCTION

The Great October Socialist Revolution ushered in a new era in the history of mankind—the era of the establishment of communism. It exerted a decisive influence on the historical destinies of the peoples of the Soviet Union and indeed of the whole of mankind. V. I. Lenin, the inspirer and organiser of the October Revolution and the founder and leader of the Communist Party of the Soviet Union (CPSU) and of the Soviet state, addressing the Third All-Russia Congress of Soviets, declared that the Congress had "consolidated the organisation of the new state power which was created by the October Revolution and has projected the lines of future socialist construction for the whole world, for the working people of all countries".[1]

We are now witnessing the fulfilment of these prophetic words. Today the peoples of many countries of Europe and Asia, together with the people of Cuba—the first socialist state in the Americas—have taken the road charted by the October Revolution. A world socialist system embracing 26 per cent of the territory of our planet, 35.2 per cent of its population and accounting for more than one-third of its industrial output has taken shape. The formation of the world socialist system has radically altered the balance of forces in the world arena in favour of socialism and the

---

[1] V. I. Lenin, *Collected Works*, Vol. 26, p. 479.

progressive forces. The Main Document adopted by the International Meeting of Communist and Workers' Parties in Moscow on June 17, 1969 noted that *"the main direction of mankind's development is determined by the world socialist system, the international working class, all revolutionary forces"*.[1]

The General Secretary of the Central Committee of the CPSU, Leonid Brezhnev, in his Report to the Party's 24th Congress, which took place in Moscow in March-April 1971, underlined that "socialism, which is firmly established in the states now constituting the world socialist system, has proved its great viability in the historical contest with capitalism".[2] He continued: "The socialist world is forging ahead and is continuously improving. Its development naturally runs through struggle between the new and the old, through the resolution of internal contradictions. The experience that has been accumulated helps the fraternal parties to find correct and timely resolution of the contradictions and confidently to advance along the path indicated by Marx, Engels and Lenin, the great teachers of the proletariat."[3]

The historical experience of the countries which are advancing along the road of socialism is clear and irrefutable testimony to the triumph of the Marxist-Leninist theory of the socialist transformation of society and to the historic significance of the Great October Socialist Revolution and the world's first socialist state to which it gave birth.

Leninism and the experience of the October Revolution and of the building of socialism in the USSR are by no means "purely Russian" phenomena, as the present-day revisionists assert. Lenin rightly pointed out that "certain fundamental features of our revolution have a significance

---

[1] *International Meeting of Communist and Workers' Parties, Moscow, 1969*, Prague, 1969, p. 13.
[2] *24th Congress of the CPSU*, Moscow, 1971, p. 9.
[3] Ibid., p. 19.

that is not local, or peculiarly national, or Russian alone, but international".[1] History has fully confirmed that forecast.

The experience of the USSR and the other socialist countries shows that the processes of the socialist revolution and the building of socialism, despite their distinctive features in particular countries, are founded upon a number of general fundamental laws. "Not only are we now theoretically aware but also have been convinced in practice that the way to socialism and its main features are determined by the general regularities, which are inherent in the development of all the socialist countries,"[2] said the Central Committee's Report to the 24th Congress of the CPSU.

Though various countries take different roads in their advance to socialism the following fundamental laws are common to all: some form of socialist revolution, including the destruction and replacement of the state machine created by the exploiting classes; the establishment of some form of the dictatorship of the proletariat, which acts in alliance with other sections of the working people, and the abolition of the exploiting classes; socialisation of the means of production and the establishment of socialist relations in production and in all spheres of public affairs in town and country; and a genuine cultural revolution—that is, full access to education and culture for all working people. Experience demonstrates that the main features of developed socialism are: the rule of the working people, with the working class playing the vanguard role, and the guidance of social development provided by the Marxist-Leninist Party; the social ownership of the means of production and on its basis the planned development of the entire national economy at an advanced technological level for the benefit of the whole people; the implementation of the principle

---

[1] V. I. Lenin, *Collected Works*, Vol. 31, p. 21.
[2] *24th Congress of the CPSU*, p. 9.

"From each according to his ability, to each according to his work"; the education of the whole people in the spirit of scientific communism and friendship with the peoples of the fraternal socialist countries and the working people of the whole world; and a foreign policy founded upon the principles of proletarian, socialist internationalism.[1]

The victorious building of socialism is impossible in any country unless the requirements predetermined by these laws are met.

Under the guise of the "creative development of Marxism-Leninism" the present-day revisionists revise and distort Marxist-Leninist theory regarding the fundamental laws of the socialist revolution and the building of socialism, and attempt to deny the fundamental objective laws governing social development which have been confirmed by life itself. They try to ignore or discredit the experience of the revolutionary workers' movement and of socialist construction. It is precisely for these reasons that they are viewed with such approbation by the imperialists.

By opposing the view that there are general laws governing the building of socialism, the revisionists try to divert the working class and the mass of the people from the only correct road of revolutionary struggle. They hope in this way to doom this struggle to defeat. The activities of the present-day revisionists amount in fact to a defence of capitalism and an attack on socialism. It is therefore necessary to make no concessions in the struggle against revisionism.

The Soviet Union—the first country in which developed socialism triumphed and the building of communism began—has the richest experience of socialist construction. The Communist Party of the Soviet Union was the first to pave the hitherto uncharted road to socialism.

The other socialist countries were in a more advanta-

---

[1] See L. I. Brezhnev, *Lenin's Cause Lives on and Triumphs*, Moscow, 1970, pp. 61-62.

geous position since they were able to use the experience of the Soviet state and the CPSU in the discovery and application of the general laws governing the development of socialism. The struggle of the Communist and Workers' parties and of the peoples of the socialist countries to build a new society was in this way made much easier.

The general principles governing the socialist revolution and the building of socialism are applied creatively in accordance with the concrete historical conditions of each country, and in the light of the distinctive features and traditions of each nation. The development of the socialist states confirms the Leninist postulate that "all nations will arrive at socialism—this is inevitable, but all will do so in not exactly the same way, each will contribute something of its own to some form of democracy, to some variety of the dictatorship of the proletariat, to the varying rate of socialist transformations in the different aspects of social life".[1]

Ridiculing anti-scientific attempts to depict the transition to socialism without the distinctive features of this transition in different countries, Lenin commented that "there is nothing more primitive from the viewpoint of theory, or more ridiculous from that of practice, than to paint, 'in the name of historical materialism', *this* aspect of the future in a monotonous grey. The result will be nothing more than Suzdal daubing".[2] Lenin frequently pointed to the need for the correct application of the fundamental laws governing the socialist development of society in a manner corresponding to the distinctive features of the nation or national state in question. "Following the victory of the socialist revolution in many countries," noted the International Meeting of Communist and Workers' Parties in Moscow in June 1969, "the building of socialism on the basis of general laws is proceeding in various forms, which take into account con-

---

[1] V. I. Lenin, *Collected Works,* Vol. 23, pp. 69-70.
[2] Ibid., Vol. 23, p. 70.

crete historical conditions and national distinctions."[1] To ignore these distinctions is to harm the cause of socialism.

But taking account of these distinctions has nothing in common with the artificial inflation of their significance. To exaggerate their role and to depart from the general laws governing socialist development, using national distinctions as the pretext, means to undermine the foundations of socialism. This is well understood by the enemies of socialism.

Theories of "national communism", "democratic socialism", "new roads" and "new models" of socialism are designed to make an absolute or fetish of the distinctive national features of particular countries. The proponents of such theories deny the existence of general laws governing the socialist revolution and the building of socialism. By doing so they seek to deny the importance of the Leninist postulates on the general laws governing the socialist reconstruction of society and the significance that the experience of building socialism in the USSR has for other countries. The real purpose of such theories is to detach the other socialist countries from the Soviet Union, to weaken and, if possible, undermine the unity of the socialist countries and to deprive the socialist countries of the opportunity to make use of the Soviet Union's rich experience. "In face of the strengthening of the international positions of socialism, imperialism tries to weaken the unity of the world socialist system. It uses the differences in the international revolutionary movement in an effort to split its ranks. It places its ideological apparatus, including mass media, in the service of anti-communism and its struggle against socialism, against all progressive forces."[2]

Championing the unity and solidarity of the socialist countries, the Marxist-Leninist parties, loyally carrying out their internationalist duty, stress the outstanding contribution which the CPSU and the Soviet Union have made to

---
[1] *International Meeting of Communist and Workers' Parties, Moscow, 1969*, p. 23.
[2] Ibid., p. 13.

the strengthening of socialism and democracy and to the defence of peace throughout the world. "... *the Communist Party of the Soviet Union and the Soviet people*," said János Kadár, First Secretary of the Central Committee of the Hungarian Socialist Workers' Party, at the International Meeting of Communist and Workers' Parties in Moscow in June 1969, "*which have equal rights with us and do not lay claim to more, bear an immeasurably greater responsibility than any of us.* Disinterestedly, acting in the spirit of internationalism, they have made, and are making, greater sacrifices than anyone else in the interests of communism, the freedom of the nations, for the prevention of a world war and for a happy future for mankind."[1] In his greeting address to the 24th Congress of the CPSU, Gustav Husák, First Secretary of the Central Committee of the Communist Party of Czechoslovakia, declared that "the Soviet Union is today the main bulwark of peace and progress throughout the world".[2]

The Report of the Central Committee of the CPSU to the Party's 24th Congress stressed that "the Communist Party of the Soviet Union has regarded and continues to regard as its internationalist duty in every way to promote the further growth of the might of the world socialist system".[3] The Report also noted that "the world socialist system has been making a great contribution to the fufilment of a task of such vital importance for all the peoples as the prevention of another world war. It is safe to say that many of the imperialist aggressors' plans were frustrated thanks to the existence of the world socialist system and its firm action".[4]

In the building and consolidation of a socialist state and in the creation and development of a socialist system of law, as in all other aspects of the life of society, the fraternal

---

[1] *International Meeting of Communist and Workers' Parties, Moscow, 1969,* p. 332.
[2] *Pravda,* April 2, 1971, p. 6.
[3] *24th Congress of the CPSU,* p. 19.
[4] Ibid., p. 9.

Marxist-Leninist parties are utilising the rich experience of the USSR and the experience of other socialist states, while taking into account the concrete historical conditions and distinctive national features of their own countries. This can clearly be seen in the field of state law.

The experience of the development of the Soviet state for the first time tested in practice and confirmed Lenin's teachings regarding the role of the Communist Party as the leading and guiding force of a socialist state and society, the alliance of the working class and the peasantry as the foundation of the dictatorship of the proletariat, the distinctive features of the forms assumed by the dictatorship of the proletariat determined by the specific conditions in a particular country, socialist democracy and its characteristic features and paths of development, the solution of the nationalities question in a socialist state, the principles underlying the building of a socialist state apparatus, the socialist reconstruction of agriculture, and other laws governing the transition from capitalism to socialism.

It is not only in the Soviet Union that Lenin's ideas constitute the theoretical basis for the solution of the most complex problems of revolutionary struggle and the building of socialism and communism. They also find triumphant expression in the achievements of the peoples of the fraternal socialist countries, and in the successes of the world communist and the national liberation movements.

"All the experience of world socialism and of the working-class and national liberation movements has confirmed the world significance of Marxist-Leninist teaching. The victory of the socialist revolution in a group of countries, the emergence of the world socialist system, the gains of the working-class movement in capitalist countries, the appearance of peoples of former colonial and semi-colonial countries in the arena of socio-political development as independent agents, and the unprecedented upsurge of the struggle against imperialism—all this is proof that Leninism is historically correct and expresses the fundamental needs of the modern age," declared the International Meeting of Communist and Workers' Parties held in Moscow in June 1969 in its Appeal marking the centenary of Lenin's birth.

"Today we have every justification for saying about Lenin's teaching what he himself said about Marxism: it is omnipotent, because it is true."[1]

Lenin never looked upon theory as a dogma. He considered it to be a guide to action. The continuing viability of his ideas derives from the fact that they are founded upon the creative development of Marxism. "For Marxists-Leninists, for all true revolutionaries, Leninism is the methodology of revolutionary thinking and revolutionary action. It is constantly enriched by the Communist Party of the Soviet Union and the international Communist movement on the basis of experience gained in the building of socialism and communism, of the living practice of the liberation movement."[2] The strength of the Leninist theory lies in its close link with life, with revolutionary practice, and in its combination of a creative, revolutionary approach with unswerving adherence to the principles of Marxism.

The experience of history shows that any departure from the principles of Marxism-Leninism and the internationalism which is characteristic of it, any attempt to substitute the bourgeois-liberal or pseudo-revolutionary phrase for scientific theory inevitably come into irreconcilable conflict with the historic tasks of the working class and the basic interests of socialism.

"Loyalty to Marxism-Leninism, to this great internationalist teaching, holds the promise of future successes of the Communist movement,"[3] declares the Appeal of the 1969 International Meeting of Communist and Workers' Parties.

---

[1] *International Meeting of Communist and Workers' Parties, Moscow, 1969*, p. 41.

[2] *On the Centenary of the Birth of V. I. Lenin*, Theses of the Central Committee, Communist Party of the Soviet Union, Moscow, 1970, p. 6.

[3] *International Meeting of Communist and Workers' Parties, Moscow, 1969*, p. 41.

CHAPTER I

STATE LAW AS A BRANCH OF LAW AND SCIENCE. METHOD OF EXPOSITION

1. INTRODUCTORY REMARKS

In defining the subject and concept of state law it is first of all necessary to establish the meaning of the term. It can mean, firstly, a *branch of law,* i.e., a particular totality of juridical norms, and, secondly, the corresponding *juridical science* which studies this branch of law.

As a branch of law, state law studies a particular sphere of social relationships. In this instance we are speaking of the subject-matter of regulation. To define the subject of state law (as a branch of law) is to describe the range of social relationships which are governed by it.

By contrast, when we refer to the subject of state law as a science, we have in mind the range of questions studied by that science. Consequently, here we have in mind the subject of investigation or study.

When we refer to state law as a branch of law, we have to bear in mind that each socialist country has its own state law which occupies a definite place in the legal system of that country and which has its own distinctive features. At the same time the state systems of the socialist countries are of the same socialist type. The state law of the socialist countries is therefore likewise of the same type, and it is consequently both possible and necessary to give a general definition of its subject-matter and concept.

2. FUNDAMENTAL ELEMENTS IN THE DEFINITION OF STATE LAW

The first requirement of a definition is that it should place the concept defined within a more general concept. "What is meant by giving a 'definition' ?" asked Lenin. "It means essentially to bring a given concept within a more comprehensive concept."[1] In accordance with this requirement the definition of state law in the first place includes an indication that it is a *branch* (part) of the socialist law of a given state. This implies that it shares all the fundamental characteristics of socialist law as a whole. Like any other branch of socialist law, state law constitutes an aggregate of juridical norms reflecting the will of the working people led by the working class and registering and regulating the corresponding social relationships.

This first element in the definition of the state law of the socialist countries—that it constitutes a *branch of the socialist law* of a particular country—is generally recognised by the socialist science of state law and gives rise to no discussion.

The fundamental difficulty lies in the clarification of the second element of the definition, in establishing the *distinctive characteristics which distinguish state law from other branches of law*. Substantive differences exist on this matter between jurists concerned with the socialist science of state law. These differences arise from differing views regarding the nature of the *subject-matter* of state law.

The delimitation of branches of law in accordance primarily with the *range of social relationships* which they govern—that is, according to the *subject of regulation*—is a generally-accepted approach in the Marxist-Leninist science of law. The subject of regulation is seen as the *fundamental criterion* in the distinguishing of this particular branch of law from the other branches.

---

[1] V. I. Lenin, *Collected Works*, Vol. 14, p. 146.

The *method of regulation* may also constitute an additional criterion. But it is applicable only in the delimitation of those branches which have substantive differences in methods of regulating the particular social relationships.[1] It helps, for example, to distinguish between the civil-legal and administrative-legal relationships which take shape in economic life. This criterion is of secondary importance in delimiting state law from other branches of law, since the difficulties of drawing a line between state law and such branches as civil, collective-farm and labour laws, recede into the background when compared with those of distinguishing between state and administrative law—branches

---

[1] The view that each branch of law has only the method of regulation which is characteristic of it is unacceptable. M. D. Shargorodsky and O. S. Joffe, for example, arguing that the method of regulation characteristic of state law differs from that characteristic of administrative law, as an example of such differences point to the general character of the norms and the absence of sanctions in state law (see *Sovietskoye gosudarstvo i pravo* No. 6, 1957, pp. 107-08). This point of view is also shared by V. F. Kotok (*Voprosy sovietskogo gosudarstvennogo prava*, USSR Academy of Sciences Publishers, 1959, p. 61). But it will be readily seen that these characteristics relate only to constitutional norms. They certainly do not relate to all the norms of state law. It should be noted that the majority of the norms of state law are, contrary to the assertion of Shargorodsky and Joffe, sufficiently concrete. Numerically general constitutional norms comprise only a part of state law. Sanctions are by no means such rare exceptions as Shargorodsky and Joffe suppose. A very large number of the norms of state law, such as those regarding the accountability of executive and administrative organs to the representative organs of state power, the rights and duties of deputies and the electoral rights of the citizens, carry appropriate juridical sanctions. The arguments of Shargorodsky and Joffe cannot therefore be considered valid. Their view that state law differs from administrative law by its distinctive method of regulation is based upon an incorrect identification of the norms of state law with constitutional norms. Criticising the view expressed by Shargorodsky and Joffe, V. S. Osnovin rightly observes that "by no means all the norms of Soviet state law regulate social relationships by means of general registration and establishment of norms" (V. S. Osnovin, *Normy sovietskogo gosudarstvennogo prava*, Gosyurizdat, Moscow, 1963, p. 41).

whose methods of regulation of the relevant social relationships are not distinguished by detectable differences.[1]

Some Soviet jurists see the subjective factor of the vested interest of the ruling class in the singling-out of an autonomous branch of law as being of significance in the grouping of legal norms in branches.[2] Such a vested interest can, however, only assist the establishment of a new branch of law within an already functioning legal system; it cannot constitute a criterion for the delimitation of different branches of law.

Only after the subject of regulation by state law has been established is it possible to define the range of social relationships governed by this branch of law and to disclose the second basic element in its definition.

3. THE SUBJECT-MATTER OF STATE LAW. STATE-LEGAL RELATIONSHIPS AND THEIR SUBJECTS

To define the subject-matter of state law means to establish which social relationships are regulated by it. Social relationships regulated by the norms of state law are state-law relationships. The definition of the subject-matter of state law is therefore inseparably bound up with the definition of these relationships.

The social relationships regulated by the norms of state law of the socialist type are numerous and varied in content. The problem is to single out the characteristic features which all of them have in common. The definition of these charac-

---

[1] Jurists from many socialist countries have indicated the special difficulties encountered in distinguishing state from administrative law. See: P. Stainov, A. Angelov, *Administrativno pravo na Narodna Republika Bulgaria. Obshcha chast*, Sofia, 1957, pp. 42-43; *Prawo administracyjne*. Praca zbiorowa pod red. M. Jaroszynskiego, Warsaw, 1952, p. 29; J. Starościak, *Prawo administracyjne*, Warsaw, 1969, p. 20.

[2] See I. V. Pavlov, *O sisteme sovietskogo sotsialisticheskogo prava* (*tezisy doklada*), Institute of Law of the USSR Academy of Sciences, Moscow, 1958, p. 7; A. I. Lepeshkin, *Kurs sovietskogo gosudarstvennogo prava*, Vol. 1, Gosyurizdat, Moscow, 1961, p. 11.

teristic features constitutes the briefest definition of the subject-matter of state law.

The characteristic feature of the social relationships regulated by state law is that they are directly linked with the organisation and functioning of the organs of state power (state or government bodies) which constitute the foundation of the entire machinery of a socialist state. It should be noted that state law likewise regulates social relationships arising from various forms of direct popular rule. But even these, as will be seen, are linked in the closest possible way with the functioning of the organs of state power.

An indication of the *direct* link between the relevant social relationships and the organisation and functioning of the organs of state power is a vital aspect of any precise definition of the subject-matter of state law. This can be illustrated by a concrete example. In the process of the implementation of the national economic plan and state budget (or local budgets) a complex system of legal relationships takes shape between various state organs, and between these organs, social (mass, non-government) organisations and citizens. All these legal relationships are *in the ultimate analysis linked* with the functioning of the organs of state power, since they serve to implement the decisions taken by these bodies regarding the plan and the budget. But among this wide range of legal relationships only those which are *directly linked* with the functioning of the organs of state power are categorised as state-legal relationships. Legal relationships in which a state agency is a direct participant (for example, the legal relationships arising between a Supreme Soviet or National Assembly and a Council of Ministers, or between a local Soviet and its Executive Committee in the discussion by representative bodies of reports on plan and budget implementation) are thus state-legal relationships. But the legal relationships between a Council of Ministers (the Executive Committee of a local Soviet) and Ministries (the departments offices of an Executive Committee) formed in connection with the fulfilment of a plan and the implementation of a budget are administrative-legal relationships, etc.

The boundaries of the subject-matter of state law are flexible. For example, in those socialist countries where during the first years after the establishment of popular rule there were either no local representative organs whatsoever, or where such organs had only limited powers, while authority in the localities was in the main exercised by administrative bodies (Poland, Bulgaria, Rumania, etc.), the relationships which arose in connection with the administrative and territorial division of the country were subject to administrative law, since this division was above all the basis for creating the system of administrative organs. After representative state bodies (councils) became the sole organs of state power in the localities, relationships arising from the territorial and administrative structure became part of the subject-matter of state law. Administrative and territorial divisions are, of course, still of great importance in administrative law. This does not, however, contradict the fact that administrative and territorial divisions now determine precisely the system of local representative organs of state power. The subject-matter of state law is constantly extending in step with the growing role of representative bodies throughout the entire system of state organs. This extension is a logical process in the evolution of the socialist state.

State-legal relationships arise between participants in these relationships who are termed their subjects. To define the range of subjects of state-legal relationships means to determine those between whom such relationships arise. We consider below who are the subjects of state-legal relationships in the socialist countries.

1. In the first instance, they are *the socialist state as a whole,* and also *national-state and national-administrative formations* incorporated in it.[1]

---

[1] In those socialist countries where such formations exist (see Chapter 6).

2. There is no single opinion in socialist state-legal literature as to whether or not *administrative and territorial units* constitute subjects of state-legal relationships.[1] In a number of socialist countries (the German Democratic Republic, Cuba, Yugoslavia) the constitutions lay down, in addition to the powers of local organs of power and administration, the legal status of the administrative and territorial units themselves, treating them as primary cells of the country's social and political organisation.[2] These units are therefore subjects of state-legal relationships by virtue of the law itself.

3. *Organs of the state* are likewise subjects of state-legal relationships. Organs of state power entering into legal relationships as organs of state power[3] are invariably subjects of these relationships. All other state organs are subjects of state-legal relationships only when the relationship in question is directly linked with the organisation and functioning of organs of state power. For example, when reporting on its work to a supreme organ of state power, a Council of Ministers is a subject of state-legal relationships. But when directing the work of ministries, it is the subject of an administrative-legal relationship. The relationships between a supreme organ of state power and a Supreme Court, and also a Procurator-General, relating to the election (appointment) and accountability of these organs to the supreme organ of state power, are likewise state-legal relationships.

4. State-legal relationships also arise between state organs and the *citizens*. For example, a citizen has the right to elect and be elected to organs of state power. Hence, a legal relationship arises between state organs and the citizens. Any

---

[1] See V. S. Osnovin, *Sovietskiye gosudarstvenno-pravoviye otnosheniya*, Yuridicheskaya Literatura, 1965, p. 42 ff.

[2] For a more detailed discussion, see Chapter 13 (1).

[3] A local Soviet may, for example, enter into a civil-legal relationship. But in such a case it acts not as an organ of state power, but as a juridical person.

citizen who has not been deprived of his electoral rights can be included in the electoral register, while the appropriate state body must ensure the exercise of that right. Any citizen has the right to lodge complaints regarding inaccuracies in the electoral register, while the appropriate body must examine such complaints, etc. Relationships of this kind between state organs and the citizens, governed by norms of state law, are state-legal relationships.

5. *Deputies,* who have a number of rights and obligations peculiar to them and arising from the organisation and exercise of state power, are special parties in state-legal relationships. They have the right of inquiry, for example. Deputies elected to all organs of state power must report to their constituents and may be recalled by them. In this way state-legal relationships arise between the deputies on the one hand, and organs of state or citizens on the other.

In a number of instances the norms of state law establish that no single deputy, but only a *group of deputies* may be a party in state-legal relationships. In the Polish People's Republic the submission of a draft law to the Seym requires the signatures of at least 15 deputies, and in the Rumanian Grand National Assembly at least 35.

6. *Social organisations* may also be independent parties in state-legal relationships. Thus, political parties and mass organisations of working people have the right to nominate candidates for election to organs of state power. In the majority of socialist countries (the exceptions being the USSR and the Mongolian People's Republic) organisations or organs of the People's or National Front are subjects of state-legal relationships.

A number of experts on state law also include the people among the subjects of state-legal relationships. In doing so they are prompted by the rightful desire to emphasise the role of the people. But no concrete form of state-legal relationships of which the people could be the subject has yet been indicated. The most frequently cited example is that of the referendum. But in this case it is citizens and electors who are the subjects. The *people* are not the subject of some particular state-legal relationships; they are the subject, the bearer of state power as a whole; absolutely all (and not particular) state-legal relationships in the socialist countries are directed towards ensuring the exercise of genuine people's rule.

Thus, the subjects of state-legal relationships in the socialist countries are: 1) the state as a whole, 2) national-state and national-administrative formations, 3) administrative-territorial units, 4) organs of state, 5) citizens, 6) deputies (both individually and in groups), 7) social organisations of working people.

4. THE DEFINITION OF STATE LAW. THE PLACE OF STATE LAW IN THE SYSTEM OF SOCIALIST LAW

Having established that the social relationships, which arise directly from the organisation and functioning of organs of state power, constitute the subject of regulation by state law, we are able to give a brief definition of state law itself. *The state law of each socialist country is that branch of its socialist law which regulates relationships directly arising from the organisation and functioning of the organs of state power.*

This definition reflects the essence of state law. Guided by it, we are able precisely to define the subject of regulation of state law and the subjects of regulation of other branches of law. This definition, however, does not demarcate the actual limits of the range of social relationships which comprise the subject-matter of state law. As Lenin observed, "... very brief definitions, although convenient, for they sum up the main points, are nevertheless inadequate, since we have to deduce from them some especially important features of the phenomenon that has to be defined".[1] A fuller definition of state law is therefore necessary.

---

[1] V. I. Lenin, *Collected Works*, Vol. 22, p. 266.

In formulating such a definition it is first of all necessary to decide whether all constitutional norms form part of state law.

It may at first sight seem that constitutional norms such as those relating to the economic basis and the principal forms of socialist ownership are "primarily" norms of civil and co-operative law, while those relating to the participation of People's Assessors in court proceedings, the public hearings, etc., are norms of procedural law. But in reality they primarily relate to representative organs of state power. The constitutional norms dealing with the economic basis of society and with the forms of socialist ownership place upon the supreme representative organ the obligation of observing and ensuring the implementation of these norms in the course of its legislative activity and in controlling other state organs. There are no civil-legal relationships which arise as a result of the *direct* application of constitutional norms. Such relationships arise as a result of the application of conventional laws and other normative acts which lay down the civil-legal methods by which the corresponding constitutional norms are implemented. Constitutional requirements regarding the elective nature of courts, the hearings with the participation of People's Assessors, etc., are likewise *not applied directly* in any socialist country. The organs of state power have in accordance with these requirements adopted legislative acts which lay down the procedure for the establishment and functioning of the courts. The relevant constitutional norms should therefore be considered norms of state law, since they lay down *direct legal obligations*.[1] It would therefore seem incorrect to exclude any constitutional norms from the category of state-legal norms.

So state law in the first instance embraces all constitutional norms. These norms, as an analysis of their content

---

[1] This does not preclude the interaction of a number of branches of law in the implementation of constitutional norms.

shows, establish the *constitutional foundations* of the social structure, of the organisation of nations within the framework of a socialist state, of the legal status of citizens, of the organisation and functioning of all state organs,[1] and of the participation of social organisations of working people in the exercise of state functions.[2] This requires some clarification. In the first place, why do we employ the concept "constitutional foundations" instead of the traditional concepts of "principles" or "fundamental principles"?

No socialist constitution *contains norms laying down all the principles* which govern the organisation and functioning of state organs. The principles governing the functioning of the courts, for example, include the adversary system and continuity of proceedings. But these principles are not mentioned in a single socialist constitution.

The statement that state law establishes only the fundamental principles of the juridical regulation of the relevant spheres of social relationships, although in substance the more correct, at the same time leaves considerable scope for subjective views. In the view of some, a particular principle may be fundamental, and hence the corresponding legal norms pertain to state law, while in the view of others it may not be fundamental.

Discussion on which principles of social structure and of the organisation and functioning of organs of state power, etc., are fundamental and which are not can be of value in the drawing up of new constitutions, or in the pre-

---

[1] Of course the concept of the constitutional foundations of the organisation and functioning of state organs embraces the structure of these bodies.

[2] There is no need specially to stipulate the affirmation of the sovereignty of the people among these constitutional norms, as do some authorities on state law (e.g. V. F. Kotok). The sovereignty of the people is an inseparable component part of a socialist social structure. It is safeguarded by the entire system of the organisation and functioning of the organs of the state, the fundamental rights of citizens, etc.

paration of amendments and addenda to existing constitutions.

In establishing the range of *operative* norms of state law, the sole criterion of fundamental principles, rights, etc., is their registration in the fundamental law—the constitution. It is for that reason that the concept of "constitutional foundations" is employed in the present work.

The subject-matter of state law includes only the constitutional foundations of the social structure. It does not include the social structure in its entirety, as some definitions of state law assert. The social structure embraces a complex aggregate of social relationships, some of which are regulated by law, while others are not. It will hardly be disputed that the functioning of the socialist economic system and the attitude to labour as a matter of honour are by no means exclusively the consequence of legal regulation. Moreover, the legal regulation of the socialist economic system, and of the organisation and payment of labour is implemented by many branches of law, including administrative, civil and labour.

The role of state law in relation to the social structure is limited to the establishment of its constitutional foundations.

Instead of the traditional concept of "state structure", that of the "national and territorial organisation of the state" will be employed in the present work. The point is that in Russian, as in many other languages, the terms "state structure" and "state system" are identical. They were used in this way by Lenin.[1] Socialist legal writings have justly pointed to the artificiality of a concept of "state structure", which embraces only a few aspects of the state structure that are mainly concerned with its national and territorial organisation, and also with citizenship and the territorial-administrative subdivision. They have also noted

---

[1] See V. I. Lenin, *Collected Works*, Vol. 8, p. 31; Vol. 24, pp. 107, 461 ff.

the contradiction between such a restricted understanding of this term and the Leninist concept of state structure.[1]

The inclusion in the definition of state law of the *constitutional foundations of the participation of mass organisations in the exercise of state functions* reflects the real processes taking place in the evolution of the socialist state and state law. It may be doubted whether it is worth while to refer to these constitutional foundations, and whether or not they are submerged by the constitutional foundations governing the organisation and functioning of state bodies. Indeed, the participation of the working people in the work of state bodies is one of the constitutional foundations of the latter's organisation and functioning. In particular, the people participate in the organisation and functioning of state bodies with the aid of mass organisations. But at the present time the role of these organisations is not confined to participation in the functioning of state bodies. The social organisations independently fulfil a large number of tasks which formerly lay within the competence of state organs. Hence, the establishment of this process in socialist constitutions cannot be reduced to one of the principles of the organisation and functioning of state organs.

State law is not, however, confined only to constitutional norms. As is rightly pointed out in socialist legal literature, it also embraces numerous norms of other juridical acts: laws, decrees, etc. In addition to constitutional norms, state law includes all juridical norms determining the national-territorial organisation of the socialist state, the forms in which direct popular rule is exercised, the organisation, functioning, competence and purposes of the organs of state power and the means by which mass orga-

---

[1] See K. Gościniak, J. Jarosz, "Prawo państwowe krajów demokracji ludowej", *Panstwo i Prawo*, No. 11, 1958, p. 842; N. P. Farberov, "O nekotorykh spornykh voprosakh v teorii sovietskogo gosudarstvennogo prava", *Sovietskoye gosudarstvo i pravo*, No. 9, 1961, pp. 138-40.

nisations participate in the formation and work of these bodies.

The subject-matter of state law—that is, the range of social relationships governed by it—should be divided into two groups. To the first group belong relationships comprising the constitutional foundations of the social structure, of the citizens' legal status, of the organisation and functioning of all state organs, and of the participation of social organisations in the exercise of state functions. In this area the subject-matter of state law is restricted by constitutional foundations. The remaining social relationships pertaining to the social structure, the organisation and functioning of the organs of the state, etc., are governed not only by state law but also by other branches of law. For example, the detailed juridical norms which govern the participation of social organisations in the formation and functioning of state power organs pertain to state law, while the functioning of administrative bodies is governed by administrative law, etc. But side by side with this first group there exists a second category of social relationships regulated exclusively by the norms of state law. Thus, relationships bearing on the national-territorial organisation of a socialist state, on the forms in which direct popular rule is implemented, and on the organisation, powers and functioning of state organs and forms of the participation of social organisations in the formation and functioning of those organs, are regulated *only* by the norms of state law. In this area state law is not restricted to the establishment and regulation of constitutional foundations, but embraces the entirety of the social relationships named.

Thus from one group of social relationships state law regulates only that part which comprises the constitutional foundations of the whole of that group. The other group is governed by state law alone. The existence of these two distinctive groups of social relationships comprising the subject-matter of state law must be reflected in a full definition of this branch of law.

Hence, socialist state law is that branch of socialist law which establishes the constitutional foundations of the social structure, the legal status of the citizen, the organisation and functioning of all state organs and of the participation of social organisations in the exercise of the state's functions; it is that branch of socialist law which establishes the national-territorial organisation of the socialist state, the forms in which direct popular rule is exercised, the organisation, authority and functioning of the organs of state power and the forms of the participation of social organisations in the formation and work of these organs.

Since the subject of regulation by state law is not confined to relationships comprising the constitutional foundations of the system, and therefore state law embraces not only constitutional norms but also numerous norms of conventional laws and other normative acts, the term "constitutional law" as applied to this branch of law is imprecise. It may be doubted whether relationships arising from the organisation of nations within the framework of a socialist state and from the exercise of various forms of direct popular rule may be included within the range of relationships directly bearing on the organisation and functioning of the organs of state power. It would seem that this is not only possible, but necessary.

In determining the status of national component parts of a socialist state and investing them with the appropriate range of rights and obligations, socialist state law lays down that the implementation of these rights and obligations in the first instance rests with the organs of state power of these national units, to which all other organs are subordinate. The national-territorial organisation of a socialist state primarily determines the structure of the representative organs of state power. Hence the relationships arising from the organisation of nations within the framework of a socialist state are directly linked with the organisation and functioning of the organs of state power.

As regards the forms in which direct popular rule is

exercised, we must not lose sight of the direct link which exists between these forms and the functioning of the organs of state power. The submission of a state issue to a referendum (a nationwide poll) or to a poll among the inhabitants of a particular administrative-territorial unit rightly lies within the competence of the organs of state power. The drafts of laws and other normative acts adopted as a result of a direct vote by electors must first be considered by representative state bodies. The promulgation of legal acts approved by a direct vote of the electors must also be a matter for the organs of state power. Thus, the relationships arising in the process of the exercise of various forms of direct popular rule—of course, to the extent to which these relationships are regulated by law[1]—are *directly* linked with the functioning of the organs of state power.

Each branch of law occupies a definite place in the system of law of the state in question. This place is determined by the range of social relationships which it governs.

As has already been said, state law is that branch of the law which reflects and lays down the constitutional foundations of the social structure of a socialist state, the legal status of citizens, the organisation and functioning of all organs of the state, etc. This determines the place of state law as a leading branch of law in the system of law of each socialist state.

To make this more clear, we will analyse the norms of state law and clarify their relationship with those of other branches.

Among the constitutional foundations of the socialist social structure the norms of state law of many socialist countries lay down the socialist ownership of the main instruments and means of production and socialist economic forms as the economic foundation of the state; they lay down that

---

[1] For example, decisions of a village meeting may impose obligations of a non-juridical nature upon the villagers.

the national economy shall be planned by the state and that foreign trade shall be a state monopoly; they establish the forms of socialist ownership and the items subject to such ownership; they lay down the right of peasants, handicraftsmen and artisans to own and to inherit means of production and the right of the citizens to own and inherit personal property. In this way state law lays down the basic principles of civil law.

By laying down the constitutional foundations of the organisation and functioning of the organs of state administration, state law determines the basic principles of administrative law.

The norms of state law which establish the citizen's right to labour, leisure, material security in old age and in case of sickness or disability are basic principles of labour law.

The norms of state law which lay down that judges shall be elected, independent and subject only to the law, that cases shall be adjudicated with the participation of People's Assessors, that hearings shall be public and that the accused shall be entitled to defence establish the basic principles of the law relating to criminal and civil procedure.

A similar relationship between the norms of state law and all other branches of law exists in every socialist country.

State law is therefore the leading branch of the law in all socialist countries. It sets down the basic principles for all other branches.

5. THE SOURCES OF THE STATE LAW OF THE SOCIALIST COUNTRIES

In the ultimate analysis the source of law, in the sense of the reason for particular norms, are the material conditions of the life of society. This is so in the case of state law as well. But as distinct from this concept of the source of law in this sense, the concept of the source of law in the juridical sense is also employed.

By the term source of state law in the juridical sense

we mean the forms in which the will of the state expressed in norms of state law is externally manifest.

In this sense, the sources of the state law of the socialist countries are:

1. The *constitutions* (Fundamental Laws) of the socialist republics, which are the basic sources of the state law of each country.

This is because, firstly, the fundamental laws establish the constitutional foundations of the social structure, the national-territorial organisation of the socialist state, the legal status of citizens, the organisation and functioning of all the organs of the state and of the participation of social organisations in the exercise of the functions of the state, that is to say, they set down the most important norms of the entire system of state law.

Secondly, constitutions, as Fundamental Laws, are the legal basis for all current legislation and predetermine the fundamental content of conventional laws and all other normative acts.

2. *Laws and other normative acts* adopted by the supreme representative organs of state power of the socialist states.

As examples, we may cite the law of the USSR dated October 12, 1967 "On the Approval of the Statute on Standing Committees of the Soviet of the Union and the Soviet of Nationalities of the Supreme Soviet of the USSR", the laws of 1968 adopted by the Union Republics on village and settlement Soviets of Working People's Deputies and the Republican laws of 1971 on district, city and ward Soviets of Working People's Deputies; and the Polish law "On National Councils" (January 25, 1958) and the "Statute on Elections to the National Councils" (October 31, 1957). Other normative acts adopted by supreme organs of state power in the form of resolutions and which constitute a source of state law include the Regulations of the Seym of the Polish People's Republic, of the People's Chamber of the German Democratic Republic and of the supreme organs of people's representation in several other socialist states.

3. *Decrees and resolutions* adopted by the higher collegiate organs of state power accountable to supreme organs of state power.

These include the decree of the Presidium of the Supreme Soviet of the USSR "On the Approval of the Statute on Elections to the Supreme Soviet of the USSR" (January 9, 1950) and subsequent amendments, the decree of the Council of State of the German Democratic Republic "On Elections to the People's Chamber and Local Representative Bodies of the German Democratic Republic (Statute on Elections)" (July 31, 1963) and subsequent amendments.

4. *Resolutions and instructions of the governments* of the socialist states, for example, the instruction of the Council of Ministers of the Polish People's Republic dated November 30, 1972, on the principles and procedure governing the election of *soltys* and *podsoltys*,[1] and on their terms of reference, rights and duties.

Mention should be made of the *joint resolutions of governments and central committees of Communist and Workers' parties*. Their special significance lies in that they simultaneously constitute normative legal acts and Party directives.

5. *Decisions of local organs of state power.* Some socialist experts on state law consider that decisions of local organs of state power cannot constitute a source of state law. For example, Professor B. Spasov (Bulgaria) writes: "If it is borne in mind that norms of state law govern the social relationships which relate to the foundations of our state and social system and which hence must be regulated in a uniform manner throughout the entire country, cases can scarcely arise in which primary measures of local organs of state power will establish norms of state law."[2] Professor Spasov concedes such a possibility only in cases when the

---

[1] Officials elected by rural community meetings.
[2] B. Spasov, A. Angelov, *Derzhavno pravo na Narodna Republika Bulgaria*, Sofia, 1968, p. 37.

measures of such bodies reproduce and carry further norms laid down by superior bodies.

But socialist state law, as has already been noted, is not confined to the regulation of the fundamentals of the state system, and regulates social relationships in a number of areas in an all-embracing manner. In particular, the juridical norms regulating the organisation and functioning of the representative organs of state power are all norms of state law. As an example of acts which comprise norms of state law and are directly established by local organs of state power we may cite decisions laying down the numerical composition of rural and city National Councils adopted by *voivod* National Councils in the Polish People's Republic.

Measures of local organs of state power are sources of state law only when they establish juridical norms regulating the organisation and functioning of representative organs of state power.

Some socialist experts on state law express the view that all legal acts which develop the constitution, make its principles more concrete and provide additional guarantees for its implementation are sources of state law.[1]

But in a socialist state all normative acts in greater or lesser degree promote the implementation of constitutional principles. Hence, to adopt this point of view would mean to include all normative acts of state bodies among the sources of state law. State law would thus absorb all other branches of law.

Some authors also consider custom[2] to be a source of socialist state law. Custom plays an important part in the organisation and functioning of representative organs of state power. Thus, it has become the custom in the majority

---

[1] See *Konstitutsionnoye pravo sotsialisticheskikh stran. Sbornik statei*, USSR Academy of Sciences Publishers, Moscow, 1963, p. 83.

[2] See *Gosudarstvennoye pravo stran narodnoi demokratii*, edited by V. F. Kotok, Gosyurizdat, Moscow, 1961, pp. 32-33.

of socialist countries for the government to resign at the first session of a newly-elected supreme representative body and for joint candidates of a People's (National) Front to be nominated for the elections to the organs of state power, although the law of several socialist countries contains no norm to this effect.

But despite the fact that custom constitutes a rule of behaviour, this rule does not have the criteria necessary for a juridical norm and therefore cannot be considered a source of law.[1] The observation of custom cannot be enforced by the coercive force of state power. The norms of socialist law are established, amended and repealed through the adoption of normative acts by the appropriate organs of state. Custom, on the other hand, grows up through practice, and its amendment and repeal does not require the promulgation of any normative acts.

Custom nevertheless plays an important part in the shaping of norms of state law. For example, many customs relating to the work of supreme organs of state power have subsequently been set down in their Regulations.

Hence, the sources of the state law of the socialist countries are their constitutions, the laws and other normative acts of their supreme organs of state power, the decrees, resolutions and instructions of their governments and the decisions of local organs of state power.

Constitutions are a source of state law *in their entirety*.

Not all the normative acts mentioned above constitute sources of state law, but *only those which contain norms of state law*.

A normative act may be a source of state law not in its entirety, but only to the extent to which it contains norms of state law.

---

[1] Academician S. Rozmaryn convincingly demonstrates that custom does not satisfy the requirements of a juridical norm (see S. Rozmaryn, *Konstytucja jako ustawa zasadnicza Polskiej Rzeczypospolitej Ludowej*, Warsaw, 1967, pp. 146-47).

6. THE SCIENCE OF THE STATE LAW OF THE SOCIALIST COUNTRIES, ITS SYSTEM AND PARTY SPIRIT

The science of the state law of the socialist countries is a branch of Marxist-Leninist legal science with its own specific field of study.

What is its subject-matter? Above all, it is the state law of the socialist countries as a branch of the law of each of those countries. Special attention is given to the analysis of the essence, distinctive characteristics and purpose of the constitutions of the socialist countries as a fundamental and most important source of the state law of these countries.

The science of the state law of the socialist countries is not confined to the study of the norms of state law. Its study of these norms is inseparably linked with a study of the social relationships which they regulate.

In studying the norms of state law in close connection with their practical application, the science of the state law of the socialist countries formulates the appropriate theoretical generalisations and brings to light the essence and significance of various state-legal acts and institutions.

The Marxist-Leninist teaching on state and law is the theoretical foundation for the science of the state law of the socialist countries.

Marx's and Engels' propositions regarding the relationship between the economic basis and the political superstructure, the class nature and interrelationships of the state and law and their role in the development of society, and the general laws governing the transition from capitalism to socialism, are of fundamental significance in the study of state law.

Lenin played a particularly important role in laying the theoretical foundations of the science of state law of a socialist type. In his writings he examined key problems of this branch of learning: its Party spirit; the nature and significance of the socialist constitution; the dictatorship of the proletariat as a special form of class alliance under the leadership of the working class; the varied state forms of the dictatorship of the proletariat, and the relationship between the dictatorship and democracy; the leading and guiding role of the Communist Party in the socialist state and society; the reconciling of the basic interests of the individual and the socialist state, and the fundamental principles determining the legal status of the citizen in a socialist state; the principles underlying the state-legal forms of the solution of the nationalities question in a socialist state and socialist federation and autonomy; the part played by organs of people's representation in the system of socialist democracy; and the principles governing the structure and functioning of a state apparatus of a socialist type. The guidelines formulated by Lenin, as will be shown in subsequent chapters, indicate the right road to the solution of appropriate state-legal problems in all the socialist countries, and retain their relevance to this day. Lenin made a substantial contribution to the development of a methodology for the study of state and law.

A concrete historical approach to the study of social phenomena is an essential feature of Marxism-Leninism. Lenin argued that the most important thing in ensuring a genuinely scientific approach to the study of social problems was "not to forget the underlying historical connection, to examine every question from the standpoint of how the given phenomenon arose in history and what were the principal stages in its development, and, from the standpoint of its development, to examine what it has become today".[1]

The science of the state law of the socialist countries therefore studies the institutions of state law in the process

---

[1] V. I. Lenin, *Collected Works*, Vol. 29, p. 473.

of their evolution. Its fundamental task is, of course, to study the currently operative state law of the socialist countries. Yet study of currently operative norms alone does not make it possible to understand fully and correctly their significance or to determine the direction in which this branch of law is evolving. It is necessary to compare currently operative norms with those of the past, to discover why norms were repealed or amended and why it became necessary to adopt new norms. The science of state law, unlike the general history of state and law which in a detailed and systematic fashion studies the historical development of the state and law (including the state and law of socialist countries), focuses attention upon those aspects of the emergence and development of the institutions of state law which are of the greatest significance in clarifying the present-day state law of the socialist countries and its developmental trends.

The very existence of a socialist state and the achievement of the aims set before it are inconceivable without the leading and guiding role of the Communist Party and the broad participation of mass organisations in the exercise of state functions. Socialist state law therefore concentrates on the study of the role of Marxist-Leninist parties and mass organisations in the functioning of the institutions of state law. Particular attention is paid to the new experience gained by the socialist countries.

In establishing and developing its own state law, each socialist country, while taking account of its own specifics draws upon the rich experience of the USSR—the first socialist state—and of other socialist states. Every socialist countries has now acquired its own experience of development in this field, and has evolved new forms for the organisation and functioning of representative organs of state power and for the involvement of the working people and their organisations in the exercise of state power. Some of this experience is of purely national significance because it is the product of distinctive features of the development of a particular country. But at the same time new state legal forms of the solutions for important problems of the development of the state have emerged in many socialist countries which have a significance extending beyond a single country, and which can be applied in other socialist countries.

The study of these new forms is a most important task for the science of the state law of the socialist countries, which should adhere to a concrete historical approach, refraining from any universal prescriptions and recommendations, since a solution which has proved valuable in one country may prove unsuitable in another. Moreover, the science of the state law of the socialist countries must pay particular attention to the study of the new experience gained during the development of each socialist state. It must comprehensively examine new state-legal institutions in each of these countries so that those working in state bodies have the necessary material to enable them to decide whether, in the conditions of their own country, it is expedient to draw upon the experience of other socialist countries. "World socialism", the General Secretary of the Central Committee of the CPSU, Leonid Brezhnev, told the International Meeting of Communist and Workers' Parties held in Moscow in June 1969, "absorbs all the wealth and diversity of the revolutionary traditions and experience deriving from the creative activity of the working people of different countries. In this connection we should like to say that our Party constantly studies that experience and utilises everything of value that may be applied in the conditions obtaining in the Soviet Union, everything that really helps to strengthen the socialist system and embodies the general laws of socialist construction, which have been tested by international experience".[1]

---

[1] *International Meeting of Communist and Workers' Parties, Moscow, 1969*, p. 148.

The comprehensive study of the state-legal institutions of the socialist countries enables us to assess better both the advantages and disadvantages of the solutions to particular problems adopted in different countries. It is a valuable aid in drafting measures designed to improve state law.

The study and critical generalisation of theoretical concepts relating both to state law as a whole and to its particular institutions are of great importance in gaining a deeper insight into the role and efficacy of the solution of problems of socialist state development in the state law of each country. Nor must this be confined to the consideration of the theoretical concepts and views of the jurists of a single country. The science of socialist state law has, of course, the longest traditions in the USSR, the first socialist state. But today it is being developed and enriched by the collective efforts of the jurists of all the socialist countries. The achievements of all the socialist countries must be utilised if the socialist science of state law is to develop successfully.

It may therefore be concluded that *as a science the state law of the socialist countries studies the operative state law of these countries in the light of the social relationships which it regulates, and also fundamental aspects of the emergence and development of institutions of state law, with the view to revealing their significance and the laws governing their development.*

A major task of this field of study is to thoroughly analyse and disseminate the most efficacious solutions of current problems of state development in the socialist countries in order to assist the improvement of the state law in these countries.

The system of the science of the state law in the socialist countries is primarily determined by the system of state law as a branch of juridical science.

"In a modern state," wrote Engels, "law must not only correspond to the general economic condition and be its expression, but must also be an *internally coherent* expression which does not, owing to inner contradictions, reduce itself to nought."[1]

The demand for internal coherence applies both to the entire system of law and to the system of a particular branch of that law in a given country. The system of state law as a branch of law finds expression in the interrelationship and coherence of all state-legal norms, grouped together in accordance with the corresponding state-legal institutions.

Both state-legal norms comprising a definite state-legal institution and all institutions of state law are internally coordinated and interrelated.

This interrelationship and coherence is a feature intrinsic in operative law itself. It is therefore impossible to share the view of those who consider that state-legal norms and state-legal relationships are amalgamated in separate institutions by the science of state law.[2]

Such a point of view introduces subjectivism into the concept of a system of law. In reality, science *does not amalgamate* the norms of state law into institutions of state law, but *brings to light* the relationships and internal coherence which *actually exist* between the various norms comprising particular institutions of state law.

An analysis of the content of state-legal norms from the viewpoint of their interrelationship enables us to establish that the main groups of these norms are made up of norms laying down: 1) the constitutional foundations of the social structure; 2) the national-territorial organisation of the socialist state; 3) citizenship and the constitutional foundations for the legal status of the citizen; 4) the constitutional foundations for the participation of social organisations in

---

[1] K. Marx and F. Engels, *Selected Works*, Vol. 3, Moscow, 1974, p. 492.
[2] See *Gosudarstvennoye pravo stran narodnoi demokratii*, edited by V. F. Kotok, p. 34.

the exercise of the functions of the state and the forms of their participation in the organisation and functioning of the representative organs of state power; 5) the constitutional foundations of the organisation and functioning of all the organs of the state, and also the organisation and functioning of the organs of state power.

The system of the science of state law takes as its starting point the system of operative state law, but at the same time is not identical with it. In considering the subject-matter of the science of state law, we have already established that it is not confined to the norms of state law and the relationships which they regulate. Hence, the system of the science must be *wider* than the system of the operative law. In addition, the system of the science may deviate from the system of the operative law, prompted by the need to achieve the maximum consistency in the study of the operative law. This makes it possible, in particular, to carry out a comparative study of the fundamental institutions of the state law of the socialist countries in accordance with a single system, despite the special characteristics of the structure of the system of the operative law in each of these countries.

Finally, in common with all other branches of law, the system of the science of state law embraces general theoretical principles (subject-matter, concept, sources, etc.).

The whole system of the science of the state law of the socialist countries is presented in the following way.

1. The subject-matter, concept, sources and system of state law.

2. The constitutions of the socialist countries.

3. The constitutional foundations of the social structure.

4. The place and role of the Communist parties and democratic parties allied to them and also of mass organisations in the political organisation of society.

5. Citizenship and the constitutional foundations of the legal status of the citizen.

6. The national-territorial organisation of multi-national socialist states.

7. The system of state organs and the constitutional foundations for their organisation and functioning.

8. The organisation and functioning of organs of state power.

The science of the state law of the socialist countries is deeply imbued with the Party spirit.

Marxism-Leninism teaches that in a class society any ideology reflects class interests. The theory of the state and hence of state law is one of the theories which most directly affect class interests. "In the question of the state, in the doctrine of the state, in the theory of the state, when you have become familiar with it and have gone into it deeply enough," wrote Lenin, "you will always discern the struggle between different classes, a struggle which is reflected or expressed in a conflict of views on the state, in the estimate of the role and significance of the state."[1]

The Marxist-Leninist Party spirit requires that in appraising events we should base ourselves firmly and frankly upon the point of view of the working class and the mass of the working people which it leads and wage an irreconcilable struggle against any distortion of Marxist-Leninist theory.

The spirit of the Communist Party differs fundamentally from that of the bourgeoisie. Firstly, it reflects the interests of the working class and the entire working people and hence of the overwhelming majority of society and, after the abolition of the exploiting classes and the establishment of the socialist unity of the people, of the entire people. The bourgeois partisanship, on the other hand, reflects the interests of a negligible minority of society.

Secondly, Marxism-Leninism explicitly affirms its partisanship precisely because it voices the interests of the people.

---
[1] V. I. Lenin, *Collected Works,* Vol. 29, p. 472.

Thirdly, Marxist-Leninist partisanship is linked inseparably with a genuinely scientific approach.

This is because the Marxist-Leninist science expresses the interests of the class which is consistently revolutionary—the working class and the working masses which it leads, whose interests wholly coincide with the objective laws governing the development of society. That is why the working class and all the working masses have a vital interest in the discovery and application of the objective laws of social development in the interests of society. A proletarian, communist partisanship is therefore inseparable from a strictly scientific approach.

* * *

The present volume describes the main features of the state law of the socialist countries.[1]

The exposition begins with an explanation of the concept and subject-matter of socialist state law and a description of its juridical sources.

The general processes characteristic of all the countries building socialism also determine the common principal features (common foundations) of their state law.

In addition to common fundamental principles, the state law of each particular socialist state has its own distinct features deriving from its national characteristics, historical traditions and from the actual conditions under which it is building socialism.

The present volume expounds the material in accordance with the uniform system of the fundamental institutions of the state law of the socialist countries, which are subjected to comparative analysis.

In examining each theme and each institution of state law and its component parts, a comprehensive analysis of

---

[1] Progress Publishers have issued a number of books dealing with aspects of the state system of the USSR. The present volume therefore discusses Soviet state law only in outline, in comparative terms.

the state-law material of all the socialist countries is given and classified in a manner making it possible clearly to indicate: 1) the features common to all socialist countries; 2) the distinct features of institutions of state law relating to particular groups of countries; 3) the distinct features of the state law of individual countries. The method of the comparative study of the main institutions of the state law of the socialist countries enables us clearly to highlight both the fundamental features and the specific characteristics of their state law.

CHAPTER II

THE CONSTITUTIONS OF THE SOCIALIST COUNTRIES

1. THE ESSENCE OF THE CONSTITUTIONS OF THE SOCIALIST COUNTRIES

The assumption of state power in a number of countries by the people headed by the working class, and the tremendous revolutionary transformations which have taken place in their economic, social and political life have brought about a fundamental change in the balance of class forces in these countries in favour of the working class and the mass of the working people which it leads.

It therefore became necessary to draw up constitutions (fundamental laws) which reflect this change, are based upon the principles of socialist democracy and establish the state power of the people led by the working class.

The essence of constitutions (fundamental laws) lies in that "the fundamental laws of the state in general, and the laws governing elections to and the powers of the representative institutions, etc., express the actual relation of forces in the class struggle".[1]

Major shifts in the balance of class forces in a particular country bring in their train the creation of a relevant constitution (fundamental law) of that country.

Changes in the balance of class forces can be of two kinds.

Firstly, such changes may find expression in the *transition of state power from the hands of one class (or group of*

---

[1] V. I. Lenin, *Collected Works*, Vol. 15, p. 336.

classes) into the hands of another class (or group of classes).
Changes of this kind, which are the most radical, make it necessary to adopt constitutions of *a new type*. For instance, the transition of state power in a number of countries from the capitalists and landowners to the working class and the mass of the working people led by it made it necessary to adopt new constitutions of a socialist type which expressed and enacted the genuine rule of the people.

The first socialist constitution in the history of mankind was that adopted on July 10, 1918 by the Fifth All-Russia Congress of Soviets—the Constitution of the Russian Soviet Federative Socialist Republic (RSFSR). "All constitutions that had existed till now safeguarded the interests of the ruling classes. The Soviet Constitution was the only one that served and would constantly serve the working people and was a powerful weapon in the fight for socialism,"[1] said Lenin. This Constitution reflected and consolidated the achievements which the first socialist state in the world had made during the first eight months after the October Socialist Revolution. Its clauses were not drafted in the tranquillity of chanceries but in the revolutionary struggle for the building of a new socialist society and state. "The Soviet Constitution, ratified in July, is, as we know ... not the creation of lawyers, nor is it copied from other constitutions. The world has never known such a constitution as ours. It embodies the workers' experience of struggle and organisation against the exploiters both at home and abroad,"[2] said Lenin.

In Russia the old state apparatus was destroyed completely and immediately during the October Socialist Revolution. The pre-revolutionary institutions of state law were repealed by the very first acts of Soviet power.

The same was true in some of the other socialist states which emerged after the Second World War. In Yugoslavia

---

[1] V. I. Lenin, *Collected Works*, Vol. 42, p. 105.
[2] Ibid., Vol. 28, pp. 145-46.

the bourgeois-monarchist state apparatus was destroyed during the national-liberation struggle against the nazi occupation forces and their collaborators—a struggle which simultaneously became a struggle against the bourgeois monarchist system. The very first measures of popular rule in Yugoslavia in effect totally revoked the bourgeois-monarchist constitution of pre-war Yugoslavia.

By contrast, in a number of other socialist countries which emerged after the Second World War, where the working class and the mass of the working people under its leadership won power in comparatively peaceful circumstances (without an armed uprising or civil war), the destruction of the old state apparatus and the building of the new one took place gradually. Some of the clauses and articles of the bourgeois-democratic constitutions remained in force until the adoption of new, socialist constitutions. In People's Poland the Constitutional Law of February 19, 1947 "On the Structure and Powers of the Supreme Organs of the Polish Republic" expressly stated which articles of the bourgeois-democratic Constitution of 1921 remained in force relative to the supreme organs of the Republic. In Czechoslovakia, the Presidential Decree of August 3, 1944 "On the Restoration of the Rule of Law" re-established the Czechoslovak Constitution of February 29, 1920. In Bulgaria the Tyrnovo Constitution of 1879 (as amended in 1923) was restored.[1]

A clear distinction must be made between what is laid down by articles in a constitution and their class content. Legal forms must not be confused with the reality of the social relationships which they express.

---

[1] In no country, however, was a pre-war constitution restored in full. Clauses which were at variance with the principles of popular democracy were not enforced. In Czechoslovakia and Rumania, for example, clauses relating to the bicameral structure of the supreme representative organs of state power remained inoperative, while changes in the constitutional norms governing electoral law were made just before the first elections, etc.

Thus, the Polish Constitutional Law of 1947 stipulated that, Arts. 40, 42-44, 46-53 and also in part Art. 45 of the bourgeois-democratic 1921 Constitution should apply as regards the terms of reference of the President of the Polish Republic. These articles defined the powers of the President, how they should be exercised, etc. Clearly, the class content of these articles as implemented by a President of People's Poland, where the President is the representative of the working people, differs fundamentally from the class content of the same articles as implemented by a President of bourgeois-landowner Poland, where the President represented the interests of the landowners and capitalists.

The utilisation of certain articles of the bourgeois-democratic constitutions during the first period of the existence of the socialist states cannot, therefore, be seen as the retention of bourgeois state-legal institutions, because the old forms were injected with a completely new content. But this process of employing old, bourgeois-democratic forms and their injection with a new content must not be seen in an over-simplified light. It took place against the background of a bitter struggle waged by the working class, and the mass of the working people it led, against reaction which sought, by clinging to bourgeois legal forms, to preserve not only these forms but also the old order.

Secondly, *major changes in the balance of class forces can also take place while state power remains in the hands of the same class (or group of classes).* State power was already in the hands of the working class and the working masses which it led when the Constitutions of the RSFSR (1918), the USSR (1924), the Mongolian People's Republic (1940), the Federal People's Republic of Yugoslavia (1946), the People's Republic of Bulgaria (1947), the Czechoslovak Republic, the Rumanian People's Republic and the Korean People's Democratic Republic (1948), and the German Democratic Republic (1949) were adopted. But when new advances in the building of socialism had led to further major changes in the class structure of society, the further strengthening of the alliance of the working class and the peasantry and the consolidation of the leading role of the working class in that alliance, and when conditions had been created for the further development and deepening of socialist democracy, these countries adopted new constitutions. Examples include the USSR Constitution of 1936 and the 1937 Constitutions of the Union Republics, the Constitution of the Rumanian People's Republic of September 24, 1952 followed by that of the Socialist Republic of Rumania adopted on August 21, 1965, the Constitution of the Czechoslovak Socialist Republic (July 11, 1960), the Constitution of the Mongolian People's Republic (July 6, 1960), the Constitution of the German Democratic Republic (April 6, 1968), the Constitution of the People's Republic of Bulgaria (May 16, 1971), the Constitution of the Korean People's Democratic Republic (December 28, 1972), and the Constitution of the Socialist Federal Republic of Yugoslavia (February 21, 1974).[1]

---

[1] Prior to the adoption of new constitutions partial amendments were made to those already in force. The USSR Constitution of 1924 was amended in 1925, 1927, 1931 and 1935 to take account of the increase in the number of Union republics and also of changes in the structure of state organs and their functions. A number of clauses in the 1948 Constitution of the Czechoslovak Republic were repealed, amended or supplemented by the Constitutional Laws of 1950, 1952, 1953, 1954, 1956 and 1960. The Constitutional Law on the fundamental principles of social and political structure of the Federal People's Republic of Yugoslavia and Union organs of power of 1953 repealed Chapters VI-XII and XV of the Yugoslav Constitution of 1946 and also all clauses in that Constitution which were at variance with the law's provisions. The norms of the 1946 Yugoslav Constitution were also supplemented and amended by the 1954 Law on the Judicial System, the 1955 Law on the structure of communities and districts, etc. The 1963 Yugoslav Constitution was substantially amended in 1967, 1968 and 1971. Some articles of the 1952 Rumanian Constitution were amended many times. The most important amendments were contained in the law of March 21, 1961. The 1949 Constitution of the GDR was amended and supplemented in 1955, 1958 and 1960. The 1940 Constitution of the Mongolian People's Republic was also frequently amended, especially important amendments being made in February 1949.

In these instances it is a question of changes in the relationship of class forces while state power is in the hands of the working people headed by the working class, with the socialist character of the state remaining unchanged. We therefore have the replacement of one constitution of a socialist type by another of the same socialist type corresponding to the new stage in the development of class relationships.[1]

The essence of the constitutions of the socialist countries lies in that they embody a relationship of class forces in which state power is in the hands of the working people led by the working class and is utilised to further the building of socialism and communism. The constitutions of these countries are therefore *constitutions of a socialist type*.

At the present time the following fundamental laws are in force in the socialist countries: the Constitution of the USSR (December 5, 1936), the Constitution of the People's Republic of Albania (March 14, 1946, as amended on July 4, 1950), the Constitution of the People's Republic of Bulgaria (May 16, 1971), the Constitution of the People's Republic of China (January 17, 1975), the Fundamental Law of the Republic of Cuba (February 7, 1959), the Constitution of the Czechoslovak Socialist Republic (July 11, 1960), the Constitution of the Hungarian People's Republic (August 18, 1949, as amended on April 19, 1972), the Constitution of the German Democratic Republic (April 6, 1968), the Constitution of the Korean People's Democratic Republic (December 28, 1972), the Constitution of the Mongolian

---

[1] At the same time, experience has shown that deformations of the socialist political system are incompatible with progressive evolution of socialist constitutions. It is not by chance, therefore, that the Maoist group which is exercising a military bureaucratic dictatorship in China, has discarded the socialist-type 1954 Constitution of the People's Republic of China and replaced it by the 1975 Constitution orienting "the development of China along a route which has already cost the great Chinese people dear and which has seriously deformed socialism in that country" (I. Alexandrov, "Slogans and Practice. On the New Constitution of the PRC", *Pravda*, February 5, 1975).

People's Republic (July 6, 1960), the Constitution of the Polish People's Republic (July 22, 1952), the Constitution of the Socialist Republic of Rumania (August 21, 1965), the Constitution of the Democratic Republic of Vietnam (December 31, 1959), and the Constitution of the Socialist Federal Republic of Yugoslavia (February 21, 1974).[1]

2. FUNDAMENTAL FEATURES OF THE CONSTITUTIONS OF THE SOCIALIST COUNTRIES

The constitutions of the socialist countries have *common fundamental features characteristic of all constitutions of a socialist type*, regardless of their distinctive features. Jurists from the socialist countries rightly underline this identity of fundamental principles.

The common features of the socialist constitutions are:
1. These constitutions serve the socialist basis, therefore they are founded on the principles of socialism, affirmed by the successes achieved in the building of socialism: the socialist ownership of mineral wealth,[2] state forests,

---

[1] Some of these constitutions were amended and supplemented in subsequent years. The 1936 USSR Constitution has been amended many times to take account of the formation of new Union republics, their incorporation in the USSR, and the extension of their rights, the improvement of the system of state organs and the further specification of their powers, and the development of the constitutional rights of Soviet citizens and of their guarantees. The most significant changes made to the constitutions of the other socialist countries are: Czechoslovakia—by Constitutional Laws regulating the federalisation of the country and other matters (1968-71); the German Democratic Republic—by the 1974 Law on constitutional changes and amendments, in particular, abolishing the private sector in the economy, consolidating the GDR's position in the world and introducing changes in the system of state organs; Poland— by laws amending the territorial structure, electoral system, the system of organs of control and the system of local state bodies (1954, 1957, 1960, 1963, 1972, 1973); Rumania—by laws reforming the territorial subdivision of the country and the organisation and functioning of state organs (1968, 1969, 1971, 1972, 1974). A number of amendments have also been made to the Albanian Constitution since 1950.

[2] In the USSR and the Mongolian People's Republic—of all the land also.

factories, mines and other basic means and instruments of production; full employment; labour as a duty and matter of honour for every able-bodied citizen in accordance with the principle "from each according to his ability, to each according to his work"; the right to work, leisure, education, etc.

2. The constitutions of the socialist countries proceed from the fact that state power in these countries is vested in the working people of town and country, that the basis of popular rule is the alliance of the working class and the working peasantry in which the former plays the leading role, and that the laws of these countries, expressing the will and interests of the working people, lay down the social order which is advantageous and beneficial to the working people.

3. The constitutions of the socialist countries are profoundly internationalist. They take as their starting point the fact that all citizens in these countries, irrespective of their race or nationality, enjoy equal rights in all spheres of the economic, social, political and cultural life of society.

They prohibit any discrimination whatsoever on grounds of racial or national origin.

The equality of citizens of all nationalities is also manifested in the establishment of national-territorial state and administrative formations within the framework of the multi-national socialist states. This ensures the genuine equality of nationalities and guarantees that due account is taken of their distinctive features and interests.

The genuine proletarian internationalism of the socialist constitutions is also seen in the fact that they express the principle of the solidarity of the working class and working people of the whole world.

4. The establishment of the equality of all citizens regardless of sex, property status, education, residence, etc., is a characteristic feature of the constitutions of the socialist countries. Not wealth, but personal ability and labour determine the status of the citizen.

5. The constitutions of the socialist countries do not merely proclaim the rights and freedoms of the citizen; they place their main emphasis on guaranteeing these rights and on the means for their implementation.

6. The constitutions of the socialist countries are constitutions of peace. This feature arises from the peaceloving character of the socialist states. The socialist constitutions give local expression to the peace policy pursued by the socialist states. The Mongolian Constitution now in force, for example, establishes that "the Mongolian People's Republic shall pursue a peaceloving foreign policy aimed at ensuring stable peace, friendship and co-operation with all peoples on the basis of the principles of peaceful coexistence...." The Constitution of the Polish People's Republic declares that the Polish people and all the organs of power of the Polish working people must be guided by the country's Fundamental Law with the aim of "preventing aggression and consolidating universal peace". In affirming the peace policy of the socialist countries, their constitutions lay down that their supreme governmental organs may proclaim a state of war only a) in the event of armed attack, or b) when necessary to fulfil international treaty obligations providing for mutual defence against aggression.[1] They therefore give legal form to the prohibition of aggressive war.

7. The inclusion of programmatic provisions referring to the building of socialism and communism is an important specific feature of the constitutions of the socialist countries. Some jurists hold that a fundamental feature of constitutions of a socialist type is that they survey the path traversed by their countries. This, however, is a characteristic of all constitutions, not merely socialist ones. Lenin pointed out that bourgeois constitutions are likewise "merely a record of the *results* of struggle".[2] Hence the fact that they record results rather than set out programmes is not a distinctive

---

[1] See *Constitution of the Union of Soviet Socialist Republics*, Art. 49 (XIII); *Constitution of the Socialist Republic of Rumania*, Art. 64 (8).

[2] V. I. Lenin, *Collected Works*, Vol. 18, p. 564.

feature of constitutions of the socialist type. Socialist constitutions differ fundamentally from bourgeois constitutions not in that they review the path that has been traversed, but in the nature of the achievements they record.

Many experts on socialist state law rightly stress the importance of the programmatic clauses contained in socialist constitutions.[1]

Clearly, programmatic provisions regarding the building of socialism and communism should be seen as fundamental features of socialist constitutions. The necessity for their inclusion is dictated by the very nature of socialist fundamental law and its active, creative role. Unlike bourgeois constitutions, whose role is confined only to the affirmation of the status quo, socialist constitutions, while setting down the achievements of the working people, are at the same time instruments for the further transformation of society. It is this which objectively necessitates the inclusion into socialist fundamental laws of programmatic clauses regarding the development of the new system.

8. The concordance between their provisions and reality is likewise a characteristic feature of socialist constitutions.

Bourgeois constitutions legalise the state power of the exploiting minority under cover of hypocritical references to the rule of the people (or nation), equality, etc. Progressive and democratic clauses have been incorporated into the constitutions of a number of bourgeois states such as Italy and Japan as a result of popular pressure. But the ruling classes of these countries try to reduce these clauses to a dead letter. Their desire to camouflage their dictatorship and their unwillingness to give effect to the concessions

---

[1] See V. F. Kotok and D. A. Gaidukov, "Novy etap v razvitii Sovietskogo gosudarstva i Konstitutsii SSSR", *Soviety deputatov trudyashchikhsya* No. 8, 1959; P. S. Romashkin, "Novy etap v razvitii Sovietskogo gosudarstva", *Sovietskoye gosudarstvo i pravo* No. 10, 1960; N. P. Farberov, "O novykh sotsialisticheskikh konstitutsiyakh", *Sovietskoye gosudarstvo i pravo* No. 4, 1961; S. Rozmaryn, *Konstytucja jako ustawa zasadnicza...*, pp. 75-86; B. Spasov, A. Angelov, *Derzhavno pravo na Narodna Republika Bulgaria*, Sofia, 1968, pp. 60-61.

which they are obliged to make to the working people give rise to a discrepancy between the democratic rights formally proclaimed in these constitutions and the rights actually enjoyed by the working people.

By contrast, in the socialist countries, where state power is in the hands of the working people, the constitutions expressly formulate the nature of that power and the guarantees which ensure its implementation. All the objective conditions exist in these countries for the effective implementation of constitutional requirements. This is, of course, not an automatic process. The main political guarantee for the fulfilment of constitutional requirements is the consistent Marxist-Leninist policy of the Communist and Workers' parties which stand at the helm of the socialist state and society. It is the policy of the development and extension by every means of socialist democracy being pursued by the Communist and Workers' parties of the socialist countries which ensures the increasingly effective realisation of the democratic principles proclaimed in the fundamental laws of these countries.

In accordance with the Marxist-Leninist view of the role of constitutions, a great deal of work is being done in the majority of socialist countries to ensure the fullest and most effective realisation of constitutional norms.

3. DISTINCTIVE FEATURES OF THE CONSTITUTIONS OF THE SOCIALIST COUNTRIES

While having common fundamental features characteristic of constitutions of the socialist type, the constitutions of socialist countries at the same time have their own *distinctive features which arise from the progress the particular country has made in the building of socialism, and also from its national traditions and historical development.*

From the point of view of progress made in the development of socialism, the present constitutions of the socialist countries may be divided into two categories: 1) those adopted during the period of transition from capitalism to socialism—that is, constitutions of socialism as yet in the process of construction; 2) those adopted in the period of the completion of the laying of the foundations of socialism and of the building of a developed socialist society.[1]

The first category reflects the multistructural nature of the economy, the survival of remnants of the exploiting classes, and other characteristic features of the period of the transition to socialism. Constitutions in this category contain programmatic provisions regarding eventual abolition of the remnants of the exploiting classes, the future building of socialism, the fuller realisation of the socialist principle "from each according to his ability, to each according to his work", etc. Such provisions are to be found in the constitutions of the Polish People's Republic and the Democratic Republic of Vietnam.

By contrast, the constitutions of those socialist states where the foundations of socialism have already been laid record the victory of socialism and contain provisions setting the aim of the building of a developed socialist society and the creation of the prerequisites for the gradual transition to communism.

The 1936 USSR Constitution belongs to the category of constitutions of victorious socialism. But during the period which has elapsed since its adoption the Soviet people have achieved new successes in the building of a new social system. A developed socialist society has been built, the construction of the material and technical basis of communism has begun, the state of the dictatorship of the proletariat has grown over into the state of the whole people and great changes have taken place in the international position of the USSR. "There are grounds for considering," said Leonid Brezhnev in his report *The Fiftieth Anniversary of the Union of Soviet Socialist Republics* on December 21,

---

[1] For a more detailed classification, see I. P. Ilyinsky, *Konstitutsii mira i sotsialisma*, Mezhdunarodniye Otnosheniya Publishers, Moscow, 1967.

1972, "that all these changes in the life of our Motherland and the tasks confronting our society under the new conditions must be reflected in the Constitution of the Union of Soviet Socialist Republics. We expect to submit the appropriate proposals for the new text of the Constitution for nation-wide discussion before the next Party Congress.

"This will doubtlessly be a great, historic event in the life of the Soviet Union. It will not only help Soviet people and the whole world to get a better understanding of what we have achieved and sum up the results of what we have accomplished, but also shed new light on the further progress of our Soviet socialist society, advancing to communism."[1]

In addition to distinctive characteristics arising from the stage reached in the building of socialism, the constitutions of each of the socialist countries also have distinctive features arising from the particular historical evolution of each country, from their different approaches to the solution of particular constitutional problems and from their different national traditions.

The national characteristics of the constitutions of the socialist countries take the form of specific provisions dealing with social structure, national-territorial organisation, the electoral system, the organs of the state and the fundamental rights and duties of citizens.[2]

The range of relationships regulated by fundamental laws likewise varies in the socialist countries. For example, public (comrades') courts function in the USSR and in almost all the European socialist countries, but only in the German Democratic Republic is reference made to such courts in the Constitution. Organs of workers' self-administration function in Poland, Yugoslavia and other socialist countries. This institution is dealt with at length in the Yugoslav Constitution.

---

[1] L. I. Brezhnev, *The Fiftieth Anniversary of the Union of Soviet Socialist Republics*, Moscow, 1972, pp. 83-84.

[2] To avoid repetition, these features are examined in later chapters dealing with the corresponding institutions of state law.

In examining the national features of the socialist constitutions, it should be borne in mind that in addition to characteristics arising from the current economic and political conditions of a particular country, these constitutions also have distinctive features arising from the national traditions of that country. These include flags and national emblems, national-territorial organisation, the system of state organs, their structure and forms of work, etc.

These national traditions are imbued with a new socialist content.

The distinctive national characteristics of the constitutions of the socialist countries find expression not only in the content, but also in the structure of these constitutions.

4. THE JURIDICAL NATURE OF THE CONSTITUTIONS OF THE SOCIALIST COUNTRIES

In analysing the constitutions of the socialist countries, the first question to arise is whether all their provisions are *normative in character*—that is, whether they constitute *legal norms.*

Certain distinctive features in the structure of the constitutions of the various socialist countries must first be noted. Some merely contain articles set out in appropriate chapters and sections. The constitutions of the USSR and its constituent Union and Autonomous republics and of Rumania and the Korean People's Democratic Republic fall into this category. The constitutions of other socialist countries contain introductory sections (declarations, preambles). In so far as these introductory sections, unlike other parts of the constitutions, are not usually in the form of articles and contain more general provisions than those to be found in articles, some jurists consider that they contain no legal norms whatsoever. Others, while rightly critical of this erroneous point of view, go to the other extreme, asserting that everything written into a constitution is normative in character.

An examination of the introductory sections of the constitutions of the socialist countries shows that they contain *both norms of law and provisions which do not fall into this category*. For instance, the statements contained in the introductory section to the Polish Constitution to the effect that "the Polish People's Republic shall be a republic of the working people" and that "the alliance of the working class and the working peasantry shall constitute the foundation for the rule of the people in Poland. In this alliance the leading role is played by the working class", etc., are undoubtedly norms of law. Other provisions, such as that declaring that "the Polish working people under the leadership of the heroic working class and basing themselves upon the alliance of the workers and peasants, for decades fought for liberation from the national enslavement imposed by the Prussian, Austrian and Russian invaders and colonisers and for an end to exploitation by Polish capitalists and landowners", cannot be considered either as legal norms or even as component parts of legal norms. This in no way implies that non-normative provisions are not a component part of a fundamental law, or that they have no legal significance. A law, be it fundamental or otherwise, may contain postulates which are not norms. In a socialist state a law is also a means of educating the broad mass of the working people in the spirit of socialism. This fully justifies the inclusion of postulates which are not norms, but which nevertheless have educational importance.

These postulates are likewise important in that they set out the fundamental principles upon which the legislator bases the entire constitution. The introductory sections are therefore of great significance in correctly interpreting the constitutional norms set out in subsequent chapters.

As has already been noted, socialist constitutions contain *programmatic provisions*. This gives rise to the question of their legal significance. Many jurists consider that since they deal with the future development of the state and society, programmatic provisions cannot constitute legal norms. Such a view is, however, without foundation. The Polish jurist Rozmaryn has rightly pointed out that a legal norm always relates to the future, because it is intended to regulate the behaviour of people in the future, after its promulgation, even when it is retroactive. Thus all legal norms are perspective and even if some clauses are considered programmatic in that they define relatively remote aims and the paths of future development, this in no way constitutes grounds for denying that they are norms.[1] Furthermore, the inclusion of such norms in a socialist constitution is of particular significance in the light of the active, creative role of socialist law as a whole and of constitutions in particular.

Soviet literature relating to state law, in distinguishing between constitutions and programmes merely observes that a constitution, although it refers to the future, in the main relates to the present, while a programme, although it refers to the present, in the main relates to the future.[2] This is correct. But it is not a question of merely quantitative criteria (i.e., which contains the greatest number of postulates relating to the future). It is above all a matter of qualitative distinctions. The *programmatic provisions* of a constitution, unlike those of a programme (which do not constitute legal norms), are expressed in legal form and *have the force of norms of law*. Those constitutional principles which require the promulgation of a law for their implementation do not remain "merely programmatic" either. These principles constitute valid legal norms, while the non-promulgation of the laws which they envisage constitutes their violation.

Many of the norms of socialist constitutions differ substantially in structure from the norms of conventional laws in that they are characterised by a high degree of abstrac-

---

[1] See S. Rozmaryn, *Konstytucja jako ustawa zasadnicza...*, pp. 75-79.

[2] See N. I. Farberov, "O novykh sotsialisticheskikh konstitutsiyakh", *Sovietskoye gosudarstvo i pravo* No. 4, 1961, p. 52.

tion and in that they contain no sanctions (that is, they indicate no measures to prevent their infringement). Many jurists therefore argue that they are not normative in character.

But neither a high degree of abstraction nor the absence of sanctions constitutes grounds for such an assertion.

Any juridical norm, in so far as it constitutes a general rule of behaviour, is to a greater or lesser degree abstract. The relatively high degree of abstraction which characterises constitutional norms as compared with the norms of conventional law springs inevitably from the nature of constitutions as *fundamental* laws. Measures to prevent the infringement of constitutional principles are customarily laid down by laws specially adopted for that purpose.[1]

What is the place of constitutional norms in the system of socialist law as a whole? Since a constitution is a *fundamental* law, its norms have *supreme juridical force*. All the norms established by conventional laws and other legal acts must be in accordance with constitutional norms.

As a fundamental law, a socialist constitution is the *legal basis* for the whole of current legislation. This means that the fundamental law plays a definitive role in current legislative activity, indicating the main direction and establishing the constitutional principles of legislation.

5. THE DEMOCRATIC PROCEDURE OF DRAFTING, ADOPTION AND AMENDMENT OF THE CONSTITUTIONS OF THE SOCIALIST COUNTRIES

The genuinely popular character of the constitutions of the socialist countries finds expression not only in their con-

---

[1] For a detailed discussion of this point, see S. Rozmaryn, op. cit. This is the most fundamental study of the normative character of constitutional principles in socialist legal literature. The Hungarian jurist I. Kovács has also made an interesting analysis of new elements in the development of socialist constitutions (I. Kovács, *A szocialisto alkotmányfejlödés uf elemei,* Budapest, 1962).

tent but also in the manner in which they are drafted, discussed and adopted.

The drafts were drawn up by constitutional commissions in which the leading role was played by representatives of the Communist and Workers' parties, the most determined champions of the interests of the people.

The drafts were drawn up with the broadest active participation of the mass of the people. Before being submitted to the supreme organs of state power for final approval, they were the subject of nation-wide discussion. More than 50 million citizens participated in the nation-wide discussion of the draft of the 1936 Constitution of the USSR, and some 2 million proposals were made. The 1960 draft Constitution of Czechoslovakia was discussed at more than 47,000 meetings attended by 4,040,170 people; 732,800 people contributed to the discussion. In Mongolia, the 1960 draft Constitution was discussed at 1,166 meetings attended by more than 208,000 people; 2,902 citizens submitted amendments.[1]

The drafts were submitted for final approval only after consideration had been given to the proposals and amendments put forward during the nation-wide discussion.

As fundamental laws, the constitutions of the socialist countries are adopted and amended exclusively by the supreme organs of state power. These are the sole bodies exercising legislative authority in these countries.[2]

In expressing the sovereign will of a socialist state, a supreme representative body may transfer its powers regarding the adoption of a constitution only to the sovereign— that is, to the people. The constitutions of Bulgaria and the German Democratic Republic were adopted as a result of

---

[1] In assessing the public participation, it is of course necessary to take account of the relative size of populations.

[2] The current Fundamental Law of Cuba was approved on February 7, 1959 by the Revolutionary Government because a supreme representative body had not yet been constituted.

referenda, held in Bulgaria on May 16, 1971 and in the German Democratic Republic on April 6, 1968. The results were a demonstration of popular support for the constitutions of these countries. In the German Democratic Republic 94.5 per cent of the electorate approved the draft Constitution, while in Bulgaria 99.7 per cent of the electorate voted and 99.96 per cent of the valid votes cast were in favour of the new constitution. The original drafts of both constitutions had been submitted for nation-wide discussion, as a result of which they were amended by the constitutional commissions of the People's Chamber of the German Democratic Republic and the Bulgarian National Assembly. As a result of the discussion, 118 amendments were made to the Preamble and to 55 articles.[1] Amendments were made the subject of referenda in both countries. This enabled the electorates not only to vote for or against their draft constitutions, but also to play a direct part in determining their content.

Constitutions are not ordinary but fundamental laws forming the juridical basis for all legislation. A substantially larger number of votes is therefore required for their approval and amendment by supreme organs of state power than is customary in the case of conventional legislation. For instance, in Bulgaria, and the German Democratic Republic the adoption of ordinary laws requires a simple majority vote at a session attended by more than a half of the members of the legislative body concerned, whereas constitutional amendments require a majority of at least two-thirds of all members (not only of those present).

This special procedure is designed to ensure the stability of the fundamental laws of the socialist countries and the approval of constitutional principles by a qualified rather than merely a simple majority of people's representatives elected to the supreme organs of state power.

---

[1] See *Neues Deutschland*, March 27, 1968, p. 2.

The requirement that constitutional amendments affecting the interests of the republics and autonomous provinces forming part of the Federal Republic must be approved by the representative bodies of these republics and autonomous provinces constitutes a specific guarantee that account will be taken of these interests. Only when a constitutional amendment relates exclusively to the legal status of republics and their relations with the federation is the consent of the supreme representative bodies of republics sufficient and the consent of those of the autonomous provinces not required.

It must be stressed that the procedure for constitutional amendment is laid down in the fundamental laws themselves and so represents a *constitutional norm.* It is therefore impossible not to agree with those jurists who rightly consider any constitutional amendment introduced in a manner not in accordance with that laid down by the constitution itself (in particular by a decree having the force of law) to be an infringement of constitutional principles. Provisions in the constitutions of socialist countries which directly prohibit amendments of this kind are commendable in this respect.

In considering the procedure for the amendment of the constitutions of the socialist countries, it should be borne in mind that in some of these countries laws are adopted which while not always amending the text of constitutions, in effect amend particular clauses. For instance, amendments to the 1963 Yugoslav Constitution adopted in 1967, 1968 and 1971 were in the form of separate acts. Constitutional laws amending the Czechoslovak Constitution likewise do not in several cases amend the actual text of articles, but are independent acts. The current Czechoslovak Constitution includes articles of the 1960 Constitution which have retained their validity, and some provisions of constitutional laws adopted subsequently.

CHAPTER III

THE CONSTITUTIONAL FOUNDATIONS OF THE SOCIAL STRUCTURE OF THE SOCIALIST COUNTRIES

1. INTRODUCTORY REMARKS

For a certain period of time consideration of social structure in socialist legal literature was as a rule confined to three aspects—the economic basis, the political basis and the class structure. Many authors still adhere to this "tripartite" system.

In accordance with this system, principles of social structure such as state planning, the socialist principle of the organisation of labour and distribution according to labour form part of the economic basis.

But state planning embraces not only the economy but also problems of cultural development, the training of personnel, etc.; when the building of socialism has still not been completed, it is directed towards the restriction and ousting of the remnants of the exploiting classes. It is therefore incorrect to reduce planning simply to the development of the economic basis, or to consider it part of the problem of the economic basis. In the socialist countries state planning is directed towards the achievement of both economic, political and social aims.[1]

Nor is the organisation of labour and of distribution under socialism simply an economic question. Can, for example, the creation of a new, socialist attitude to labour

---

[1] Recent constitutions and legislations of several socialist countries (e.g. Rumania and Poland) mention socio-economic rather than economic development plans.

be regarded simply as a part of the problem of the economic basis?

A growing number of authors therefore rightly treat planning, and also the organisation of labour and of distribution according to work done as independent principles of the social structure (that is, relatively independent, since all the principles of social structure are closely interrelated).[1]

The most important question of social structure, given the existence of a state, is that of the nature of the state, its purposes and functions. Unless this question is answered, it is impossible fully to understand the structure of society. But the "tripartite" system either finds no place at all for this problem or it is considered merely as a component part of the problem of the class structure of society,[2] or as an aspect of the problem of the political basis.[3] Even authors who do not favour the "tripartite" approach either do not consider the problems of the class nature, purposes and functions of the state when they deal with the social structure,[4] or consider them only to be aspects of the problem of the political basis.[5]

This problem cannot, however, be regarded as an aspect of the problem of the class structure of society (the purposes and functions of the state cannot be compressed within the framework of the class structure of society; the class structure of socialist society is itself a result of the functioning of the socialist state). Neither can it be regarded as an aspect of the problem of the political basis (the political

---

[1] See *Sovietskoye gosudarstvennoye pravo*, Gosyurizdat, Moscow, 1950; V. F. Kotok and A. G. Mozokhina, *Razvitiye osnovnykh institutov gosudarstvennogo prava Polskoi Narodnoi Respubliki*, USSR Academy of Sciences Publishers, Moscow, 1955; A. I. Denisov, M. G. Kirichenko, *Sovietskoye gosudarstvennoye pravo*.

[2] See Y. N. Umansky, *Sovietskoye gosudarstvennoye pravo*, Gosyurizdat, Moscow, 1955, pp. 107-10.

[3] See *Sovietskoye gosudarstvennoye pravo*, Chapter III (3), Gosyurizdat, Moscow, 1958.

[4] See V. F. Kotok and A. G. Mozokhina, op. cit.

[5] See A. I. Denisov and M. G. Kirichenko, op. cit., Chapter III (7).

basis of the state itself arises from its nature, purposes and functions).

The present chapter therefore examines the following constitutional foundations of the social structure of the socialist countries:

1) the nature, purposes and functions of the socialist state;
2) representative bodies as the foundations of the state apparatus;
3) the economic basis and the nature of the economy;
4) the class structure of society;
5) state planning of economic and cultural development, and
6) work as a duty and a matter of honour for every able-bodied citizen and the socialist principle of distribution according to labour.

The sequence in which the fundamental principles of the social structure are examined in the present chapter, corresponds in the main to that in which they are laid down in the constitutions of the socialist countries and is determined by their objective relationship. We first examine the problems of the nature, purposes and functions of the state and of the basis of the entire system of the socialist state bodies, because a socialist economy does not emerge spontaneously but is created as a result of the planned operation of the socialist state. We then consider economic structures, followed by changes in the class system brought about by changes in the economy.

Not all the constitutions of the socialist countries set down the constitutional foundations of the social structure enumerated above in a single chapter entitled "The Social Structure". Such chapters are to be found in the constitutions of the USSR and Czechoslovakia. But in the Polish Constitution the fundamental principles of the social structure are set down in two chapters: Chapter 1, "The Political Structure", and Chapter 2, "The Social and Economic Structure". The fundamental principles of the social structure are set out in two groups: 1) the fundamental principles of the social and political structure (the class nature, purposes and functions of the state, and the representative system as the basis of the entire state apparatus), and 2) the fundamental principles of the social and economic structure (the economic foundations and the nature of the economy, state planning, and the socialist principle of the organisation of labour and of renumeration). Problems of class structure are dealt with in both chapters. An approximately similar categorisation of the constitutional foundations of the social structure is to be found in the Bulgarian Constitution and in the Constitution of the Democratic Republic of Vietnam, which contain chapters on "The Social and Economic Structure", while the fundamental principles of the social and political structure are set out in different chapters. In the Bulgarian Constitution the relevant chapter bears the title "The Social and Political Structure", and in the Constitution of the Democratic Republic of Vietnam—"The Democratic Republic of Vietnam".

The Constitution of the German Democratic Republic lays down the fundamental principles of the social structure in Section 1: "The Fundamental Principles of the Socialist Social and State System", which consists of two chapters, "The Political Foundations" and "The Economic Foundations, Science, Education and Culture".

In the Yugoslav Constitution the fundamental principles of the social structure are set down in "The Fundamental Principles" and in a number of chapters in Part II of the Constitution which bears the title "The Social Structure". In the Fundamental Law of the Republic of Cuba a number of clauses dealing with the social structure are contained in Section 4, "Labour and Property", and in articles in other sections. In the Rumanian Constitution the fundamental principles of the social structure are set down in Chapter 1 entitled "The Socialist Republic of Rumania".

Both the socio-economic structure and the socio-political structure are thus integral parts of the social structure. The identification of the socio-economic structure with the social structure as a whole found in the writings of some jurists cannot therefore be considered correct.[1]

Nor must it be forgotten in analysing the constitutional foundations of the social structure that these fundamental principles are also frequently set down in norms to be found in the introductory sections of the constitutions of a number of socialist countries.

The varying methods of systematisation of the norms establishing the fundamental principles of the social structure in the constitutions of the socialist countries (in one or two chapters and partly in the introductory sections) should not, however, be allowed to obscure the fact that the fundamental principles of all the socialist countries have a basic uniformity with, of course, distinctive features arising from the conditions of a particular country. This enables us to examine the constitutional foundations of the social structure of the socialist countries in a single chapter, abstracting ourselves from the distinctive features of the method of systematisation employed in each particular constitution.

2. THE CLASS NATURE, PURPOSES AND FUNCTIONS OF THE STATE IN THE SOCIALIST COUNTRIES

The constitutions of the socialist countries, being constitutions of a socialist type, explicitly establish the class nature of the socialist states.

The sovereignty of the working people, i.e., the concentration in its hands of plenary powers, is clearly set down in articles which define the nature of state power in the socialist countries. "The Union of Soviet Socialist Republics shall be a socialist state of workers and peasants.... All power in the USSR shall be vested in the working people of town and country...."; "All power in the Czechoslovak Socialist Republic shall be vested in the working people"; "In the Polish People's Republic power shall be vested in the work-

---
[1] See, for example, *Gosudarstvennoye pravo stran narodnoi demokratii*, edited by V. F. Kotok, Chapter III.

ing people of town and country"; "The Socialist Republic of Rumania shall be ... a state of the working people of town and country". It should be stressed that the sovereignty of the people is not merely proclaimed in articles or groups of articles. It is safeguarded by a wide range of guarantees. The first essential for the implementation of genuine popular rule is the creation of the economic and social conditions which enable the working people to take an active part in state administration. These conditions are ensured by the domination of the national economies of the socialist states by socialist forms of ownership and socialist relations of production which preclude any possibility of the exploitation of man by man and which constitute the economic basis for the rule of the people, and by far-reaching and effective rights and freedoms, which ensure that the citizens of the socialist countries are able to play an active part in all spheres of their countries' economies, politics and public affairs. The entire system of state organs is organised in a way which ensures effective rule by the people. The participation of mass organisations in the exercise of state functions plays an important part in ensuring the sovereignty of the working people. The fundamental guarantee of the sovereignty of the people is the leading role played by the Marxist-Leninist parties in the state and society.

The exercise of popular sovereignty is thus ensured not merely by a single norm or group of norms written into the constitutions of the socialist countries, but by all the norms contained in these constitutions, and indeed by all the norms of the state law of these countries.[1]

The experience of the USSR and the other socialist countries confirms the fundamental Marxist-Leninist postulate that the transition to socialism cannot take place without the establishment of the dictatorship of the proletariat. The at-

---

[1] In order to avoid unnecessary repetition, the present work therefore does not contain a special chapter dealing with the guarantees of popular sovereignty, since all the institutions of state law considered in the appropriate chapters constitute such guarantees.

tainment of the dictatorship of the proletariat by the Soviet people as a result of the October Revolution is explicitly affirmed by Art. 2 of the USSR Constitution. As a rule, the actual term "dictatorship of the proletariat" is not used in the constitutions of the other socialist countries. But by affirming the determination of the peoples of these countries to build a socialist and communist society and establishing the state power of the working people based on the alliance of the working class and the working peasantry under the leadership of the former, these constitutions in fact affirm the dictatorship of the proletariat.

As Lenin foresaw, the form of the dictatorship of the proletariat undergoes changes in accordance with the actual historical conditions of each particular country.[1] Below we shall analyse the forms these changes take.

1. "The dictatorship of the proletariat," Lenin writes, "is a specific form of class alliance between the proletariat, the vanguard of the working people, and the numerous non-proletarian strata of the working people (petty bourgeoisie, small proprietors, the peasantry, the intelligentsia, etc.), or the majority of these strata ... an alliance for the final establishment and consolidation of socialism."[2]

The dictatorship of the proletariat is, therefore, a particular form of class alliance.

The scope of this class alliance may vary, depending upon the actual historical conditions in a particular country.

In the Democratic Republic of Vietnam and the German Democratic Republic the democratic, patriotic section of the national (middle) bourgeoisie came to understand the need for socialist change and to acknowledge the leading role of the working class. It joined the alliance of the working class and the peasantry. This alliance, led by the working class, forms the class basis of the rule of the people in the socialist countries. It is the supreme principle of the proletarian dictatorship. Any attempt to deny the leading role of the prole-

---

[1] See V. I. Lenin, *Collected Works*, Vol. 23, pp. 69-70.
[2] V. I. Lenin, *Collected Works*, Vol. 29, p. 381.

tariat in this alliance amounts in effect to a revision of Marxism-Leninism, since it leads to the denial of the dictatorship of the proletariat itself.

2. The mechanism of the dictatorship of the proletariat also undergoes changes in various countries in the light of actual conditions. For instance, in the majority of socialist countries there exist special organisational forms of the People's (National) Front.

There are also other variations in the mechanism of the proletarian dictatorship. In some countries there are only Communist (Workers') parties. In others (Bulgaria, the German Democratic Republic, the Democratic Republic of Vietnam, etc.) there exist, as a result of the special characteristics of their historical development, other parties which acknowledge the leading role of the Communist and Workers' parties.

But despite these variations, the leadership of society and the state by the Communist (Workers') parties is a fundamental, universal feature of the mechanism of the dictatorship of the proletariat in the socialist countries without which the building of a new social system is inconceivable.

3. The state forms of the dictatorship of the proletariat are likewise extremely varied. This may be seen in the structure of the supreme organs of the state (for example, the institution of President exists in Cuba, the Democratic Republic of Vietnam, Yugoslavia, Czechoslovakia, the Korean People's Democratic Republic and Rumania, while in the other socialist countries there exist only collegiate bodies), in the organisation and activities of local government bodies and other state organs, in the electoral system and in the national-territorial structure.

But despite this variety, the general rule is that the state forms of proletarian dictatorship must ensure the fullest democracy for the working people in a manner corresponding to the actual historical conditions in each particular country.

In their attempts to distort the essence of the dictatorship of the proletariat, the present-day revisionists resort to an old manoeuvre: they counterpose "dictatorship in general" to "democracy in general". On this basis they allege that the dictatorship of the proletariat is a denial of democracy.

In reality it is impossible to counterpose "dictatorship in general" to "democracy in general" because in practice they always have a specific class content. "If we are not to mock at common sense and history," Lenin wrote, "it is obvious that we cannot speak of 'pure democracy' as long as different *classes* exist; we can only speak of *class* democracy."[1]

However much bourgeois theoreticians and politicians may sing the praises of bourgeois democracy, it nevertheless remains democracy for the exploiters and a dictatorship over the vast majority of the population—over the working and exploited masses.

By contrast, the dictatorship of the proletariat is democracy for the overwhelming majority, for the working people; it is a dictatorship over a small minority, over the exploiters.

By attempting to depict the dictatorship of the proletariat as a denial of democracy, the bourgeois ideologists and present-day revisionists are in effect seeking the restoration of bourgeois democracy in the socialist countries. They do not always dare to declare this openly at a time when the class consciousness of the working people is growing; they often couch their demand in more veiled terms. These include the concepts of "integral democracy" and "pluralist democracy" which allegedly combine features of both bourgeois and socialist democracy and include legal political opposition. In fact these concepts demand toleration in the socialist countries of the activities of political parties and other organisations which are hostile to the people and which would campaign against socialism. The Marxist-Leninist parties naturally reject such recipes.

A dogmatic interpretation of the dictatorship of the pro-

---

[1] V. I. Lenin, *Collected Works*, Vol. 28, p. 242.

letariat which idealises the methods of coercion throughout the entire period of the transition from capitalism to socialism and which neglects the development of socialist democracy likewise harms the cause of socialism. Lenin's thesis that "socialism is impossible without democracy"[1] must not be ignored.

While constituting democracy for the vast majority of the population, for mass of the working people, the dictatorship of the proletariat is of course a dictatorship directed against the enemies of the working people. This is frankly acknowledged by Communists.

Thus, variations in the form of the dictatorship of the proletariat in the different socialist countries are expressed in different types of the class alliance under the leadership of the proletariat, in distinctive features of the mechanism of the proletarian dictatorship, and in various forms of national-territorial structure and the organisation and functioning of the state bodies.

But the supreme principle of the dictatorship of the proletariat—the alliance of the working class and working peasantry under the leadership of the former, the leadership of the state and society by a Marxist party and the broad democracy for the mass of the working people—remains constant in all the socialist countries, whatever variety may exist in external forms.

Unlike the dictatorship of the exploiting classes, which strives to preserve the system of exploitation and hence to perpetuate itself, the dictatorship of the proletariat has as its main aim the building of a classless society in which there will be no one to suppress, and thus creates the conditions for its own evolution into a state of the whole people. With each new success in the building of socialism, the social basis of the socialist state broadens. Ultimately, following the abolition of the exploiting classes, and with the complete and final victory of socialism and the onset of the

---

[1] V. I. Lenin, *Collected Works*, Vol. 23, p. 74.

period of the building of developed socialism, with the creation of a stable socialist unity of the entire people, the socialist state gradually evolves from a state of class dictatorship into a state of the whole people, and proletarian democracy becomes socialist democracy for the whole people. This stage has been reached in the USSR. "... The dictatorship of the proletariat has fulfilled its historic mission and has ceased to be indispensable in the USSR from the point of view of the tasks of internal development. The state, which arose as a state of the dictatorship of the proletariat, has, in the new, contemporary stage, become a state of the entire people, an organ expressing the interests and will of the people as a whole."[1]

The evolution of the state of the proletarian dictatorship into a state of the whole people and of socialist democracy into democracy for the whole people in the USSR, does not imply that the state and democracy have lost their class character. Nor does it imply the emergence of a "supra-class state" or of a non-class, "pure" democracy. As Lenin pointed out, "'pure democracy' is not only an *ignorant* phrase, revealing a lack of understanding both of the class struggle and of the nature of the state, but also a thrice-empty phrase, since in communist society democracy will *wither away* in the process of changing and becoming a habit, but will never be 'pure' democracy".[2] The socialist state of the whole people and socialist democracy for the whole people in the USSR retain their class character as a state of the working people and as democracy for the working people. They have become a state of the whole people and democracy for the whole people not as a result of a withdrawal from the class positions but because today the entire Soviet people consists exclusively of working people.

The evolution of the state of the dictatorship of the proletariat into the state of the whole people is one of the most important theoretical and practical problems of the building

---
[1] *The Road to Communism*, Moscow, 1962, p. 547.
[2] V. I. Lenin, *Collected Works*, Vol. 28, p. 242.

of communism posed and resolved in the Programme of the CPSU adopted at the 22nd Party Congress.[1]

The present-day dogmatists, making use of quotations from the writings of the founders of Marxism-Leninism taken out of context, abbreviated and misinterpreted are trying to "prove" that in accordance with Marxist-Leninist teachings on the socialist revolution and the dictatorship of the proletariat the dictatorship of the working class must allegedly be retained right up to the complete victory of communism. Such a point of view, however, testifies to their characteristic failure to understand the essence of Marxist-Leninist teachings on the dictatorship of the proletariat, their fear of any creative development of Marxism-Leninism and their isolation from reality.

In reality the proposition of the CPSU Programme regarding the evolution of the state of the dictatorship of the proletariat into a state of the whole people, representing a further creative development and enrichment of Marxist-Leninist teachings on the socialist revolution and the socialist state, is not at variance with the fundamental, initial propositions on these problems contained in the writings of the founders of Marxism-Leninism. On the contrary, it is wholly in accord with them.

In attempting to prove that the dictatorship of the proletariat is allegedly necessary right up to the complete building of communism, the dogmatists usually refer to Marx's well-known comment that "between capitalist and communist society lies the period of the revolutionary transformation of the one into the other. Corresponding to this is also a political transition period in which the state can be nothing but *the revolutionary dictatorship of the proletariat*".[2] Reference is also made to Lenin's proposition that "the transition from capitalism to communism is certainly bound to yield a tremendous abundance and variety of political forms,

---

[1] See *The Road to Communism*, pp. 248-50, 546-47.
[2] K. Marx and F. Engels, *Selected Works*, Vol. 3, p. 26.

but the essence will inevitably be the same: *the dictatorship of the proletariat*"[1] and other similar passages. The present-day dogmatists use these quotations to give a semblance of "validity" to their assertions that it is necessary to retain the dictatorship of the proletariat during the entire period up to the onset of the higher phase of communism.

But the dogmatists' attempts to attribute to the founders of Marxism-Leninism the view that it is necessary to preserve the dictatorship of the proletariat right up to the complete building of communism are unfounded.

Marx and Lenin, taking a dialectical view of the creation of a communist society, distinguished two phases of communism—the first, socialist phase and the second, higher phase—that of communism proper.[2] Therefore in order correctly to understand their postulates regarding the historical period during which the dictatorship of the proletariat is necessary, we have to clarify precisely to which phase reference is being made. An examination of a whole series of writings leave no doubt that the founders of Marxism-Leninism considered that the dictatorship of the proletariat was necessary in the period of the transition from capitalism to socialism. Lenin, for example, points out that "Marx spoke of an entire period of the dictatorship of the proletariat as the period of transition from capitalism to *socialism*",[3] and that the dictatorship of the proletariat is created "for the final establishment and consolidation of *socialism*"[4] (italics mine —*A.M.*). Many other similar remarks by Lenin can be cited. To do so is however unnecessary. In a theoretical discussion the most convincing arguments are not quotations, but the clarification of the substance of the matter and arguments directed towards this end. In order to determine in genuinely scientific fashion the period during which the

---

[1] V. I. Lenin, *Collected Works*, Vol. 25, p. 413.
[2] See, for example, V. I. Lenin, *Collected Works*, Vol. 25, pp. 465-67, 471, 474.
[3] V. I. Lenin, *Collected Works*, Vol. 29, p. 388.
[4] Ibid., Vol. 29, p. 381.

dictatorship of the proletariat is necessary, we must consider Marxist-Leninist teachings regarding the dictatorship of the proletariat, the causes prompting its necessity, and its aims and purposes.

The need for the dictatorship of the proletariat arises from the conditions of the class struggle between the proletariat and the mass of the people which it leads on the one hand, and the exploiting classes on the other. When it has won political power, the proletariat cannot organise the building of a socialist society without breaking the bitter resistance of the exploiting classes. Lenin pointed out that the meaning and purpose of the proletarian dictatorship was "to break the resistance of the capitalists"[1] and that it "arises out of the need ... to forcibly suppress the resistance of the class that is losing its political sway".[2]

The dictatorship of the proletariat is of course not merely coercion directed against the exploiters. Indeed, this is not even its main characteristic. But the constructive tasks performed by the socialist state and its organisational, economic, cultural and educational functions can also be fulfilled without the dictatorship of the proletariat. Lenin, while indicating the great importance of the constructive tasks of the dictatorship of the proletariat, at the same time emphasised that "the indispensable characteristic, the necessary condition of dictatorship is the *forcible* suppression of the exploiters as a *class*".[3] The purpose of the dictatorship of the proletariat was also clearly formulated in the Programme adopted by the 8th Congress of the Russian Communist Party (Bolsheviks), which declared that "the dictatorship of the proletariat which enables it to suppress any resistance by the exploiters"[4] is an essential condition for the socialist revolution.

---

[1] Ibid., Vol. 25, p. 65.
[2] Ibid., Vol. 28, p. 464.
[3] Ibid., p. 256.
[4] *KPSS v rezolyutsiyakh i resheniyakh syezdov, konferentsii i plenumov TsK*, Part 1, Gospolitizdat, Moscow, 1954, p. 410.

From this it is clear that the abolition of the exploiting classes, the complete and final victory of socialism and the transformation of a society made up of antagonistic classes into a society in which there are only two friendly classes—the working class and the collective-farm peasantry, together with the social stratum of the working intelligentsia—means the disappearance of the conditions which give rise to the need for the dictatorship of the proletariat, which has already happened in the USSR.

Today in those socialist countries in which all the main tasks of the transition from capitalism to socialism have been accomplished, where a developed socialist society is being built and the conditions for communist construction are being created, the state of the dictatorship of the proletariat is growing over into a socialist state of the whole people.

But this evolution must not be depicted in an over-simplified fashion. It would be wrong to think that the socialist state is immediately transformed into a state of the whole people on the day after the abolition of the last exploiting class. The term "the abolition of the exploiting classes" means not their physical destruction, but the ending of their ownership of the instruments and means of production which enabled them to exploit the working people. The confiscation of landed estates, the nationalisation of the capitalist-owned factories, banks, etc., meant the abolition of the class of landlords and the class of urban capitalists. But the people who had belonged to these classes remained alive, embittered by the fact that popular rule had deprived them of their land and factories and of the means which enabled them to live by the exploitation of the working people. These people do not immediately lay down their arms. On the contrary, they attempt to wage a struggle against the rule of the people. Their re-education takes a long time. The abolition of the kulaks (rich peasants) as a class likewise does not mean that all formerly rich peasants immediately became loyal supporters of popular rule, renouncing struggle against it for all time. Therefore the state function of suppressing the resistance of the exploiting classes does not wither away immediately after the abolition of the latter, but continues for a certain time until the re-education of the members of the former exploiting classes has been completed. The transformation of the socialist state from a state of the dictatorship of the proletariat into a state of the whole people is completed only when the indestructible social and political unity of the whole people has taken shape. The duration of this process is also influenced by external factors. Imperialism tries to revive and activise anti-popular elements in the socialist countries by every possible means.

From this it is clear that the period of the transformation of the state of the dictatorship of the proletariat into that of the whole people is of substantial duration. The onset of this period in a number of socialist countries does not mean that they no longer need the dictatorship of the proletariat. *In all the socialist countries except the USSR the state essentially remains a state of the dictatorship of the proletariat.* This is stressed in the documents of the congresses of the Communist and Workers' parties of the socialist countries.

The socialist state is the main instrument for the socialist transformation of society. It organises and unites the masses, exercises the planned guidance of economic and cultural development, and ensures the defence of the revolutionary achievements of the people. This historic role of the socialist state determines its aims and functions, which are set down in the constitutions of the socialist countries.

In examining a particular socialist state, it is necessary in determining its functions to take into account the stage which the country has reached in the building of socialism and the changes of functions associated with this. In addition, the concrete conditions of a particular socialist state determine the specific implementation of its functions. The special characteristics of particular functions of the socialist state also depend upon the features of the international situation in a given period. Thanks to the assistance of the USSR and the mutual co-operation of the socialist countries, the economic, organisational, cultural and educational work of their state organs assumed great scope almost from the first days of their existence. The exercise of the function of the defence of the socialist homeland against imperialist aggression is greatly facilitated by the fact that each socialist state can now rely not only upon its own armed forces, but also upon the strength of the world socialist system, which is a reliable bulwark in the anti-imperialist struggle. With the creation and development of the world socialist system the socialist states have acquired a new function—that of fraternal mutual assistance and co-operation with the socialist countries and the reinforcement of the world socialist system. Owing to the new balance of forces in the world the transition to socialism in the majority of the socialist states which emerged after the Second World War was taking place peacefully, without civil war. The function of the suppression of the resistance of the overthrown exploiting classes did not therefore assume the form of armed suppression in the majority of these countries.

At the same time the means by which a particular function is implemented do not remain unchanged, but are adapted to prevailing circumstances. In Hungary, where the transition to socialism took place by peaceful means, the suppression of the resistance of the exploiting classes in the main assumed juridical forms. But when in 1956 the counter-revolution organised an uprising and launched armed struggle, the function of the suppression of the exploiting classes was primarily implemented through the military defeat of the counter-revolution's armed groups.

In the USSR the function of the suppression of the resistance of the exploiting classes has withered away as a result of the total abolition of the remnants of these classes and the creation of the social and political unity of the Soviet people.

The need for the all-round consolidation of the socialist state arises from its historical role as the main instrument for the building of socialism and communism and for the defence of the gains of the working people against the attacks of internal and external enemies. The constitutions of the socialist states therefore set down in legal form the obligation of all citizens and government state bodies to strengthen the socialist state in every way. The introductory section of the Polish Constitution lays down that the people and all the organs of working people's rule shall be guided by the Constitution in "strengthening the people's state as the main force safeguarding the fullest prosperity of the Polish nation and its independence and sovereignty".

The socialist states rely on disinterested mutual aid and support in the fulfilment of their functions. The Soviet Union, as the first country to complete the construction of socialism and begin the building of a communist society, and as the most powerful socialist state with the greatest experience in socialist construction, continues to give fraternal aid and support to the other socialist countries.

The importance of the strengthening and development of the unity and co-operation of the socialist countries is stressed in the Declaration of the Meeting of Representatives of the Communist and Workers' Parties held in Moscow in November 1960, in the Main Document approved by the International Meeting of Communist and Workers' Parties on June 17, 1969, by the 24th Congress of the CPSU and by the congresses of the fraternal Marxist-Leninist parties of the other socialist countries.

The unity of the socialist countries is the guarantee of their invincibility and of their successes and achievements. That is why the enemies of socialism make every effort to undermine this unity.

The identity of their economic bases, political systems, and Marxist-Leninist ideology, and their common interest in the defence of their revolutionary gains and national independence against the attacks of imperialism create a firm objective foundation for the development of relations of a new type between the socialist countries marked by genuine equality, close ties, the reciprocal exchange of experience, close economic co-operation and fraternal mutual assistance. Proletarian internationalism is the fundamental principle governing the relations between the socialist countries.

The establishment of a new type of international relations within the world socialist system is not, however, the automatic outcome of the interaction of the objective prerequisites enumerated above. It is a complex process. It is a question of overcoming national antagonisms and mistrust which have been nurtured for centuries, during the domination of these countries by the exploiting classes. The imperialists resort to every means to cause discord and estrangement between the socialist countries. The successful development of relations of a new type between the socialist countries depends above all upon the ruling Communist parties of these countries and upon their loyalty to Marxism-Leninism and proletarian internationalism.

Uncompromising struggle against Right and "Left" opportunism, both of which share the common characteristic of concessions to nationalism and sometimes of outright adherence to nationalistic attitudes, is of great importance in strengthening the unity and solidarity of the socialist countries. Lenin showed the close link which exists between opportunism and nationalism. "The ideological and political affinity, connection, and even identity between opportunism and social-nationalism are beyond doubt,"[1] he wrote.

Despite certain difficulties, a healthy process of the consolidation of the unity of the socialist countries is under way, thanks to the consistent internationalist policies of the CPSU and the fraternal Marxist-Leninist parties of the other socialist countries. "Communists are aware of the difficulties in the development of the world socialist system," says the Main Document of the International Meeting of Communist and Workers' Parties held in Moscow in June 1969. "But this system is based on the identity of the socio-economic structure of its member-countries and on the identity

---

[1] V. I. Lenin, *Collected Works*, Vol. 21, p. 154.

of their fundamental interests and objectives. This identity is an earnest that the existing difficulties will be overcome and that the unity of the socialist system will be further strengthened on the basis of the principles of Marxism-Leninism and proletarian internationalism."[1]

Fraternal co-operation and mutual assistance between the socialist countries assume diverse forms. An important role is played by the Council for Mutual Economic Assistance (CMEA) formed in January 1949 by Albania,[2] Bulgaria, Czechoslovakia, the German Democratic Republic, Hungary, Poland, Rumania and the Soviet Union, joined in 1962 by Mongolia and in 1972 by Cuba. Yugoslavia also participates in certain areas of CMEA's work. In 1964 the Yugoslav Federal Executive Council (Government) instituted a permanent mission in CMEA.[3]

In 1971 the CMEA member-countries adopted a comprehensive programme for the development of socialist economic integration.

The Warsaw Treaty signed on May 14, 1955 is a guarantee of peace and of the security of the socialist countries. Its signatories include the Soviet Union and the majority of the European socialist countries.[4]

The Warsaw Treaty member-countries undertook to act in a spirit of friendship and co-operation for the further development and strengthening of their economic and cultural ties, adhering to the principles of mutual respect, independence, sovereignty and non-interference in each other's internal affairs. They affirmed their readiness sincerely to co-operate on all international matters relating to the safe-

---

[1] *International Meeting of Communist and Workers' Parties, Moscow, 1969*, p. 24.

[2] Albania subsequently withdrew from CMEA.

[3] See *Sluzhbeni list SFRY*, Item 47/1964.

[4] Of the European socialist countries only Yugoslavia did not join the Warsaw Treaty Organisation. Albania, although formally remaining a member, in fact played no part in it for a number of years and withdrew in 1968.

guarding of peace and security, and to work for effective measures to reduce armaments and bring about the prohibition of weapons of mass destruction. They undertook to consult together on all important international issues affecting their common interests and to give immediate assistance in the event of an armed attack upon one of their number.

A Political Consultative Committee, made up of representatives of the member-countries, was established to conduct the consultations envisaged by the Treaty and to consider issues arising in connection with its implementation. A Joint Command of the Armed Forces of the member-countries was also established under the terms of the Treaty.

Meetings of the Political Consultative Committee consider key international issues which have a direct bearing upon the strengthening of peace and the development of peaceful co-operation between peoples and upon the struggle against the aggressive policy of imperialism. These joint efforts enable the socialist countries to achieve significant successes which strengthen the international position of socialism and the cause of peace in Europe and throughout the world.

A conference of the Political Consultative Committee held in March 1969 approved the Statute on the Committee of Defence Ministers, a new Statute on the Joint Armed Forces and the Joint Command and other documents designed to improve the structure and administration of the Warsaw Treaty's defence organisation.

The importance of the Warsaw Treaty Organisation is stressed in the Main Document adopted by the International Meeting of Communist and Workers' Parties held in Moscow in June 1969: "So long as the aggressive NATO bloc exists, the Warsaw Treaty Organisation has an important role to play in safeguarding the security of the socialist countries against armed attack by the imperialist powers and in ensuring peace."[1]

---

[1] *International Meeting of Communist and Workers' Parties, Moscow, 1969*, p. 23.

The socialist countries have also concluded a number of bilateral treaties and agreements on economic, cultural and military assistance.

The 24th Congress of the CPSU opened up new prospects for the development of fraternal co-operation and mutual assistance between the socialist countries. "The Congress instructs the CC CPSU," said the resolution on the Report of the Central Committee, "to go on strengthening and developing co-operation with the Communist and Workers' Parties of the socialist states, on which primarily depend the unity and cohesion of the world socialist system; to extend to the utmost co-operation with the socialist states in the sphere of international policy and economic relations, including the development of economic integration; to strengthen scientific and cultural ties."[1]

The foreign policy of the socialist countries seeks to ensure a stable democratic peace between peoples, strengthen friendly co-operation between peace-loving peoples by every possible means, defend the national sovereignty of large and small nations and resist imperialist aggression. The struggle for peace is its basis. Its cornerstone is alliance and friendship with all the socialist states and the strengthening of the unity and solidarity of the world socialist system. This finds expression in the fundamental laws of a number of socialist countries. "The Czechoslovak Socialist Republic," declares Art. 1(3) of the Czechoslovak Constitution, "shall be a part of the world socialist system; it desires friendly relations with all peoples and the establishment of a stable peace throughout the world." Article 12 of the Bulgarian Constitution declares that "the People's Republic of Bulgaria belongs to the world socialist community, which constitutes one of the most important prerequisites for its independence and all-round development."

The peace-loving character of the socialist states has been clearly demonstrated by their laws in defence of peace, their

---

[1] *24th Congress of the CPSU*, pp. 213-14.

governments' decisions to reduce their armed forces and by their numerous measures to avert world war and strengthen peace.

The campaign for peaceful coexistence between states with differing social systems cannot be counterposed to the revolutionary struggle against imperialism, as is done by some present-day "Left" opportunists.

The policy of peaceful coexistence between states and the revolutionary struggle against imperialism are in reality closely linked. The work for peace and peaceful coexistence weakens imperialism, isolates its most aggressive spokesmen from the mass of the people and assists the revolutionary struggle of the working class and the national liberation movement.

The policy of peaceful co-existence, says the Main Document of the International Meeting of Communist and Workers' Parties held in 1969, "does not imply either the preservation of the socio-political status quo or a weakening of the ideological struggle. It helps to promote the class struggle against imperialism on a national and world-wide scale".[1]

3. REPRESENTATIVE ORGANS AS THE FOUNDATION OF THE STATE APPARATUS OF THE SOCIALIST COUNTRIES

The representative organs of state power, both central and local,[2] which have the closest possible links with the people, are the foundation of the entire state apparatus of a socialist state.

Under the constitutions of the socialist countries, the supreme representative organs of state power are: the Supreme Soviet of the USSR, the Supreme Soviets of the Union Republics incorporated in the Soviet Union and also of the

---

[1] *International Meeting of Communist and Workers' Parties, Moscow, 1969*, p. 31.

[2] In Cuba nation-wide elections have not yet been held. Nor have representative organs of state power been established. This was done as an experiment in 1974 in the Province of Matanzas.

Autonomous Republics incorporated in the RSFSR and of the Azerbaijan, Georgian and Uzbek Union Republics, the People's Assembly of Albania, the People's Assembly of Bulgaria, the Federal Assembly of Czechoslovakia, the Czech and Slovak National Councils in the Czech and Slovak socialist republics incorporated in Czechoslovakia, the People's Chamber of the German Democratic Republic, the State Assembly of Hungary, the Supreme People's Assembly of the Korean People's Democratic Republic, the People's Great Khural of the Mongolian People's Republic, the Polish Seym, the Grand National Assembly of Rumania, the National Assembly of the Democratic Republic of Vietnam, the Federal Skupshina (Assembly) of Yugoslavia, the Skupshinas of the socialist republics which form part of the Socialist Federal Republic of Yugoslavia and the Skupshinas of the Socialist Autonomous Provinces which form part of the Socialist Federal Republic of Yugoslavia and the Skupshinas of the Socialist Autonomous Provinces which form part of the Socialist Republic of Serbia. In the People's Republic of China the All-China Assembly of People's Representatives is the supreme organ of state power. It is not an elected body but is formed through "democratic consultations" (i.e., actually through appointment and "invitation") which makes the representative nature of this slogan extremely doubtable.

Local representative organs of state power are the Soviets of Working People's Deputies in the USSR, the People's Councils in Albania, Bulgaria, the Democratic Republic of Vietnam and Rumania, the National Committees in Czechoslovakia, People's Representative Bodies in the German Democratic Republic,[1] Councils in Hungary, People's Assemblies in the Korean People's Democratic Republic, the Khurals of People's Deputies in the Mongolian People's Republic, the

---

[1] "People's representative bodies" is a collective term. There are Regional and District Assemblies, City and Ward Assemblies, and Community Councils (in villages).

National Councils in Poland and Skupshinas of communities, urban and regional inter-community associations in Yugoslavia. In the People's Republic of China All-China Assemblies of People's Representatives are considered to be local organs of state power. They are formed in a non-democratic way and lack a representative nature.

The constitutions of the socialist states which establish the state power of the working people of town and country under the leadership of the working class lay down that the working people exercise this power through the representative organs of state power they elect.

The representative institutions of the working people in the centre and in the localities constitute a unified system of organs of state power. This is due above all to the social and political uniformity of these institutions as organs of the working people. Yet not only the representative system, but the entire system of the state organs of the socialist state is uniform from this point of view. The representative organs have in addition a number of special features which are common to all such bodies and which distinguish them from other organs of the state. Representative organs of state power *are formed by means of elections on the basis of common fundamental principles of electoral law.* According to the constitutions of the socialist countries, the representative organs at all levels are *organs of state power*, to which other organs are subordinate. The *specific forms of work* of these organs (plenary meetings, deputies' inquiries, the hearing of reports by organs of state administration, etc.) are features common to representative organs at all levels. The organisational unity of the entire system of representative organs of state power is also reflected in the fact that it is based on the principle of *democratic centralism.* This ensures that due account is taken of local characteristics and provides scope for local initiative, while at the same time ensuring uniformity in the work of all the organs of state power. In accordance with this principle, organs of state power at a higher level are invested with powers to control, supervise and co-ordinate the work of those at a lower level.[1] These features indicate the uniformity of representative organs at all levels. They demonstrate that in each of the socialist countries these organs constitute an integrated system.

The status of representative organs as the foundation of the entire state apparatus of a socialist state is manifest in that all other organs are, firstly, formed either directly by the representative bodies or by organs accountable to them, and secondly, are subordinate to them, accountable to them and are under their control.[2] It should be emphasised that the role of foundation of the entire state apparatus in the socialist countries is performed by all the representative organs of state power of the state in question, not by any individual representative organ. Superior organs of state administration are not, of course, subordinate to inferior representative organs of state power. But the representative organs of state power as a whole constitute the backbone of the entire system of the organs of a socialist state.

In the socialist countries governments are formed either directly by the supreme representative bodies (the USSR, Poland, Hungary, etc.) or must submit their programme to such bodies for their approval (for example, in Czechoslovakia, where the government is appointed by the President). In this way in the ultimate analysis both the composition of the government and its programme are approved by the supreme representative body, which controls the government and to which it is accountable, in all the socialist countries.[3]

The Supreme Court and Procurator-General are in the socialist countries elected (appointed) by the supreme rep-

---

[1] For the distinctive features of the relationships between the representative organs at various levels in the Socialist Federal Republic of Yugoslavia, see Chapter XIII (6) of this book.

[2] For the position of the Presidium of the Socialist Federal Republic of Yugoslavia, see Chapter XI.

[3] For the distinctive features of the formation and legal status of the governments of the Republic of Cuba and the KDPR, see Chapter XII of this book.

resentative body or a collegiate organ of state power elected by it. The Supreme Court and Procurator-General are responsible and accountable to the supreme representative body or a collegiate organ of power elected by it.

The executive and administrative bodies are as a rule formed and controlled by local representative organs of state power and may be recalled by them. In the majority of socialist countries, local representative bodies elect the judges of the courts of the area.

In this way, all the links in the state apparatus are derivative from the representative bodies, and are subordinate to them.

Why do representative bodies, rather than any other state organs, constitute the foundation of the entire state apparatus in a socialist state?

The answer lies in the genuinely popular character of socialist democracy.

Destroying the old state apparatus of the exploiting classes, which was designed to facilitate the exploitation and oppression of the working people, the socialist revolution creates a new type of state apparatus, capable of fulfilling the task confronting it—that of the complete emancipation of the working people from all oppression and exploitation.

The apparatus of a socialist state is constructed in a manner wrich ensures the widest participation of the working people in the exercise of power and the administration of the state. Understandably, this apparatus must be based on organs of state which are linked in the closest, most direct fashion with the working people, which provide them with the fullest opportunities to build and administer their own state, and which are in the most direct sense organisations of the majority of the people, promoting the political activity of the mass of the working people to the fullest possible extent.

Representative bodies formed by means of democratic elections, under the constant and direct control of the people, who may at any time recall those who have not justified the confidence of the electors, are organs of this kind.

Like the Soviets in the USSR, the representative organs in the other socialist countries combine features of both state and mass organisations. The building of a new, just social system demands the fullest development of the creative initiative of the working people and their increasingly active participation in the administration of the socialist state. The constant enhancement of the role of the organs of popular representation in the system of state bodies, the further strengthening of their ties with the people, the improvement of their democratic foundations and the increased application of the social principles in their activities are therefore an objective general law governing the building of socialism and communism. It is in this direction that the work to improve the system of popular representation organs is proceeding under the leadership of the Communist and Workers' parties in the majority of socialist countries.

The organisation and functioning of the organs of popular representation in the socialist countries is based on the principles of socialist democracy common to all state organisations of a socialist type,[1] regardless of variations of form depending upon the distinctive national and national-state characteristics of particular countries.

The uniformity of the principles which underlie the organisation and functioning of both the Soviets in the USSR and of the organs of popular representation in the other socialist countries indicates that all these agencies are organs of *one and the same Soviet type*. This is in no way contradicted by their differing nomenclature. Lenin pointed out that the title "Soviet" is not an obligatory feature of an organ of the Soviet type. Addressing the soldiers of the Izmailovsky Regiment in April 1917, he said: "All power in the state, from the bottom up, from the remotest little village to every street block of Petrograd, must belong to the Soviets of Workers', Soldiers', Agricultural Labourers', Peasants' and other Deputies. The central state power uniting these local Soviets must be the Constituent Assembly, National Assem-

---
[1] See Chapters VIII, IX, X and XIII.

bly, or Council of Soviets—*no matter by what name you call it*"[1] (italics mine—*A.M.*).

The principle that the representative organs of state power in all the socialist countries are state organs of a Soviet type must not, of course, be interpreted in an over-simplified fashion which depicts these bodies as copies of the Soviets as they exist in the USSR. The representative organs in each socialist country have their own distinctive features. Even in the Soviet Union itself, there are distinctive features in the juridical regulation of the organisation and work of Soviets in the different Union republics.

The Soviet type of representative body implies the uniformity of the fundamental principles underlying the structure and functioning of the representative organs of the socialist state. Yet it by no means rejects, but on the contrary presupposes consideration of the actual historical circumstances and national characteristics of each country in determining the forms to be assumed by the state legal institutions within the system of representative bodies. This was well expressed by Lenin when he pointed out that "the Soviet type is not yet Soviets as they exist in Russia, but the Soviet type is becoming international".[2]

Jurists of the socialist countries rightly point out that the fundamental principles underlying the organisation and functioning of the Soviets in the USSR and of the representative organs of state power in the other socialist countries are the same, and therefore all the latter are organs of a Soviet type.[3]

---

[1] V. I. Lenin, *Collected Works*, Vol. 24, p. 107.
[2] V. I. Lenin, *Collected Works*, Vol. 29, pp. 172-73.
[3] Thus, B. Spasov in his article "On the Concept of a Representative System and Representative Organs" notes that "representative organs in the socialist countries, including those in the People's Republic of Bulgaria, are organs of the Soviet type" (*Godishnik na Sofiiskiya universitet. Yuridicheski fakultet*, Vol. V, 1964, p. 29). The Polish Professor Rybicki also takes this principle as his starting point when he stresses that "both the general principles of the structure and functioning of Soviets and certain distinctive features arising from the circumstances in which these

Organs of popular representation are in themselves only a form of state organisation, and everything in fact depends upon their content.

They can fulfil their role as the foundations of the socialist state apparatus only if they are guided by a Marxist-Leninist party.

That is why the anti-socialist forces, having realised the futility of an open attack upon the organs of the socialist state, are attempting to undermine the leading role of the Marxist-Leninist party in these bodies. During the counter-revolutionary uprising in Hungary in October-November 1956 the counter-revolution did not attack the Councils, but directed its main blows against the party organisations in the Councils. The anti-socialist forces which became active in Czechoslovakia in 1968 likewise tried to weaken and undermine the leading role of Communists in every way.

The Communist and Workers' parties are firmly resisting these attacks. They stress the decisive significance of the leading role of the Communist Party in the socialist state's fulfilment of its historic role. "The consistent exercise of the leading role of the Party at all levels of the state is the basic guarantee that the socialist state will fulfil its functions and that it will express the interests of the working class and the working people," said the directives adopted by the May, 1969, Plenary Meeting of the Central Committee of the Communist Party of Czechoslovakia.[1]

---

bodies emerged and subsequently developed find expression" in the system of representative organs of state power in Poland (Z. Rybicki, *Dzialalność i organizucja rad narodowych w PRL*, Warsaw, 1965, p. 29). On the basis of an analysis of the fundamental features and distinctive characteristics of the representative organs of state power of the socialist countries, Professor I. Kovács, Corresponding Member of the Hungarian Academy of Sciences, also concludes that "at the present stage of the development of the countries of people's democracy—including the Hungarian People's Republic—power is exercised through a system of Soviet-type organs (Beér J., Kovács I., Szamel L., *Magyar államjog*, Budapest, 1960, p. 158).

[1] *Rudé právo*, June 3, 1969, Supplement, p. 5.

4. THE ECONOMIC FOUNDATION AND STRUCTURE OF THE SOCIALIST COUNTRIES

The socialist ownership of the basic instruments and means of production and the socialist economic system constitute the economic basis of a state of the socialist type.

This definition has never been disputed in the case of states where the foundations of socialism have already been laid. In the case of states where these foundations are still being laid, many authors believe that prior to the victory of socialism in branches of the economy and in conditions of the plurality of social and economic structures, both socialist and private ownership constitutes the economic basis.[1]

We believe this view to be incorrect. The question of which forms or, more precisely, what type of ownership and which corresponding economic system constitute the economic basis of a given state can be correctly answered only in the light of Marxist-Leninist teachings regarding the relationship between the economic basis and the political superstructure.

Only the form of ownership which constitutes the foundation of the economic basis (that is, the aggregate of the production relations), of which the given state is the political superstructure, can constitute the economic basis of a state.

Therefore only socialist (state and co-operative) ownership of the instruments and means of production and a socialist economic system can constitute the economic basis of a state which is laying the foundations of socialism.

The socialist ownership of the instruments and means of production and a socialist economic system thus form the economic basis of all the socialist states, although, of course, the scope and strength of this economic system depends directly upon the successes achieved in the building of socialism.

---

[1] V. Maslennikov, *Mongolskaya Narodnaya Respublika na puti k sotsializmu*, Gospolitizdat, Moscow, 1951, p. 33; *Konstitutsiya i osnovniye zakonodatelniye akty Mongolskoi Narodnoi Respubliki*, Inostrannaya Literatura Publishers, Moscow, 1952, p. 20.

The economic basis of the socialist states is set down in legal form in their constitutions. "The socialist economic system and socialist property in the instruments and means of production, firmly established as a result of the abolition of the capitalist economic system, private ownership of the instruments and means of production and the exploitation of man by man, shall constitute the economic foundation of the USSR", declares Art. 4 of the USSR Constitution. Art. 8 of the 1960 Constitution of the Mongolian People's Republic lays down that "the socialist economic system and the socialist ownership of the means of production established as a result of the prolonged and arduous struggle of the working people of the Mongolian People's Republic and as a result of the abolition of the private ownership of the means of production and of the exploitation of man by man shall constitute the economic foundation of the Mongolian People's Republic". The Polish Constitution of 1952 lays down that social ownership shall be the inviolable foundation of the development of the state and the source of the nation's wealth and strength (Art. 77 i).

The special creative role of the socialist state as the instrument of the establishment and planned growth of the socialist economy is clearly manifest in the creation and development of socialist economic forms.

The people's governments, basing themselves upon the objective economic law of the correspondence of production relations to the level of the productive forces, nationalised the key branches of the national economy.

Nationalisation was carried out on the basis of legislative acts, under the terms of which large and medium-sized industrial and commercial enterprises, banks, rail, water and air transport and the means of communication became state property.

In many socialist countries the key economic branches were actually transferred to the working people's state considerably in advance of the adoption of relevant legislation. In Poland and Yugoslavia, for example, as the country's territory was liberated from the nazis, the new people's governments which formed in the course of the national liberation struggle, with the participation of the working people themselves, took over industrial, transport and other enterprises which were mainly owned by the nazi invaders or their collaborators. Only some time later did this *de facto* nationalisation find expression in the appropriate legislation. This in no way diminishes the role of the subsequent legislative acts, the significance of which lay in that they set down in legislative form the nationalisation which had already taken place.

The establishment of socialist economic forms had distinctive features in each socialist country, which arose from the special characteristics of its historical development.

In the Mongolian People's Republic, for example, where the transition from feudalism to socialism was direct, bypassing the capitalist stage, industry was built up by the people's government and was therefore socialist from the outset.

The nationalisation of the instruments and means of production belonging to the big capitalists is a fundamental law governing the building of socialism in all countries.

Small and medium capitalist undertakings may become socialist in a variety of ways, depending upon the conditions in each country.

The German Democratic Republic, for example, nationalised capitalist property owned by the monopoly bourgeoisie and also by other strata of the bourgeoisie which had supported the nazi regime. But property belonging to the democratically and patriotically inclined middle strata was at first transformed into socialist property through the transitional form of state-private enterprises. Then in the spring of 1972 private undertakings and also private holdings in joint state-private enterprises were bought up by the socialist state.

As a means of bringing about the peaceful, gradual transformation of the privately-owned capitalist property of the national (middle) bourgeoisie into socialist property, state capitalism has also been used in the Democratic Republic of Vietnam.

The Korean People's Democratic Republic nationalised industrial, transport and communications enterprises, and banks owned by Japanese imperialists and the Korean compradore bourgeoisie. The remaining capitalists and traders were ruined during the 1950-53 war and found themselves in such a plight that they could not re-establish themselves without the help of the state and the socialist sector; nor could they do so without combining their efforts, means of production and finances. The introduction of co-operatives in agriculture and in the artisan industry made it impossible for them to buy raw materials and supplies on the private market. In these circumstances the Labour Party of Korea transformed capitalist industry and trade belonging to the national and petty bourgeoisie into various forms of co-operatives.

Co-operation has also been widely used in many socialist countries to turn the farms of rural capitalists (kulaks) into socialist farms.

Socialist ownership of the instruments and means of production and socialist economic forms also emerged as a result of the voluntary association of working people in production co-operatives of a socialist type, and as a result of the voluntary socialisation of the instruments and means of production belonging to the members of these co-operatives.

Socialist ownership is growing steadily stronger and is augmenting in the socialist countries. The extended reproduction of socialist (state and co-operative) enterprises is the most important source of this growth and development.

As a rule, the constitutions of the socialist countries lay down two main forms of socialist property: state property and co-operative property.

Property owned by mass organisations of the working people is likewise a form of socialist property. But the constitutions of the socialist countries, with the exception of those of the German Democratic Republic, Bulgaria and Yugoslavia, make no reference to this form since the fundamental law only lays down the basic forms of socialist property.

State property is the highest form of socialist property[1], that is, it constitutes the property of the whole people, the "national wealth", as it is described in the constitutions of the socialist countries.

In the socialist countries, mineral deposits, part of the land comprising state land (in the USSR and the Mongolian People's Republic, all land), water, state forests, mines, roads, rail, water and air transport, means of communication, banks, state industrial and commercial enterprises, state farms, machine stations and municipal enterprises and installations, are state property.

The state is the subject of the right to state property. In the socialist countries state enterprises are not the owners of the property at their disposal; they merely run it.

The constitutions of some socialist countries do not use the term "state property". The Polish Constitution, although referring to state socialist industry and to state industrial, agricultural and commercial enterprises, does not use the term "state property", but speaks of "public" and "national property". The Yugoslav Constitution establishes the "social ownership of the means of production". But, despite the especially wide powers exercised by enterprises and institutions over the public property at their disposal (a distinctive feature of the Yugoslav economic system), the Yugoslav Constitution stipulates that no one has the right of ownership of the social means of production.

But the fact that a socialist enterprise is not, in the state-legal sense, the owner of the public property which it controls, in no way implies that it should not have the autonomy necessary to run this property to achieve the maximum benefit.

Under a planned economy, a socialist enterprise cannot of course have unlimited entrepreneural freedom and act as the "collective proprietor" of the means of production placed

---

[1] This in no way implies an underestimation of the significance of the other form—co-operative property.

under its administration, as some present-day revisionists insist should be the case. The recognition of an enterprise's rights of ownership of the public property it administers would in effect mean the fragmentation of that property, which would become the property of individual enterprises rather than of the whole people. The real meaning of such proposals was demonstrated by Lenin, who pointed out that "any direct or indirect legalisation of the rights of ownership of the workers of any given factory or any given trade on their particular production ... is a flagrant distortion of the basic principles of Soviet power and a complete rejection of socialism".[1]

While resisting revisionist distortions, the Marxist-Leninist parties of the socialist countries also reject dogmatic conceptions.

Such conceptions, which restrict the autonomy of socialist enterprises necessary for the successful development of the socialist economy, underestimate the role of material incentives and favour a crude administrative approach, hold up the growth of socialist production and therefore obstruct the building of socialism.

A variety of measures, experiments and discussions have been undertaken over a number of years in many socialist countries to discover the most effective socialist economic model appropriate to the conditions of each particular country and ensuring both the unity of the economic system as a whole and the autonomy and initiative which enterprises and their amalgamations need in order to achieve the most successful development of socialist production.

Co-operative ownership—ownership by particular co-operatives and co-operative associations—is another form of socialist property to be found in the socialist countries.

Agricultural producer co-operatives, through which the transition is effected from small individual peasant farming to large collective farming, are of particular importance in the building of socialism.

---
[1] V. I. Lenin, *Collected Works*, Vol. 42, pp. 100-01.

The retention of the private ownership of land is an important distinctive feature of the evolution of agricultural producer co-operatives in the socialist countries which emerged after the Second World War.

In these countries the land, with the exception of relatively small areas (land belonging to state farms, machine and tractor stations, research establishments, etc., and also the land of major cities and the state reserve land), is not state property, but private property. Mineral resources (coal, ores and other mineral deposits) are, however, state property.

This is due to historical conditions in these countries. In Russia the principle of the private ownership of land had still not become firmly rooted in the consciousness of the peasantry before the October Socialist Revolution. It was therefore possible to nationalise all land immediately (Decree on Land, November 8 [October 26] 1917). But the countries which took the socialist road after the Second World War had firmly established traditions of private land ownership. The slogan of the nationalisation of all land would not have been immediately comprehensible to the peasantry. Lenin, having in mind countries with strong traditions of private land ownership, warned against precipitate and incautious moves to nationalise all land: "In most capitalist countries, however, the proletarian state should not at once completely abolish private property; at all events, it guarantees both the small and middle peasantry, not only the preservation of their plots of land but also their enlargement to cover the total area they usually rented...."[1]

The land reform legislation in these countries provided for the confiscation of large landed estates and land owned by collaborators, and for its distribution to the landless and land-hungry peasants, i.e., to the poor and middle peasants. Only a relatively small part of land became state land, while by far the larger part became the property of the working peasantry. Kulak land was as a rule not confiscated. The

---

[1] V. I. Lenin, *Collected Works*, Vol. 31, p. 157.

principle of "the land belongs to those who till it" became the most important principle of the land reforms and found legal expression in the constitutions of these countries. The buying and selling of land, its leasing or mortgaging, was, however, either restricted or prohibited.

The retention of private land ownership in states where power and the key sectors of the economy are in the hands of the working people does not constitute an obstacle to the development of producer co-operatives. As working peasants are organised in co-operatives on a mass scale and the class of rich peasants is abolished, the land is gradually transferred to agricultural co-operatives of a socialist type and to state farms. Georgi Dimitrov said in 1948:

"We consider that by gradually winning over the poor and middling peasants into co-operative farms, by developing the machine and tractor stations, by prohibiting the renting out of farms, by restricting and subsequently prohibiting the purchase and sale of land, by reducing and subsequently abolishing rent through decision of the co-operative farmers themselves when conditions permit, *the practical problem of land nationalisation will be solved by leaving all land for the perpetual use of the toiling peasants.*"[1]

All land was nationalised in the Mongolian People's Republic, where the transition from feudalism to socialism was direct, bypassing the capitalist phase, and where prior to the revolution all land belonged to the secular and clerical feudalists, while the peasantry was nomadic and had no concept of land ownership.

The distinctive feature of Rumanian legislation is that under the 1965 Constitution land belonging to peasants who are members of agricultural producer co-operatives is co-operative property (Art. 9).

In several socialist countries, against the background of the development of the agricultural producer co-operative

---

[1] Georgi Dimitrov, *Selected Works (1910-1943)*, Sofia, 1960, pp. 398-99.

movement and with the retention of private land ownership, there exist both co-operatives of the advanced type in which income is distributed in accordance with the amount and quality of labour performed, and co-operatives of a less advanced type in which a part of the income is distributed in accordance with the amount of land and the number of implements contributed by members.

But the trend is towards co-operation of the more advanced type.

The producer co-operative movement in the socialist countries was able to profit from the Soviet experience and avoid fruitless experimentation. In the early post-revolutionary years, for example, agricultural communes were set up in the USSR. Formed at a time when there was little machinery and production was inadequate, the communes adopted an equalitarian approach and took little account of the personal interest of their members. Such communes naturally could not attract mass peasant support, and during the period of large-scale collectivisation were re-organised into agricultural *artels*. In the agricultural *artel* the main means of production are held in common while each member retains personal ownership of his subsidiary farming, the size of which is determined by the Rules of the co-operative, and labour is remunerated in accordance with its quantity and quality. The *artel* has become the fundamental, main form of agricultural co-operation in the USSR and most of the other socialist countries. Experience has shown that this form best corresponds to the present level of agricultural production and the political consciousness of the peasantry.

Any infringement of the voluntary principle or of the material interest of the peasantry during the socialist reconstruction of agriculture, or any resort to equalitarian distribution causes serious disruption of agricultural production.

In the past a substantial part of the aid which the state gave to the co-operatives was used not to expand production, but to boost the incomes distributed to members. This discredited agricultural producer co-operatives in the eyes of the working people. Mistakes led to the infringement of the principle of the material incentives of co-operators and to dogmatism and stereotyped attitudes in agricultural science and practice.[1]

The overcoming of these harmful trends promoted the development of agricultural producer co-operatives.

The co-operative system has triumphed in all the socialist countries except Poland, Yugoslavia and Cuba.

There were 10,203 registered producer co-operatives in Poland as of September 30, 1956. Some were not economically viable and, as was noted at the Eighth Plenary Meeting of the Polish United Workers' Party (October 1956), had discredited the idea of agricultural co-operation. The Eighth Plenary Meeting emphasised the need for the strict observance of the principle of voluntariness in setting up agricultural co-operatives. It called for the winding-up of non-viable co-operatives and for support for those which were viable and which genuinely demonstrated the advantages of socialist economic forms.

The majority of co-operatives broke up immediately after the Eighth Plenary Meeting. Not only non-viable co-operatives, but also a number which were economically strong were dissolved under the pressure of anti-socialist forces.

Some of them were subsequently re-established; new co-operatives were set up as well. At the beginning of 1970 there were 1,090 registered producer co-operatives in Poland.

Simpler forms of co-operation—various types of association for the performance of particular farming operations— are growing up in the Polish countryside in accordance with the decisions of the Eighth Plenary Meeting, carried further in the decisions of subsequent Central Committee plenary

---

[1] See J. Kadár, "Socialist Reconstruction of Agriculture of Hungary", *World Marxist Review*, Vol. 4, No. 6, London, 1961, pp. 6, 7, 10; T. Zhivkov, *Report of the Central Committee of the Bulgarian Communist Party to the Eighth Party Congress*, Russ. ed., Gospolitizdat, 1963, pp. 59-60; *VIII Plenum Komitetu Centralnego PZPR*, October 19-21, 1956; *Nowe Drogi*, No. 10, 1956, pp. 34-37.

meetings and congresses of the Polish United Workers' Party. These include associations for the joint use of machinery, the joint performance of land-improvement work and for the production of building materials. Farmers' circles are playing an important role in the socialist reorganisation of Polish agriculture. They are a distinctive form of voluntary peasant organisation set up to raise farm output by means of the correct co-ordination of peasants' individual efforts with mutual aid and co-operation in the use both of the peasants' own resources and of social resources. The circles popularise farming know-how, purchase agricultural machinery, organise the cultivation of fallow land, participate in the distribution of the financial and material aid given by the state for agricultural development, etc. The circle members are individual owners of their means of production, while co-operation through the clubs enables them to step up output on their holdings. But the common ownership of the instruments and means of production (machinery and other equipment bought by the circles as common property) is also emerging and the habits of collective work are gaining firmer ground. Farmers' circles exist in 90 per cent of the villages and embrace almost 55 per cent of all holdings. Resolutions and other statements of the Polish United Workers' Party show that the socialist transformation of agriculture is the major aim set by the Party's programme in the countryside, and that the Party will continue patiently but persistently to work to win the Polish peasantry for producer co-operation in farming.

In Yugoslavia the policy of mass collectivisation adopted in 1948 was in 1953 replaced by one of encouraging other, simpler forms of co-operatives, mainly supply and marketing. At present attention is mainly focussed upon the development of farming co-operatives of a general type described as agricultural co-operatives. They operate co-operative farms, and also organise various forms of joint work on land belonging to individual peasants, buy farm surpluses in the villages, process farm produce, and supply the villages with implements and other facilities for farming needs and also with consumer goods. In 1969 there were 1,111 agricultural co-operatives in Yugoslavia.

In both Poland and Yugoslavia the socialist sector in agriculture, represented mainly by state farms and also co-operatives, is comparatively small in terms of cultivated area (15 per cent in Poland and 14 per cent in Yugoslavia). But its share of marketable farm output is substantially greater. In Yugoslavia the socialist sector in 1970 contributed over 20 per cent of total farm output and 45 per cent of procurements. In Poland state holdings accounted for about 40 per cent of the procurements and deliveries of grain in 1973, while their share of total marketable farm output was about 20 per cent.

The distinctive features of the socialist re-organisation of agriculture in Cuba arise from special objective and subjective factors. The larger part of the republic's cultivated land—70 per cent—belongs to the state farms. In 1965 these farms owned 50 per cent of the cattle. State farms grew 75 per cent of the sugar cane, and all the cotton, kenaf and henequen. Their contribution will further increase in the near future, because their output is growing considerably faster than that of the individual farms. These circumstances, coupled with the various means by which the state influences the development of the individual farms provide the socialist economy with a sound position in agriculture and guarantee it against the influence of small-commodity production. A hasty campaign to introduce mass co-operation in the countryside, which could do nothing but harm, is therefore unnecessary. The main stress is at present laid on increasing output on the state farms, and also on aid of all kinds for the varied forms of simple co-operatives Producer co-operatives in Cuba have not been developed to any significant extent; in 1971 they only numbered several dozen. Marketing, credit and service co-operatives are much more common. Moreover, in 1971 there were nearly 10,000 mutual aid teams which covered nearly 45 per cent of all peasant farms.

Such teams were first set up in 1964 to carry out work requiring large amounts of labour on the holdings of each of their members in turn.

The state and co-operative sectors of the national economy together make up the socialist economic system, in which the relations of production are relations of co-operation and mutual assistance between people freed from exploitation and are socialist relations of production.

Socialist production relations have over a short period of time demonstrated their decisive superiority over those of capitalism. The rapid growth of industrial production in the socialist countries is clear evidence of this.

High rates of growth in output is a general law of socialism now confirmed by the experience of all the socialist countries.

By their economic achievements the socialist countries are making a major contribution to the world revolutionary movement. By expanding their economies under the conditions of peace which they themselves have secured, and by improving the people's living and working conditions, they are giving the working people of the capitalist countries a practical demonstration of the advantages of socialism and are in this way winning more and more millions of working people in these countries for socialism. Lenin's forecast that "we are exercising our main influence on the international revolution through our economic policy"[1] is coming true. Thus, life itself shows that the interests of socialism are promoted by the peaceful coexistence of states with differing social systems and, in this context, by the economic competition between the socialist and capitalist systems.

In the USSR, socialist production relations triumphed in all branches of the national economy in the second half of the 1930s. Since then the Soviet people have created the economy of a developed socialist society. Its distinctive features are: the absolute predominance of socialist property and the

---

[1] V. I. Lenin, *Collected Works*, Vol. 32, p. 437.

eradication of all exploiting elements, the complete establishment of the socialist principle of distribution in accordance with the quantity and quality of work done, the attainment of a level of economic development immeasurably higher than that in the first period of the victory of socialism, the building of a powerful material and technical base, notably diversified industry and large-scale socialist agriculture, advanced science and highly qualified personnel, and the achievement of a qualitatively new level of production on the basis of the scientific and technological revolution. The building of the economy of a developed socialist society in the USSR has made it possible to begin the practical work of laying the material and technical basis of communism and much more fully to achieve the aim of socialist production—the aim, in Lenin's words, of ensuring the "*full* well-being and free, *all-round* development for *all* the members of society".[1]

In the majority of other socialist countries the main tasks of the period of transition from capitalism to socialism have been carried out: socialist relations of production have triumphed in all sectors of the national economy. The building of a developed socialist society is under way.

In a number of socialist countries (Poland, the Democratic Republic of Vietnam, Yugoslavia and Cuba) capitalist elements still exist in various forms. In Poland capitalist elements in industry and trade are infinitesimal, and kulak farms amount to less than two per cent of the total. In Yugoslavia private trading enterprises amount to seven per cent of the total, while their share in the retail trade turnover is only 0.5 per cent. Privately-owned handicraft workshops can make only limited use of hired labour. The maximum depends upon the nature of the work, but cannot exceed five. The 1953 law "On Agricultural Land and on the Allotment of Land to Economic Organisations"[2] reduced the

---

[1] V. I. Lenin, *Collected Works*, Vol. 6, p. 54.
[2] See *Sluzhbeni list SFRY*, Item 22/1953.

maximum permissible size of private land holdings from 50-70 to 25 acres. This was written down into the Constitution.

In Cuba, an important contribution to the abolition of the capitalist structure in agriculture was made by the law of October 5, 1963 nationalising private holdings of over five *caballerias*.[1] "The existence of a rural bourgeoisie is incompatible with the interests and aims of the socialist revolution," the law declares. But there are still private farms which exploit hired labour. This is not the case, however, with other branches of the Cuban economy. The last small privately-owned industrial and trading enterprises were nationalised in March 1968.

In the Democratic Republic of Vietnam, the privately-owned undertakings of the national bourgeoisie are being transformed into state-capitalist undertakings.

The socialist economic system thus plays the decisive role in the economies of all the socialist countries.

The socialist constitutions permit small private farms based on personal labour. The share of such small-commodity production is now very small in the majority of socialist countries and only in Poland, Yugoslavia and Cuba, where most peasant holdings are individually-owned, is it possible to speak of a small-commodity structure.

In establishing the main forms of ownership, the constitutions of the socialist countries clearly define the attitude of the socialist state to the citizens' personal property—that is, to the ownership of articles of personal consumption.

In its campaign against socialism bourgeois propaganda falsely asserts that socialism means the complete abolition of personal property. In reality, socialism does not abolish personal property; on the contrary, it grows thanks to the steady improvement of the people's living standards in a socialist

---

[1] See *Pravda*, October 6, 1963. 1 *caballeria* equals approximately 32 acres. The maximum private holding was therefore set at approximately 165 acres.

state. The inviolability of the personal property of citizens derived from their labour, and the right to inherit such property, is guaranteed by the fundamental laws of the socialist countries. "The laws shall protect the right of citizens to have personal property in the form of earned income and savings, a house and a house-garden plot, articles of household and personal use and convenience, and also the right of citizens to inherit personal property," declares Art. 10 of the USSR Constitution.

Art. 10 of the Czechoslovak Constitution establishes:

"1. The personal ownership by citizens of consumer goods, in particular of articles of personal and household use, individual dwelling-houses and also of earned savings, shall be inviolable.

"2. The inheritance of personal property shall be guaranteed."

5. THE CLASS STRUCTURE OF SOCIETY IN THE SOCIALIST COUNTRIES

The revolutionary transformations and the successes gained in the building of socialism and communism have radically changed the class structure of society in the socialist countries. In most of them there are now only two friendly classes—the working class and the working peasantry. The position of the working class has changed fundamentally during the years of people's rule.

The *working class* is no longer a class deprived of the instruments and means of production, oppressed and exploited by the landowners and capitalists. It has become a class which, together with all other working people, owns the instruments and means of production, a class free from exploitation. It has become the organiser and leader of the building of socialism, the leading force of the people.

From the point of view of its class consciousness, the working class is not homogeneous at the time when the working people win political power. Its core consists of politically aware, experienced workers. It also includes strata which have a lower level of political awareness. Prolonged imperialist domination had a harmful ideological effect upon a certain section of the workers, blunting their class consciousness and infecting them with nationalism and chauvinism. Ruined by capitalism, the petty bourgeoisie who joined the ranks of the proletariat brought with them their petty-bourgeois views and habits. It is clear, therefore, that in guiding the socialist construction the Communist and Workers' parties of the socialist countries had to give prominence to the task of the socialist education of the leading force of the nation—the working class—and the complete eradication of bourgeois ideological influence over it.

In the Mongolian People's Republic the transition from feudalism to socialism bypassed the capitalist phase and the working class grew up after the establishment of popular rule. The Mongolian People's Revolutionary Party has always paid great attention to the development of the workers' class consciousness.

Socialist industrialisation causes a rapid increase in the size of the working class. In the USSR, workers constitute more than 60 per cent of the country's population, in the German Democratic Republic workers and office employees make up 87 per cent of the gainfully employed population and in Czechoslovakia workers account for 58 per cent of the population. The structure of the working class is also changing. During the period of the rapid economic development hundreds of thousands of former peasants and representatives of other social strata have joined the ranks of the working classes of the socialist countries. Clearly, they need some time to catch up with veteran workers both as regards skill and class consciousness. The moulding of the workers' class consciousness in conditions of popular rule is neither simple nor automatic. The Communist and Workers' parties must therefore pay great attention in their day-to-day work to enhancing the level of organisation and awareness of the working class, and to raising its authority among the people.

The working class of the socialist countries constantly promotes from its own midst capable leaders for all sectors of state and social activities. In the USSR, for example, in 1971 over 80 per cent of secretaries of the Central Committees of the Republican Communist parties and territorial and regional Party committees, Chairmen of Councils of Ministers and territorial and regional Executive Committees, and about 70 per cent of Ministers and Chairmen of State Committees of the USSR had started their careers as workers or peasants. In the German Democratic Republic, 69 per cent of Ministers and State Secretaries, 87 per cent of chairmen of district councils, 92 per cent of Directors-General of amalgamations of people's enterprises and key combines, nearly 75 per cent of judges, over 71 per cent of Procurators and 80 per cent of officers in the National People's Army have come from among the workers.

The leading role of the working class in state and society finds legislative embodiment in the constitutions of the socialist countries. The Hungarian Constitution (Art 2, iii) stipulates that the working class, which exercises power in alliance with the co-operative peasantry, together with the intellectuals and other working strata of the population, is the leading class in the Hungarian People's Republic.

The working class of the socialist countries exercises its leading role with the aid of its militant headquarters—the Communist (Workers') Party.[1]

The position of the *working peasantry*—land-hungry and middle peasants—has also changed radically. As a result of the land reform the working peasants have been freed from the landowners' bondage and received land from the people's government. The peasantry has in practice seen that only popular rule under the leadership of the working class can satisfy their vital needs. The alliance of the working class and the peasantry and the leading role of the work-

---

[1] See Chapter IV of this book.

ing class have grown stronger in the course of the land reform.

The replacement of individual peasant farming by socialist, co-operative farming is necessary in order to achieve the final emancipation of the working peasantry from all forms of exploitation, to ensure a steady improvement in the material well-being and cultural level of the working peasantry and a sharp increase in agricultural output.

Today, as a result of mass co-operation, the peasants have become a class of co-operative farmers in the majority of the socialist countries. The alliance between the working class and the peasantry has in consequence grown still stronger and reached a new and higher level of development.

In those socialist countries where co-operation has not yet been implemented on a mass scale, the state gives all-out assistance to the individual working peasant and protects him against exploitation by the kulaks and other capitalist elements. This aid takes varied forms. The state exempts the smallest peasant farms from taxation and establishes differential tax rates under which land-hungry and middle peasants pay substantially less tax than kulaks. The working peasants also receive substantial assistance in the form of credits, contracts, allocations of goods in short supply, etc. Efforts are at the same time being made to draw the peasants into co-operative farms.

Radical changes have taken place in the composition and status of the *intelligentsia* in the socialist countries. The overwhelming majority of the present-day intellectuals are playing an active part in the building of socialism.

The Communist and Workers' parties entrust the intellectuals with the solution of important problems, both in the creation of the material and technical foundation for the new society and in the ideological moulding of the new man. The new society is being built on the basis of the most advanced science and culture. The contribution of the intellectuals to the economic, scientific and cultural development of the socialist countries will therefore continue to grow.

The *exploiting classes* have been abolished in the majority of the socialist countries. This process testifies to the iron necessity of the fundamental general laws governing the building of socialism and to the creative contribution made by the various socialist countries to the achievement of this goal.

The class of landowners was abolished during the agrarian reform. In the Democratic Republic of Vietnam, where a section of the patriotically-minded landowners participated in the national liberation struggle, a differentiated approach to the different categories of landowners was a distinctive feature of this process. The land of those who had taken part in the liberation struggle was bought up, while that of others was confiscated or requisitioned.

As a result of the nationalisation of the key branches of the national economy, all socialist countries have abolished big urban capitalists and most of these countries have also done away with middle urban capitalists.

The situation is different in a number of countries (the German Democratic Republic, the Democratic Republic of Vietnam) as regards the property of patriotic elements among the middle (national) bourgeoisie who took part in the anti-fascist, anti-imperialist struggle and the democratic transformations and who understood the inevitability of the transformation of society along socialist lines. Their property is not nationalised, but is gradually transformed into socialist property through various forms of state capitalism (joint state-private undertaking) and is bought up, while the representatives of the national bourgeoisie are being re-educated and becoming working people.

In the final, highest form of state capitalism state-capitalist enterprises are fully run by the state, while their former owners receive a certain proportion of their profit. The payment of this unearned income will be terminated as a result of advances in the socialist re-education of the national bourgeoisie. As was noted, in the German Democratic Republic private-capitalist and state-private property had been transformed into socialist property by 1972.

The kulaks have been abolished as a class in the majority of the socialist countries.

In Cuba, Poland and Yugoslavia, as was earlier the case in other socialist countries, a policy of restricting and ousting the kulaks is being pursued. This takes the form of establishing maximum size for privately-owned holdings, restrictions on the use of hired labour, higher taxes on kulak holdings, etc.

Former kulaks who have honestly resolved to find their new place in socialist society are accepted into producer co-operatives managed by the small and middle peasants. In countries where co-operation has been completed, the majority of the former kulaks joined the co-operatives voluntarily. The small section which attempted to obstruct the co-operative movement received a fitting rebuff. The kulaks who join the co-operatives are re-educated and gradually absorbed into the mass of the working peasantry. They enjoy the same rights as the latter. In Hungary, for example, former kulaks may after two years of honest work in an agricultural producer co-operative, become full-fledged members and even be eligible for election to its management. This is of great significance in bringing about the complete merging of former poor peasants, middle peasants and kulaks in a single class of working co-operative peasantry. Opposing any dogmatic approach to the Leninist slogan of reliance upon the poor peasant, alliance with the middle peasant and struggle against the kulak, János Kadár declared: "We have faithfully followed this Leninist precept throughout the long years of class struggle, but to apply this principle literally, in our conditions [those of the complete victory of the co-operative system in the countryside and the abolition of the kulaks on that basis—*A.M.*], as a ready-made pattern at the present time would be a grave mistake indeed. Lenin never suggested that we should base ourselves on the *former* poor peasant to form an alliance with the *former* middle peasant, or to combat the *former* rich peasant. If we, instead of furthering the coming together now under way, were to divide the peasants according to their former class affiliations we would be setting one co-operator against another, reviving their old differences springing from past class distinctions. It is precisely in accordance with Lenin's teachings that we put the emphasis on the complete eradication of all vestiges of the old differences."[1]

The building of a socialist society takes place in the process of class struggle. "The proletariat does not cease the *class struggle* after it has captured political power, but continues it until classes are abolished—of course, under different circumstances, in different form and by different means."[2]

The class struggle continues for a certain period even after the abolition of the exploiting classes. By the abolition of the exploiting classes Marxism-Leninism implies the ending of the economic conditions which enable them to exploit the labour of others, not their physical extermination. There remain living people who do not immediately renounce the exploitationist ideology they have inherited. Some attempt to continue the struggle against the rule of the people which has deprived them of the opportunity of living on the labour of others. The re-education of such people requires a considerable time.

Ideological struggle is an important form of class struggle. Even after the abolition of the exploiting classes the struggle against the survivals of bourgeois ideology in the minds of individuals, for the complete overcoming of bourgeois and petty-bourgeois morality continues to be a most important task. Imperialist propaganda tries to re-vitalise

---

[1] J. Kadár, "Socialist Reconstruction of Agriculture of Hungary", *World Marxist Review*, Vol. 4, No. 6, London, 1961, p. 10.
[2] V. I. Lenin, *Collected Works*, Vol. 29, pp. 420-21.

the hangovers of bourgeois way of life and thinking. This intensifies the ideological struggle. This struggle is conducted in forms which correspond to its manifestations. In socialist countries where there are still individuals whose outlook is predominantly bourgeois and whose attitude is politically motivated by hostility to socialism, the contradiction between their outlook and the ideology of socialism is antagonistic. But it is resolved not by measures of class suppression, but by ideological struggle, provided these people do not violate the socialist rule of law. If they do, this brings due retribution in its train.

In their struggle against the socialist system the reactionary elements have the backing of international imperialism, which resorts to any means to undermine socialism. The organisation of conspiracies and sabotage, ideological manoeuvres designed to erode the foundations of socialism—all are used by imperialism in its anti-socialist campaigns.

Great vigilance is therefore necessary regarding the intrigues of internal and external anti-popular forces.

"The formation of the socialist world constitutes an integral part of the class struggle being waged in the international arena. The enemies of socialism are keeping up their attempts to undermine the foundations of the socialist state power, thwart the socialist transformation of society and restore their own rule. To give a firm rebuff to these attempts is an essential function of the socialist state, which relies on the broad masses led by the working class and its Communist vanguard,"[1] said the Main Document adopted by the International Meeting of Communist and Workers' Parties in Moscow in June, 1969.

The acuteness of the class struggle is influenced by both internal and external factors. Today, when socialism has become a world system, the balance of forces between social-

---

[1] *International Meeting of Communist and Workers' Parties, Moscow, 1969*, pp. 22-23.

ism and capitalism in the world arena has radically changed in favour of socialism. Within the socialist countries, the working people are uniting more closely around the working class, led by the Communist and Workers' parties. The old reactionary political forces which opposed the people were defeated and isolated. In this situation many of the old exploiting classes realise with increasing clarity that they are faced with the only alternative: either to continue a hopeless struggle against popular rule and face deserved retribution, or to renounce the struggle and take the path of loyalty to popular rule. Therefore more and more former exploiters, albeit slowly and with hesitation, are beginning to play their part in the building of socialism.

But the process of winning over former exploiting elements to socialism is complex and difficult. Should there appear the slightest hope of taking advantage of more or less serious difficulties for their own ends, or of intervention by foreign imperialists, the reactionary elements again raise their head and a significant section of the former exploiting elements who have been won over to socialism again take the side of reaction.

In the majority of the socialist countries which emerged after the Second World War the establishment of the dictatorship of the proletariat was not accompanied by civil war. The working people, under the leadership of the Communist and Workers' parties, taking advantage of the favourable situation created by the victory of the USSR in the Second World War, overthrew the anti-popular regimes after the ousting of the fascist occupation forces, and established people's rule, which in the process of bitter class struggle, though not of civil war, developed into a new form of the dictatorship of the proletariat.

Such a relatively peaceful development of the revolution (without civil war) was positive in that it avoided the tremendous human and material losses inevitable in civil war.

But the peaceful development of the revolution without civil war enabled the bourgeoisie to preserve its cadres, who, given a suitable opportunity, can come forward as an active political force in opposition to the rule of the people.

The consolidation of the socialist forces and the weakening of the resistance of the remnants of hostile classes is a general tendency of the class struggle within the socialist countries.

But this general tendency does not proceed in a straight line, and the bitterness of the class struggle does not diminish evenly. It can at times become more acute as a result of changes in the internal or external situation. This is illustrated by the Czechoslovak events of 1968.

The socialist unity of the people takes shape and grows stronger, and hence the social basis of the socialist state gains increasing strength, as the building of socialism and communism progresses. This process has naturally developed further in the USSR, where the exploiting classes were abolished and the social and political unity of the Soviet people began to take shape even before the start of the socialist revolution in the other socialist countries. New achievements in the consolidation of the unity of the Soviet people were recorded at the 24th Congress of the CPSU: "*A new historical community of people, the Soviet people*, took shape in our country during the years of socialist construction. New, harmonious relations, relations of friendship and co-operation, were formed between the classes and social groups, nations and nationalities in joint labour, in the struggle for socialism and in the battles fought in defence of socialism. Our people are welded together by a common Marxist-Leninist ideology and the lofty aims of building communism. The multi-national Soviet people demonstrate this monolithic unity by their labour and by their unanimous approval of the Communist Party's policy."[1]

---

[1] *24th Congress of the CPSU*, p. 92.

6. STATE PLANNING OF ECONOMIC AND CULTURAL DEVELOPMENT

The planned development of the national economy is a fundamental principle of the social system of the socialist countries. It finds legal embodiment in their constitutions.

The planned, proportionate development of the national economy is an objective economic law of socialism which arises on the basis of the new economic conditions—on the basis of the socialisation of the means of production.

By socialising the means of production and creating socialist economic forms, the socialist state abolishes the economic conditions in which the law of competition and anarchy of production operated, and creates the conditions for the emergence and operation of the objective law of the planned, proportionate development of the national economy. The sphere of operation of this law constantly extends as the socialist economic forms grow and become stronger.

The main aims of planning are set down in legislative form in the constitutions of the socialist countries. They are the steady expansion of the country's productive forces, the enhancement of social wealth, the steady improvement of the material well-being and cultural level of the working people and the building up of the strength, defence potential and independence of the socialist countries.

But state planning in the socialist countries is not merely a matter of economic development; it also embraces cultural development, training, etc. Where remnants of the exploiting classes still exist, state planning is also directed towards their restriction and ousting.

The Soviet Union gives substantial assistance to the other socialist countries in the fulfilment of their economic plans and in the steady improvement of the living standards of their people. It gives them credits on favourable terms; it supplies machinery and equipment, raw materials, and the latest technological documentation; it trains personnel and sends its own specialists to the socialist countries. The Soviet

Union has also given free aid to a number of these countries.

Co-operation between the Soviet Union and the other socialist countries is not simply a question of aid on equal terms, but of fraternal mutual assistance, which is the highest expression of proletarian internationalism.

In developing its own economy, each socialist country relies not only on the aid and support of the Soviet Union, but also on the aid and co-operation of the other socialist countries. The law of planned, proportionate development operates not only within each individual socialist country. It is also applicable to the economy of the entire socialist community which constitutes an integrated economic system.

Through mutual co-operation, each socialist country can develop those branches of the economy for which the conditions are most favourable. The correct organisation of co-operation and specialisation of production among the socialist countries ensures the most rational utilisation of their resources and economic potentialities to accelerate their rates of economic growth. A new, socialist-type international division of labour is evolving as a result of co-operation of this kind.

During the first period of the development of the world socialist system economic ties between the socialist countries in the main took the form of bilateral trade and scientific and cultural exchanges. Subsequently they began to assume more advanced forms. An important step in this direction was the acceptance by the member-countries of the Council for Mutual Economic Assistance (CMEA) of agreed basic indices for the development of particular branches over the period 1956-1960. The national economic development plans of CMEA member-countries have been co-ordinated since 1959. Plan co-ordination has become the main means of establishing stable and mutually advantageous economic links between CMEA member-countries.

The most important requirement of plan co-ordination is that it should take due account of the objectively necessary proportions of the economic development of each socialist state in particular and of the world system of socialism as a whole.

Important decisions regarding the further development of economic co-operation between the socialist countries were adopted at the special 23rd session of CMEA held in Moscow in April 1969. They defined the main aims and directions of a comprehensive, long-term programme for the further development of socialist economic integration. In line with these decisions, the 25th session of CMEA held in Bucharest in July 1971 approved a comprehensive Programme for the Further Extension and Improvement of Co-operation and the Development of Socialist Economic Integration by the CMEA Member-Countries. This programme, to be carried out in stages over 15-20 years, expresses the resolute determination of the socialist countries to implement the long-term fundamental aims of their all-round fraternal co-operation. The fulfilment of the measures outlined in the Programme will enable the CMEA member-countries to make fuller use of the advantages of the socialist economic system and of the international socialist division of labour in order further to enhance their economic and defence potential, raise the living standards of their peoples and strengthen the unity of the socialist community.

The experience of the co-operation of the Soviet Union and the other socialist countries shows that it is based on the sincere desire to assist one another and achieve economic progress for all. This co-operation results in the high rates of industrial development achieved by the socialist countries. Countries which were in the past economically backward have been able, relying on the experience and fraternal mutual assistance of the other socialist states, rapidly to develop their economies and culture and to overtake the other socialist countries. From this springs the exceptionally important theoretical conclusion that the development of the socialist states within the framework of a single world system of socialism and the utilisation of the laws and advantages of that system enable them *"to reduce the time necessary for the construction of socialism and offers them the prospect of effecting the transition to communism more or less simultaneously, within one and the same historical epoch*".[1]

Alongside achievements in economic and cultural development, there have also been serious shortcomings in planning in some socialist countries, due to the insufficiently correct utilisation of the objective economic law of the planned, proportionate development of the national economy. Some countries exhibited certain imbalances in their economic development. For example, in Poland during the 1950-55 Six-Year Plan and in Hungary during the 1950-54 Five-Year Plan insufficient attention was paid to agriculture, the consumer goods industry, the supply of industrial raw materials and the improvement of living standards. The Communist and Workers' parties brought these shortcomings to light and took steps to eradicate them.

Disregard of objective laws, and any manifestation of voluntarism in planning are utterly impermissible.

Many socialist countries take measures to improve planning with a view to enhancing the efficiency of the socialist economy and giving greater scope to the working people's initiative. In essence, these measures restrict the use of administrative methods and increase the role of economic incentives and the role and responsibility of enterprises and their workers in the drawing up and fulfilment of plans. The principle of the active participation of the masses in the compilation and implementation of national economic plans is embodied in the law of the socialist countries.

While opposing undue centralism and an excessive use of administrative methods and calling for the wider application of economic incentives in regulating economic development, the Communist and Workers' parties of the socialist countries also resist parochialism and any relaxation of the necessary principle of centralism, which ensures the unity of the country's socialist economy.

---

[1] *The Road to Communism*, p. 579.

7. LABOUR—A DUTY AND MATTER OF HONOUR FOR EVERY CITIZEN. THE SOCIALIST PRINCIPLE OF DISTRIBUTION ACCORDING TO WORK DONE

The constitutions of the socialist countries give legal expression to one of the fundamental principles of socialism—work as a duty and matter of honour for every able-bodied citizen.[1]

Socialism is inconceivable without work. Only the labour of all members of society and the constant raising of its productivity can create the abundance of material and cultural values necessary to satisfy the constantly growing needs of society. "In the last analysis," Lenin said, "productivity of labour is the most important, the principal thing for the victory of the new social system."[2] Socialism can finally triumph and overcome the capitalist economic system because it achieves a higher productivity of labour.

The material and moral prerequisites necessary for the growth of labour productivity have been created in the socialist countries.

The overthrow of the rule of the capitalists and landowners and the establishment of the power of the working people headed by the working class, coupled with the fundamental revolutionary transformations have given the working people of these countries the opportunity to work not for the exploiters, but for themselves, with the aid, furthermore, of the latest technological and cultural achievements.

The new, socialist attitude to work as a matter of honour and valour evolved in the struggle to carry through socialist transformations in the socialist countries.

The new attitude to work is fostered in the course of the struggle against the traditions and habits inherited from the old bourgeois-landowner system, in the struggle against class enemies who resort to every means to preserve and revive

---

[1] See *Constitution of the USSR*, Art. 12.
[2] V. I. Lenin, *Collected Works*, Vol. 29, p. 427.

the hangovers of the old bourgeois ideology in the minds of backward sections of the working people.

The education of the working people on the best examples of work, the affirmation in the mind of every member of society of the concept of work for the social benefit, work as a sacred duty, remains an important task even after the socialist state has evolved into a state of the whole people.

In socialist society increased productivity of labour means an improvement in the material and cultural level of the working people who, therefore, have a vital interest in raising productivity.

The struggle against so-called economism launched by the "Left" opportunists—by which they mean the natural desire of the workers and peasants to improve their living standards—has nothing in common with Marxism-Leninism. The slogan "Ignore bad living conditions!" they have coined is incompatible with scientific socialism. It contradicts the socialist principle of the steady improvement of the material and cultural standards of the people.

The socialist system creates both the incentives and conditions for increasing labour productivity through the large-scale introduction of advanced techniques and technological processes, the improved organisation of labour, the raising of the educational and cultural level of the working people and of their industrial qualifications. The unity of interest between the socialist state and the mass of the working people is the source of the powerful upsurge in their activity and creative initiative. This finds expression in the extensive development of labour emulation and its constant evolution into higher forms.

The socialist organisation of labour is inseparably linked with the unswerving implementation of the strictest control over the measure of labour and consumption, and with the implementation of the fundamental principle of socialism: "From each according to his ability, to each according to his work." This principle, set down in the constitutions of the socialist states, harmoniously combines the personal and social interests of the working people.

Implementing the socialist principle of payment for work in accordance with its quantity and quality, the people's power resists equalitarianism, and pursues a policy of differentiated wages depending upon the nature of the industry and the qualifications of the worker. It establishes incentives for improvement of skills, increased labour productivity and a conscientious attitude to labour duties.

This fundamental principle of socialism is more and more coming into its own as the capitalist elements are being ousted, as socialist forms grow and become stronger in all branches of the national economy and as workers participate more actively in management and wages systems improve.

CHAPTER IV

THE ROLE OF THE COMMUNIST AND ASSOCIATED DEMOCRATIC PARTIES AND MASS ORGANISATIONS IN THE POLITICAL STRUCTURE OF SOCIETY IN THE SOCIALIST COUNTRIES

1. THE COMMUNIST (WORKERS') PARTIES— THE LEADING AND GUIDING FORCE IN THE SOCIALIST STATE AND SOCIETY

The success achieved by the working people of the socialist countries in the struggle to win state power, create and consolidate a socialist state, build socialism and ensure the independence and build up the defence potential of their countries, was made possible above all thanks to the Communist (Workers') parties—parties of a Marxist-Leninist type— which were and remain the leading and guiding force among the workers' organisations in these countries.

The proletariat needs a Communist Party not only for the conquest of state power; it is even more necessary if that power is to be retained and consolidated in the interests of the complete victory of socialism, since leadership of a Communist Party is the basic prerequisite without which the very existence of a socialist state and the successful building of a new socialist and communist society is impossible.

"Practice has shown that socialist transformations and the building of the new society are a long and complex process, and that the utilisation of the tremendous possibilities opened up by the new system depends on the Communist Parties in the leadership of the state, on their ability to resolve the problems of socialist development the Marxist-Leninist way,"[1] said the Main Document approved by the Internation-

---

[1] *International Meeting of Communist and Workers' Parties, Moscow, 1969*, p. 22.

al Meeting of Communist and Workers' Parties in Moscow in June 1969.

The Communist Party, as the highest form of political organisation of the working people, as their advance guard, must ensure that the work of all other mass organisations of the working people—state, trade-union, youth, co-operative, etc.—follows a uniform line to achieve the common purpose of completing the building of socialism and communism.

The constitutions of the socialist countries in one way or another give legal expression to the leading role of the Communist and Workers' parties in state and society.

It is directly affirmed in the constitutions of almost all socialist countries. Article 126 of the USSR Constitution declares that the Communist Party of the Soviet Union is "the vanguard of the working people in their struggle to build communist society" and is "the leading core of all organisations of the working people, both governmental and non-governmental". Article 1 (ii) of the Bulgarian Constitution states that "the Bulgarian Communist Party is the leading force in society and the state". According to Art. 82 of the Constitution of the Mongolian People's Republic, the Mongolian People's Revolutionary Party "is the advance guard and leader of all governmental and other mass organisations of the working people".

In a number of socialist states which emerged after the Second World War, there were two workers' parties during the period immediately following the establishment of people's rule. This was not an accidental phenomenon.

Under capitalism, the bourgeoisie, realising that the strength of the proletariat lies above all in its unity and organisation, tried in every way to obstruct the rallying of the proletariat around Communist and Workers' parties of a Marxist-Leninist type—the true spokesmen for the interests of the working class and all working people—because such a unification would inevitably lead to the overthrow of capitalism. In its attempts to undermine the labour movement, the bourgeoisie supported the establishment of anti-communist Right-wing Socialist (Social-Democratic) parties. The Right-wing leaders of such parties in effect defend and support capitalist rule.

But the majority of rank-and-file members of the Right-wing Socialist parties are as a rule workers. This provides the soil for the growth of Left-wing, revolutionary tendencies within these parties. Left-wing groups are formed which seek to throw off the reactionary leadership, transform the Social-Democratic Party into a real working-class party and direct it along the revolutionary path. The roots of the development of revolutionary currents in the Social-Democratic parties lie in the growth of the class consciousness of their working-class members and their increased solidarity with communist workers as a result of the Communist parties' consistent criticism of the treacherous behaviour of the Right-wing socialist leadership and of the participation of socialist workers (Social-Democrats) in joint struggle against the capitalist system together with Communists, despite the opposition by their Right-wing leaders.

Co-operation between Communist and Social-Democratic workers became closer during the struggle against fascism for freedom and genuine people's democracy in a number of countries.

After the establishment of people's rule and as a result of bitter struggle, the revolutionary Left wing within the Social-Democratic parties secured final victory over the Right-wing elements. This opened the way for the unification of the Social-Democratic and Communist parties.

The unification of the working-class parties was preceded by their purge of alien elements and by a struggle against ideological influences alien to Marxism-Leninism. They united on the basis of Marxist-Leninist ideology and Leninist organisational principles.

In 1946 the German Communist and Social-Democratic parties united to form the Socialist Unity Party of Germany.

In 1948 the Communist and Social-Democatic parties in Czechoslovakia, Bulgaria, Rumania and Hungary amalgamated; so, too, did the Polish Workers' Party and the Polish Socialist Party.

The specific feature of the formation of the Labour Party of Korea in 1946 which united parties of North Korea was an amalgamation, not of two workers' parties, as was the case in the European countries, but of a working-class party —the Communist Party of North Korea—and the New People's Party—a party of the working peasantry and working intellectuals. In 1949 the Labour Party of North Korea and the Labour Party of South Korea united to form the Labour Party of Korea.

The formation of a united Marxist-Leninist party in Cuba also had its distinctive features. It was the result of the amalgamation of three revolutionary organisations—the working-class Popular Socialist Party, the July 26 Movement (Fidel Castro's Movimiento 26 de Julio), mainly representing the peasantry, and the Revolutionary Directorate, predominantly representative of progressive Cuban students. The result of the amalgamation was first the formation of the United Revolutionary Organisations and then of the United Party of the Cuban Socialist Revolution, which in 1965 became the Communist Party of Cuba.

In the other socialist countries united proletarian parties existed from the outset. Hence, there are now united working-class parties in all the socialist countries.

These parties bear various names, but the important thing is not what they are called, but the ideological and organisational principles underlying their work and the policies which they pursue.

Only a party equipped with Marxism-Leninism, the sole scientific theory of social development, can fulfil the role of true leader of the working people in their struggle to build a socialist and communist society. That is why the genuinely Marxist Communist and Workers' parties wage a resolute campaign against all symptoms alien to Marxism-Leninism.

These parties consistently observe and develop the Leninist standards of Party life, the principle of collective leadership, and the democratic principles underlying the functioning of all Party bodies and organisations from top to bottom. They have resolutely condemned the personality cult which led to the abuse of power and to violations of socialist democracy and revolutionary legality. The strict observance of the Leninist standards of Party and state life and extensive links with the masses are the guarantee against such abuses. While condemning the personality cult, the Marxist-Leninist parties repudiate attempts to exploit this criticism to the disadvantage of the people and of socialism, for revising the principles of Marxism-Leninism.

The purity of the Marxist-Leninist ideology and of the social composition of the Marxist-Leninist parties is essential if these parties are to fulfil their leading role in the socialist state and society. Great harm was done to the Hungarian labour movement as a result of the penetration of alien elements into the Hungarian Working People's Party formed by amalgamation of the Communist Party with the Social-Democratic Party in 1948, and by the failure to wage an open resolute struggle on fundamental issues within the Party against the anti-Party ideology of the Imre Nagy group. In consequence the Hungarian Working People's Party proved inadequately effective at the time of the October 1956 counter-revolutionary revolt in Hungary.[1] The Hungarian Socialist Workers' Party which was formed in November 1956 from the best members of the Hungarian Working People's Party and which conducted a determined campaign for the purity of Marxism-Leninism and the unity of the Party, led the revolutionary forces of the Hungarian people.

A serious crisis emerged in 1968 in the Communist Party of Czechoslovakia as a result of the growth within the Party of Right-wing opportunist trends against which no resolute

---

[1] See the "Report of János Kadár to the Plenary Meeting of the Central Committee of the Hungarian Socialist Workers' Party held to mark the fiftieth anniversary of the foundation of the Hungarian Communist Party", *Pravda*, November 25, 1968.

campaign was waged. Ideological divisions within the Party's leading bodies and the lack of unity in action weakened the Communist Party of Czechoslovakia. This, coupled with the increasing militancy of anti-socialist forces, gave rise to a serious threat. The plenary meetings of the Central Committee of the Communist Party of Czechoslovakia held in April, May and September of 1969 and in January 1970 marked a decisive turning point, a transition to uncompromising struggle against the Right-wing opportunist elements for the consolidation of Party unity on the basis of Marxist-Leninist principles. A detailed analysis of these events is contained in the document "The Lessons of the Crisis Development in the Communist Party of Czechoslovakia and Czechoslovak Society Following the 13th Congress of the Party" approved by the December 1970 Plenary Meeting of the Central Committee of the CPCz.[1]

The importance of the struggle for the ideological purity of the Marxist-Leninist parties and for the unity of their ranks has been emphatically underlined in the Programme of the CPSU and in the decisions of its congresses and Central Committee plenary meetings, in the decisions of the Communist and Workers' parties of the other socialist countries and in documents of the international communist and working-class movement. All these documents give a fundamental appraisal of revisionism and dogmatism and of Right- and "Left"-wing opportunism.

The Programme of the CPSU characterises revisionism as "Right opportunism ... a reflection of bourgeois influence.... The revisionists, who mask their renunciation of Marxism with talk about the necessity of taking account of the latest developments in society and the class struggle, in effect play the role of pedlars of bourgeois-reformist ideology within the Communist movement. They seek to rob Marxism-Lenin-

---

[1] See "Poučeni z krizového vývoje ve straně a společnosti po XIII sjezdu KSČ. Schváleno plenárnim zasedánim UV KSČ 11 prosince 1970", *Rudé Právo*, January 14, 1971 (Supplement).

ism of its revolutionary spirit, to undermine the faith which the working class and all working people have in socialism, to disarm and disorganise them in their struggle against imperialism. The revisionists deny the historical necessity of the socialist revolution and of the dictatorship of the proletariat. They deny the leading role of the Marxist-Leninist party, undermine the foundations of proletarian internationalism, and drift to nationalism."[1]

The Communist and Workers' parties, while defending Marxism-Leninism against revisionist attacks, at the same time resolutely oppose dogmatism and sectarianism. The dogmatists, who attempt to depict themselves as the only consistent Marxists, are in reality opponents of genuine creative Marxism. They see Marxism not as a living, creative philosophy, but as an ossified collection of formulas and recipes which are applied mechanically regardless of the actual conditions and national characteristics of particular countries at various stages of their development. Dogmatism in theory and the consequent sectarianism in practice lead, in the words of the Programme of the CPSU, "to the dissociation and isolation of Communists from the masses, doom them to passive expectation or incite them to Leftist adventurist actions in the revolutionary struggle, and hinder a correct appraisal of the changing situation and the use of new opportunities for the benefit of the working class and all democratic forces. Dogmatism and sectarianism, unless steadfastly combated, can also become the chief danger at particular stages in the development of individual parties".[2]

The necessity and importance of an unremitting campaign against revisionism and dogmatism is therefore apparent.

The Communist and Workers' parties exercise their leadership of the socialist state within the framework of the constitutions of their respective countries.

The Communist and Workers' parties promote their best members and the finest representatives of the working class

---

[1] *The Road to Communism*, p. 488.
[2] Ibid., p. 489.

and other sections of the working people to leading posts in the state. They verify the work of the organs of state power and administration and rectify shortcomings, assist state bodies in their work and mobilise the working people to play an active part in the campaign to accomplish the tasks confronting the organs of the socialist state. The Communist parties do not issue directives to the organs of the state; they give instructions to their members in these organs who, thanks to the great authority and influence which the Communist and Workers' parties have among the people, are able to ensure that the organs of the socialist state carry out the policy of the parties and adopt decisions in accordance with that policy.

Members of the Communist and Workers' parties play a leading role in the state bodies because the working people, in forming the organs of their own power, place their trust above all in members of these parties.

The fact that it is they who initiate the most important measures of the socialist state is one of the manifestations of the leading role of the Communist and Workers' parties. It is on their initiative and under their leadership that the constitutions—the fundamental laws of the socialist countries—and laws on national economic plans, electoral laws, laws relating to local government bodies, laws in defence of peace and other key legislation, are drafted and approved.

The Communist and Workers' parties guide the activity not only of state bodies, but also of the mass organisations, such as trade unions and co-operatives. This does not of course imply the formal subordination of these organisations to the Party. But, thanks to the authority enjoyed by the Communist and Workers' parties, their members as a rule occupy leading posts in the mass organisations and are able to carry out the Party's policy through these organisations.

In order to ensure the leading role of the Communist and Workers' parties in the state and society, Party groups (clubs, factions) are formed in all government bodies and non-government organisations in which there are at least three Party members. Their purpose is to enhance the influence of the Party and implement its policy among non-members, strengthen Party and state discipline, campaign against bureaucracy and verify the fulfilment of Party directives. The Party groups are subordinate to the appropriate Party organ (central, regional, district, city and other Party committees) and are guided by the decisions of leading Party bodies in all their work.

The leadership of the organs of the socialist state by a Marxist-Leninist party in no way implies the replacement of state organs by those of the Party or the merging of the functions of Party and state bodies.

The correct delineation of the functions of Party and state organs is of primary importance for a proper functioning of the socialist state as a whole. This is demonstrated by the experience of both the Soviet Union and the other socialist countries. The CPSU and Lenin repeatedly stressed the importance of this question.

As early as March 1919, the decisions of the Eighth Congress of the Russian Communist Party (Bolsheviks) pointed out that "the functions of Party organs must on no account be merged with those of state bodies, such as the Soviets. Such a merger would have fatal results.... The Party must implement its decisions through Soviet bodies, *within the framework of the Soviet Constitution*. The Party strives to *guide* the work of the Soviets, but not to take their place.... Party organisations must never resort to petty tutelage over the Soviets".[1]

The necessity for the precise delineation of the functions of Party and government bodies was also noted frequently in a number of subsequent CPSU decisions.[2]

---

[1] *KPSS v rezolutsiyakh i resheniyakh syezdov, konferentsii i plenumov TsK*, Part 1, pp. 446-47.
[2] Ibid., pp. 627-28, 704-05 ff.

Lenin clearly defined the principles governing this delineation. In 1922 he noted that "it is necessary to delimit much more precisely the functions of the Party (and of its Central Committee) from those of the Soviet Government; to increase the responsibility and independence of Soviet officials and of Soviet government institutions, leaving to the Party the general guidance of the activities of all state bodies, without the present, too frequent, irregular and often petty interference".[1]

Basic principles regarding the Communist Party's guidance of the legislative activity of the organs of the socialist state are set out in Lenin's report to the 10th Congress of the Russian Communist Party (Bolsheviks) on the replacement of the surplus-appropriation system by a tax in kind. Lenin pointed out that the Party lays down the basic line, while detailed proposals are drawn up and adopted by government bodies. Referring to the implications of freedom for local economic exchange he declared: "We shall find the answer in our legislation; it is our task to lay down the principle to be followed and provide the slogan."[2] In concluding his report, he again emphasised that "we cannot issue a law now ... laws are not written at Party congresses".[3]

The following conclusions regarding Party guidance of the socialist state organs flow from the guidelines laid down in decisions of CPSU congresses and the works of Lenin:

(i) the functions of Party and government bodies must be clearly delineated;

(ii) it is impermissible to replace government bodies by Party organs in taking decisions which lie within the competence of the former;

(iii) party guidance of government bodies with regard to the drafting and promulgation of normative acts must take

---

[1] V. I. Lenin, *Collected Works*, Vol. 33, p. 253.
[2] Ibid., Vol. 32, p. 218.
[3] Ibid., p. 227.

the form of laying down the fundamental principles and guidelines, without restricting the initiative of Party members working in government bodies as regards the drafting of detailed measures which are to ensure the best possible implementation of the basic policy;

(iv) tutelage by Party organs of the organs of state power with respect to minor matters is harmful, in that it fetters the initiative and diminishes the responsibility of the functionaries of the government bodies.

These principles, as the experience of the USSR and other socialist countries shows, retain their importance for state development in all the socialist countries.

The implementation of the policy of a Marxist-Leninist party by the organs of a socialist state in no way implies the mechanical obedience of such bodies to the directives of the appropriate Party committee, as the enemies of socialism allege. A study of the organisation and work of the representative organs of state power in the socialist countries clearly demonstrates how substantial is the constructive work which they do.[1] The guidance given by the leading organs of Communist and Workers' parties to Party groups (clubs, factions) in the organs of state power concerns fundamental issues of Party policy and the basic principles of draft legislation. This basic guidance in no way restricts the initiative and work of deputies (members) of the organs of state power as regards the optimal implementation of Party policy. On the contrary, it stimulates and guides the deputies' work.

While striving to enhance their influence in the state bodies, the Communist and Workers' parties of the socialist countries condemn the attempts of some Party bodies to take the place of organs of state power and take decisions on concrete issues which properly lie within the competence of government bodies.

The delineation of the functions of Party and state bodies

---

[1] See Chapters X and XIII of this book.

in no way implies the diminution of the leading role of the Communist Party in a socialist state. On the contrary, the correct delineation of functions enhances this role.

The constant enhancement of the leading role of the Communist and Workers' parties is a general rule governing the building of socialism and communism. This fundamental postulate is stressed in decisions and other documents of the leading bodies of the Marxist-Leninist parties of the socialist countries. "The experience of the development of the socialist system", declares the Resolution of the 24th Congress of the CPSU on the Report of the Central Committee of the CPSU, "shows with ever greater clarity the need constantly to consolidate the leading role of the Marxist-Leninist Party in socialist society, ceaselessly to improve the forms and methods of Party leadership, and to take a creative Marxist-Leninist approach in tackling the urgent problems of socialist development."[1]

The enhancement of the leading role of the Marxist-Leninist parties in the state and society is inseparably bound up with the raising of the scientific level of Party guidance and with the deep-going analysis and elaboration of the scientific principles of Party policy. The Communist and Workers' parties of the socialist countries are waging a determined struggle against manifestations of subjectivism and voluntarism, for the sound scientific principles to underlie their policies and reflect the objective needs of social development. Congresses of the Communist and Workers' parties of the socialist countries have stressed the importance of the raising of the scientific level of Party leadership, and of the in-depth study of the fundamental tasks confronting Party policy, which most fully reflect the actual conditions and requirements of each socialist country.

The unity and solidarity of the Communist and Workers' parties of all countries is of great importance in building socialism and communism and in strengthening the socialist

---

[1] *24th Congress of the CPSU*, p. 213.

system and the forces of democracy and peace throughout the world.

The Communist and Workers' parties of the socialist countries bear a special responsibility in this respect, because, as has been rightly stressed by the General Secretary of the Central Committee of the CPSU, Leonid Brezhnev, "active relations between ruling Communist Parties are the nucleus, the cornerstone for promoting many-sided co-operation among socialist states".[1]

The overwhelming majority of the Communist and Workers' parties resolutely champion the international solidarity of the revolutionary vanguard of the world's working class. The CPSU is making great efforts to strengthen the unity and solidarity of the international communist movement.

This movement has many times been subjected to grave trials; it has withstood them with honour and emerged still stronger. The Communist Party of the Soviet Union jointly with the other fraternal Marxist-Leninist parties has scored new successes in the struggle to strengthen the unity of the communist movement.

The Main Document adopted by the 1969 Meeting of Communist and Workers' parties stated: "The successes of socialism, its impact on the course of world events and the effectiveness of its struggle against imperialist aggression largely depend on the cohesion of the socialist countries. Unity of action of the socialist countries is an important factor in bringing together all anti-imperialist forces."[2] From this it follows that concern for the consolidation of the world socialist system is at the same time concern for the development of the world revolutionary process and for effective struggle against imperialism.

The participants in the Meeting re-affirmed that "relations between the fraternal Parties are based on the princi-

---

[1] *International Meeting of Communist and Workers' Parties, Moscow, 1969*, p. 146.
[2] Ibid., p. 23.

ples of proletarian internationalism, solidarity, and mutual support, respect for independence and equality, and non-interference in each other's internal affairs. Strict adherence to these principles is an indispensable condition for developing comradely co-operation between the fraternal Parties and strengthening the unity of the communist movement".[1]

2. THE ROLE OF MASS ORGANISATIONS IN THE POLITICAL STRUCTURE OF THE SOCIETY; THEIR PARTICIPATION IN THE IMPLEMENTATION OF THE FUNCTIONS AND TASKS OF THE SOCIALIST STATE

In the socialist countries the mass organisations operating under the guidance of the Communist (Workers') parties link the guiding force of the political mechanism of these countries—the Communist (Workers') Party—with the working class and all the working people.

The role of the mass organisations is so great that it would be no exaggeration to say that the rule of the people would be impossible without such organisations which, as Lenin expressively termed it, are " 'transmission belts' running from the vanguard to the mass of the advanced class, and from the latter to the mass of the working people".[2]

The "transmission belt" conception is, of course, used figuratively, merely to express the fact that all mass organisations, firstly, work in one direction under the uniform leadership of the Communist Party and, secondly, link the Party with the broad mass of the people. But this concept does not fully reflect the role of mass organisations in a socialist state. Mass organisations are a powerful means for fostering the people's initiative and activity. They play a creative role in the building of socialism and are a major form of the working people's participation in the organisation and work of government bodies and in the exercise of state functions.

The mass organisations in the socialist countries carry out

---

[1] *International Meeting of Communist and Workers' Parties, Moscow, 1969*, p. 36.

[2] V. I. Lenin, *Collected Works*, Vol. 32, p. 21.

the policy of the Communist Party and play an active part in its formulation on a scientific basis, helping the Party bring to light the interests of various sections of the working people and relate them to the interests of the building of socialism and communism which are common to the people as a whole.

It was noted at the 24th Congress of the CPSU that the Draft Directives of the Congress for the 1971-75 Five-Year Economic Development Plan took account of many proposals submitted by the Soviet trade unions.[1]

The growing role of mass organisations in the political, economic, social and cultural advance of socialist society is an objective law governing their development.

The principal mass organisations which link the Communist (Workers') parties with the working class and the working people as a whole are the trade unions, youth, cooperative and women's organisations and other mass bodies.

Each has its distinctive features reflected in its membership, tasks and methods of work.

The *trade unions* under socialism are organisations of the entire working class. Their functions are mainly organisational, economic and educational. They draw the broad mass of the working people into the organisation of labour and the management of production, into active control of the measure of work and consumption. They play an important part in educating the working people in the spirit of the conscientious observance of state discipline and public law and order, and a care for socialist property; they concern themselves with the raising of workers' qualifications, the protection of the material interests and rights of the working people and the improvement of their cultural and leisure services.

The trade unions encourage the active participation of factory and office workers in economic, social and political life.

---

[1] See speech of V. I. Prokhorov (Secretary of the All-Union Central Council of Trade Unions) to the 24th Congress of the CPSU, *Pravda*, April 8, 1971, p. 2.

The *youth leagues* are independent, non-party, mass organisations of working youth associated with the Communist (Workers') Party.

United youth organisations now exist in the majority of socialist countries: in the USSR—the All-Union Leninist Young Communist League, in Bulgaria—the Dimitrov Young Communist League, in Albania the Union of Working Youth, in Cuba the Union of Young Communists, in Czechoslovakia the Socialist Union of Youth, in the German Democratic Republic the Free German Youth, in Hungary the Communist Youth Union, in the Korean People's Democratic Republic the Union of Democratic Youth, in the Mongolian People's Republic the Mongolian Revolutionary Youth Union, in Rumania the Union of Communist Youth, and in Yugoslavia the Yugoslav League of Youth.

In the Democratic Republic of Vietnam, all youth organisations have united in the Federation of Vietnamese Youth of which the Ho Chi Minh Union of Working Youth is the core.

In Poland, five youth organisations: the Union of Socialist Youth, the Union of Rural Youth, the Socialist Union of Polish Students, the Union of Polish Harcerzes and the Socialist Union of Army Youth, in April 1973, on the basis of decisions of their earlier congresses, set up a Federation of Socialist Unions of Polish Youth.

The programmes and other documents of the youth leagues of the socialist countries clearly lay down that they are guided by Marxism-Leninism and acknowledge the leading role of the Communist (Workers') Party in the youth movement.

Under the leadership of the Communist (Workers') parties, the youth leagues educate young people in the spirit of socialism and communism, in the spirit of love for their socialist homeland, loyalty to the principles of socialist internationalism, fraternal friendship between the peoples of the Soviet Union and the other socialist countries and of the struggle for world peace.

As the aides of the Communist (Workers') parties, the youth leagues play their part in political and economic developments in the socialist countries. They make extensive use of the rights which they enjoy, taking part in the discussion by the appropriate bodies of matters relating to the work of factories, machine and tractor stations, state farms, agricultural producer co-operatives, institutions, educational establishments, etc., with a view to eradicating shortcomings and helping to improve work.

The youth leagues help the Communist (Workers') parties in the training of young reserves and put forward their representatives for work in the mass organisations of the working people and in government bodies. Their best members join the Communist (Workers') parties.

The distinctive feature of *co-operative organisations*—agricultural producer, industrial, consumer, housing and others—is that they are at one and the same time both economic and social organisations. This is reflected in their Rules. As a social organisation, a co-operative is an important component of the political mechanism of society in the socialist countries. Not being confined to economic tasks, a co-operative is one of the most important forms of socialist and communist education, a school of public self-administration.

Despite their distinctive characteristics, the mass organisations have common fundamental features: organisational unity, the recognition of the leading role of the Communist (Workers') Party, a common aim—that of actively assisting the building of socialism and communism—and the genuinely democratic principles which govern their organisation and work.

The structure and work of the mass organisations is founded upon genuinely democratic principles.

The most important of these are laid down in the constitutions of the socialist countries, which establish that 1) only working people may form mass organisations; 2) all such organisations are based on the principle of voluntary membership; 3) the work of all such organisations must have as its main aim the strengthening and development of the socialist system and the increasing involvement of the mass of the working people in the building of socialism and the strengthening of peace.

Some of the basic principles governing the work and structure of these organisations are also contained in laws and other normative acts which deal specifically with particular mass organisations, such as those relating to trade unions, co-operatives, model rules of agricultural producer co-operatives, etc.

The structure and forms of work of mass organisations are laid down in detail in the rules they adopt.

The establishment in law of the fundamental principles governing the structure and activities of the mass organisations does not restrict their freedom, but on the contrary creates conditions and guarantees which ensure the maximum freedom for their work. This arises from the very nature of the socialist state and from the laws governing the building of socialism and communism, which can only proceed successfully with the active participation of millions of the working people.

The genuinely democratic, popular character of the normative acts laying down the principles governing the organisation and activity of the mass organisations in the socialist countries is manifested as follows:

1. The mass organisations play a decisive role in the preparation of these acts. The Polish draft Law on the Trade Unions adopted on July 1, 1949 was drawn up and submitted by the Polish trade unions.[1] The Collective Farm Model Rules approved by the Central Committee of the CPSU and the Council of Ministers of the USSR on November 28, 1969 were adopted by the Third All-Union Congress of Collective Farmers.[2] The Model Rules of United Agricultural Co-

---

[1] See *Dziennik Ustaw RPL* No. 41, 1949, Item 293.
[2] See *SP SSSR*, No. 26, 1969, Item 150.

operatives approved by the Czechoslovak Government on April 26, 1961 were adopted on March 26, 1961 by the Fifth Congress of United Agricultural Co-operatives of Czechoslovakia.[1] The 1964 amendments to these Rules were adopted by their Sixth Congress.[2]

2. The socialist countries have repealed all the restrictions on the working people's freedom to unite in mass organisations and on the activities of such organisations which existed in these countries prior to the victory of the people's revolution. Art. 1 of the Polish Law of July 1, 1949 on the trade unions lays down that "all regulations bequeathed by capitalist rule which restrict the right of factory and office workers voluntarily to associate together in trade unions, which establish administrative supervision over trade union activities and which encourage division in the trade union movement shall be repealed". The law guaranteed the right of factory and office workers voluntarily to associate together in trade unions.

3. The normative acts of the socialist countries lay down genuinely democratic principles governing the organisation and activity of the mass organisations.

In addition to the above-mentioned principles laid down in the constitutions of these countries, the basic principles also include democratic centralism, collective leadership and the free and businesslike discussion of the activities of mass organisations at their meetings, conferences, congresses, etc.[3]

4. The legislation of the socialist countries is to an increasing extent vesting mass organisations with powers

---

[1] See *Sbírka zákonů ČSSR*, Item 49/1961.

[2] See *Sbírka zákonů ČSSR*, Item 169/1964.

[3] This does not, however, imply that these basic principles are in law applied with equal force to all mass organisations. There is firstly an important distinction arising from the nature of the organisation (for example, unlike trade unions and co-operatives, youth organisations are not governed by special legislation; they are subject only to the general constitutional rules relating to mass organisations). Secondly, the laws governing the organisation and activities of mass organisations in the various socialist countries differ substantially.

which not only enable them to play an active role in the implementation of state tasks and functions, but also enable them independently to carry out many functions hitherto lying within the competence of state bodies. This clearly demonstrates the identity and class homogeneity of the aims of non-government and government organisations in a socialist state. It exemplifies the law-governed process of the gradual eradication of the distinction between government and non-government organisations during the period of building communism.

The establishment of mass organisations by the working people of the socialist countries and the activity of these organisations play a great role in the implementation of one of the most important constitutional principles governing the political system of these countries—the participation of the working people in the activity of state organs. Through their mass organisations the working people variously participate in the formation and work of organs of the socialist state.

The participation of the mass organisations in the exercise of state functions is becoming more widespread, in step with the successes gained in the building of socialism and communism, the consolidation of the socialist state and the increased activity and awareness of the masses.

This participation takes three main forms: 1) through "pure" public activity conducted in ways and with means peculiar to mass organisations; 2) through the granting to mass organisations of the power to influence the formation and work of government bodies; 3) through the exercise by mass organisations of the powers of government bodies which have been transferred to them, while retaining the possibility of resorting to measures of state compulsion.

In the first instance, mass organisations participate (within definite limits) in the exercise of all the main functions of a socialist state together with state organs. Thus, co-operatives, trade unions, youth leagues, women's unions and scientific and technical societies play an active part in the exercise of the economic and organisational function of the state by purely social measures.[1] Youth leagues, trade unions, scientific and enlightenment, atheist and other mass organisations play an active part in the exercise of the educational function alongside government bodies. In stressing the interaction of government and non-government bodies in this area, the Czechoslovak Constitution explicitly stipulates that "the state *together with mass organisations* [italics mine—*A.M.*] shall in every way encourage creative activity in science and art, strive to ensure that the working people should receive an increasingly broad and profound education and play an active part in scientific and artistic work, and shall endeavour to ensure that this work would serve the people as a whole" (Art. 16 ii). The Constitution also lays down that *"the state and the mass organisations* [italics mine—*A.M.*] shall systematically direct their efforts towards the eradication of the survivals of the exploiter society in the minds of the people" (Art. 16 iii).

The youth leagues and the voluntary defence organisations which educate young people in the spirit of selfless loyalty to their homeland, patriotism and readiness to resist the attack of any enemy, play an important part in the exercise of the function of defence.

The societies of friendship with other socialist countries and other bodies play their part in the exercise of the function of strengthening the friendship, fraternal co-operation and mutual assistance of the socialist countries.

The legislation of the socialist countries endows the mass organisations with far-reaching rights as regards the formation of socialist state organs.

---

[1] This does not however imply that all these organisations take part in the exercise of the functions of the state only by social measures. For example, the work of the trade unions in organising socialist emulation and socialist labour teams and shock-workers, the wide introduction of advanced production methods, etc., constitutes participation in economic, organisational, cultural and educational work by exclusively social means. At the same time, in exercising their powers with regard to labour protection, the trade unions may also resort to measures of state compulsion.

These rights above all include the right enjoyed by mass organisations in the formation of the elected organs of state power which constitute the basis of the entire state apparatus of the socialist countries. The mass organisations have the right to nominate candidates for election to all representative bodies; they are represented in the election commissions which conduct the elections and see to it that electoral law is observed; their authorised persons have the right to be present in polling stations, both while votes are being cast and during the count. Mass organisations supervise the activity of those whom they have nominated throughout their term of office and have the right to propose their recall.

The legislation of the socialist countries also envisages the participation of mass organisations in the formation of other, non-elected state organs. In the USSR, representatives of the trade unions, Young Communist League and other organisations serve on committees of people's control at all levels, including those of autonomous and Union republics and the People's Control Committee of the USSR.[1]

According to a Polish law of April 13, 1960 on the establishment of a Labour and Wages Committee,[2] representatives of the Central Council of Trade Unions, delegated by and also subject to recall by the Presidium of the Central Council, serve on this Committee alongside senior government officials. The membership of the Committee, in addition to its chairman and his three deputies, includes five government officials and five trade union representatives. In the German Democratic Republic representatives of the appropriate trade union bodies serve in the State Planning Committee, the Labour and Wages Committee, Regional Economic Councils, etc. In accordance with a decision of the

---

[1] See Arts. 15-17 of the Statute on Organs of People's Control in the USSR, approved by the Central Committee of the CPSU and the Council of Ministers of the USSR on December 19, 1968 (*SP SSSR* No. 1, 1969, Item 2).

[2] See *Dziennik Ustaw RPL* No. 20, 1960, Item 119.

Central Committee of the Socialist Unity Party of Germany and the Council of Ministers of the German Democratic Republic "On the Establishment of a Workers' and Peasants' Inspection", adopted in May 1963, the Committee of the Workers' and Peasants' Inspection of the German Democratic Republic and its local bodies include representatives of the trade unions, the Union of Free German Youth, the Democratic Women's League of Germany and the National Front.[1]

Mass organisations also take part in the formation and work of other state bodies, including consultative bodies attached to organs of state power and administration.

In law, the active participation of mass organisations of socialist countries in the work of state bodies arises from the constitutions of these countries, which lay down that all state bodies shall base themselves upon the politically conscious and active participation of the broad mass of the people and constantly reinforce their ties with them. The constitutions also establish that mass organisations unite citizens for active participation in the political, social, economic and cultural life. General rules governing the participation of mass organisations in the work of state bodies are also to be found in the ordinary legislation and other normative acts which regulate the work of these bodies.[2]

Broad regulations of this kind give great scope and are of great importance in establishing proper relationships between government and non-government bodies with respect to the fulfilment of state functions. But general regulations do not impose upon a government body the specific obligation to seek the view of a mass organisation in each concrete instance or to co-operate with it in any other way,

---

[1] See *Gesetzblatt der DDR*, Part II, No. 40, 1963.
[2] See, for example, the 1971 Hungarian Law on Councils (iii) (*Magyar Közlöny*, 1971, Item 11) and Art. 3 of the 1968 Rumanian Law on the Organisation and Work of People's Councils (*Buletinul oficial al RSR*, Part 1, 1968, Item 168).

while the mass organisation may express its opinion regarding the settlement of a particular issue by a government body, but it is not obliged to do so.

A different situation arises when the law imposes upon government bodies the *actual legal obligation* to co-operate in some form or other with mass organisations in the settlement of particular questions, or when a particular government body *does not have the right to settle* a whole range of issues without the participation of a mass organisation. The Resolution of the Central Committee of the CPSU and the Council of Ministers of the USSR of October 4, 1965 "On the Supplementary Transfer to Councils of Ministers of Union Republics of Matters Relating to Economic and Cultural Development" lays down that a number of these issues may be resolved by the Councils of Ministers of the Union Republics only *with the agreement* of the republican Council of Trade Unions.[1] The Czechoslovak Social Security Law of 1964 envisaged the promulgation of a series of detailed legal regulations, to enforce this law, by the Ministry of Labour and Public Affairs *by agreement with* the Central Council of Trade Unions.[2] The Polish Law of April 13, 1960 "On the Establishment of the Labour and Wages Committee and Introducing Changes in the Administration of Social Insurance, Pensions and Social Security" laid down (Art. 8, iv) that the Polish Council of Ministers shall issue regulations governing the powers and procedures of the Institute of Social Insurance and its departments *by agreement with* the Central Council of Trade Unions.[3]

With the imposition upon government bodies of a legal obligation to involve mass organisations in the settlement of a specific range of questions, the role of the latter is of course

---

[1] See Arts. 17, 30, and 33 of the Resolution (*SP SSSR* Nos. 19-20, 1965, Item 154).

[2] For the newly published text, see *Sbírka zákonů. ČSSR. ČSR. SSR*, Item 5/1972, as amended: *Sbírka zákonů. ČSSR, ČSR. SSR*, Item 99/1972.

[3] See *Dziennik Ustaw PRL* No. 20, 1960, Item 119, as amended: *Dziennik Ustaw PRL* No. 11, 1972, Item 81.

greatly enhanced, since such involvement, and also its *degree and form*, which is likewise of great importance (for example, consultation, agreement or joint decision), is not subject to the discretion of the government body, but is *mandatory* for it.

Hence, the legal prescriptions extending and specifying the forms of participation by non-government organisations in the work of government bodies testify to the growing role of mass organisations in the exercise of state functions in the socialist countries.

A distinction should also be drawn between *consultative* participation and *decision-making* participation.

Laws establishing *mandatory consultative participation* by non-government organisations in the work of government bodies have undergone substantial evolution in the socialist countries. Under the terms of Art. 11 of the Resolution of the Central Committee of the CPSU and the Council of Ministers of the USSR of October 4, 1965 "On the Supplementary Transfer to Councils of Ministers of Union Republics of Matters Relating to Economic and Cultural Development", the Councils of Ministers of the Union Republics shall take trade unions' proposals into account when planning housing construction and developing municipal, cultural and other amenities and public health facilities associated with the construction of major industrial enterprises in non-urban areas. The Polish Law of July 2, 1958 on Vocational Training[1] lays down that its application to minors employed in agriculture shall be determined by the Minister of Agriculture on the receipt of conclusions drawn up by the Union of Farming Circles and Organisations. In this instance, the government body must first consult the mass organisation (receive its opinion) but the latter's consent to issue an act (take a decision) is not mandatory. Nevertheless, this form of participation is of great importance in ensuring that government bodies adopt correct decisions.

---

[1] See *Dziennik Ustaw PRL* No. 45, 1958, Item 226, as amended *Dziennik Ustaw PRL* No. 32, 1961, Item 160; No. 12, 1969, Item 85.

Decision-making participation is a more advanced form than consultative participation. This implies that a measure (decision) *cannot be adopted without the consent of the mass organisation*. Participation of this kind may assume various forms.

One is the *submission of proposals* by a mass organisation, if this is a *mandatory requirement* for the promulgation of particular measures by government bodies. We refer here not to any proposals (these may be submitted without a special legal prescription), but to proposals without which a government body may not take a decision on a particular question. For example, a Polish decree of November 10, 1954[1] lays down that prescriptions governing labour safety and hygiene shall be issued by the Council of Ministers on the basis of proposals drawn up by the Central Council of Trade Unions.

Another form is the adoption of measures by government bodies *by agreement* with voluntary organisations. In this instance, it is not a question of the joint adoption of measures by government and non-government bodies, but of the adoption of measures by government bodies alone. But in so far as the prior consent of agencies of mass organisations is *mandatory* for issuance of such acts, this may be said to be a form of decision-making participation, rather than of that in a purely consultative capacity. There are many legal prescriptions in the socialist countries which lay down that government bodies shall resolve particular issues with the agreement of mass organisations. The Decision of the Central Committee of the CPSU and the Council of Ministers of the USSR of October 4, 1965 referred to above requires that the Councils of Ministers of the Union republics shall take decisions on a number of economic and cultural issues by agreement with the republican Trade Union Councils. A decision of the Polish Council of Ministers of March 25, 1957[2], while

---

[1] See the integrated text of the decree in *Dziennik Ustaw PRL* No. 8, 1968, Item 47, as amended: *Dziennik Ustaw PRL* No. 12, 1971, Item 115.

[2] See *Monitor Polski* No. 28, 1957, Item 189.

authorising the Minister of Finance to issue regulations regarding the granting of credits to co-operatives, at the same time laid down that such regulations must have the consent of the Chairman of the All-Poland Council of Producer Co-operatives. A decision of the Polish Council of Ministers dated July 27, 1959 laid down that the regulations governing the utilisation of the agricultural development fund shall be drawn up by the Minister of Agriculture with the consent of the Chief Organisational Committee of Farming Circles, the All-Poland Council of Producer Co-operatives, etc.

A still more advanced form of co-operation between government and non-government bodies is the adoption of *joint resolutions and decisions* by the agencies of non-governmental organisations and gevernment bodies. Examples include the joint decision of the CC CPSU, the Council of Ministers of the USSR and the All-Union Council of Trade Unions "On the Measures to Improve Labour Conditions and Employ Mechanisers in Agriculture on a Permanent Basis", adopted in April 1971;[1] the joint decision of the Government of the Hungarian People's Republic and the All-Hungarian Council of Trade Unions dated November 17, 1957, "On Factory Councils";[2] and the joint regulation of the Czechoslovak Central Council of Trade Unions and the State Institution of Social Security of January 16, 1958, "On the Insurance in the Event of Disease and the Pensions to Seasonal and Auxiliary Workers".[3]

The growing role played by mass organisations in the functioning of the socialist state is especially clearly seen in the development of legal regulations establishing the decision-making participation of non-governmental organisations in the work of government bodies.

We can distinguish between two forms of the participa-

---

[1] See *Izvestia*, April 20, 1971.
[2] See *Magyar Közlöny*, 1957, Item 121.
[3] See *Úřední list ČSR*, Item 7/1958.

tion by mass organisations of the socialist countries in state activities, depending on its type:

a) participation in the creation of law (in the legislative activities of government bodies), and

b) participation in the work of government bodies concerned with the application of law.

In the former case, their participation is expressed in their independent elaboration of draft laws and other normative acts adopted by government organs, in discussing or submitting conclusions on the normative acts drafted by government bodies, in the adoption by government bodies of normative acts jointly or in agreement with the agencies of non-government organisations, and in the independent issuance by non-governmental organisations of normative legal acts whenever this right is granted them by special legal regulations.

Thus, the drafts of Model Rules of Agricultural Producer Co-operatives, approved by the governments of several socialist countries, were adopted by the national congresses (conferences) of these co-operatives. The Fundamentals of Labour Legislation of the USSR and the Union Republics, approved by the Law of the Supreme Soviet of the USSR dated July 15, 1970, were drafted by the Council of Ministers of the USSR and the All-Union Central Council of Trade Unions.[1] The Regulations on the Rights of the Factory and Local Committee of Trade Unions, approved by the Decree of the Presidium of the Supreme Soviet of the USSR dated September 27, 1971, were submitted by the All-Union Central Council of Trade Unions.[2] The Polish laws "On Trade Unions"[3] of July 1, 1949, "On the Social Labour Inspection" of February 4, 1950, and "On Workers' Self-Management"[4] of December 20, 1958, were drafted

---

[1] See *Pravda*, April 16, 1970.

[2] See *Vedomosti Verkhovnogo Sovieta SSSR* No. 38, 1971, Item 382.

[3] See *Dziennik Ustaw PRL* No. 6, 1950, Item 52, as amended: *Dziennik Ustaw PRL* No. 52, 1954, Item 260; No. 13, 1965, Item 91.

[4] See *Dziennik Ustaw PRL* No. 77, 1958, Item 397.

and submitted by trade unions. The drafting of the Bulgarian Law on Pensions[1] adopted on November 4, 1957, was accompanied by examination of the proposals which were submitted by the Central Council of Trade Unions and discussed in enterprises and institutions and of proposals submitted by other mass organisations. The Union of Yugoslav Trade Unions organised a broad discussion of the draft Law on legal relationships in labour in all trade union organisations following its preliminary discussion in December 1964 in the appropriate committees (commissions) of the Federal Assembly of the Federal Skupshina.[2]

In several socialist countries the trade unions, as represented by their central organs, are given the rights to issue normative acts determining the procedure for applying labour legislation.

Non-government organisations take an active part in the work of government organs concerned with the *realisation of law*. In particular, trade unions, organs of workers' self-administration, co-operative and other organisations, as well as various bodies of people's control, take part in the exercise of the functions of state administration. The role played by mass organisations in the implementation of state tasks cannot be reduced solely to their participation in state bodies.

The extension of socialist democracy is accompanied by the *complete transference of a number of state functions to the mass organisations*. In such cases, it is a question *not of participation*, but of the *independent exercise* by non-government organisations of functions hitherto lying within the competence of government bodies.

Moreover, some functions in both law-making and law-application are transferred to mass organisations. The Czechoslovak Labour Code of June 16, 1975[3] vested the Czecho-

---

[1] See *Izvestia na Presidiuma na Narodnoto Sobranie*, 1957, Item 91. Subsequently many amendments were made in this Law.

[2] See *Yugoslav News* No. 4, Belgrade, 1965, p. 1.

[3] For the text of this law with subsequent amendments see *Sbírka zákonů. ČSSR. ČSR. SSR*, Item 42/1970, Item 100/1970.

slovak Central Council of Trade Unions with the right to promulgate normative acts relating to a number of problems of industrial safety and health. Under the terms of the Polish Decree of November 10, 1954 "On the Transference to the Trade Unions of Functions of Law Enforcement in the Sphere of Labour Protection, Safety and Health, and also of Labour Inspection",[1] the Central Council of Trade Unions was authorised to publish universally binding regulations laying down the procedure for the imposition of sanctions for the infringement of labour safety and health regulations, defining which infringements should be considered grave, etc.

Labour inspection, the administration (wholly or partially) of social insurance and other functions previously exercised by government bodies have in the socialist countries been transferred to the trade unions.

This transference of functions from government bodies to non-government organisations is one of the most important elements in the gradual transformation of state functions into functions of public self-administration.

But the transference of a function from a government body to a non-government organisation does not of itself mean that the function has become social. For instance, the trade union labour inspection bodies which operate in the socialist countries may, although they are social, resort to measures of state compulsion, such as the compulsory administrative implementation of their decisions and the imposition of fines. Thus, although labour inspection has been transferred to the trade unions, it has not yet become a function of public self-administration, because state coercion is used in exercising it.

On the other hand, the transference, for example, of the Polish governmental agricultural bodies responsible for advisory work which required no state coercive measures to the farming circles meant that this function had completely lost its state character and is carried out by organs of mass

---

[1] For the text of the Decree see *Dziennik Ustaw PRL* No. 8, 1968, Item 47, as amended: *Dziennik Ustaw RPL* No. 12, 1971, Item 115.

organisations exclusively by means appropriate to these organisations.[1]

A function transferred from a state organ to a mass organisation moves from the sphere of state activity to that of public self-administration only when it is exercised exclusively through measures of social influence, without any resort whatsoever to measures of state coercion.

It is not of course possible immediately and completely to renounce resort to measures of state coercion to ensure the fulfilment of functions transferred from the state to mass organisations. But even while this possibility is retained, the transference of particular matters from government to non-government bodies plays an important part in fostering the growth of public communist self-administration. Mass organisations acquire new experience and skills in the exercise, with the aid of measures of social influence, of a growing number of new functions hitherto exercised by the state.

In examining the question of the transference of state functions to mass organisations, it should however be borne in mind that such a step can under certain conditions lead to consequences which are both desirable and undesirable from the point of view of the extension of socialist democracy. The transference of functions from government to non-government bodies, when the latter are given the power to apply measures of state coercion, introduces a coercive element into their work which is alien to their overall voluntary character. Such elements, if introduced on too large a scale, may harm the voluntary character of the work of the organisation. Therefore the use of such methods should, in our view, be strictly limited. This aspect is taken into account when deciding whether or not a particular function should be transferred to a mass organisation. Account is also taken of whether such a transfer will lead to an improvement or a deterioration of the area of activity concerned.

[1] This was rightly pointed out by J. Starościak in his *Decentralizacja administracji*, Warsaw, 1960, p. 241, and also by A. Lopatka, *Państwo socjalistyczne a związki zawodowe*, Poznań, 1962, pp. 215-22.

The extension of the varied forms in which the mass organisations in the socialist countries participate in the formation and work of state organs and in the exercise of the functions of the socialist state, is of great significance in the extension of socialist democracy. "The building of socialism and its further development rests on the support, participation and initiative of the broadest masses inspired and led by the working class. The Communist Party is the vanguard of socialist society as a whole. The forces of socialism are strengthened and unity of will and action of the people is promoted by the steadily increasing political activity of the working people, by the greater activity of their social organisations, extension of the rights of the individual, irreconcilable struggle against manifestations of bureaucracy and by the all-round development of socialist democracy."[1]

3. THE PLACE AND ROLE OF NON-COMMUNIST DEMOCRATIC PARTIES IN THE POLITICAL STRUCTURE OF THE SOCIETY AND FORMS OF THEIR CO-OPERATION WITH THE COMMUNIST (WORKERS') PARTIES

The existence of political parties other than the Communist and Workers' parties is a distinctive feature of the political mechanism of many socialist countries.[2]

The leadership of the state and society by Marxist-Leninist parties is an inviolable general law characteristic of all

---

[1] *International Meeting of Communist and Workers' Parties, Moscow, 1969*, p. 22.

[2] The Agrarian People's Union in Bulgaria; the Democratic and Socialist Parties in the Democratic Republic of Vietnam; the Democratic Peasants' Party, the National Democratic Party, the Liberal Democratic Party and the Christian Democratic Union in the German Democratic Republic; the Democratic Party and the Chenudan Party in the Korean People's Democratic Republic; the United Peasants' Party and the Democratic Party in Poland; the Czechoslovak People's Party, the Czechoslovak Socialist Party, the Slovak Renaissance Party and the Slovak Freedom Party in Czechoslovakia. There are eight non-Communist parties in the People's Republic of China.

socialist countries without exception, regardless of any other special characteristics which they may have. The form of their leadership may, however, vary in accordance with the conditions prevailing in a particular country. As the experience of socialist countries has shown, the leading role of the Communist (Workers') parties does not of necessity imply the establishment of a one-party system in each socialist country. In many socialist countries the leadership of state and society by a Marxist-Leninist Party is exercised within the framework of a multi-party system.

The question of a one-party or multi-party system is decided in each socialist country in the light of the actual conditions of the class struggle, the historical traditions and the special national characteristics of each country.

The Russian Communist Party (Bolsheviks) and Lenin envisaged the possibility of the existence of several parties within the framework of the dictatorship of the proletariat.[1]

The objective possibility of co-operation between Communist and petty-bourgeois parties in revolutionary socialist transformations arises from the fact that the interests of the proletariat are in no way antagonistic to those of the petty-bourgeois working people. The latter, on the contrary, benefit from these social changes. This was stressed by Lenin in his letter to *Pravda* on November 18 (December 1), 1917: "Touching on the question of an alliance between the Bolshevik workers and the Left Socialist-Revolutionaries, whom many peasants at present trust, I argued in my speech that this alliance *can* be an 'honest coalition', an honest alliance, for there is *no* radical divergence of interests between the wage-workers and the working and exploited peasants. Socialism is fully able to meet the interests of both. *Only* socialism can meet their interests."[2]

But in order that the objective possibility of such co-operation should become reality, subjective factors are also neces-

---

[1] See V. I. Lenin, *Collected Works*, Vol. 26, pp. 269, 277-78, 287, 295, 301, 306, 331-34, 457; *KPSS v rezolyutsiyakh...*, Part 1, p. 402.

[2] V. I. Lenin, *Collected Works*, Vol. 26, p. 333.

sary—the readiness of the leadership of the petty-bourgeois parties to co-operate with Communists on the basis of the recognition of the need to build socialism. Only the honest acknowledgement by the non-Marxist parties of a programme of socialist changes creates the conditions for their stable co-operation with Communist parties in the building of socialism. "We stand firmly by the principle of Soviet power, i.e., the power of the *majority* obtained at the last Congress of Soviets," Lenin said in November 1917. "We agreed, and *still agree*, to share power with the minority in the Soviets, provided that minority loyally and honestly undertake to submit to the majority and carry out the programme, *approved by the whole* Second All-Russia Congress of Soviets, for gradual, but firm and undeviating steps towards socialism."[1]

It is clear that the non-Marxist parties' acknowledgement of a programme of socialist change must also include the acknowledgement of the leading role of the working class and its party in the building of socialism, without which the building of a socialist society is inconceivable.

Our party therefore considered the existence of a multiparty system within a socialist state to be quite permissible in principle on condition that the non-communist parties 1) represent the interests of classes and sections of society which are in alliance with and under the leadership of the proletariat in the building of socialism; 2) support the building of socialism; 3) acknowledge the leading role of the Communist Party in the building of socialism.

On the other hand, the attitude of the petty-bourgeois parties to co-operation with a Communist Party and to a programme of building socialism depends upon actual circumstances, above all upon whether the Left wing of these parties, which reflects the interests of the working masses of the petty bourgeoisie, who are the natural allies of the proletariat in the struggle for socialism, succeed in winning the lead-

---

[1] V. I. Lenin, *Collected Works*, Vol. 26, p. 307.

ership, or whether the leadership is seized by the Right wing, which represents the capitalists.

In Russia, the Communist Party of Bolsheviks showed tremendous patience and persistence. It repeatedly called upon the petty-bourgeois Mensheviks and Socialist-Revolutionaries to co-operate in the building of socialism.[1] Several Left Socialist-Revolutionaries were included in the Council of People's Commissars in December, 1917. They resigned of their own accord in March, 1918 in protest against the signing of the Brest Peace. Of the 305 members of the Third All-Russia Central Executive Committee (CEC) 162 were Bolsheviks, 122 Left Socialist-Revolutionaries, five Mensheviks, five Right and Centre Socialist-Revolutionaries, three United Internationalists, three Communist-Anarchists and six Socialist-Revolutionary-Maximalists. Of the 207 members of the Fourth CEC, 141 were Bolsheviks, 48 Left Socialist-Revolutionaries, four Maximalists, four Right and Centre Socialist-Revolutionaries, three Communist-Anarchists, four United Mensheviks and two Menshevik Internationalists.[2] From these figures it is clear that the petty-bourgeois parties had a substantial number of seats in the supreme government organ of the Soviet state. The fact that co-operation between the RCP(B) and these parties came to nothing was the responsibility solely of the leadership of these parties, in which the Right wing gained the upper hand, drawing them to the position of open counter-revolution. This naturally led to the isolation of these parties from the people and to their extinction.

A multi-party system emerged in those socialist countries where the Left, revolutionary wing came to the leadership of the petty-bourgeois parties, ridding them of Right-wing elements, overcoming the influence of bourgeois ideology and

---

[1] See V. I. Lenin, *Collected Works*, Vol. 26, pp. 269, 277-78, 287, 295, 301, 306, 331-34, 457; Vol. 28, pp. 217, 219; Vol. 32, p. 161.
[2] See *Syezdy Sovietov Vserossiiskiye i Soyuza SSR v postanovleniyakh i rezolyutsiyakh*, Moscow, 1935, pp. 27, 57.

leading them along the road of honest co-operation with the
Marxist-Leninist party of the working class.

Clearly, there can be no place for counter-revolutionary
parties in the socialist states.

During the counter-revolutionary revolt in Hungary in
1956 internal reaction attempted to re-establish a multi-
party system by creating numerous "political parties". To
deceive the public, reaction set up a number of parties bearing the names of parties which had existed in Hungary previously and whose activities had at certain periods contained
progressive elements (Social-Democratic Party, Small Farmers' Party, Peasants' Party). But their leadership was seized
by Right-wing elements who strongly opposed the dictatorship of the proletariat. In such circumstances reaction's
attempt to re-establish a multi-party system in Hungary was
a move directed against the dictatorship of the proletariat.

After the defeat of the counter-revolutionary uprising the
openly reactionary bourgeois parties disintegrated. Organisations which acted on behalf of the Social-Democratic Party,
the Peasants' Party and the Small Farmers' Party, attempted
to carry on their activities for some time in certain districts.
But this only served to demonstrate their anti-popular character.

Naturally, the Hungarian Socialist Workers' Party resolutely opposed the re-establishment of a multi-party system.

Thus, as János Kadár rightly observed, the question of a
one-party or multi-party system does not stem from a general law; it is a practical political issue which must be resolved in the light of the political and social conditions of
each particular country.[1]

---

[1] See János Kadár, *Political Report of the Central Committee of the Hungarian Socialist Workers' Party to the Seventh Party Congress;* See also Hermann Matern, "The Multi-Party System in the German Democratic Republic", *World Marxist Review*, Vol. 2, No. 4, 1959, pp. 26-33; B. N. Topornin, *Politicheskaya sistema sotsializma,* Moscow, 1972, Chapter VI; G. K. Shakhnazarov, *Sotsialisticheskaya demokratiya. Nekotoriye voprosy teorii,* Moscow, 1974, Chapter 2.

The multi-party system which exists in the socialist countries differs fundamentally from that in capitalist countries.

Irreconcilable struggle between proletarians and capitalists is a characteristic features of bourgeois society, which is divided into antagonistic classes. Hence, there is likewise irreconcilable struggle between the parties which reflect the interests of these antagonistic classes.

By contrast, the social and economic transformations carried out in the socialist countries have created the conditions for the political unity of the majority of the nation rallying around the Communist and Workers' parties on the basis of a programme for the building of socialism. This unity grows stronger with each new success in the building of socialism and communism. This is also the basis for the new relationships which exist between the parties in the socialist countries.

The non-communist parties, while remaining independent political parties, are closely allied to the Marxist-Leninist Party and acknowledge its leading role in the building of socialism.[1]

These relationships are the result of the attitudes taken up by the classes and strata whose interests these parties represent.

To define in a genuinely scientific manner the relationships between the various parties, it is necessary first to identify the classes or strata whose interests these parties

---

[1] This is reflected in the official documents of the non-proletarian democratic parties of the socialist countries. See, for example, the resolutions of the 12th Congress of the German Christian Democratic Union, the Ninth Congress of the German National Democratic Party, the Eighth Congress of the German Democratic Peasants' Party, the Declaration of the 10th Congress of the German Liberal Democratic Party (*Das System der Sozialistischen Gesellschafts- und staatsordnung in der Deutschen Demokratischen Republik. Dokumente*, Berlin, 1969, pp. 249, 251, 254-56), materials of the 31st Congress of the Bulgarian Agrarian People's Union (*Zemedelsko zname*, April 28, 1967).

express and defend, and secondly to define the relationships between these classes and strata in a given society at a particular stage in its development.

To answer these questions, we shall consider the party systems in Poland and Bulgaria.

Which classes and strata of society are represented by the non-proletarian parties in these countries? In Poland the United Peasants' Party represents a section of the working peasantry, while the Democratic Party unites a section of the working intelligentsia and of the working masses of the urban petty bourgeoisie. The Bulgarian Agrarian People's Union is an organisation of the rural working people of socialist Bulgaria.

The relations between these parties and the advanced detachment of the working class and all working people— the Marxist-Leninist party—in the period of the dictatorship of the proletariat are determined by the relations which exist between the proletariat and the mass of the working peasants, the urban petty bourgeoisie and the intelligentsia.

In voicing the interests of some sections of the working peasantry, the working intelligentsia, artisans and others who are working to build socialism and communism in alliance with, and under the leadership of, the working class, the non-communist parties are the allies of the Marxist-Leninist party. Together with it, they mobilise the non-proletarian sections of the working people for active work to achieve the aims of people's rule. These parties support the building of socialism and acknowledge the leading role of the Marxist-Leninist party.

The situation is similar in other socialist countries where there is still a multi-party system. The parties which function alongside the Communist and Workers' parties recognise the leading role of the latter in the building of socialism and are their allies.

A close alliance with the Marxist-Leninist party and the acknowledgement of its leading role does not of course mean that there is complete identity of views on all matters between the Communist and other democratic parties. There are certain differences, because it is impossible immediately after the victory of the socialist revolution completely to overcome the contradictions between the working class and the petty bourgeois strata of the working people in town and country. But these contradictions are not antagonistic and are gradually being overcome in the process of building socialism and communism.

It is not these contradictions, but a firm unity on basic issues, an identity of fundamental interests in the common struggle to build socialism and communism which is the main characteristic feature of the alliance between these classes and strata on the one hand and the working class on the other, and hence of the relations between the Marxist-Leninist parties and the non-communist democratic parties.

In socialist countries where a multi-party system exists other democratic parties are represented in state organs in accordance with their political weight alongside Communists and non-Party members.

The present relations between the political parties existing in the socialist countries took shape as a result of the long and bitter struggle of the Left, revolutionary wing of the non-communist parties to rid those parties of Right-wing elements which represented the interests of the capitalists, and to overcome bourgeois ideology.

Although the fundamental interests of the non-proletarian working people objectively coincide with those of the proletariat, considerable time and persistent struggle are necessary in order to free them from bourgeois ideology and to overcome their hesitations. The bourgeoisie fights by every means in its power to retain its influence over the peasant and other petty-bourgeois parties, to safeguard its position in their leadership and to use them in the struggle to ensure its own domination.

That is why there was a bitter and irreconcilable struggle between the Left, revolutionary wing of the peasant and other petty-bourgeois parties and the Right, reactionary wing to transform these parties. As a result of the victory of the Left, revolutionary wing, these parties were purged of reactionary elements and transformed into parties of the working people, playing a vigorous role in the building of socialism.

Thus, there is a general law governing the development of the multi-party system in all the socialist countries: the transformation of non-proletarian political parties into parties of the working people which play an active part in the building of socialism and acknowledge the leading role of the Marxist-Leninist party in socialist construction.

It should at the same time be noted that the evolution of the non-communist political parties is not simple; like the process of overcoming class contradictions, it does not proceed in a straight line.

Reaction strives to take advantage of any internal or international difficulties which confront a people's government in order to attack the foundations of the socialist system. In countries where a multi-party system has been retained, reaction, in addition to other methods, also tries to revive bourgeois ideology within the non-proletarian parties and to open the way to reactionary elements. Such attempts were made in Poland in 1956 and in Czechoslovakia in 1968. But the sound forces within the non-proletarian democratic parties of these countries gave a fitting rebuff to the Right-wing, reactionary elements.

In the socialist countries all parties present a united front.

Their activities are co-ordinated through the drafting of joint decisions and joint measures to carry them out. Varied forms of inter-party co-operation have emerged.

Among them we should in the first instance note that of the People's (National) Front, which will be discussed below. In Poland there are also central and local co-ordinating commissions representing the political parties. In the German Democratic Republic there is co-operation between the parties within the framework both of the National Front and of the Democratic Bloc of parties and mass organisations.[1]

The fact that leaders of allied parties are invited to the congresses of other parties is of importance in co-ordinating their work. A delegation from the Agrarian People's Union headed by its secretary attended the 10th Congress of the Bulgarian Communist Party; a delegation from the United Peasants' Party, headed by the chairman of its Supreme Committee and another from the Democratic Party, headed by the chairman of its Central Committee, attended the Sixth Congress of the Polish United Workers' Party.

Leaders of the Marxist-Leninist parties are in their turn invited to congresses of the other democratic parties.

Joint conferences and meetings of representatives of party leading bodies draw up common policies on fundamental issues. Representatives of the Politbureau of the Central Committee of the Polish United Workers' Party met representatives of the Presidium of the Supreme Committee of the United Peasants' Party to discuss the women's movement (July, 1957); representatives of the leadership of the Polish United Workers' Party and the Democratic Party met in January, 1961 to discuss current political problems of interest to both parties; representatives of the Central Committee of the Polish United Workers' Party met representatives of the Supreme Committee of the United Peasants' Party, and also representatives of the Central Committee of the Democratic Party in February, 1971 to discuss inter-party co-operation

---

[1] The Democratic Bloc of parties and mass organisations embraces all five political parties in the German Democratic Republic and also three mass organisations—the Free German Trade Unions, the Free German Youth and the Democratic Women's League. The scope of the National Front is wider. It embraces not only all political parties and mass organisations, but also all democratic and patriotic citizens who are not members of any party or mass organisation.

and the forthcoming session of the Seym. In the German Democratic Republic political, economic and cultural issues are discussed at conferences of representatives of the parties and mass organisations of the Democratic Bloc, at which the representatives of each constituent body preside in turn. Prior to the Fifth Congress of the Socialist Unity Party of Germany, its leadership informed the leaders of other democratic parties of the main issues to be submitted to the congress, and they were discussed by the representatives of these parties in a businesslike manner. Such conferences are not mere formalities. This is indicated by the fact that a resolution of the Fifth Congress reflected a proposal submitted by a representative of the German National Democratic Party regarding the further development of producer co-operatives in a manner taking account of the interests of particular groups of artisans.[1]

The adoption of joint resolutions by their leading bodies is an important form of inter-party co-operation. For instance, the Political Bureau of the CC of the Polish United Workers' Party and the Presidium of the Supreme Committee of the United Peasants' Party took joint decisions on agricultural problems between 1971 and 1975 (April 1971), on the development of agricultural circles (September 1971), and on improving the performance and further development of producer co-operatives. At their joint sitting in November 1971, the Political Bureau of the CC PUWP and the Presidium of the Democratic Party adopted a decision on the economic policy for 1971-1975, to expand craftsmen's services to the population.[2]

Joint sessions and conferences of local leading bodies of democratic parties are also held in the localities to discuss co-operation between the local organisations of these parties.

---

[1] See *World Marxist Review* No. 4, 1959, p. 81.

[2] See P. Winczorek, "Funkcje stronnictw sojuszniczych w systemie politycznym z perspektywy 30-lecia PRL", *(Państwo i Prawo* No. 7, 1974, p. 77).

Special forms of co-operation between representatives of the various parties in state bodies have been evolved in the socialist countries.

In a number of countries, where deputies are associated in party factions (clubs, groups), their work is co-ordinated by their representatives on the steering bodies of the people's representation. In the German Democratic Republic, all factions are represented on the Presidium of the People's Chamber. Chairmen of factions may also attend meetings of the Presidium. The chairman or his deputy must be invited to a meeting of the Presidium if the representative of the faction in question cannot attend.[1]

In Poland, members of the United Peasants' Party and of the Democratic Party are represented on the Presidium of the Seym. In addition, the Seym has a special body—the Council of Elders—which includes members of the Presidium and the chairmen (or their deputies) of the deputy groups of the three parties. The Council of Elders is a consultative body of the Presidium of the Seym, reponsible for the efficient functioning of the Seym and for co-operation between the party groups on procedural matters. In particular, it examines the drafts of meetings, dates and agendas, proposals for the Seym's election of its organs, procedural recommendations for separate items of the agenda, and also considers other matters referred to it by the Presidium.[2]

In the Bulgarian National Assembly, which has two parliamentary groups—the Communist Party and the Agrarian People's Union—the chairman is a member of the Bulgarian Communist Party, while one of his deputies is a member of the Agrarian People's Union.

---

[1] See Part 2, (xxiii) and Parts 2 and 3, (xxiv) of the Standing Orders of the People's Chamber of the German Democratic Republic, October 7, 1974, *Gesetzblatt der DDR*, Part 1, No. 50, 1974.

[2] See Art. 24 and Art. 25 of the Standing Orders of the Seym of the Polish People's Republic, March 1, 1957, as subsequently amended (unified text—*Monitor Polski*, No. 24, 1972, Item 136).

4. THE PEOPLE'S ((NATIONAL) FRONT[1]

The People's Front must be considered firstly as an alliance of certain classes and strata of society[2] and secondly as an organisational form of that alliance.

As an alliance of certain classes and strata of society, the People's Front is not peculiar to any particular group of countries making the transition to socialism. The alliance between the working class and the bulk of the peasantry and other sections of the working people is one of the principal laws governing the socialist revolution and the building of socialism in all countries.[3]

In the socialist states which emerged after the Second World War, the People's (National) Fronts were formed during the struggle for national liberation (or reunification),[4]

---

[1] The term "People's Front" is here used as a general term, since it is known variously in the different socialist countries: in Bulgaria and the Democratic Republic of Vietnam as the Fatherland Front, in Hungary as the Patriotic People's Front, in the German Democratic Republic and Czechoslovakia as the National Front, in the Korean People's Democratic Republic as the United Democratic Fatherland Front, in Poland as the Polish People's Unity Front, in Rumania as the Socialist Unity Front, in Yugoslavia as the Socialist Alliance of the Working People of Yugoslavia and in Albania as the Democratic Front. In Cuba, a similar organisation is called the Committee for the Defence of the Revolution.

[2] The People's Front is referred to as an alliance of certain classes and strata of society in the Declaration of the Meeting of Representatives of Communist and Workers' Parties held in Moscow in November, 1960 and also in other documents of the Communist and Workers' parties (see *Struggle for Peace, Democracy and Socialism*, Moscow, 1963, pp. 15, 63-64, 68-69).

[3] See *Struggle for Peace, Democracy and Socialism*, pp. 13-14.

[4] It should, however, be recalled that the People's Front has deep historical roots in these countries. It was born in the course of the long struggle of the peoples of these countries against imperialist reaction and fascism, during which the people learnt from their own experience that a united front was necessary in the fight to win and defend their freedom and national independence. See G. Dimitrov, Report to the Second Congress of the Fatherland Front, February 2, 1948 (Georgi Dimitrov, *Soch.*,

which facilitated the broadening of their social basis. This struggle helped rally around the proletariat not only the non-proletarian working people, but also the middle strata of society which had not in the past been supporters of socialism, but who on the basis of their own experience had come to realise that only under the leadership of the proletariat and only by building socialism was it possible to achieve genuine national independence and prosperity.

As the people's revolution developed the class structure of the People's Front was transformed in line with the regrouping of class forces.

The People's Fronts of the socialist countries today unite the patriotic intelligentsia, artisans, small producers and all other patriotic and democratic sections of the people around the alliance of the working class and working peasantry. The scope of this unity varies in accordance with the particular conditions of each country. But everywhere the class basis of the People's Fronts is the alliance of the working class and the working peasantry under the leadership of the working class.

The organisational forms (organisations or organs) assumed by the People's Front are distinctive features of the political organisation of society in the socialist countries which have emerged since the Second World War.[1] These forms are extremely varied in different socialist countries. A number of works dealing with this subject contain substantial inaccuracies: specific features of separate socialist countries are brushed aside and reference is made to the

---

Vol. 13, pp. 461-67); see also the decision of the Fourth Congress of the Bulgarian Fatherland Front (*Chetverty kongres na Otechestveniya front 11-12 fevruari 1957 god*, Sofia, 1957, p. 261); A. Zawadski's speech to the All-Poland Committee of the National Unity Front, January 4, 1958 (see *Trybuna Ludu*, January 5, 1958) and also statements by other political leaders of the socialist countries.

[1] That is, the specific organisational forms of the People's Front itself (its organisation and organs), and not the general question of the organisational forms of the alliance of the various classes and strata of society under the leadership of the working class.

existence of some uniform social and political organisation of the People's Front, to the electivity of the leading bodies, a discipline binding on all members, that the People's Fronts normally have their own rules, etc.[1]

Only in some socialist countries has the People's Front assumed the *form of a mass social and political organisation.*

Any mass organisation is marked by the following distinctive features: a charter, existence of primary organisations, institution of membership and discipline binding upon all members.

These features are to be found in the organisational forms assumed by the People's Front in Yugoslavia and Albania. Hence, in these countries, the People's Front may be said to become a mass social and political organisation.

But in many socialist countries the Front has neither primary organisations nor membership or charter. In Hungary, the Front has its charter, but it has neither primary organisations nor membership. It cannot therefore be said that the People's Front in these countries is a mass social and political organisation. It is a mass social and political *movement* without primary organisations, the institution of membership or binding discipline.[2]

But as a mass movement the Front has its organisational forms in the shape of local or central committees or councils. In a number of countries it also holds congresses and conferences.

Organs of the People's Front exist therefore both where it takes the form of a mass social and political organisation and where it takes the form of a mass movement.

---

[2] See, for example, *Gosudarstvennoye pravo stran narodnoi demokratii*, edited by V. F. Kotok, pp. 93-95; L. D. Voyevodin, D. L. Zlatopolsky, N. Y. Kuprits, *Gosudarstvennoye pravo stran narodnoi demokratii*, IMO Publishers, Moscow, 1960, p. 82.

[2] In *DDR. 300 Tragen—300 Antworten*, Berlin, 1959, p. 32, it is categorically stated that the National Front "*is not an organisation* but a broad non-party *movement*" (italics mine—*A.M.*). Article 1 of the Charter of the Patriotic People's Front likewise states that "the Patriotic People's Front is a political mass *movement*" (italics mine—*A.M.*).

In Bulgaria, the Fatherland Front from 1948 constituted a social and political organisation. The July 1968 Plenary Meeting of the Central Committee of the Bulgarian Communist Party and the BCP's 10th Congress concluded that against the background of the building of a developed socialist society the Fatherland Front must also make use of the methods and means characteristic of a nationwide movement. On the recommendation of the Central Committee of the Bulgarian Communist Party, the leading bodies of a number of movements (the Committee of Bulgarian Women, the National Peace Committee, the Vietnam Solidarity Committee, the Afro-Asian Solidarity Committee, the Temperance Committee) affiliated to the Front, while retaining their titles and organisational independence. In addition to the trade unions and the Komsomol (Young Communist League), the Central Co-operative Union, the Union of Labour Producer Artels and almost all the mass organisations and creative unions became collective members of the Front. The Front in this way came to embrace the entire Bulgarian people and is developing as the very widest type of social and political organisation and nationwide movement.

As organisations or movements, the Fronts unite all democratic political parties and mass organisations, and also non-party citizens who do not belong to mass organisations but who work for peace, democracy and socialism.

Since the Communist (Workers') parties of the socialist countries are the acknowledged leading core of all the mass organisations, and since all the other democratic parties recognise their leading role in the building of socialism, they also clearly constitute the leading force of the People's Front. The activity of the organisations and organs of the Front is in each country determined by the policy of the Communist (Workers') Party.

In the majority of socialist countries the People's Front does not have a programme in the form of a particular single document. This does not mean, however, that it does not have clearly defined aims and purposes. In countries where the Front has no programme but has a charter (Bulgaria, Hungary), its main aims and purposes are set down in the charter. Where the Front has neither programme nor charter (Czechoslovakia, Poland), its aims and purposes are clearly set out in election appeals and other documents adopted by its central bodies.

An examination of the documents of the People's Fronts of the socialist countries shows that, in addition to the particular tasks arising from the conditions in each country, the Fronts also pursue certain common aims: the defence of the independence and unity of their country, the consolidation and extension of the achievements of socialism, the strengthening of friendship with the Soviet Union and other socialist countries, and the struggle for peace throughout the world.

Since, as has already been noted, the People's Front in a number of socialist countries constitutes a mass movement without registered members or binding discipline, this naturally gives rise to the question of how the fulfilment of its decisions, appeals and declarations is ensured.

The fulfilment of its decisions is ensured by the fact that all the parties and organisations united in the Front participate in their drafting and adoption. Issues under dispute are resolved through comradely discussion, which continues until agreement is reached. The social character of the parties and organisations united in the Front objectively makes it fully possible to achieve unanimity on all fundamental issues. This is also the main method of decision-making in those socialist countries where the charter of the Front makes its decisions binding upon affiliated bodies.

The People's Front has demonstrated its viability and effectiveness as a means of uniting the broad mass of the people under the leadership of the working class and its party.

The Communist and Workers' parties of the socialist

countries therefore see as one of their most important tasks the strengthening and development of the People's Front, whose role steadily increases with each new success in, and the concluding stage of, the socialist construction.[1]

The People's Front plays an important part in mobilising the mass of the people for participation in the *formation and work of the organs of state power*.

The People's Front takes part in the formation of all central and local organs of state power in the socialist countries. The political parties and mass organisations exercise their right to nominate candidates to deputies of state organs within the framework of the Front through the nomination of joint candidates on behalf of the Front. This is provided for in different forms in the legislation of the socialist countries.

According to one form, legislation lays down that the protocols of nomination meetings shall be sent in the first instance to the appropriate body of the People's Front, which alone sends the nomination papers to the electoral bodies. This is the case of Czechoslovakia, for example, where the registration of candidates outside the framework of the Front is not allowed.

In Hungary and Rumania candidates are nominated for registration in a somewhat different manner, but also by the Front's organs.

In the German Democratic Republic the People's Front does not have the right under the law to nominate its own candidates. Nor does the law require that the Front register candidates nominated by meetings of other organisations. In this instance the law, while establishing the right of

---

[1] See "Otcheten doklad na Tsentralniya Komitet na Bulgarskata komunisticheski partiya pred Desetiya kongres na partiyata. Doklad na perviya sekretar na TsK dr. Todor Zhivkov", *Rabotnichesko delo*, April 21, 1971, p. 7; "XIV sjezd Komunistické strany Československa. Zpráva o činnosti strany a vývoji společnosti od XIII sjezdu Komunistické strany Československa a další úkoly strany, přednesene na XIV sjezdu KSČ soudrukem Gustávem Husákem dne 25. května 1971", *Rudé Pravó*, April 26, 1971, p. 6.

democratic parties and mass organisations to nominate candidates, provides only for the unification of their proposals and the nomination of joint candidates by the Front. A similar procedure is established in Bulgaria.

Despite these differences in procedure, in practice only joint candidates of the Front are nominated. This is because the class structure of society has changed radically in the course of the revolutionary transformations in the socialist countries as a result of which the social and political unity of their peoples is growing still stronger.

These differences in legal form are not due to any differences in the actual role played by the Front in the nomination of candidates in the socialist countries. They merely arise from differences in the legal approach to the question.

The People's Front bodies take part in the organisation of election meetings and in the election campaign both through the co-ordination of the work of affiliated organisations and through the work of canvassers nominated directly by the Front's committees. More than 420,000 of the Fatherland Front's activists took part in the campaign to elect deputies to state power organs and district courts in Bulgaria in 1971.[1]

The People's Front plays an active part in the establishment of electoral bodies (commissions, committees and presidiums), which bear direct responsibility for the organisation and supervision of elections. There are distinctive features in the laws governing this question in the various socialist countries. In some countries, Poland for example, the electoral law provides for the setting up of electoral commissions made up of representatives of political parties and mass organisations, without referring to People's Front bodies. Elsewhere, in Rumania for example, the law envisages the setting up of electoral commissions including representatives of the People's Front as well as of its organisations and representatives elected at the constituents' meetings. In yet other socialist countries, for

[1] See *Rabotnichesko delo*, June 30, 1971.

example Hungary, the law assigns a still larger role to People's Front bodies, establishing their sole right to nominate or even appoint the members of the electoral bodies.

Despite these differences in the legislative provisions, practice shows that the active participation of the People's Front in the setting-up of electoral bodies is a feature common to all socialist countries.

The People's Front participates in the supervision of elections not only through its own representatives on the electoral bodies (commissions, committees), but also through representatives specially selected for this task.

The People's Front fulfils important functions *not only in the field of the organisation, but also in that of the day-to-day work of state organs.* Close ties exist between local government bodies and the corresponding People's Front bodies. The People's Front plays an active part in the preparation and proceedings of sessions of local government bodies. The bodies of the People's Front submit proposals regarding the draft agendas which are taken into account in drawing them up.

The People's Front bodies organise meetings between deputies and their constituents to discuss matters on the agenda of sessions of local government bodies.

Representatives of the People's Front are invited to the meetings of local government bodies in an advisory capacity.

When necessary, local government bodies and People's Front bodies hold joint sessions.

The People's Front assists the Standing Committees of local government bodies in selecting and organising activists. In some socialist countries the law requires that Standing Committees shall seek the aid of the committees or other organisations of the People's Front.

The committees or organisations of the People's Front maintain regular contact with the Standing Committees, make recommendations and assist their investigations.

Co-operation between the committees and the executive and administrative bodies of the National Councils takes various forms. In order to co-ordinate the work of the executive and administrative bodies of the Councils and of the People's Front bodies, the Councils' Executive Committees supply the Front bodies with plans of their work. These plans are discussed by the Front bodies, which note the part to be played by the Front in their implementation.

Recommendations and proposals from the People's Front bodies are taken into consideration during the drawing up of agendas for meetings of the Councils' Executive Committees and in the preparation of reports to be delivered at these meetings.

Representatives of the People's Front are whenever necessary invited to attend meetings of the executive and administrative bodies of the National Councils. Such an invitation is mandatory when matters tabled by a Front body are to be discussed.

Proposals submitted by People's Front bodies are taken into account during the drawing up of working plans by executive and administrative bodies. The Front bodies participate in the preparation of these plans.

The executive and administrative bodies of the National Councils hold meetings jointly with the People's Front bodies to consider important issues. In accordance with Art. 56 of the Instructions of the Presidium of the Bulgarian National Assembly of April 29, 1965 regarding the structure and work of the National Councils, the Executive Committees of the Councils and the bureaux of the committees of the Fatherland Front conduct joint meetings to discuss such issues as public health and amenities, building, trade, the work of libraries, etc.

Bodies and organisations of the People's Front do a great deal to explain and publicise the decisions of the National Councils and their executive and administrative bodies and to mobilise the public to carry them out.

The work of public control carried out by the bodies and organisations of the People's Front is of great assistance to the organs of state power and administration.

The Front bodies play an active part in the maintenance of a permanent link between deputies and their constituents. They regularly organise meetings at which deputies report on their work and listen to the criticisms, comments and proposals of their constituents.

In a number of socialist countries (for example the German Democratic Republic and Hungary) the law requires deputies to organs of state power and these organs themselves to work in close co-operation with the People's Front bodies. In case of need, the Front bodies take the initiative in securing the recall of a deputy who has not justified the confidence of his constituents.

The bodies and organisations of the People's Front pay great attention to bringing to light the needs of constituents. They help to collect the proposals and mandates of electors, draw up plans to implement them and verify that the members of local government bodies carry out these mandates. The Front bodies' representatives inform Council members of the most important mandates from electors at meetings of local government bodies.

The Front bodies discuss the progress being made in the implementation of mandates at the electors' and their own meetings. The latter meetings also assess the work of Council members. The implementation of electoral mandates is also discussed at joint sessions of the local representative organs of state power—councils and Front bodies, or at a meeting of the Council to which representatives of the Front are invited.

Of great importance in the fulfilment of the economic and cultural functions of the local government bodies in the socialist countries is the organisation of mass voluntary public work by the People's Front.

The Front bodies play a major role in organising the preliminary discussion of drafts of important normative acts adopted by the supreme organs of state power and administration.

In the German Democratic Republic, for example, the

committees of the National Front in co-operation with the Democratic Bloc of parties and mass organisations organise the discussion of measures outlined by the People's Chamber and the Government, during which members of the public express their opinion and submit proposals.

Joint sessions of supreme state bodies and the central organs of the Front are held. A report on the visit of a Bulgarian Party and Government delegation to the Soviet Union was made on November 23, 1972, at the joint sitting of the CC of the Bulgarian Communist Party, the Managing Council of the Bulgarian Agrarian People's Union, the National Council of the Fatherland Front, the National Assembly, the Council of State and the Council of Ministers of the People's Republic of Bulgaria[1].

Representatives of the Front sit on central organs of state administration and play a direct part in their work.

The great importance of the People's Fronts in the social and political life of the socialist countries is reflected in the constitutions of a number of these countries, which give a legal expression to the establishment of People's Front and define its main functions. The Yugoslav Constitution lays down in detail the various forms of social and political activity and public self-administration implemented within the framework of the People's Front.

The varied forms of the participation of the People's Front in the organisation and work of the state organs indicate the great role it plays in the functioning of these organs in the socialist countries. When account is also taken of the fact that the People's Front is the broadest movement or organisation embracing the very widest sections of the public in these countries, it becomes especially clear how important is the development of these varied forms for drawing the broadest masses of the people into the administration of the state.

---

[1] See *Rabotnichesko delo*, November 24, 1972.

CHAPTER V

CITIZENSHIP AND THE CONSTITUTIONAL FOUNDATIONS OF THE LEGAL STATUS OF CITIZENS IN THE SOCIALIST COUNTRIES

1. INTRODUCTORY REMARKS

The present chapter examines two inseparably linked institutions of state law: the institution of citizenship—that is, the totality of juridical norms regulating the procedure for the acquisition and loss of citizenship—and the institution of the constitutional foundations of the legal status of citizens—that is, the constitutional norms relating to the rights and duties of the citizen.

Until recently authors dealing with socialist state law usually considered the institution of citizenship under the heading of "State Structure", which included national-territorial and administrative-territorial structure as well as citizenship. Such an aggregation of diverse issues derived from the view of the functions of Soviet state law which was widespread in the past—a view which in essence reduced these functions to that of providing commentaries on the 1936 Constitution of the USSR. In drawing up the structure of the science of state law and in drafting the syllabus for its study, the category to which a particular norm should be ascribed was decided simply by reference to the chapter of the Constitution in which it appeared. Art. 21 of the 1936 USSR Constitution establishing a uniform Union citizenship forms part of the chapter dealing with the state structure; this was seen as sufficient justification for declaring the institution of citizenship to be a component part of state structure. This example was followed in a number of other socialist countries.

In reality, even the 1936 Constitution gave no grounds for considering the institution of citizenship to be a part of state structure, since Art. 21 defined the relationship between Union and republican citizenship, not the procedure for the acquisition or loss of citizenship.

Objectively, the norms of state law relating to the acquisition and loss of citizenship are most closely linked to those regulating the fundamentals of the citizens' legal status. The constitutions and other legislation of the socialist countries, which harmonise the interests of society and the individual, give rights to, and place duties upon, precisely the citizen. Citizenship of the state in question is the necessary prerequisite for the exercise of these rights and the fulfilment of these duties. Hence the inseparable connection between the institution of citizenship and that of the constitutional foundations of the legal status of the citizen.

It is because of this objective connection that these institutions are considered in the same chapter.

2. CITIZENSHIP

In the science of state law citizenship means firstly the corresponding institution of state law—that is, the aggregate of legal norms governing the procedure for the acquisition and loss of citizenship; secondly, it means the corresponding legal relationship between a physical person and the state. In this second meaning citizenship implies the juridical allegiance of a physical person to a particular state. He enjoys all the rights and is subject to all the duties of a citizen of that state, regardless of whether he is on its territory or not.

Citizenship of a socialist state implies a person's legal allegiance to a state in which power belongs to the people. It implies that that person is afforded the extensive rights guaranteed by the constitution and other legislation of the socialist state in question for active participation in the administration of the state and in all aspects of the country's political, economic, cultural and social life. Of course, citizenship of a socialist state also implies corresponding duties.

But even these duties likewise differ radically from those of the citizens of a capitalist state.[1]

The procedure for the acquisition and loss of citizenship is laid down by the legislation of each particular state.

With the exception of the Fundamental Law of the Republic of Cuba, the constitutions of the socialist countries contain no rules establishing this procedure. Part II of the Fundamental Law of the Republic of Cuba, entitled "Citizenship", contains articles relating to this question (Arts. 11-17). In the other socialist countries this procedure is governed by current legislation: the Law on Citizenship of the USSR of August 19, 1938,[2] the Law on Bulgarian Citizenship of October 7, 1968,[3] the Law on Polish Citizenship of February 15, 1962,[4] the 1957 Law on Hungarian Citizenship,[5] the Law on Citizenship of the German Democratic Republic of February 20, 1967,[6] and the Law on Rumanian Citizenship of December 17, 1971.[7]

The legislation of the socialist countries lays down in the first place that those who were subjects or citizens prior to the establishment of the socialist system and who have not lost their citizenship under the terms of new legislation became citizens of the new state. Citizenship of the socialist states is now acquired by origin (birth to parents who are citizens of the republic in question) or by naturalisation. In the majority of socialist countries naturalisation lies within the competence of the supreme collegiate organs of state power (Presidium of the Supreme Soviet of the USSR or the Presidium of the Supreme Soviet of a Union republic, the Presidium in Hungary, the Council of State in Bulgaria

---

[1] See Section 6 of the present chapter.

[2] *Vedomosti Verkhovnogo Sovieta SSSR* No. 11, 1938, Item 3. For the currently valid text see *Sbornik zakonov SSSR. 1938-1967*, Vol. 1, pp. 200-01.

[3] See *Derzhaven Vestnik*, 1968, Item 79.

[4] See *Dziennik Ustaw RPL* No. 10, 1962, Item 49.

[5] See *Magyar Közlöny*, 1957, Item 64.

[6] See *Gesetzblatt der DDR*, I, No. 2, 1967.

[7] See *Buletinul Oficial de RSR*, Part I, Item 157/1971.

and Poland, and the Presidium of the Great People's Khural in the Mongolian People's Republic). However, in Czechoslovakia naturalisation is a matter for the Ministry of the Interior of the appropriate republic (Czech or Slovak), in Yugoslavia for the Federal Secretariat of Internal Affairs, in the German Democratic Republic for the Council of Ministers, and in Rumania for the President.

The regulation of the relationship between federal and republican citizenship is a distinctive feature of the citizenship legislation of the Soviet Union, Yugoslavia and Czechoslovakia. This is due to their federal structure. The law of August 19, 1938 on USSR citizenship lays down that each citizen of a Union republic is simultaneously a citizen of the USSR (Art. 1, ii). According to Art. 1 of the law of September 15, 1964 on Yugoslav citizenship[1] citizens of the Socialist Federal Republic of Yugoslavia, have uniform Yugoslav citizenship. Art. 2 lays down that only a citizen of Yugoslavia may have republican citizenship, and that loss of the former also entails loss of the latter.

The Czechoslovak law of December 19, 1968 on the principles governing the acquisition and loss of citizenship[2] lays down that every citizen of the Czech Socialist Republic and of the Slovak Socialist Republic is a citizen of the Czechoslovak Socialist Republic. Any person who acquires the citizenship of one of the republics simultaneously becomes a Czechoslovak citizen. The loss of the citizenship of one of the republics (unless arising from the acquisition of that of the other) entails the loss of Czechoslovak citizenship.

Loss of citizenship arises for the following reasons.

1. Through the action of the law regardless of the wishes of the person concerned. For example, in accordance with Art. 4 and Art. 11 (v) of the law of January 8, 1951 on Polish citizenship,[3] persons who on August 31, 1939 were

---

[1] See *Sluzhbeni list SFRY*, Item 38/1964.
[2] See *Sbírka zákonů ČSSR*, Item 165/1968.
[3] See *Dziennik Ustaw RPL* No. 4, 1951, Item 25.

Polish citizens but who were permanently resident abroad and who had acquired, in accordance with an international agreement amending the Polish frontiers, the citizenship of another state lost Polish citizenship.

Under the terms of Art. 16 (ii) of the law on Bulgarian citizenship, Bulgarian citizens of non-Bulgarian nationality who settle in other countries lose Bulgarian citizenship from the moment of settlement.

In these cases no application by the persons concerned is required, nor is any special decision by government bodies necessary.

2. On application by the person concerned. The competent authorities (in the USSR the Presidium of the Supreme Soviet of the USSR, in Bulgaria and Poland the Council of State, in the German Democratic Republic the Council of Ministers, in Yugoslavia the Federal Secretariat for Internal Affairs, and in Rumania the President) consider the application and permit the renunciation of citizenship. Citizenship is held to have been renounced from the moment permission is received.

It is necessary to distinguish between loss of citizenship and deprivation of citizenship. Deprivation of citizenship constitutes a punishment for a grave offence. The citizenship laws of the majority of socialist countries enumerate actions which constitute grounds for deprivation of citizenship. These include disloyalty, actions and behaviour infringing the vital interests of the socialist state, illegal departure abroad after the establishment of people's rule, refusal to return in response to a summons by the competent authorities, evasion of military service and conviction abroad for a criminal offence.

The laws of the majority of socialist states prohibit dual citizenship, and hence do not recognise this institution. Dual citizenship is however permitted by the Yugoslav citizenship law of September 15, 1964. The question of the citizenship of persons hitherto holding dual citizenship is decided between socialist states in the spirit of true internationalism and in accordance with the voluntary principle. Conventions have been concluded under the terms of which persons who are simultaneously citizens of two socialist states freely decide which citizenship they shall retain.

3. THE SOCIALIST DEMOCRATIC CHARACTER OF THE CONSTITUTIONAL RIGHTS AND DUTIES OF CITIZENS OF SOCIALIST COUNTRIES

The definition of the legal status of the citizen is of great significance in ensuring the rule of the people. Without effective safeguards for far-reaching and genuine rights for the citizen in all spheres of political, economic and cultural life, there can be no question of genuine popular sovereignty.

The constitutions of the socialist states embody the far-reaching and effective rights and freedoms which the working people of these countries have won in revolutionary struggle and in the struggle to build a new social system.

The rights and duties of the citizen are not confined to those laid down in the constitutions of the socialist countries. The constitutions, as fundamental laws, lay down only the basic rights and duties which constitute the *foundation, the legal basis* for all the other rights and duties which are regulated in detail by the appropriate branches of the law.

The constitutional (basic) rights and duties of the citizen in the socialist countries include not only those set down in the special chapter of the constitution entitled "The Fundamental Rights and Duties of Citizens", but also all those set down in the basic law, regardless of the chapter in which they appear. In particular, rules regarding the constitutional rights of the citizen may be found in the chapters dealing with the social structure, the electoral system and the fundamental principles of the structure and work of state bodies.

The rights and duties of the citizen of a socialist state are founded on the principles of socialist democracy. The further strengthening of the socialist state and the exercise of its functions, the building of a socialist and communist society are inconceivable without the involvement of the broadest mass of the working people in the administration of the state and the exercise of its functions, without the full development of the people's creative activity and initiative in all spheres of political, economic, cultural and social life. From this springs the genuinely popular character of the citizen's constitutional rights and freedoms—which are rights and freedoms for the working people—and the objective trend towards the constant extension of the rights and freedoms set down in the socialist constitutions.

The harmonious co-ordination of the rights and duties of the citizen with the interests of the socialist society and state is eloquently formulated in the Czechoslovak Constitution (Art. 19, i): "In a society of the working people, in which the exploitation of man by man has been eliminated, the development and interests of each of its members shall correspond to the development and interests of society as a whole. The rights, freedoms and duties of the citizen shall contribute to the free and all-round development of the individual and simultaneously to the strengthening and development of socialist society; as it develops, they shall become fuller and more far-reaching."

The constitutions of the socialist countries do not confine themselves to setting down the rights of the citizen; they attach decisive importance to providing guarantees for those rights and the means to exercise them.

The steadily developing and strengthening socialist economic system, state power in the hands of the working people headed by the working class and the leading role in the state of the Communist and Workers' parties is the *main guarantee* enabling the working people of the socialist countries to exercise the rights and freedoms inscribed in their constitutions.

The constitutions also provide a number of special *legal and material guarantees* for particular rights and freedoms.

The observance of laws, said Lenin, is guaranteed firstly by supervision over the observance, and secondly, by punishment of infringements.[1] The establishment of strict control over the observance of the law and effective punishment for its infringement constitutes a *legal guarantee* for the observance of the law and its enforcement.

The legislation of the socialist countries establishes strict responsibility for the infringement of the citizen's rights.[2] It must be emphasised that the socialist state's systematic campaign to strengthen socialist legality is of the greatest significance in reinforcing the legal guarantees for the rights and freedoms of the citizen.

The constitutions of the socialist countries do not confine themselves to the establishment of legal guarantees. They also lay down *material guarantees* (material resources) enabling the citizen to exercise his legal rights and freedoms. Moreover, the constitutions of certain socialist countries formulate a number of the rights of the citizen from the point of view of the constant extension of the scope for their realisation and of their material guarantees. Art. 57 of the Polish Constitution states that "the Polish People's Republic, while strengthening and enhancing the achievements of the working people, shall reinforce and extend the rights and freedoms of the citizen".

It is necessary to clarify the *legal significance* of the material guarantees for the basic rights and freedoms of the citizen. These are clearly created not by the fundamental laws but through the efforts of the people itself, with the organising role of the socialist state guided by a Marxist-Leninist party. But the significance of constitutions cannot be reduced to the recording of what in fact exists. The constitutional provisions regarding material guarantees for the basic rights and freedoms of the citizen are *legal norms* which impose a *legal obligation* upon the organs of the socialist state to provide and extend such guarantees.

---

[1] See V. I. Lenin, *Collected Works*, Vol. 2, p. 295.
[2] This responsibility is in the main defined not in the constitutions but in the ordinary legislation of these countries.

While guaranteeing the most far-reaching rights and freedoms for the citizen, the constitutions of the socialist countries stress that reactionary elements shall not take advantage of them to harm the interests of the people and their state.

4. THE EQUALITY OF CITIZENS IRRESPECTIVE OF SEX, RACE, NATIONALITY OR RELIGIOUS PERSUASION

Genuine equality for all citizens, irrespective of sex, nationality, race or religious persuasion is one of the most important principles of socialist democracy and it is established in law by the constitutions of the socialist countries.

What is the significance of this constitutional provision from the point of view of the basic rights of the citizen? Until recently the majority of experts on state law placed these provisions in "a special category of basic rights". Adhering to the sequence of articles in the constitution, they examined the question of equal rights after examining the basic rights of the citizen in the economic and cultural spheres and before considering the political rights and personal freedoms of the citizen,[1] while some included articles dealing with the equality of citizens among political rights.[2]

There are, however, no grounds for the separation of these articles in a special group of basic rights, to be considered together with basic rights in the economic and cultural fields and before political rights and personal freedoms. The articles on equality do not give the citizen any additional basic rights; they lay down that all the rights set down in all other constitutional articles apply equally to all citizens and provide a guarantee of equality.

Nor are there grounds for including the articles dealing with equality in the category of political rights, because these articles expressly establish equality in all spheres and

---

[1] See *Sovietskoye gosudarstvennoye pravo*, Yurizdat, Moscow, 1948; *Sovietskoye gosudarstvennoye pravo*, Gosyurizdat, Moscow, 1950; *Sovietskoye gosudarstvennoye pravo*, Gosyurizdat, Moscow, 1958.

[2] See Y. N. Umansky, *Sovietskoye gosudarstvennoye pravo*, p. 278 ff.

not merely in politics. Therefore in the present work the constitutional provisions regarding the equality of the citizens are not treated as "a special category of citizen's rights" but are considered before the examination of the basic rights of the citizen as one of the main principles of socialist democracy applicable to all basic rights.[1]

The constitutions of the socialist countries lay down that women enjoy equal rights with men in all spheres of state, political, economic, social and cultural activities. This equality is ensured by equal working conditions, equal pay for equal work, paid leaves, etc.

In establishing the conditions for the genuine equality of women, the socialist states initiated the large-scale construction of crèches and kindergartens, catering and other facilities to free women from housework. In tsarist Russia on the eve of the First World War there were in all only some 4,550 children in permanent crèches and kindergartens; in the USSR in 1973 the figure was 9,360,900. In Hungary in 1938 there were only 37 crèches for 1,000 children, and in 1971 there were 1,052 for 44,749 children. In Bulgaria in 1939/40 there were only 254 kindergartens for 13,000 children, while in 1972 there were 7,613 for 336,000 children. This enabled women to take an active part in production and in social and political life.

While establishing the equality of the citizens irrespective of nationality and race, the constitutions of the socialist countries impose strict responsibility for the infringement of this principle. Any direct or indirect privilege or any

---

[1] In the constitutions of a number of socialist countries the basic rights of the citizen are preceded by the general articles relating to equality (see, for example, Arts. 35 and 36 of the Bulgarian Constitution, Art. 20 of the Fundamental Law of the Republic of Cuba, Art. 17 of the Rumanian Constitution, Art. 154 of the Yugoslav Constitution, Art. 76 of the Constitution of the Mongolian People's Republic, Arts. 19 and 20 of the Constitution of the German Democratic Republic, and Art. 51 of the Constitution of the Korean People's Democratic Republic. This sequence of constitutional norms relating to the legal status of the citizen is very logical.

restriction of the rights of the citizen on grounds of race or nationality, any incitement to racial or national hatred or contempt or any attempt to humiliate a person on grounds of nationality is prohibited by the constitutions of these countries and is punishable under the law. There are strict penalties for those who infringe the equality of the citizen on racial or national grounds.

Not only are national minorities given equal rights with all other citizens; they are also assured of equal opportunity to exercise them. For example, the principle of equal opportunity for the national minorities in the field of education is ensured by provision of teaching in their native languages and by the training of teachers able to give education in their mother tongues.

In the schools of the USSR education is conducted in 57 languages of the country's national minorities. During the 1971/72 academic year in Yugoslavia there were 1,529 schools in which teaching was carried on in Albanian, Hungarian, Italian, Rumanian, Slovak, Bulgarian, Roucenian, Turkish or Czech. In Rumania there are over 2,000 schools and school departments teaching in Hungarian, German and other national languages.

The Communist and Workers' parties of the socialist countries, with the support of the mass organisations, are waging a resolute campaign against every manifestation of bourgeois nationalism and cosmopolitanism, educating the public in the spirit of proletarian internationalism.

The constitutions of the socialist countries guarantee freedom of conscience and religious belief.

Genuine equality irrespective of religious persuasion can exist only when there is complete freedom of conscience. Freedom of conscience implies the freedom to hold any religious beliefs and to profess any religion or none, and also freedom of anti-religious propaganda. Any infringement of freedom of conscience implies an infringement of the equality of the citizen on religious grounds. Indeed, if any state prohibits the profession of any religion, it infringes the freedom of conscience and at the same time places that section of the population which professes the prohibited religion in an inequitable position *vis-à-vis* other sections of the population (prohibition is accompanied by corresponding sanctions and restrictions applicable to those who profess the prohibited faith).

When a state establishes direct or indirect privileges for a particular faith this implies similar privileges for that section of the population which professes it and places other sections of the population in an inequitable position.

The constitutions of the socialist countries prohibit all acts limiting or restricting freedom of conscience and religious belief, and all acts creating privileges or imposing restrictions on religious grounds. The constitutional separation of church and state is an essential prerequisite for freedom of conscience.

While guaranteeing freedom of conscience and religious belief, the people's governments cannot of course tolerate attempts by anti-popular forces to take advantage of these freedoms for political purposes contrary to the interests of the people. Needless to say, rites are prohibited which threaten the people's health or violate public order.

5. CONSTITUTIONAL RIGHTS IN THE SOCIALIST COUNTRIES

The primary basic rights inscribed in the constitutions of the socialist countries include the right to work, leisure, medical care and assistance in the event of sickness or disability, the right to education, access to the achievements of science and culture and creative participation in the development of national culture. It is noteworthy that the constitutions of the socialist countries as a rule begin their exposition of the basic rights of the citizen with those rights which ensure a prosperous and cultural life for the working people and which therefore form the basis which enables the citizen to take advantage of his other rights and freedoms.

The citizens of the socialist countries have the right to work—that is, the right to receive work with remuneration in accordance with its quantity and quality. This means that they are free from unemployment and fear for the morrow, that they are assured of stable living standars and that the state guarantees a fair wage without artificial equalitarianism. The people's governments, having nationalised the key branches of the national economy and systematically building and reinforcing the socialist economy to ensure the maximum satisfaction of the material and cultural needs of the working people, have completely eradicated the unemployment bequeathed by capitalism and guaranteed the right to work. The steadily expanding socialist economy offers immense opportunities for increased employment of factory and office workers.

The right to leisure is indivisibly linked with the right to work. In laying down the right to leisure, the constitutions of the socialist countries envisage the material and cultural provisions necessary for the maximal use of this right by the working people. It is guaranteed by the legislative limitation of working hours,[1] legislative provision for holidays, annual paid leave, and the provision of leisure and cultural facilities.

The constitutions of the socialist countries guarantee the citizen's right to medical care and assistance in case of sick-

---

[1] For instance, the 5-day working week totalling 41 hours has been introduced in the USSR. Art. 162 of the Yugoslav Constitution establishes a maximum 42-hour working week. A 5-day working week of similar duration is in force in Czechoslovakia. Measures are being taken to implement these constitutional requirements. The transition to a 5-day working week of 42.5 hours is taking place in Bulgaria between 1973 and 1975. A 5-day working week of not more than 43 3/4 hours was introduced in the German Democratic Republic from 1967. The Cuban Fundamental Law establishes a maximum 44-hour working week (Art. 66), a 46-hour working week has been introduced in Poland and the transition to an average 44-hour working week has been completed in Hungary.

ness or disability. The improvement of social insurance provisions relating to sickness, old age and disability and also the development of various forms of social security, the constant improvement of industrial health and safety, far-reaching measures to prevent and cure illness, the growing availability of free medical aid and the increasing number of hospitals, polyclinics, rural health centres, sanatoria and other facilities, all contribute to the fuller realisation of this right.

The people's governments are unstinting in their allocation of resources to public welfare. The following figures give a clear picture of the rapid expansion of public health facilities in the socialist countries. Tsarist Russia on the eve of the First World War had only 18 doctors and 130 hospital beds per 100,000 population; in the USSR in 1972 the corresponding figures were 280 and 1,110. In Poland in 1938 there were 37 doctors and 19 nurses for every 100,000 population; in 1972 the corresponding figures were 160 and 340. Over the same period the number of hospital beds increased from 69,400 to 212,600. In Mongolia, where prior to the establishment of the people's government there were no medical facilities at all for the working people, there are now some 1,000 hospital beds and nearly 200 doctors for every 100,000 population—figures higher than those in several developed capitalist countries.

Citizens of the socialist countries have the right to education. Their constitutions provide material guarantees for the exercise of this right. The right to education is guaranteed by the provision of universal, free and compulsory education in primary and incomplete secondary schools (in the USSR, the German Democratic Republic, Rumania and the Korean People's Democratic Republic by compulsory ten-year education), by the steady expansion of general secondary education, vocational training and higher education, by government assistance to workers wishing to improve their qualifications, government grants and by the building of new boarding schools and student hostels.

The following figures show what successes have been achieved. In tsarist Russia on the eve of the First World War there were 124,000 general educational schools of all types with 9,656,000 pupils and 105 higher educational establishments with 127,000 students. During the 1971/72 academic year the Soviet Union had 184,000 schools with 49,229,000 pupils and 811 higher educational establishments with 4,597,000 students. In Korea prior to the establishment of the people's government there was not a single higher educational establishment and only a few secondary schools, but in 1974 the Korean People's Democratic Republic had more than 3,000,000 schoolchildren and over 240,000 students in colleges and specialised secondary schools. In the Democratic Republic of Vietnam there were in 1970 16 higher educational establishments with 27,000 students; under the colonial regime there was only one higher educational establishment in the whole of Indochina with 500 students. In Bulgaria the number of higher educational establishments increased from five in 1939 to 27 in the 1972/73 academic year, while the number of students grew from 10,000 to 101,000 over the same period.

The social composition of the student body in the socialist countries has undergone a radical change. While under the capitalist-landowner regime it was in the main only the offsprings of the exploiting classes who had access to education, today the overwhelming majority of those studying are the children of workers, working peasants and working intelligentsia. A special system of schools has been set up enabling workers to study while continuing to work.

The right to benefit from the achievements of national culture and to make a constructive contribution to its development is closely linked with the right to education. This right is ensured by the expansion of libraries, the press, radio, cinemas, museums, exhibitions, cultural centres, clubs and reading-rooms accessible to the working people, and by the all-out support and encouragement given to culture and talent.

The constitutions of the socialist countries guarantee freedom of speech, press, meeting and assembly, and freedom to hold street processions and demonstrations.

The building of socialism and the other tasks confronting the socialist state cannot be carried out without the active participation of the mass of the working people. The freedoms mentioned above are a necessary prerequisite for the fullest development of the activity of the mass of the people and for drawing them into the administration of the state and the building of socialism. These freedoms therefore help to reinforce the socialist system.

In establishing these freedoms, the constitutions of the socialist countries provide guarantees for their implementation by providing the working people and their organisations with printing facilities and supplies of paper, public halls and buildings, communications media, radio and the other necessary material resources.

To ensure the maximum development of the political, social, economic and cultural activity of the broadest mass of the working people the constitutions of the socialist countries guarantee the right of association in political organisations, trade unions, co-operatives, youth, women's, sports and defence organisations, cultural, technical and scientific societies, etc.

The most active and politically aware citizens from the ranks of the working people, the working peasantry and the working intelligentsia are united in the Communist and Workers' parties.

While giving the working people the widest rights of association, the constitutions of the socialist countries stress that anti-popular elements shall not take advantage of this right in their struggle against the rule of the people.

The socialist constitutions lay down that every citizen shall have the right to submit statements, lodge complaints and address petitions to all state bodies. Like all the other basic rights of the citizen in the socialist countries, this right reflects the harmonious co-ordination of the interests of the socialist state with the personal interests of the individual worker. This right is an expression of the socialist state's concern for the protection of the rights and legitimate interests of the citizen. It is also of great importance in eradicating shortcomings in the work of government bodies and economic and mass organisations, and a means of drawing the people into the administration of the state.

The inviolability of the person is guaranteed in the socialist countries. Their constitutions lay down that a citizen may be deprived of his freedom only when the law so provides. A person detained must be released if on the expiry of the period laid down by the law he is not presented with a decision of a court or a procurator authorising his arrest.

The constitutions of the socialist countries also establish inviolability of domicile, correspondence and the citizen's property. With a view to strengthening socialist legality with respect to government bodies, the fundamental laws of a number of socialist countries elevate to the level of a constitutional right the right of the citizen to appeal against decisions of courts and administrative bodies and against improper acts of officials, and to take action through the courts in respect of offences committed by officials in the course of their duties, and to demand restitution from government bodies and officials for losses caused by the improper or illegal acts of officials.

The constitutions of the socialist countries afford the citizen a number of other rights in addition to those enumerated above. Reference has already been made in Chapter III to the right to own and inherit personal property. The constitutional rights of the citizen arising directly from the formation and functioning of state bodies will, to avoid repetition, be considered in Chapters VIII and IX.

The right of asylum occupies a special place in those chapters in the constitutions of the socialist countries which deal with the basic rights and duties of the citizen. This right does not relate to the rights of the citizens of socialist countries. As the constitutions themselves indicate, it is a right granted to aliens and stateless persons. The constitutions clearly define the categories of persons to whom the socialist state may grant asylum. It is given to aliens and stateless persons persecuted for defending the interests of the working people or campaigning for social progress, for activity in support of peace, for participation in the national liberation struggle or for scientific work.

6. THE CONSTITUTIONAL DUTIES OF CITIZENS OF THE SOCIALIST COUNTRIES

In a socialist state the citizen's rights are indivisibly linked with his duties. The constitutions of the socialist countries therefore set them down in a single chapter usually entitled "The Fundamental Rights and Duties of Citizens".[1] There is genuine equality of rights and duties for all citizens in socialist countries.

The indivisible link between basic rights and duties arises from the harmonious co-ordination of the interests of the socialist state and the personal interests of the individual workers.

The citizen's precise and conscientious fulfilment of his duties is an essential prerequisite for the strengthening of the socialist state and for success in the building of socialism and therefore for the improvement of the material and cultural well-being of the working people and the strengthening of the material and legal guarantees of the citizen's rights.

Therefore the overwhelming majority of the citizens of the socialist countries carry out their duties voluntarily. The

---

[1] See Chapter X of the Constitution of the USSR, Chapter VII of the Polish Constitution, Chapter II of the Rumanian Constitution, etc. In the Yugoslav Constitution the relevant chapter is entitled "The Freedoms, Rights and Duties of the Man and Citizen"; in the Cuban Fundamental Law Part IV is entitled "Basic Rights" and refers only to rights. In the Constitution of the Mongolian People's Republic the section dealing with basic rights and duties consists of two chapters, dealing respectively with rights and duties.

basic duties laid down in the constitutions of these countries are for the vast majority of the population of these countries both legal and moral obligations.

The voluntary and conscientious fulfilment of their duties by the overwhelming majority of the population in the socialist countries is a most important source of the indestructible stability of the socialist states.

The indivisible link between the basic rights and basic duties of the citizen does not of course imply that there is no distinction between them. The distinction lies in that a citizen's evasion of his duties renders him liable to measures of state coercion.

In the socialist countries coercion is applied to an infinitesimal minority of society—to exploiting elements which attempt to harm the interests of socialism, and to some individuals from other classes infected by bourgeois ideology. Coercion is applied in the interests of the vast majority of society, on the basis of that majority's belief that it is necessary to apply such measures in relation to the minority.

The citizens of the socialist countries are required to abide by the constitutions and observe the laws of their countries. Insofar as in these countries all the legal measures of state bodies must be in accordance with the constitution and the law, it may be concluded that the citizen's obligation to abide by the constitution and observe the law extends to all legal acts promulgated by organs of the socialist state within the limits of their authority. When examining the basic rights of the citizen we have already noted the significance of the legal guarantees for these rights, in particular of the socialist rule of law.

The citizen's precise and undeviating observance of socialist law strengthens the socialist rule of law and thus helps to strengthen the legal guarantees for the rights of the citizen.

In laying down the basic duties of the citizen, the constitutions of the socialist countries take account of the fact that laws and other normative acts cannot embrace all aspects of life, and that in addition to the norms of law there are also norms of morality which regulate people's behaviour. The socialist constitutions therefore require the citizen to respect the rules of socialist (in the case of the Polish Constitution social) community living and to abide by the norms of evolving socialist morality.

The Czechoslovak and Yugoslav Constitutions require the citizen to respect the rights of his fellow-citizens, while the Constitution of the Korean People's Democratic Republic requires that the citizen shall respect the collective.

Citizens of the socialist countries are required to abide by socialist labour discipline and to protect and strengthen public (socialist) property as the sacred and inviolable economic foundation of the state, the source of the country's strength and independence and of the prosperity and culture of all the working people.

To defend their country is the supreme duty and a matter of honour for the citizens of the socialist states. Military service is the honorary duty of the citizen. Treason, violation of the oath of allegiance, desertion to the enemy, espionage and actions which impair the military strength of the state are punishable with the full severity of the law.

The constitutions of some socialist countries list the duty to pay taxes, to be vigilant regarding class enemies and strictly to protect state secrets among the basic duties of the citizen.

The Czechoslovak and Yugoslav constitutions also lay down that the citizen shall conscientiously fulfill the public function entrusted to him, while the Yugoslav Constitution also requires that the citizen shall give aid and support to a fellow-citizen in danger and play his part in joint measures to avert danger.

The Hungarian Constitution requires that citizens shall raise their educational level and safeguard the country's natural and cultural wealth.

The Constitution of the Mongolian People's Republic also lays down the following basic duties of the citizen: the practical all-out reinforcement of international friendship and the friendship and solidarity of the working people, and of the unity and solidarity of the peoples of the socialist countries headed by the Soviet Union; the education of the rising generation in the spirit of diligence, discipline and organisation, collectivism, a communist attitude to work and socialist property, devotion to the ideals of communism and the principles of proletarian internationalism, and in the spirit of respect for all working people regardless of their nationality.

The Bulgarian Constitution specifically lays down the duty, and that of the German Democratic Republic also the right, of the citizen to contribute to the maintenance and consolidation of peace.

The inclusion of these duties in the constitutions of the socialist countries underlines the great importance to the building of a socialist and communist society of the campaign to mould a new man.

It has been mentioned above that the constitutional rights of the citizens of the socialist countries are not confined to the chapters of their constitutions directly dealing with fundamental rights and duties but are also to be found in some other chapters (those dealing with social structure or the electoral system, for example). In the same way the constitutional duties of the citizens of the socialist countries are not confined to those set down in the chapters dealing with rights and duties. Some constitutional duties are contained in chapters dealing with social (or social and economic) structure. It is in this section that the majority of the constitutions of the socialist countries set down the constitutional duty to work. The Czechoslovak Constitution, in a chapter headed "Social Structure", likewise sets down the duty of the citizen to make every effort to carry out assignments under the economic plan (Art. 13, i).

In the Rumanian Constitution the citizen's duty to work is contained in the chapter headed "The Socialist Republic of Rumania" (Art. 5).

CHAPTER VI

THE NATIONAL-TERRITORIAL STRUCTURE OF THE MULTI-NATIONAL SOCIALIST STATES

1. INTRODUCTORY REMARKS

The national-territorial structure of the multi-national socialist states is one of the means by which the national question is resolved in accordance with the principle of the complete equality of nations.

The genuine equality of all the nations and nationalities of a socialist state is achieved through a wide range of political, economic, social and cultural measures. The law, and state law in particular, plays an important part in the system of these measures. State law does not of course study all the means, forms and methods of solving the national question. It deals only with a particular category of measures designed to ensure genuine national equality, viz. *the state-legal forms of solving the national question.*

These forms are varied. They include constitutional norms establishing the complete equality of all citizens irrespective of nationality, the representation of national minorities in state bodies, and the right of the citizen to use his native language in the courts. This aspect has already been discussed in Chapter V.

The norms of state law which ensure the equality of the citizens irrespective of nationality in the organisation and work of state bodies will be considered in subsequent chapters. In the present chapter we shall examine the state legal forms of the organisation of nations within the framework of a socialist state—that is, the national-territorial structure of multi-national socialist states.

In the socialist countries there are two basic forms of national-territorial organisation: the unitary state and the federal state.

2. SOCIALIST FEDERALISM

According to Marxist-Leninist teachings on the state, the best form for a socialist state is in principle that of a united centralist-democratic republic.[1] But Marxist-Leninist theory never made this principle an absolute. Marxist-Leninist theory approaches the question of the desirability of a particular national-territorial structure from the point of view of the actual historical circumstances.

Under certain historical conditions, the solution of the national question in a country entering upon the transition to socialism and communism may require the establishment of a federal rather than a unitary state.

After the victory of the October Socialist Revolution in Russia, the Communist Party found that a federal structure was the most suitable means for uniting the nations which had been part of the former tsarist empire.[2] In the first years after the Revolution several independent Soviet republics were formed on the territory of the former tsarist empire. After the establishment of the Russian Soviet Federative Socialist Republic (RSFSR), a number of other republics were formed: the Ukrainian Soviet Socialist Republic (December 1917), the Byelorussian Soviet Socialist Republic (January 1919), and the Soviet Socialist Republics of Azerbaijan (April 1920), Armenia (November 1920) and Georgia (February 1921). The three latter republics united to form the Transcaucasian Socialist Federative Soviet Republic (TSFSR) in March 1922. Life itself had shown the Soviet peoples how

---

[1] K. Marx and F. Engels, *Selected Works*, Vol. 3, pp. 435-36; V. I. Lenin, *Collected Works*, Vol. 6, pp. 454-55; Vol. 19, pp. 500-01; Vol. 20, pp. 224-25; Vol. 26, pp. 446-47.

[2] V. I. Lenin, *Collected Works*, Vol. 25, pp. 37-38, 448; Vol. 26, p. 479; Vol. 27, pp. 206-07, 227-28; *KPSS v rezolyutsiyakh...*, Part I, p. 417.

essential it was to unite in a federal state. Without the unification of all the republics it would have been impossible to defend the achievements of the revolution against imperialist intervention, to rebuild the devastated economy and achieve any economic and cultural progress. Explaining the need for the amalgamation of the Soviet republics in a single union state, Lenin pointed out that "it is necessary to strive for ever closer federal unity, bearing in mind, first, that the Soviet republics, surrounded as they are by the imperialist powers of the whole world—which from the military standpoint are immeasurably stronger—cannot possibly continue to exist without the closest alliance; second, that a close economic alliance between the Soviet republics is necessary, otherwise the productive forces which have been ruined by imperialism cannot be restored and the well-being of the working people cannot be ensured; third, that there is a tendency towards the creation of a single world economy, regulated by the proletariat of all nations as an integral whole and according to a common plan. This tendency has already revealed itself quite clearly under capitalism and is bound to be further developed and consummated under socialism."[1]

The gradual development of federal ties between the Soviet republics culminated in the formation of the Union of Soviet Socialist Republics in December 1922. On December 30, 1922 the First Congress of Soviets of the USSR approved the Declaration and Treaty on the formation of the USSR, which was joined by the RSFSR, the Ukrainian SSR, the Byelorussian SSR and the TSFSR. The Congress elected a Central Executive Committee of the USSR, referred the Declaration and Treaty to the Central Executive Committee of the Union republics for further consideration and instructed the Central Executive Committee of the USSR to approve the text of these documents in the light of their comments. It also instructed the CEC of the USSR to prepare a final draft of these documents for their approval by

---

[1] V. I. Lenin, *Collected Works*, Vol. 31, p. 147.

the Second Congress of Soviets of the USSR. The first Constitution of the USSR, consisting of the Declaration and Treaty of the formation of the USSR, was approved by the Central Executive Committee of the USSR on July 6, 1923. After having been approved by Congresses of the Soviets of the Union republics, it received the final approval of the Second Congress of Soviets of the USSR on January 31, 1924.

As a result of the national-state delimitation and the establishment of a number of Union republics in Central Asia and also of the dissolution of the TSFSR and the direct entry of its constituent republics into the USSR, a total of 11 Union republics were members of the USSR at the time of the adoption of its 1936 Constitution. The Moldavian, Lithuanian, Latvian and Estonian Republics became members in August 1940.

Yugoslavia and Czechoslovakia are also federal states.

The Yugoslav federal structure was set down in the first constitution adopted in 1946 after the country's liberation. Czechoslovakia, however, was under the terms of the 1948 and 1960 constitutions a unitary state of two equal nations —the Czechs and the Slovaks. Slovak national bodies, set up in order to take account of national and other distinctive features, functioned in the Slovak districts. Czechoslovakia became a federal state under the terms of the Constitutional Law of October 27, 1968 on the Czechoslovak Federation.[1] This law laid down the basic principles of the Czechoslovak federation, defined the powers of the federation and of the republics and set out the fundamental principles governing the organisation and work of federal and republican bodies. The law repealed a considerable portion of the provisions of the 1960 Czechoslovak Constitution. The Constitutional Law on the Czechoslovak Federation now operates as amended and supplemented by the Constitutional Laws of December 20, 1970, July 6, 1971, and December 12, 1973.[2]

---

[1] *Sbírká zákonů ČSSR*, Item 143/1968.

[2] *Sbírká zákonů ČSSR*, Item 125/1970, Item 43/1971, Item 157/1973.

The distinctive features of socialist federal states are:

1. They are union states made up of socialist republics. The USSR is made up of 15 Soviet Socialist Republics: the Russian Soviet Federative Socialist Republic, the Ukrainian, Byelorussian, Uzbek, Kazakh, Georgian, Azerbaijan, Lithuanian, Moldavian, Latvian, Kirghiz, Tajik, Armenian, Turkmen and Estonian Soviet Socialist Republics. The Socialist Federal Republic of Yugoslavia is made up of six socialist republics: Bosnia-Herzegovina, Macedonia, Serbia, Slovenia, Croatia and Montenegro. Czechoslovakia consists of two republics—the Czech Socialist Republic and the Slovak Socialist Republic.

2. In addition to a federal constitution, each constituent republic has its own constitution.[1]

3. In addition to the federal supreme state organs, each constituent socialist republic has its own supreme organs of state power and administration, as well as its own courts and Procurator's office.

4. The legal systems of the USSR, Yugoslavia and Czechoslovakia include both federal and republican legislation.

The fundamental principles of socialist federation set down in the Constitutions of the USSR and Yugoslavia and in the Constitutional Law on the Czechoslovak Federation are:

1. Federation is based on the rule of the working people. In this it differs fundamentally from bourgeois federation.

2. The subjects of federation are organised in accordance with the national-territorial principle. Each constituent socialist republic is a national or multi-national state with its own territory, compactly inhabited by the corresponding nationality or nationalities.

3. Federation is based on the voluntary principle. The USSR, Yugoslavia and Czechoslovakia are union states of peoples which have united voluntarily.

---

[1] Constitutions will be adopted by the Czech and Slovak Socialist Republics after the adoption of a new Czechoslovak Constitution (see Art. 42, ii, of the Constitutional Law on the Czechoslovak Federation).

4. The subjects of federation have equal rights. The rights and duties of each constituent socialist republic are similar. Each republic, irrespective of its size or population, has equal representation in a special chamber of the supreme federal legislative body which safeguards the equality of the republics and nations and represents their interests. In the case of the USSR, this function is fulfilled by the Soviet of Nationalities of the Supreme Soviet of the USSR, in Yugoslavia by the Chamber of Republics and Provinces of the Skupshina of the Socialist Federal Republic of Yugoslavia, and in Czechoslovakia by the House of Nations of the Federal Assembly.[1]

5. Fraternal assistance from the more developed socialist republics and from the federation as a whole to the less advanced republics.

The Constitutions of the USSR and Yugoslavia, and also the Constitutional Law on the Czechoslovak Federation include articles defining and delimiting the powers of the federations and those of their constituent republics. This delimitation on the one hand safeguards the required unity of the state as a whole and on the other establishes the necessary limits of the independence of each republic.

The unity of each federation is safeguarded by the following factors.

A constitution which is uniform for the entire federation. The constitutions of the constituent republics likewise conform to the constitution of each federation. "Every Union Republic shall have its own Constitution with due account for the specific features of the Republic and drawn up in full conformity with the Constitution of the USSR," states Art. 16 of the Constitution of the USSR. "The Republican Constitution and the Provincial Constitution shall not conflict with the Constitution of the Socialist Federal Republic of Yugoslavia," states Art. 206(i) of the Yugoslav Federal Constitution. The Constitutional Law on the Czechoslovak

---

[1] See Chapter X (2).

Federation likewise requires that republican constitutional legislation shall conform to the federal constitution (Art. 87, b).

Uniformity of territory. Under the terms of Art. 2 (ii) of the Yugoslav Federal Constitution, "the territory of the Socialist Federal Republic of Yugoslavia is uniform and includes the territory of the socialist republics". Art. 3 of the Constitutional Law on the Czechoslovak Federation similarly lays down that "the territory of the Czechoslovak Socialist Republic shall comprise the territory of the Czech Socialist Republic and that of the Slovak Socialist Republic".

Uniformity of citizenship. "Uniform Union citizenship shall be established for the citizens of the USSR. Every citizen of a Union Republic shall be a citizen of the USSR," declares Art. 21 of the USSR Constitution. "Citizens of Yugoslavia shall have uniform Yugoslav citizenship. A citizen of a constituent republic shall simultaneously be a citizen of the Socialist Federal Republic of Yugoslavia," states Art. 249 of the Yugoslav Federal Constitution. The same principle is set down in the Constitutional Law on the Czechoslovak Federation, which lays down that "Czechoslovak citizenship shall be uniform" and that "every Czechoslovak citizen shall simultaneously be a citizen of the Czech or Slovak Socialist Republic".

The extension of all-Union laws and other all-Union normative acts to the entire territory of the federation and the conformity of republican to federal legislation. In Yugoslavia and Czechoslovakia constitutional legislation places responsibility for ensuring this conformity upon special bodies—the constitutional courts.[1]

The inclusion of a definite range of questions within the competence of the federation. Measures uniform for the entire federation must be taken regarding these questions.

According to Art. 14 of the USSR Constitution, matters lying in the exclusive competence of the Union include:

---
[1] See Chapter VII (4).

a) approval of the economic plans of the USSR, approval of the single state budget of the USSR and of the reports on its execution, determination of taxes and other revenues that go to the Union, republican and local budgets; administration of banks and industrial, agricultural and trading enterprises and institutions under Union jurisdiction; general direction of industry and construction under Union-Republican jurisdiction; administration of transport and communications of all-Union importance; direction of the monetary and credit system, contracting and granting of loans, organisation of state insurance, organisation of a uniform system of national economic statistics;

b) control over the observance of the Constitution of the USSR, and ensuring conformity of the Constitutions of the Union republics with the Constitution of the USSR; definition of the fundamentals of Union and republican legislation regarding labour, marriage, and the family, the judicial system and judicial procedure, the fundamentals of civil, criminal and corrective labour legislation, the basic principles of land tenure, the use of mineral resources, forests and water, public education and health; legislation regarding Union citizenship and the rights of aliens, the promulgation of all-Union acts of amnesty;

c) admission of new republics into the USSR, the approval of changes to boundaries between the Union republics and of the formation of new Autonomous republics and Autonomous regions within Union republics;

d) representation of the USSR in international relations, conclusion, ratification and denunciation of treaties of the USSR with other states, establishment of general procedure governing the relations of the Union republics with foreign states; issues of war and peace; organisation of the defence of the USSR, direction of the Armed Forces of the USSR, formulation of principles guiding the organisation of the military formations of the Union republics; foreign trade on the basis of state monopoly; state security.

In other respects each Union republic exercises state power independently.

In Yugoslavia, the powers of the federal government include:

a) safeguarding the independence and territorial integrity of the Socialist Federal Republic of Yugoslavia, the defence of its sovereignty in international relations and decisions regarding the issues of war and peace;

b) ensuring the system of socialist self-managing socio-economic relations and the single foundation of the political system;

c) regulation of the basic rights of workers in associated labour and the basic rights and duties of organisations of associated labour, self-managing communities of interest and other self-managing organisations and communities as regards the resources in common use; regulation of the basic rights of the working people to ensure their social confidence and solidarity; establishment of principles in relation to the status, rights and duties of the social attorney of self-management;

d) regulation of the fundamentals of relations of obligation (general part) and contractual and other relations of obligation in the sphere of commodity turnover and services; of the basic relations of property rights; of the basic relations assuring the unity of the Yugoslav market, of the basic property-legal and other material legal relations in marine and inland shipping and air communication; regulation of copyright;

e) regulation of the fundamentals of the system of social planning and the establishment of Yugoslavia's social plan; establishment of basic guidelines for preparing the economy and social agencies for war-time operation; regulation of the monetary system; establishment of a legitimate means of payment and emission policy and its implementation; regulation of the balance-of-payments turnover at home and abroad, formation of monetary and devisen reserves and their disposal, if necessary, for the country as a whole; regulation of the foundations of the credit and banking system, credit and other investments made by Yugoslav citizens abroad and aliens in Yugoslavia, and promulgation of injunctions to enforce federal laws on this, when it is established by the federal law in the national interest; regulation of the foundations of the system of property and personal insurance; regulation and implementation of measures to preclude the violation of the unity of the Yugoslav market; regulation of the system of social price control and exercise of direct control over commodity prices and services of national interest; regulation and provision of federal commodity reserves to meet the country's requirements in the event of war or other extraordinary circumstances and to secure a stable market in case of its gross breaches; regulation and implementation of protection from monopolies and disloyal competition; regulation and implementation of measures to restrict the free play of market forces and free commodity and services turnover in the national interest and in case of natural calamities and shortage of goods necessary for the economy and life of its citizens, and also for national defence; regulation of the system of foreign trade and devisen activity and other economic relations with foreign countries, and enforcement of the relevant federal laws; regulation of the customs system, customs tariffs and extra-customs protection, and their implementation; regulation of conditions necessary for the opening and functioning of customs zones; regulation and assurance of crediting accelerated development of underdeveloped republics and autonomous provinces; establishment and securing of federal revenues; regulation of the foundations of the social information system, of the status and the principles governing the work of the Social Accounting Service; regulation of the foundations of the legal status and activities of the associated labour and business community organisations on Yugoslavia's single economic territory; regulation of unification of the associated labour organisations and their communities in the Economic Chamber on the Yugoslav territory; regulation of the mandatory unification of associated labour organisations when required by the system's technological unity in separate fields of activity and by the national interest; regulation of the conditions on which Yugoslav citizens go abroad to conduct economic and other activities and work on hire, and protection of Yugoslav citizens working abroad;

f) regulation of the principles of the national defence system and concern about its implementation; regulation of the basic rights and duties of the working people and other citizens, of associated labour and other self-managing organisations and communities, of socio-political and other social organisations in the field of national defence; regulation of the basic rights and duties of socio-political communities in the system of national defence; regulation of the basic rights and duties of associated labour organisations and other self-managing organisations and communities as regards the priority production and services for national defence and the production of armaments and materiel; co-ordination of territorial and urban construction plans and investment construction with national defence requirements, regulation of the foundations of planning and preparation for national defence; announcing mobilisation; regulation of the leadership and command of the Yugoslav Armed Forces and the exercise of supreme command; regulation and organisation of the Yugoslav People's Army, its leadership and command; regulation of the management and disposal of public resources used in and for the Yugoslav People's Army; regulation of the citizens' military duty and protection of the families of persons on military service; regulation of the status and other matters relating to servicemen; regulation and provision of military training and research work for the needs of the armed forces; regulation and organisation of military courts and a military Procurator's Office; regulation and organisation of the social maintenance of servicemen and their families; and the guarantee of the basic rights to war veterans, war invalids and families of those who fell in battle:

g) establishment of Yugoslavia's foreign policy and concern about its implementation; maintaining relations with other states and international organisations; promotion of co-operation with the developing countries, provision of resources for the development of economic relations with them and the strengthening of solidarity with the liberation movements; signing, ratification and fulfilment of international treaties; protection of Yugoslav citizens and their interests and the interests of Yugoslav juridical persons abroad; regulation of international relations; regulation of the organisation and functioning of the federal foreign affairs service;

h) regulation of the basic principles governing the defence of the constitutional system (state security); maintenance of the work of the state security service necessary for the implementation of the constitutional responsibility of federal bodies, and co-ordination of the activities of state security organs;

i) regulation of Yugoslav citizenship; establishment of the basic data for the civil status registry and identity cards; establishment of Yugoslav holidays and honourable titles; establishment of the Yugoslav anthem; regulation of the use of the Yugoslav seal, arms and flag.

j) regulation of the frontier regime and the status of aliens; protection of the people's lives and health from infectious diseases threatening the whole country; introduction of medicines; protection of animals and plants from diseases and pests threatening the whole country; regulation of the import and dissemination of the foreign press and other mass information and the implementation of relevant federal requirements in conformity with the federal law; regulation of the regime of territorial waters and the manner in which Yugoslavia uses her rights in relation to the continental shelf and the high seas; regulation of the legal status of foreign juridical persons, representatives of foreign states, foreign and international organisations and representations of foreign economic and other organisations; protection and improvement of the environment in the interests of the country and international community; regulation of the turnover and transportation of dangerous substances and materials when national interest is concerned; regulation of the turnover, of poisons and of the production and turnover of narcotics; regulation of the fundamentals of the water regime in the interests of two or more republics and provinces; regulation of the status of foreign information institutions and their representatives; prohibition or restriction of the unhindered use of the mass media when it is aimed against the foundations of the constitutionally established socialist democratic system or threatens the country's independence, peace or equitable international co-operation; establishment of the elements of cartographic data of importance for national defence and security and for the general utilisation of cartographic publications; regulation of the status and powers of the Yugoslav Red Cross and other organisations exercising public powers on the basis of federal laws and international treaties; designation and upkeep of the cemeteries and graves of servicemen of allied and other foreign armies on the territory of Yugoslavia;

k) regulation and assurance of the safety of air communications; regulation of basic safety of other types of transport; regulation of matters concerning shipping routes subject to the international or interstate regime; regulation of communication systems of importance to the national security and the technological integrity of the communication systems, regulation of international communication;

l) regulation of general conditions and principles of punishment for crimes and economic infringements, the system of sanctions, conditions for their expunging and rehabilitation and general rules governing the use of educational measures and the punishment of minors (general part of the criminal law and the law on economic infringements); definition of crimes against the foundations of the socialist self-managing social system of Yugoslavia and the national security, humaneness and international law, against the prestige of the Socialist Federal Republic of Yugoslavia, its organs and representatives, against the prestige of foreign states, organisations and their leaders or representatives, against the official duties of employees in federal organs, against the armed forces, and also definition of crimes and economic infringements which violate the unity of the Yugoslav market or federal requirements; establishment of the responsibility and sanctions for the violation of federal requirements; regulation of the procedure to be followed by federal organs when considering these violations, regulation of general administrative procedure, criminal procedure and other judicial procedures, except special proceedings the regulation of which is referred to the competence of republics and provinces; regulation of amnesties and pardon for crimes as provided for by the federal law;

m) regulation of the system of measures and control of measures and precious metals, regulation of the protection of inventions, technical improvements, etc., regulation of standards, technical and quality norms, etc.;

n) regulation and organisation of the retrieval and processing of statistical and other data on separate spheres of public affairs, on the condition and mobility of the population, etc.;

o) regulation of conflicts between home and foreign legislation;

p) regulation of the organisation, terms of reference and the work procedure of federal organs, their material and other relations, elections to federal organs, their rights and duties in relation to public resources used; regulation of the status, organisation and work procedure for establishments and schools set up by the federation to implement its functions, and of the relationship between them and the federal organs; regulation of the rights, duties and responsibilities of employees in federal organs, establishments and schools;

q) defence of constitutional principles and legality;

r) exercise of other constitutional rights and duties.

With the exception of matters which the Constitution places within the competence of the federal government, each republic exercises all the functions of state power, administration and justice independently on its own territory.

The Constitutional Law on the Czechoslovak Federation places the following matters within the exclusive competence of the federal government: foreign policy, the conclusion of international treaties, the representation of Czechoslovakia in international relations, and issues of war and peace; defence, currency, federal state material reserves; federal legislation and administration within the framework of the federation's authority, and also supervision of the work of federal bodies; the safeguarding of federal legality. These general principles are set out in Art. 7 (i) of the Constitutional Law and are developed in greater detail in subsequent articles.

Under Art. 8, a number of matters are placed within the joint competence of the federal government and the governments of the two member-republics. These include planning, finance, banking, prices, foreign economic relations, industry, agriculture and food, transport and communications, science and technology, labour, wages and social policy, investment, public order and security, press, information and other matters.

Matters not falling within the exclusive competence of the federal government or the joint competence of the federal and republican governments may be resolved by each republic independently.

In its own territory each republic ensures the implementation of the rights of the citizen, the observance of the constitution and of the law. It also exercises all functions in the political, economic, cultural and social spheres which are of republican significance and which do not lie within the competence of the federation.

In stressing the sovereignty of the member-republics, the constitutions of the USSR and Yugoslavia and the Constitutional Law on the Czechoslovak Federation lay down that the territory of a member-republic shall not be altered without its consent and that frontiers between republics may be altered only on the basis of an agreed decision of the supreme representative organs of state power of the republics concerned. The federation protects the sovereign rights and equality of the member-republics.

3. NATIONAL-TERRITORIAL AUTONOMY

All other socialist countries are unitary states.

The majority of socialist countries are in the main made up of a single nationality. Citizens of a different nationality do not usually constitute a significant part of the population, compactly inhabiting a particular area. In this case the state-legal forms by which the national question is resolved are limited to ensuring complete equality for all citizens irrespective of nationality in all spheres of political, economic, social and cultural life, and to affording all citizens, irrespective of their nationality, equal rights of participation in the organisation and work of the organs of the socialist state. Insofar as there are no substantial national minorities compactly inhabiting particular areas, the question of national-territorial autonomy does not arise.

But in a number of other socialist countries where there are numerous compact national minorities, autonomy within a unitary state is given to particular national regions.

The socialist theory of the unitary state by no means rejects far-reaching autonomy for those parts of a unitary state which are compactly inhabited by national minorities. Lenin, while pointing out the advantages of the unitary, centralised democratic state, also explained that Marxists championed only *democratic* centralism: "Far from precluding local self-government, with *autonomy* for regions having special economic and social conditions, a distinct national composition of the population, and so forth, democratic centralism necessarily demands *both*."[1]

---

[1] V. I. Lenin, *Collected Works*, Vol. 20, p. 46.

Lenin at the same time pointed out that autonomy could be given not only to large areas, but also to small districts, asking "why national areas with populations, not only of half a million, but even of 50,000 should not be able to enjoy autonomy; why such areas should not be able to unite in the most diverse ways with neighbouring areas of diffent dimensions into a single autonomous 'territory'...".[1]

These Leninist principles have been embodied and developed not only in Soviet autonomy, but also in the forms of autonomy to be found in other socialist countries.

Autonomy in the socialist countries is based on the *national-territorial principle*. It is granted to areas with a distinctive national character and way of life.

There are at present autonomous national-territorial formations within the borders of five constituent republics of the USSR: the RSFSR and the Azerbaijan, Georgian, Uzbek and Tadjik SSRs. Similar formations exist within the Democratic Republic of Vietnam and within the Socialist Republic of Serbia, forming part of the Socialist Federal Republic of Yugoslavia. In the People's Republic of China national-territorial autonomy is provided for in the Constitution, yet the 1975 Constitution does not specify the right of autonomy which is virtually absent.

Autonomy in a socialist state implies the granting of internal self-government to districts inhabited by national minorities regarding matters relating to their distinctive national characteristics within limits laid down by the supreme organs of the republic. The state bodies in each autonomous unit are in the main made up of representatives of the nationality exercising autonomy, or of other people who are familiar with the language, way of life, customs and traditions of the local population.

While ensuring self-government and taking account of the distinctive national, economic and cultural characteristics of the particular region, autonomy in the socialist countries

---

[1] V. I. Lenin, *Collected Works*, Vol. 20, p. 49.

promotes the genuine equality of all peoples and nationalities inhabiting the territory of the state in question, their voluntary union in a single state and their vigorous participation in the common cause of building socialism and communism.

There are two main forms of socialist autonomy: state and administrative.[1]

The state form includes autonomous socialist states. These exist within the RSFSR (16), the Azerbaijan SSR (1), the Georgian SSR (2) and the Uzbek SSR (1) in the form of Autonomous Soviet Socialist Republics. Autonomous Soviet Socialist Republics have all the attributes of a state, viz.: 1) their own constitutions, 2) their own supreme organs of state power, administration and justice in the shape of the Supreme Soviet of the ASSR, its Council of Ministers and its Supreme Court, 3) its own legislation, and 4) its own citizenship.

The administrative form of socialist autonomy includes autonomous administrative-territorial units: Autonomous regions in the RSFSR and the Azerbaijan, Georgian and Tajik

---

[1] Many Soviet authors divide autonomy into political (autonomous republics) and administrative (all other forms of national-territorial autonomy). See, for example, Y. N. Umansky, *Sovietskoye gosudarstvennoye pravo*, p. 213; D. L. Zlatopolsky, *Gosudarstvennoye ustroistvo SSSR*, p. 207.

This definition of the forms of national-territorial autonomy is unsatisfactory. It is impossible not to agree with A. I. Lepyoshkin, who takes the view that autonomous national-territorial units which are not autonomous republics nevertheless constitute a form of political autonomy (see A. I. Lepyoshkin, A. I. Kim, N. G. Mishin, P. I. Romanov, *Kurs sovietskogo gosudarstvennogo prava*, Vol. II, Moscow, Gosyurizdat, 1962, p. 177). Lepyoshkin therefore suggests that the forms of socialist autonomy should be defined as state-political (autonomous states) and administrative-political (autonomous administrative-territorial units). While noting that this suggestion is well-founded, it is however desirable to render the nomenclature more precise. Insofar as both forms are political in character and insofar as not only forms of autonomy but also all institutions of state law without exception are political in character, there is no necessity, in naming them, to continually add the word "political". It therefore suffices to define the two forms of socialist autonomy as state and administrative.

SSRs, and autonomous provinces and an autonomous district in the Democratic Republic of Vietnam. The organisation of the state bodies of these autonomous units conforms to the basic principles governing the structure and functioning of the local bodies at the corresponding level of the general administrative-territorial structure of the republic, while of course taking account of the special rights of the autonomous units.

The autonomous provinces forming part of the Socialist Republic of Serbia (one of the six making up the Yugoslav Federation) were also a form of administrative autonomy.[1] But in accordance with the 18th Amendment to the 1963 Yugoslav Constitution adopted in December 1968, an autonomous province acquired a number of features characteristic of the state form of autonomy. These features were even more clear in the 1971 amendments and especially in the 1974 Yugoslav Constitution. The Provincial Skupshina, the representative body of the province, acquired the right to adopt the Provincial Constitution and laws, which is characteristic of a supreme organ of state power. The supreme judicial organs of a province began to be termed Supreme Courts which exercise the rights and duties of a republican Supreme Court in the province. The territory of a province cannot be changed without the consent of the Provincial Skupshina. A province, like a republic, itself decides a number of major issues on the Federal level.

State-legal guarantees are of crucial importance in ensuring the practical implementation of genuine national-territorial autonomy. Lenin attached great importance to guarantees of this kind. In proposing amendments to the 1918 Draft RSFSR Constitution, Lenin wrote: "Draft with *mandatory guarantees* for the equality and rights of the minority"[2]

---

[1] The Socialist Republic of Serbia has two autonomous regions—Voyevodina, where a substantial part of the population constitutes a Hungarian national minority, and Kosovo, where the majority of the population are Albanians.

[2] *Leninsky sbornik XXI*, Partizdat, Moscow, 1933, p. 267.

(italics mine—*A.M.*) in the margin against an article envisaging that local government bodies should have the right autonomously to protect the national cultural rights of the people inhabiting the territory under these bodies' jurisdiction.

Apart from constitutional injunctions relating to the complete equality of citizens irrespective of race and nationality, state-legal guarantees of securing the national-territorial autonomy are:

1. Constitutional provisions laying down that nations and nationalities *exercising the rights of autonomy shall have the right to play a definitive role in determining the legal status of the autonomous unit in question*. The Supreme Soviet of each Autonomous Soviet Socialist Republic adopts its fundamental law—the Constitution of the ASSR. The legal status of an autonomous province is defined by its Constitution the adoption of which lies within the competence of the Provincial Skupshina. A Statute regarding each autonomous administrative-territorial formation shall be drawn up by the organ of state power of the corresponding autonomous formation elected by its population. Thus, according to the Constitutions of the RSFSR (Art. 76), the Azerbaijan SSR (Art. 85), the Georgian SSR (Art. 24) and the Tajik SSR (Art. 64), the Soviet of Working People's Deputies of each Autonomous region shall draw up a Statute on the Autonomous Region.[1] Art. 95 of the Constitution of the Democratic Republic of Vietnam lays down that the National Councils of the autonomous provinces shall draw up their own Statutes regarding autonomy and other special problems.

2. *The constitutional obligation of superior state bodies is to ensure that the organs of self-administration of the autonomous units are able to exercise their autonomous rights and to assist them in the economic, political and cultural development of the national minorities inhabiting the territories under these organs' jurisdiction.* Art. 96 of the Con-

---

[1] Such statutes have as yet not been adopted.

stitution of the Democratic Republic of Vietnam lays down that superior state bodies must ensure that the National Councils and administrative committees of districts with national autonomy have the guaranteed use of rights to autonomy. They must assist national minorities in their political, economic and cultural development and create favourable conditions for this. In Yugoslavia, the federal government must safeguard the rights and duties of autonomous provinces as laid down by the Constitution.

3. *Legislative provision for the use of the language of the nationality of the particular area by the governing bodies of the respective autonomous unit.*

4. *Representation established by law of the national minorities inhabiting autonomous units in the country's supreme organs of state power.*

This representation is provided for in various forms by the legislation of the socialist countries.

In the USSR autonomous formations are represented on a general basis in the Supreme Soviet of the Union republic of which they form part. In addition, they have special representation in the Soviet of Nationalities of the Supreme Soviet of the USSR (11 deputies from each Autonomous republic and five from each Autonomous region).

In Yugoslavia, the population of the autonomous provinces forming part of the Socialist Republic of Serbia is represented not only in the supreme organ of state power of the Republic, but also has special representation in the supreme federal organ of state power—the Skupshina of the Socialist Federal Republic of Yugoslavia. In the Skupshina's Federal Chamber there are 20 delegates representing each autonomous province and in the Chamber of Republics and Provinces of this Skupshina there are eight delegates. One representative from each autonomous province serves on the Presidency of the Socialist Federal Republic of Yugoslavia, one on the Constitutional Court, and two representatives serve on the Federal Executive Council (government).

In the Democratic Republic of Vietnam, the law on elections to the National Assembly of December 31, 1959, originally laid down (Art. 12) that approximately one-seventh of the seats shall be reserved for national minorities. In addition to this mandatory representation of the national minorities, other citizens belonging to national minorities may be (and in fact are) elected to the supreme organ of state power. In practice their share reached nearly one-sixth of the total membership of the National Assembly. In December 1974 the electoral law was changed. Now one-sixth of all seats are reserved under the law for national minorities.

The norms of state law in the various socialist countries which regulate the representation of national minorities in the supreme organs of state power, differ both in form and in content. In the Democratic Republic of Vietnam, the national minorities are guaranteed a number of seats in the supreme organ of state power corresponding to their proportion of the population as a whole.

In the supreme organs of state power of the USSR and Yugoslavia, the autonomous formations have greater representation than would be the case if it were calculated on the basis of the size of their population in relation to the population as a whole. This is seen as an additional guarantee of minority rights.

As has already been noted, national-territorial autonomy in the socialist countries is exercised within the framework of a single state, the organisational principle of which is democratic centralism.

The state-legal *guarantees for the unity of the state* in implementing the national-territorial autonomy in the socialist countries are:

1. The definition of the limits of autonomy by the supreme organs of state power of the republic. These limits are in the first instance determined by the relevant provisions in the constitutions of the socialist countries. In accordance with the Constitution of the RSFSR, each Autonomous republic has its own constitution, which takes into account the distinctive features of the Autonomous republic and which is drafted in full conformity with the Constitutions of the RSFSR and the USSR. The Yugoslav Constitution lays down that a provincial Constitution cannot be at variance with the Constitution of the Socialist Federal Republic of Yugoslavia; according to Art. 226 of the 1974 Constitution of the Socialist Republic of Serbia, a provincial Constitution cannot be at variance with the Constitution of the SRS. The Constitution of the Democratic Republic of Vietnam lays down that the organs of autonomous units shall exercise their powers of self-administration within the framework of the rights of autonomy granted to them.

2. *The conformity of the normative acts defining the legal status of autonomous units to the principles of the constitution of the state in question.* In the USSR the constitutions of Autonomous republics and the statutes on Autonomous regions are approved by the Supreme Soviet of the Union Republic of which the respective autonomous formation is part. In the Democratic Republic of Vietnam, statutes on autonomy and other matters drawn up by the National Councils of Autonomous districts are enforced after they have been approved by the Standing Committee of the National Assembly.

In Yugoslavia, there is no provision for the approval of the constitutions of autonomous provinces by republican state bodies. Conformity of the Constitution of an autonomous province to the Constitution of the SFRY and the Constitution of the Socialist Republic of Serbia is ensured by a special system of constitutional control.[1]

3. *The inclusion of the state organs of the autonomous units into a single system of the state organs of the republic in question.* The state organs of autonomous formations, despite the distinctive nature of their legal status, are links in this integrated system.

---

[1] See Chapter VII (4) of this book.

4. *The constitutional enactment of the territorial unity of the republic.* The territory of autonomous formations is recognised as being a component part of the territory of a unitary socialist state. "Areas with national autonomy shall be component parts of the Democratic Republic of Vietnam," states Art. 3 of the Constitution of the Democratic Republic of Vietnam.

5. *Laws and other normative acts adopted by the central organs of state power and administration apply throughout the territory of the republic, including autonomous formations.*

"Laws of the Georgian SSR shall apply uniformly throughout the territory of the Georgian SSR," states Art. 23 of the Constitution of the Georgian Republic. "In the event of conflict between the laws of the Abkhazian and Ajarian SSRs and those of the Georgian SSR, the latter shall prevail."

In Yugoslavia, in the event of conflict between federal law and that of a province, the latter prevails pending a decision of the Constitutional Court. Federal law is only applied if federal organs are responsible for its exercise. In the event of conflict between republican law and provincial law the former prevails.

The creation within the RSFSR of ten national areas (*okrugs*) in the territory inhabited by small Northern nationalities is a distinctive state-legal form of considering the interests of national minorities. A national area is a national-administrative unit whose population has a distinctive national character. The Soviet of Working People's Deputies of each national area is not authorised to adopt a Statute on the National Area. In accordance with Art. 102 of the Constitution of the RSFSR, the RSFSR Supreme Soviet adopts a single Statute common to all national areas. The National Area is represented in the Soviet of Nationalities of the Supreme Soviet of the USSR by one deputy. National areas are not autonomous formations under the terms of the Constitution of the USSR or that of the RSFSR.

The creation of the Bain-Ulgy *Aimak* (region) by a decree of the Presidium of the Small Khural on July 25, 1940, was a distinctive state-legal form of the solution of the national question in the Mongolian People's Republic. This is a national Kazakh region, in which 70 per cent of the population are Kazakhs and 18 per cent Tuvinians. The Bain-Ulgy *Aimak* is not an autonomous formation, but its organs of state power and administration are authorised to take concrete measures in accordance with local conditions and the distinctive national characteristics of its population. Teaching in schools and administration are conducted in the Kazakh and Tuvinian languages. These languages are also used in the press, radio and other spheres.

* * *

The examination of the forms of national-territorial structure in the multinational socialist states shows that they are very varied.

But the feature common to all is that they are designed to promote the genuine equality of all the peoples inhabiting each state, and to encourage the development of the economies and cultures, national in form and socialist in content, of peoples who were victims of oppression prior to the establishment of popular rule. The state-legal forms of national-territorial organisation in the multi-national socialist states do not weaken but on the contrary reinforce the close economic, political and cultural ties of all the nationalities inhabiting each of these countries. By helping to overcome the legacy of pre-revolutionary national oppression, economic and cultural backwardness and national hostility fostered by the bourgeois-landowner regime, and by creating the conditions for the all-round development and drawing together of all the peoples inhabiting each state, these forms contribute to their unity for the common struggle to build socialism and communism. Addressing a special session of the Central Committee of the CPSU and of the Supreme Soviets of the USSR and the RSFSR held to mark the 50th anniversary of the formation of the USSR, Leonid Brezhnev declared: "The emergence in our country of a new historical entity of men, the Soviet people, is, comrades, our great accomplishment. We are justified in regarding it as a summary of the economic and socio-political changes that have taken place in this country in the past fifty years."[1]

---

[1] L. I. Brezhnev, *The Fiftieth Anniversary of the Union of Soviet Socialist Republics*, Moscow, 1972, p. 33.

CHAPTER VII

THE SYSTEM OF STATE ORGANS IN THE SOCIALIST COUNTRIES

1. INTRODUCTORY REMARKS

In considering the system of state organs, it is first of all necessary to clarify what is meant by this concept. Some authors define the system of organs of the socialist state as the totality of all such organs. But the system of state organs and their totality are far from identical concepts.

As has already been noted in defining the subject-matter and concept of state law, its norms by no means regulate the organisation and functioning of the totality of state organs. But it is state law which lays down the *system* of state organs, that is, which defines the *forms* of the various state organs, *their place* in the state mechanism and the character of their *interrelationships*.

2. THE BASIC TYPES OF STATE ORGANS IN THE SOCIALIST COUNTRIES

The types of state organs differ in accordance with the basic forms of activity of the state. In all the socialist countries the basic types are: 1) *organs of state power*, 2) *organs of state administration*, 3) *judicial organs (the courts)*, and 4) *the procurator's office*.

Distinctions are drawn between the forms of state organs in accordance with the *basic spheres of their activity* and their characteristic *basic legal forms of work*. It is important to emphasise this because some state organs also within certain limits function in ways characteristic of other forms of state organs. For example, the basic form of activity of judicial organs is the administration of justice. But the Supreme Court may also exercise certain functions of state administration within the framework of the judicial system. A particularly clear example of this was the abolition in 1956 of the Ministry of Justice of the USSR and subsequently of the Ministries of Justice of the Union Republics and the transference of their functions to the corresponding Supreme Courts,[1] and the abolition of the Ministry of Justice of the Democratic Republic of Vietnam and the transference of its main functions to the Supreme People's Court in 1960. Certain functions of state administration in the field of the judicial system were thus transferred to Supreme Courts. But this did not imply that these Supreme Courts became organs of state administration, because their basic sphere of activity—the administration of justice—remained unchanged.

Organs of state power also have certain executive and administrative functions in addition to their main function. For example, the Constitution of the People's Republic of Bulgaria (Art. 94 ii) stipulates that the Council of State has the right to issue decrees on the fundamental executive and administrative activities of the state. But the carrying out of some executive and administrative actions by the government bodies does not alter their character as organs of state power, because, as has already been noted, the distinctions between the various forms of state organs are drawn only in accordance with their *basic* sphere of activity.

The system of the state organs of each socialist country is constructed with a view to ensuring maximum popular sovereignty. Therefore the *representative organs of state power* which are most closely linked with the people constitute the basis of the entire system of state organs. All other state organs are subordinate to them.

---

[1] The Ministry of Justice of the USSR and those of the Soviet republics have since been re-established.

The system of representative organs in the socialist countries consists of a supreme organ of state power, which stands at the head of all the state organs of the country in question, and of local organs of state power, whose functions are confined to the corresponding administrative-territorial units.

In the USSR, Czechoslovakia and Yugoslavia the system of representative organs also includes the supreme representative bodies of the republics which are members of the federations. In socialist countries where there are autonomous formations, the system of representative organs also includes the organs of state power of the autonomous units. As already noted in Chapter VI, these have special rights and cannot therefore be regarded as ordinary local organs of state power. In the USSR, in addition to the representative organs already enumerated, the system also includes the supreme organs of state power of the Autonomous republics, and, in the case of Yugoslavia, of the autonomous provinces.

In addition to representative bodies, the organs of state power also include the higher collegiate, combined collegiate and individual, or individual organs of state power elected by the supreme representative bodies and accountable to them. These include the Presidium of the Supreme Soviet of the USSR, the Councils of State in Bulgaria, Poland, the German Democratic Republic and Rumania; the Standing Committee of the National Assembly and the President of the Republic in the Democratic Republic of Vietnam; the Presidency[1] and President of Yugoslavia, etc. In the Korean People's Democratic Republic, the people's committees elected by local representative bodies are also organs of state power.

Since a general description of the representative system as the foundation of the entire state apparatus of the socialist countries has already been given in Chapter III (3), while

---

[1] The Yugoslav Presidency is not elected by the Skupshina of the SFRY, but represents the republics and autonomous provinces forming part of the Yugoslav Federation.

the organisation and functioning of organs of state power will be considered in greater detail in subsequent chapters, there is no necessity here to consider in detail the status of organs of state power in the system of state bodies.

The constitutions of the socialist countries define the status of the *organs of state administration* in the state mechanism, their general aims and structure.

The system of organs of state administration is headed by the government. In the majority of the socialist countries the government goes under the title of Council of Ministers. In the Korean People's Democratic Republic it is termed the Administration Council, and in the Democratic Republic of Vietnam—the Government Council. In Yugoslavia the system of organs of state administration is headed by the Federal Executive Council.

The higher organs of state administration are subordinate to the supreme organs of state power. They are formed either directly by the supreme representative bodies or with their decisive participation, and are accountable to the supreme organs of state power.[1]

Local organs of state administration (with the exception of some centralised bodies) are usually in dual subordination both to the local organs of state power which form them and to the appropriate higher organ of state administration.[2]

In the USSR, Czechoslovakia and Yugoslavia the system of organs of state administration also includes the republican organs of administration of the national republics and, in the case of Yugoslavia, also those of the autonomous provinces.

The distinction between organs of state power and organs of state administration in the socialist countries in no way implies the application of the principle of "the separation of authorities". On the contrary, a feature of a socialist state

---

[1] For more detail, see Chapter XII of this book.

[2] For the special characteristics of the relationships between the local organs of state administration of the various territorial units in particular countries, see Chapter XIII (6).

is the combination of legislative and executive authorities, which finds expression in the close organisational link between the organs of state power and administration, and in the genuine subordination and accountability of the latter to the former.

The constitutions of a number of socialist countries particularly stress the unity of legislative and executive authority. In accordance with the 1960 Czechoslovak Constitution, local, city, district *(okres)* and regional *(kraj)* National Committees are integrated organs of state power and state administration in their areas. To ensure the closest possible organisational link between the National Committees and their executive bodies departments of the Committees themselves, but not of the Councils which are their executive bodies, are set up. The heads of these departments are appointed and recalled by National Committees at plenary meetings.

In Yugoslavia, the unity of legislative and executive power is emphasised by the fact that the Constitution defines the Federal Executive Council as the executive organ of the Skupshina of the SFRY (Art. 346). The status of republican governments is similarly defined.

The Constitution of the Democratic Republic of Vietnam defines the government not only as "the highest state administrative body" but also as "the executive body of the supreme organ of state power" (Art. 71).

The local government organs elected by local organs of state power are usually defined as executive and administrative bodies of local organs of state power. In Poland, after the 1972-73 reform, local government bodies are not elected by the National Councils, but are considered the Councils' executive and administrative organs (Art. 42 of the Constitution of the Polish People's Republic).

The system of *court organs* in the socialist countries consists of their Supreme Courts and territorial and special courts. In the USSR, Czechoslovakia and Yugoslavia, in addition to federal Supreme Courts, there are also republican

Supreme Courts (in the USSR there are Supreme Courts not only of Union Republics but also of Autonomous Republics), while in the Socialist Republic of Serbia there are the Supreme Courts of autonomous provinces. Special self-governing courts which are not included in the system of common state courts are a distinctive feature of the Yugoslav judicial system. The Czechoslovak and Yugoslav Constitutions also make provision for special Constitutional Courts.[1]

In the socialist countries the constitutions also lay down democratic principles relating to the organisation and functioning of the courts, such as the election of judges,[2] the uniformity and equality of courts for all citizens, the independence of judges and their subordination solely to the law, the adjudication of cases with the participation of People's Assessors, the public hearing of cases, and the right of the accused to defence. A Supreme Court heads the entire judicial system and supervises the work of all the court organs of its country. Supreme Courts are elected either directly by the supreme representative organs of state power, or by the supreme collegiate organ of state power (in Poland by the Council of State), or (as in the Democratic Republic of Vietnam, Hungary and the Korean People's Democratic Republic) the Chairman of the Supreme Court is elected by the supreme representative organ of state power, while other members of the Court are appointed by the supreme collegiate organ which is accountable to the National Assembly. The Supreme Courts are accountable to the supreme representative organs of state power or, during intervals between its sessions, to the supreme collegiate organ of state power.

The constitutions of the socialist countries normally make provision for a centralised system of *organs of the procuracy*. This system is in each case headed by a Procurator-

---

[1] See Section 4 of the present chapter.

[2] In Poland only members of the Supreme Court and People's Assessors are elected. The judges of *voivodship* and county courts are appointed by the Council of State. In Hungary all professional judges are elected by the Presidium of the Hungarian People's Republic.

General (Chief or Republican Procurator) who is in the majority of cases appointed by the supreme representative organ of state power. In the USSR, the Procurator-General of the USSR is appointed by the USSR Supreme Soviet. Procurators of the Union and Autonomous republics are appointed by the Procurator-General of the USSR. In Yugoslavia, the Federal Public Prosecutor is appointed by the Skupshina of the SFRY, while republican, provincial and communal Prosecutors are appointed by the appropriate Skupshinas. A distinctive feature of the Rumanian system is the appointment of county procurators and the Procurator of the Bucharest Municipality by the appropriate People's Councils.

In Poland, the Procurator-General is appointed by the Council of State, while in Czechoslovakia the Procurator-General is appointed by the President and those of the Czech and Slovak Socialist Republics by the Presidiums of their National Councils.

The Procurator-General is responsible and accountable either directly to the supreme representative organ of state power, or to the supreme collegiate organ of state power,[1] or to both.

Other procurators and investigating officers are normally appointed and dismissed by the Procurator-General (Chief or Republican Procurator).

In those socialist countries where the procurator's office is assigned the functions of supervision over the uniform interpretation of laws and their strict observance, the appropriate constitutions lay down that the organs of the procuracy shall be independent of the organs of state administration and of local government bodies. Only in Rumania do the People's Councils of counties and the Bucharest Municipality have the authority to recall chief procurators whom they have appointed.

---

[1] In Poland, since the Procurator-General is appointed by the Council of State, the Council receives an annual report from the Procurator's Office.

According to the constitutions of the majority of the socialist countries, the main task of the organs of the procuracy is that of supervising the strict fulfilment and observance of laws and other legal measures by government bodies, officials and citizens.

The fundamental laws of the socialist countries define the general function of organs of the procuracy and the courts as being the protection of the socialist system and of the rights and lawful interests of citizens and working people's organisations.

The 1974 Constitution of the Socialist Federal Republic of Yugoslavia established a new organ the functions of which are to some extent similar to those of the Procurator's Office. This is the Federal Social Attorney of Self-Management who is elected by the appropriate Skupshina.

3. DISTINCTIVE STRUCTURE OF ORGANS OF CONTROL IN SOME SOCIALIST COUNTRIES

In some socialist countries the system of state organs includes, in addition to organs of state power and administration, the courts and the procuracy, a distinctive type or system of state organs—*organs of control*.

The function of control is in various degrees and forms inherent in all the organs of a socialist state. The organs of state power not only adopt normative acts but also control their implementation; they not only form executive and administrative bodies but also supervise their work.

It has been noted that the organs of the procuracy exercise general supervision over the work of government bodies. The courts carry out a controlling function by bringing to light shortcomings in the work of factories and offices during the hearing of cases, by the adoption of riders on such shortcomings and by bringing them to the attention of the officials concerned, and by hearing complaints against officials submitted in accordance with existing procedures.

Special organs of state control have a particular role to

play in the system of organs of the socialist state. In the majority of socialist countries such organs are included in the system of organs of state administration. The head of the institution charged with the function of state control is a member of the government, while the institution itself is subordinate to the government.

In Poland, the organs of state control are separated from the system of state administration bodies. In outlining measures to enhance the role of the Seym, the Eighth Plenary Meeting of the Central Committee of the Polish United Workers' Party (October 1956) called attention to the need to reform the organisation of state control. With a view to strengthening the control of the Seym over all other state organs, it was decided to entrust the function of state control not to a ministry, which formed part of the Council of Ministers and hence could not control the government, but to a body accountable to the Seym—the Supreme Chamber of Control.[1]

On December 13, 1957 the Seym adopted a law amending the Constitution, according to which the Constitution was supplemented by a new chapter ("The Supreme Chamber of Control"); a law on the Supreme Chamber of Control; and a decree regarding the procedure by which the Chamber received instructions from the Seym and reported to it.[2] These acts lay down the Chamber's organisation and procedure. The Chairman of the Chamber is appointed by the Seym, and his deputies by the Council of State. The Chamber is subordinate to the Seym, and within the limits laid down by the law its work is supervised by the Council of State.[3] This organisational structure strengthened the position of organs of state control within the system of state organs.

---

[1] See *Nowe Drogi* No. 10, 1956, p. 7.

[2] See *Dziennik Ustaw RPL* No. 61, 1957, Items 329, 330; *Monitor Polski* No. 99, 1957, Item 578.

[3] For the relations between the Supreme Chamber of Control and the Seym, see Chapter X (5) of this book.

In Bulgaria, in accordance with a decision of the National Assembly of July 8, 1971[1] the Committee of State Control occupied a unique place in the system of state organs. The First Deputy Chairman of the Council of State is now the Committee's Chairman. The Deputy Chairman of the Committee is a member of the Council of Ministers with ministerial status. The Committee is thus linked organisationally not only with the Council of Ministers, but also and more particularly with the Council of State.

The main lines of development of organs of control in the socialist countries are: 1) the establishment of closer links between themselves and the public, combining state and public control; 2) closer co-operation between organs of state and Party control.

Closer links between the organs of control and the public are achieved through the growing participation of public controllers in the work of these organs and through the integration of government and non-government control bodies in a unified system.

Closer co-operation between the organs of state and Party control takes varied forms: co-ordination of work, joint checks, the participation of representatives of organs of Party control in the work of organs of state control, and of representatives of the latter in the work of Party control bodies.

In the German Democratic Republic, a Committee of the Workers' and Peasants' Inspection of the Central Committee of the Socialist Unity Party of Germany and the Council of Ministers was set up in May, 1963 on the basis of a decision of the Central Committee and the Council of Ministers. Similar bodies were set up in the localities, while commissions of the workers' and peasants' inspection were set up at major factories.[2]

In Rumania, a law on the organisation and functions of

---

[1] See *Derzhaven vestnik*, Item 55/1971.
[2] See *Gesetzblatt der DDR*, II, No. 40, 1963.

the Central Council of Workers' Economic and Social Control was adopted at the end of 1972.[1] This body is authorised to exercise uniform control over the implementation of the economic and social policies of the Party and state, functioning under the leadership of the Central Committee of the Communist Party and the State Council. Workers' Control Councils were also set up in counties and in Bucharest, as well as at factories and industrial amalgamations.

The organisational merger of organs of Party and state control has not, however become widespread in the majority of socialist countries. The Committee of Party and State Control of the Central Committee of the CPSU and the Council of Ministers of the USSR[2] set up in November 1962 was subsequently re-organised as the Committee of People's Control of the USSR.[3] A similar development has taken place in Bulgaria.[4]

4. SPECIAL ORGANS OF CONSTITUTIONAL CONTROL IN CERTAIN SOCIALIST COUNTRIES

A most important task of all the government bodies of a socialist state, a task that is established legislatively as these bodies' major obligation, is that of ensuring the observance of the constitution and of the law. Each government body performs this task within its sphere of competence.

---

[1] See *Buletinul oficial al RSR*, Part 1, No. 161, 1972.

[2] See *Vedomosti Verkhovnogo Sovieta SSSR* No. 48, 1962, Item 503.

[3] The organisation and functioning of people's control bodies in the USSR is at present governed by the Statute on Organs of People's Control in the USSR, approved by the Central Committee of the CPSU and the Council of Ministers of the USSR on December 19, 1968 (*SP SSSR*, No. 1, 1969, Item 2).

[4] See the Law of December 17, 1966 on Changes and Amendments to the Law on Party and State Control (*Derzhaven Vestnik*, 1966, Item 101). Under the terms of this law, the Committee of State Control is a purely state organ.

The Yugoslav Constitution, the Constitutional Law on the Czechoslovak Federation and the Fundamental Law of the Republic of Cuba nevertheless make provision for special organs—*organs of constitutional control.*

In Yugoslavia, these are the Yugoslav Constitutional Court and the republican and provincial constitutional courts.

The Yugoslav Constitutional Court is elected by the Skupshina of the SFRY, and those of the republics are elected by the Republican Skupshinas.

The Chairman and judges of the Yugoslav Constitutional Court are elected for an eight-year term and may not be re-elected for a second term. The Court is made up of two representatives from each republic and one from each autonomous province.

To ensure the independence of the judges of the Constitutional Court, the Yugoslav Constitution lays down that they may be removed before the expiry of their term of office only at their own request, if they are sentenced to a term of imprisonment for a criminal offence, or if they become incapable of work.

Similar rules govern the election and removal of judges of republican constitutional courts.

The judges of the Yugoslav Constitutional Court and of republican constitutional courts have the same immunities as delegates of the Federal, republican and provincial Skupshinas.

The powers of the Yugoslav Constitutional Court include: a) making decisions on whether laws are constitutional, on whether republican and provincial laws run counter to federal legislation, on whether instructions and other general measures adopted by organs and organisations conform to the Yugoslav Constitution, and on whether they contradict federal legislation for whose implementation the federal organs are responsible;

b) settlement of disputes regarding rights and duties between the federation and a republic or a province, between republics, between republics and autonomous provinces, and between territorial units on the territory of different republics (if the jurisdiction of another court is not established by law); settlement of jurisdictional disputes between republican, *resp.* provincial constitutional courts, between courts and federal bodies, between federal and republican or provincial organs and also between courts and other state bodies on the territory of different republics or provinces.

If the Yugoslav Constitutional Court rules that a federal, republican or provincial law runs counter to the Constitution of the SFRY or that a republican or provincial law contradicts the federal law, the appropriate Skupshina must, within six months of the ruling, take steps to bring the law into line with the Constitution or remove the discrepancy between the republican or provincial law and the federal law. If it does not do so, then the appropriate law or its separate parts become invalid, with a special ruling of the Constitutional Court to that effect.

If it is established that an instruction or a general measure other than the law is at variance with the Constitution of the SFRY or that a measure of a federal body is at variance with a federal law, the Constitutional Court repeals or annuls these norms or instructions. When normative acts are at variance with a republican (or provincial) constitution or republican (or provincial) legislation, the matter is considered by the appropriate republican or provincial Constitutional Court.

Under Art. 387 of the Yugoslav Constitution the right to institute proceedings in the Yugoslav Constitutional Court belongs to the Skupshina of the SFRY and to any other Skupshina; to the Presidency of the SFRY and to republican and provincial presidencies; to the Federal Executive Council and to republican and provincial executive councils (except for matters relating to instructions adopted by the Skupshina which elects the Council in question); to a republican or provincial Constitutional Court, if the issue regarding the conformity to the constitution and legality has arisen in its proceedings; to the Federal Procurator; to the republican, provincial or military Procurator if the matter has arisen in the course of his work; to the social attorney of self-management; to an organisation of associated labour, local collective or any other self-managing organisation or association, provided the Constitution of the SFRY or the federal law has established that its rights have been violated; and to other organs and institutions. Moreover, the Constitutional Court may institute proceedings on its own initiative.

The organisation and procedure of the Yugoslav Constitutional Court and of republican constitutional courts is set down in detail in the federal, republican and provincial laws dealing with the constitutional courts, and also by the regulations of those courts.

The Constitutional Law on the Czechoslovak Federation makes provision for the establishment of a Czechoslovak Constitutional Court, and for Constitutional Courts in the Czech and Slovak Socialist Republics elected by the Federal Assembly and the Czech and Slovak National Councils, respectively.

Members of the Czechoslovak Constitutional Court serve for a term of seven years, and may not serve for more than two consecutive terms. Half the members of the Court and their deputies must be citizens of the Czech Socialist Republic, and half citizens of the Slovak Socialist Republic. The Chairman and Deputy Chairman of the Czechoslovak Constitutional Court, elected directly by the Federal Assembly, must represent different republics. Members enjoy the same immunities as deputies of the Federal Assembly.

The Czechoslovak Constitutional Court ensures that laws of the Federal Assembly and legislative decrees of its Presidium, and the constitutional and other legislation of the Czech and Slovak National Councils conform to the Czechoslovak Constitution. It also ensures that the decisions of the Government of the Czechoslovak Socialist Republic, the generally obligatory legislative measures of federal ministries and other federal bodies of state administration, and also decisions of republican governments and the generally obligatory legislative measures of the ministries and other central organs of state administration of the republics conform to the Czechoslovak Constitution and to the laws of the Federal Assembly.

The Court also considers jurisdictional disputes between federal bodies and bodies of one or both republics, and between organs of both republics.

If the Constitutional Court rules that any of the above-named measures do not conform to the Constitution or to the laws of the Federal Assembly, the discrepancy must be removed by the body concerned within six months. If not, the measure or that part of it which is at variance with the Czechoslovak Constitution or the law of the Federal Assembly, becomes invalid.

The Czechoslovak Constitutional Court must institute proceedings on the basis of appeals from the chambers of the Federal Assembly, the Presidium of the Federal Assembly, the Czechoslovak Government or other federal body; the Czech or Slovak National Councils, their Presidiums or the governments of the republics; the courts; the Procurator-General; and also from citizens on matters relating to electoral law. The Court may also institute proceedings on its own initiative or on that of mass organisations.

CHAPTER VIII

THE CONSTITUTIONAL PRINCIPLES GOVERNING THE ORGANISATION AND FUNCTIONING OF STATE ORGANS IN THE SOCIALIST COUNTRIES

1. INTRODUCTORY REMARKS

One of the most important tasks confronting the working people headed by the working class after their achievement of political power is that of building a new, socialist state machine. If the socialist state is to fulfil its task successfully, its organs must be structured and must function in the appropriate way. The importance of the correct organisation of the state machine in safeguarding the interests of the working people was stressed by Lenin who pointed out that "in revolutionary times of all times it is necessary accurately to analyse the question as to the very essence of the state, as to whose interests it shall protect, and *as to how it should be constructed* in order effectively to protect the interests of the working people"[1] (italics mine—*A.M.*).

The fundamental principles governing the organisation and functioning of the organs of the socialist state are determined by the character of the state. These are the principles of socialist democracy, which are common to all socialist states. From this flows the universality of the constitutional principles which are set down in the fundamental laws of these countries and govern the organisation and functioning of the socialist state organs. This universality does not exclude distinctive features peculiar to particular countries.

---

[1] V. I. Lenin, *Collected Works*, Vol. 24, p. 557.

2. THE CONSTITUTIONAL FOUNDATIONS (PRINCIPLES) UNDERLYING THE ORGANISATION AND FUNCTIONING OF THE ORGANS OF THE SOCIALIST STATE

An analysis of the fundamental laws of the socialist countries shows that they set down the following constitutional foundations (principles) underlying the organisation and functioning of state organs: 1) the active participation of the mass of the working people in the organisation and functioning of these bodies; 2) democratic centralism; 3) proletarian (socialist) internationalism; 4) socialist legality.

Insofar as neither in the USSR nor in the other socialist countries is there unanimity regarding the constitutional (fundamental) principles governing the organisation and functioning of the organs of the socialist state, it is necessary to explain why these four principles are singled out.

A number of jurists both in the USSR and in other socialist countries include the leading role of the Communist Party among these fundamental principles.[1] But this is unacceptable, because the Communist Party is the leading force not only of the socialist state, but also of socialist society. The leading role of the Communist Party is the most important general law governing all the processes of the socialist revolution and the building of socialism, and it cannot be placed on the same level as the organisational principles of the structure and functioning of the state machine.

The leadership of the Communist (Workers') Party ensures the effective and complete realisation of the four principles we have enumerated.

The leading role of the Communist Party is not, therefore, one of the principles governing the organisation and functioning of the state organs. It permeates all these principles and is the prerequisite for their realisation and development.

---

[1] See *Sovietskoye gosudarstvennoye pravo*, Yurizdat, Moscow, 1948, pp. 285-86; *Gosudarstvennoye pravo stran narodnoi demokratii*, edited by V. F. Kotok, p. 130.

Nor is it possible to agree with the very many jurists who include the principle of the planned development of the national economy among the constitutional (fundamental) principles governing the organisation and functioning of the organs of the socialist state.[1]

The planned development of the national economy is an important aspect of the functioning of state organs, but not a principle governing it.

The functioning of state organs and the principles governing this functioning are two different concepts and must not be confused. The principles governing the functioning of state organs are the basic postulates which underlie all the work of the state organs. The principle of socialist legality, for example, is equally mandatory for all state organs without exception. It cannot, however, be asserted that the principle of economic planning finds expression in, for example, verdicts and decisions of the courts regarding homicide, divorce, etc., or in the mandatory decisions of a Soviet relating to the maintenance of public order.

Instead of the "principle of the decisive participation of the mass of the working people", some jurists in the socialist countries introduce the concept of "the principle of the democratic character of the state apparatus" or of "socialist democracy", seen as embracing the diverse forms of mass participation in the organisation and functioning of state organs.[2]

The introduction of these concepts, however, serves no purpose. The democratic character of the mechanism of the socialist state is by no means confined to the participation of the masses in the organisation and functioning of state organs. There is no need to demonstrate the indisputable

---

[1] See *Sovietskoye gosudarstvennoye pravo*, Yurizdat, Moscow, 1948, pp. 292-94; *Gosudarstvennoye pravo stran narodnoi demokratii*, edited by V. F. Kotok, pp. 136-37; B. Spasov, A. Angelov, *Derzhavno pravo na Narodna Republika Bulgaria*, pp. 178-80.

[2] See B. Spasov, A. Angelov, *Derzhavno pravo na Narodna Republika Bulgaria*, p. 173.

truth that the democratic character of the organisation and functioning of state bodies is manifested in democratic centralism, in proletarian internationalism and in socialist legality. Socialist democracy is a much wider concept than that of the participation of the masses in the organisation and functioning of state bodies. It embraces all the democratic principles governing the organisation and functioning of the socialist state machine, and cannot be reduced to any one of them.

Some writers also include the principle of the equality of nationalities among the fundamental principles governing the organisation and functioning of the organs of a socialist state. It is, however, more correct to refer not to the principle of the equality of nationalities, but to that of socialist internationalism as being one of these fundamental principles. This principle undoubtedly includes that of the equality of nationalities, but is not confined to this principle alone. Thus, in the relations between socialist states and hence in the corresponding functions of their organs, it is not a question of equality alone, but also of fraternal friendship and mutual assistance, and of the consolidation and development of the world socialist system. Within the multi-national socialist countries, the work of state bodies in giving fraternal aid to once backward peoples in the development of their economies and cultures and in uniting all nationalities in a united family likewise goes beyond the equality of nationalities.[1]

---

[1] In their "State Law of the Hungarian People's Republic" J. Beér, I. Kovács and L. Szamel include the principle of proletarian internationalism among the "fundamental principles of the exercise of state power". The point, however, is not fully developed, it being merely stated that "in a socialist state it flows from the principle of proletarian internationalism that the principle of the complete equality of nationalities is realised to the full in all aspects of the work and development of the state" (*Magyar államjog*, p. 162). The impression is given that here, too, the application of the principle of socialist internationalism in the organisation and functioning of state bodies is confined to the equality of nationalities.

All the principles governing the organisation and functioning of the organs of the socialist state are indivisibly linked and by their interaction ensure the socialist democratism in the organisation and functioning of the entire mechanism of the socialist state.

3. THE ACTIVE PARTICIPATION OF THE MASS OF THE WORKING PEOPLE IN THE ORGANISATION AND FUNCTIONING OF THE ORGANS OF THE SOCIALIST STATE

The principle of the active participation of the mass of the working people lies at the basis of the organisation and functioning of the state organs of the socialist countries. This principle is set down in their constitutions. "Representative bodies and all other organs of the state shall base their activity upon the creative initiative and the direct participation of the working people and their organisations," states Art. 2(iv) of the Czechoslovak Constitution. Art. 5 of the Constitution of the Mongolian People's Republic contains a general norm to the effect that "all state organs shall base themselves upon the mass of the working people and constantly reinforce their links with them". Similar requirements are set down in the fundamental laws of other socialist countries.

The principle of the active participation of the mass of the working people is also set down in conventional laws and other normative acts of the socialist countries which establish the procedures for the organisation and functioning of state organs.

The active participation of the mass of the working people arises from the very nature of the socialist state, which expresses the will of the majority of society, or of society as a whole.

In the hands of the working people headed by the working class, the socialist state is the main instrument for the building of socialism and communism. The immense tasks confronting it can be carried out only with the active participation of the very broadest masses of the working people in the exercise of the functions of the socialist state. As new achievements are won in the building of socialism and communism, the scale of the economic, organisational, cultural and educational tasks whose successful fulfilment is impossible without the day-to-day systematic participation of the mass of the people in the work of state bodies, grows steadily.

Not only the objective necessity for the increasingly extensive participation of the mass of the working people in the work of state bodies, but also the creation of the objective conditions for this participation arises from the essence of the socialist state. Immediately it comes into being the socialist state implements far-reaching democracy for the vast majority of the population—the working people. With each new success in the building of socialism, the social basis of the socialist state becomes broader and the bounds of socialist democracy are correspondingly extended.

The participation of the mass of the people in the organisation and functioning of state bodies assumes varied forms, among which the following main ones may be singled out:

1. *Direct participation.* This includes meetings at which candidates for election to representative bodies and people's courts are nominated, and also elections to these bodies,[1] and the nationwide discussion of draft constitutions and other legislative measures.

2. *Participation through the elected representatives.* In a socialist state, the function of the elector is not confined to voting. Those who are elected must throughout their entire term maintain contact with their electors and report to them. The working people exert a systematic influence on the work of state bodies by means of mandates, discussion of reports, the submission of proposals and comments regarding the work of their elected representatives and of the state bodies on which they serve and through the prior discussion

---

[1] See the following chapter.

with deputies of issues to be decided by plenary meetings of state power bodies. The policy of the Communist and Workers' parties of the socialist countries regarding the gradual extension of the elective principle and the principle of accountability to representative bodies and the electorate, is of great importance in extending this form of participation.

3. *Participation through conferences, commissions, councils, etc.*, convened or set up under state bodies on a social basis and with consultative functions. These include conferences (meetings) dealing with various aspects of state and economic life convened by governments, ministries, local government bodies, etc.

4. *Participation through mass organisations.* The varied organisational forms assumed by participation of this kind have already been considered in Chapter IV.

5. *Participation through organs of mass self-activity* such as comrades' (public) courts, voluntary groups for protecting public order, house (block, street, village) committees, parents' committees in schools, etc.

This form of participation differs from that referred to in Section 4 above in that there is a distinction between mass organisations and the organs of mass self-activity. Their mass character and their clearly defined organisational structure are features common to both. But the organs of mass self-activity lack the nationwide centralised structure characteristic of mass organisations.

The system of mass self-activity bodies differs in various socialist countries. The most widespread forms are house (street, block) committees, parents' councils, etc.

Voluntary public order groups *(druzhiny)*[1] have been set up in the USSR in accordance with the decision of the Central Committee of the CPSU and the Council of Ministers of the USSR of March 2, 1959, "On the Participation of the

---

[1] Special statutes governing the organisation and work of these groups have been adopted by the Union republics. See, for example, the RSFSR Statute on Voluntary Public Order Groups (*SP RSFSR* No. 14, 1960, Item 56).

Working People in the Maintenance of Public Order".[1] They are set up at factories, building sites, transport undertakings, offices, educational establishments, house-management boards and at collective and state farms. Their operative work is guided by their district (ward) or city headquarters, while general guidance is effected by Party bodies. Premises, means of communication and transport are made available by the Executive Committees of local Soviets of Working People's Deputies.

Similar groups were set up in Bulgaria, by a joint decision of the Central Committee of the Bulgarian Communist Party and the Council of Ministers "On the Participation of the Working People in the Maintenance of Public Order"[2] adopted in March 1960. They were placed under the control of organisations of the Bulgarian Communist Party, with the broad participation of the People's Councils, the Fatherland Front, the Young Communist League, the trade unions and other mass organisations. Similar voluntary groups that assist state organs in maintaining public order exist in Hungary, the German Democratic Republic and other socialist countries.

Courts operating on the principles of a social organisation have in recent years become increasingly widespread in the socialist countries.

They deal with minor offences, applying mainly social sanctions.

6. The establishment of *elected, broadly representative bodies* at enterprises. These bodies, which are a form of the democratisation of management, enable all the workers to participate in the discussion and settlement of issues relating to the work of their enterprises. The establishment of these bodies is of great importance in implementing the principle of working people's participation in the work of state organs and in the accomplishment of the state tasks.

---

[1] *SP SSSR* No. 4, 1959, Item 25.
[2] See *Izvestiya na Presidiuma na Narodnoto Sobraniye, 1960*, Item 22.

Bodies of this kind include standing production conferences in the USSR and the Mongolian People's Republic, workers' councils and conferences of workers' self-management in Poland, economic committees in Bulgaria and production committees in the German Democratic Republic.

The organisation and work of these bodies ensures the combination of the maximum participation by the workers and the principle of one-man management of a particular enterprise.

Organisational forms of the enterprises' representative bodies which meet both these requirements were in some socialist countries evolved in the course of struggle against both dogmatic and anarcho-syndicalist and other anti-socialist tendencies.

In Poland, for example, when the workers' councils were being set up in 1956, in the course of the discussion of the "Polish economic model" proposals designed to improve this model were put forward. But other proposals harmful to the cause of the building of socialism were also put forward calling for the transfer of the state-owned enterprises to the group ownership of those who worked in them, and for the establishment of a hierarchical structure of workers' councils in each branch of the economy. In the early period of their activity, many workers' councils devoted most of their attention to the personal matters; attempts were made to replace managements by workers' councils; and there were tendencies towards non-co-operation with factory councils. The Ninth Plenary Meeting of the Central Committee of the Polish United Workers' Party (May 1957) repudiated these views and tendencies and helped the workers' councils to find their proper place in the factories.[1]

The Fourth Congress of Polish Trade Unions held in April 1958 adopted measures to improve the organisation and functioning of workers' self-management.[2] The deficiencies

---

[1] See *Trybuna Ludu*, May 21, 1957.
[2] Ibid., April 15, 1958.

in the organisation and work of the workers' councils were noted, and it was pointed out that they were not the only forms of workers' self-management: the working class also has both Party and trade union organisations. In order to ensure the proper interaction of all these organisations, and to reinforce the leading role of the Polish United Workers' Party, its Central Committee proposed that conferences of workers' self-management be set up at factories. All members of the workers' council, the factory (trade union) council and of the Polish United Workers' Party committee at the factory should be permanent delegates to the conference. The conference would be superior to the workers' council, and its decisions would be binding upon the workers' and the factory councils and the Party committee. The Central Committee also proposed that the workers' councils, in addition to directors, should include the chairmen of factory councils and representatives of Party committees. This new form of workers' self-management was established by the Law on Workers' Self-Management adopted by the Seym on December 20, 1958.[1]

Workers' participation in the management of industrial enterprises through workers' self-management in Poland does not mean that factories are administered by the workers' self-management bodies. Their participation actually implies supervision and control over the factory administration, while leaving individual responsibility for operative management in the hands of the director.

Workers' self-management bodies have extensive powers in Yugoslavia. Workers' self-management in organisations of associated labour and other forms of uniting labour and resources is a constitutional principle.

Self-management is exercised both directly (general meetings, referenda, etc.) and through the organs set up by the workers (workers' councils and their executive bodies) which

---

[1] See *Dziennik Ustaw RPL* No. 77, 1958, Item 397.

guide the work of the administration, though the latter has its own sphere of competence.

Various forms of directly involving workers in the administration of their factories and production amalgamations are to be found in other socialist countries.

It should be emphasised that the concept of permanently functioning, broadly representative bodies elected by workers at particular enterprises and on their behalf playing an active part in the administration of such enterprises is being increasingly applied in practice in the socialist countries.

4. DEMOCRATIC CENTRALISM

The system of the socialist state organs is based on the principle of democratic centralism. The constitutions of the majority of socialist countries contain no specific reference to this principle. But an analysis of those parts of their constitutions which deal with the organisation and functioning of state organs and their interrelationships demonstrates that the principle of democratic centralism is established as a fundamental constitutional principle of the system of state organs in all these countries. In addition, this principle is directly affirmed in the constitutions of some of these countries (Bulgaria, Czechoslovakia, the Korean People's Democratic Republic). Art. 18 (i) of the Czechoslovak Constitution lays down that "the centralised leadership of society and the state on the basis of democratic centralism shall be effectively combined with far-reaching powers and responsibility of lower bodies, coupled with the active participation of the working people and the encouragement of their creative initiative".

Democratic centralism is a harmonious combination of two inseparably linked features—centralism and democracy. The building of socialism and communism in any country is inconceivable without the centralised leadership of the work of the state organs, mass organisations and the people as a whole directed towards the building of a new social system.

Lenin many times called attention to the necessity for such centralised leadership.[1] But a socialist state requires not just mere centralism, but democratic centralism, which will ensure both unity in the solution of fundamental, major issues and also the opportunity for the fullest account to be taken of local distinctive features and the development of local initiative and independent activity.

"... Centralism, understood in a truly democratic sense," said Lenin, "presupposes the possibility, created for the first time in history, of a full and unhampered development not only of specific local features, but also of local inventiveness, local initiative, of diverse ways, methods and means of progress to the common goal".[2]

There is no conflict between the need for the centralised leadership of the building of socialism and communism on a countrywide scale on the one hand and on the other for account to be taken of local conditions and distinctive features. On the contrary, with democratic centralism, Lenin teaches, "the unity of essentials, of fundamentals, of the substance, is not disturbed but ensured by *variety* in details, in specific local features, in methods of *approach,* in *methods* of exercising control".[3]

The principle of democratic centralism is embodied in state law through the establishment in the norms of state law of such a system, terms of reference and procedure for the organisation and functioning of state organs which ensure a combination of centralised leadership on fundamental issues with the maximum development of the initiative and activity of local bodies and of the mass of the people, with the vigorous participation of the working people in the administration of the state and the management of the economy.

---

[1] See V. I. Lenin, *Collected Works*, Vol. 27, pp. 207-08, 384; Vol. 28, pp. 36, 350, 400, 405; Vol. 30, pp. 245-46 ff.
[2] Ibid., Vol. 27, p. 208.
[3] Ibid., Vol. 26, p. 413

Democratic centralism demands a proper balance between centralism and decentralisation. This is important for the proper organisation and functioning of the socialist state.

But the balance between centralism and decentralisation does not remain constant. It depends upon concrete circumstances.

At the Seventh All-Russia Congress of Soviets, Lenin, while stressing the undoubted need for centralised leadership in the socialist state, noted the existence of differences of opinion regarding "how much more or how much less centralism is needed in a certain field at a certain moment".[1]

The degree of centralisation varies in different spheres of state activity and at different periods of the evolution of the socialist state. Civil war, acute class struggle, the lack of qualified local personnel, etc. make a higher degree of centralism an objective necessity. The consolidation of the socialist state, economic and cultural progress and the development of experienced personnel in the localities create wider opportunities for independent and enterprising action by local bodies and by the mass of the people, while retaining the necessary measure of centralism.

Hence, the establishment of a correct balance between centralism and decentralisation requires a precise estimate of the objective circumstances of a particular country at a particular time and in each particular sphere of state activity.

The retention of excessive centralism when the prerequisites for the encouragement of the initiative and activity of the masses have been created becomes a brake upon the development of the socialist state and society. The Communist and Workers' parties of the socialist countries, having launched a struggle against the harmful influence of dogmatism, have taken steps to overcome excessive centralism.

At the same time they resolutely opposed the revisionists, who on the pretext of resistance to excessive centralism attempted to undermine the very principle of democratic cen-

---

[1] V. I. Lenin, *Collected Works*, Vol. 30, p. 246.

tralism. The revisionist attacks received a fitting rebuff in the state-legal literature of the socialist countries.[1]

Excessive decentralisation of political and economic leadership likewise does harm to the building of socialism and communism. Therefore the Communist and Workers' parties of the socialist countries, while developing democratic centralism in every way, in their decisions emphasise the need to retain a proper degree of centralisation and resist parochial tendencies.

5. PROLETARIAN (SOCIALIST) INTERNATIONALISM

The principle of proletarian (socialist) internationalism in the organisation and functioning of the state organs is set down in various forms in the state law of the socialist countries: in the general injunctions relating to the main lines of the work of the socialist state, and in more detailed norms which give more concrete expression to this principle and contain guarantees for its realisation.

As has already been noted, this principle is not confined to internal policy; it also finds expression in foreign policy. This is mirrored in the constitutions of the socialist countries. Alongside the affirmation in general form of this principle as applied to internal policy,[2] the fundamental laws of the socialist countries also lay down that state organs shall be guided by this principle in foreign policy. The Preamble to the Constitution of the Mongolian People's Republic declares that "the Mongolian People's Republic shall pursue a

---

[1] See J. Beér, *A helyi tanácsok kialakulása és fejlödése Magyarozszágon (1945-1960)*, Budapest, 1962, IX, bejezet.

[2] See, for example, Art. 3 of the Constitution of the Democratic Republic of Vietnam, which requires that "the state shall safeguard and develop the unity between nationalities", that "the state shall afford every assistance to national minorities to ensure their speediest possible attainment of the level of economic and cultural development of the people as a whole".

peaceloving foreign policy directed towards ... the consolidation by every means of the fraternal relations of indestructible friendship, close co-operation and mutual assistance which have been established and which are developing between the peoples of the countries of the world socialist system on the basis of the inviolable principle of proletarian internationalism". Art. 6 (ii) of the Constitution of the German Democratic Republic lays down that "the German Democratic Republic in accordance with the principle of socialist internationalism shall maintain and develop all-round co-operation and friendship with the Union of Soviet Socialist Republics and the other socialist states".

The general injunctions set down in the constitutions of the socialist countries regarding proletarian internationalism are given concrete form in the more detailed norms of the constitutions and in other state-legal norms. These include:

1. Norms relating to the equality of citizens, irrespective of race or nationality.

These norms have already been considered from the point of view of the legal status of citizens in socialist countries. When applied to the organisation and functioning of state organs, the equality of citizens irrespective of nationality implies the equal participation of all citizens in the election of representative organs of state power, equality of rights as regards employment in state organs, the absence of any discrimination on grounds of nationality in relations between the citizen and state organs, and the right of the citizen to use his native language when appealing to state bodies.

2. Norms defining the particular state-legal forms of the organisation of nations compactly inhabiting particular areas on the territory of a multi-national socialist state. These have already been considered in Chapter VI.

3. Norms relating to the special structure of state organs in multi-national states designed to ensure that the fullest possible consideration is given to the interests of all nations inhabiting the state in resolving matters of concern to the

state as a whole. The supreme representative organs of federal socialist states (Czechoslovakia, USSR and Yugoslavia) have, as has already been noted, special chambers—the House of Nations of the Czechoslovak Federal Assembly,[1] the Soviet of Nationalities of the Supreme Soviet of the USSR and the Chamber of Republics and Provinces of the Skupshina of the SFRY.

In the Presidium of the Supreme Soviet of the USSR the 15 deputies to the Chairman are representatives of all the Union Republics. The Presidency of the SFRY includes one representative from each republic and from each autonomous province. Half the Presidium of the Czechoslovak Federal Assembly (20 members) is elected by the House of Nations, which elects ten members of the Presidium from deputies elected in the Czech Socialist Republic and ten from deputies elected in the Slovak Socialist Republic. If the Chairman of the Federal Assembly, who also presides over the Presidium, is a citizen of the Czech Socialist Republic, then a citizen of the Slovak Socialist Republic is elected as his first deputy, and vice versa.

The Chairmen of the Councils of Ministers of all the Union Republics are *ex officio* members of the Council of Ministers of the USSR. An equal number of representatives from each republic and a corresponding number of members from each autonomous province are elected to the Federal Executive Council (the Yugoslav Government). The Chairmen of the Governments of the Republics are in practice elected as Deputies to the Chairman of the Government of Czechoslovakia.

The Chairmen of the Supreme Courts of the Union Republics are *ex officio* members of the Supreme Court of the USSR. Two members from each of the six republics and one from each of the two autonomous provinces are elected to the Yugoslav Constitutional Court, made up of a Chairman and 13 members. The Federal Court of the SFRY is formed

---

[1] For their composition and powers, see Chapter X (2).

on the basis of a parity representation of the republics and corresponding (also parity) representation of the autonomous provinces. The Czechoslovak Supreme Court is, as a rule, made up of an equal number of representatives from both republics.

In the Democratic Republic of Vietnam and the Mongolian People's Republic where, as has already been noted, there are a substantial number of national minorities, there are special standing committees of the supreme organs of state power whose task is to assist these bodies in resolving issues relating to the minorities.

In the Mongolian People's Republic mandatory provision for the establishment by the supreme representative body of a standing committee dealing with matters relating to the national minorities is contained in the Constitution. In the Democratic Republic of Vietnam, neither the Constitution nor the law on the organisation of the National Assembly adopted in July 1960[1] make specific provision for a standing committee of the National Assembly dealing with matters of concern to the national minorities. These acts make mandatory for the National Assembly to establish only two standing committees. The formation of others is left to the discretion of the National Assembly itself. The standing committees set up by the National Assembly include one dealing with the affairs of the national minorities.

A special body whose function is systematically to promote the economic, political and cultural development of the national minorities was set up under the government of the Democratic Republic of Vietnam—the Administration of National Minority Affairs attached to the Government Council.

4. The principle of socialist internationalism as applied in the external sphere of the functioning of the socialist state is manifested both in the activity and in the system of its

---

[1] See *Vysshiye organy gosudarstvennoi vlasti stran narodnoi demokratii (sbornik normativnykh aktov). Vypusk 2. Strany Azii*, Gosyurizdat, Moscow, 1961, pp. 10-11, 36.

organs. Special bodies attached to the governments of the socialist countries ensure the co-ordination of their economic efforts.

5. The granting of asylum to citizens of capitalist countries persecuted for their democratic activities and participation in the national-liberation struggle is a duty of the state organs of the socialist countries arising from the principle of proletarian internationalism.

The consistent application of the principle of proletarian internationalism is in the forefront of the attention of the Marxist-Leninist parties. In the Report of the Central Committee of the CPSU to the 24th Party Congress, the General Secretary of the CC CPSU Leonid Brezhnev emphasised that "the Party shall continue to educate all the working people in the spirit of socialist internationalism, intolerance of nationalism, chauvinism, national narrowness and conceit in any form, in a spirit of profound respect for all nations and nationalities".[1]

6. SOCIALIST LEGALITY

The fundamental laws of the socialist countries include the principle of socialist legality among the basic constitutional principles governing the organisation and functioning of the organs of the socialist state. Art. 113 of the Constitution of the USSR lays down that all ministries and institutions subordinated to them, and also all officials shall strictly observe the law. "All state organs," declares Art. 7 of the Constitution of the Mongolian People's Republic, "shall strictly observe the Constitution and laws of the Mongolian People's Republic." The constitutions of the other socialist countries contain similar injunctions.

The principle of socialist legality implies the strict and unswerving observance of laws and other juridical measures based upon them, by all government bodies, mass organisations and citizens.

---
[1] *24th Congress of the CPSU*, p. 92.

The significance of socialist legality is determined by the essence of the laws of the socialist state, which express the will of the people. This is mirrored in the constitutions of the socialist countries. Art. 4 of the Polish Constitution lays down:

"1. The laws of the Polish People's Republic shall be the expression of the interests and will of the working people.

"2. The strict observance of the laws of the Polish People's Republic shall be a fundamental duty of every organ of the state and of every citizen.

"3. All organs of state power and administration shall function on the basis of the requirements of the law."

This definition of the essence of socialist laws and the affirmation of the obligation to observe them aptly underlines the importance of the principle of socialist legality.

Socialist law, expressing the will and interests of the people, is a potent instrument for the building of socialism and communism. It is this which makes the strict observance of the law by state organs, mass organisations and citizens necessary and significant.

In its content and scope of application socialist legality is not merely a principle governing the organisation and work of state bodies. In a socialist state the strict and unswerving observance of the law is ensured by the joint efforts of state organs, mass organisations and citizens.

As new advances are made in the building of socialism, as the socialist state grows stronger and as the role of socialist democracy in ensuring socialist legality expands, the role of educational work in maintaining the rule of law and preventing crime increases. So also does the role of mass organisations. Art. 17 (ii) of the Czechoslovak Constitution, therefore, makes special provision for this role: mass organisations, in carrying out their tasks, shall educate citizens in the spirit of the observance of laws and labour discipline, of respect for the rules of socialist community living seeking to avert and check infringements."

But at the present stage the socialist state is the main means of ensuring socialist legality. The responsibility for safeguarding legality therefore rests mainly upon state organs.

In the context of the work of state organs, socialist legality means firstly the strict observance of the law in the functioning of the state organs themselves; secondly, it means ensuring (within the limits of their authority) that the law is strictly observed by all those subject to it (state organs, organisations, citizens). At the same time, it is not only through the efforts of state organs themselves that the principle of socialist legality is applied in their work. Great assistance is given by mass organisations and citizens, who point out shortcomings and deficiencies in the work of the state machine, assist in the campaign against violations of the law and conduct educational work. "It is not only the task of the state apparatus to strengthen legality," said the Report of the Central Committee of the CPSU to the 24th Party Congress. "Party organisations, the trade unions and the Komsomol are in duty bound to do everything to ensure the strictest observance of laws and improve the working people's knowledge of the law."[1]

Socialist legality is an essential component of socialist democracy.[2] A violation of socialist law is a violation of the will and interests of the people as expressed in those laws and hence a violation of socialist democracy. Measures to strengthen and develop socialist democracy are therefore an inseparable part of measures to strengthen socialist legality.

The Communist and Workers' parties of the socialist countries are taking energetic steps to reinforce socialist legality and establish effective guarantees.

---

[1] *24th Congress of the CPSU*, p. 97.

[2] This point is discussed at length by, *inter alia*, N. G. Alexandrov, *Pravo i zakonnost v period razvernutogo stroitelstva kommunizma*, Gosyurizdat, Moscow, 1961, and A. Burda, *Demokracja i praworządność*, Wrocław-Warzawa-Kraków, 1965.

Socialist legality is one of the most important principles governing the organisation and work of every organ of the socialist state. Its strict and punctilious observance is a most important guarantee of the full and consistent practical implementation of all the democratic principles governing the organisation and work of the organs of the socialist state, since all these principles are embodied in the appropriate legal instruments.

The active role played by law in the building of the new society is becoming greater as new advances are made in the building of socialism. From this springs the need for the constant reinforcement of socialist legality. That is why the fraternal Communist and Workers' parties of the socialist countries stress the importance of the further all-round strengthening of the rule of law and socialist legality.

CHAPTER IX

THE PRINCIPLES AND PROCEDURE GOVERNING THE FORMATION OF REPRESENTATIVE ORGANS OF STATE POWER IN THE SOCIALIST COUNTRIES

1. THE CONCEPT OF AN ELECTORAL SYSTEM

The representative organs of state power in the socialist countries are formed on the basis of a genuinely democratic electoral system.

There is as yet no unanimity among jurists in the socialist countries regarding the nature of the electoral system. In Soviet literature the view is exexpressed that it is a specific aggregate of legal norms.

Some believe that the electoral system embraces only a part of the norms of electoral law.[1] The only grounds for such a definition are to be found in the title of Chapter XI of the 1936 Constitution of the USSR. But the chapter "The Electoral System", like other chapters in the Fundamental Law, sets down only the constitutional basic norms governing the relevant sphere of social relations. Thus the definition of the electoral system as the aggregate of norms which constitute only part of electoral law is based merely on a purely grammatical interpretation of the title of Chapter XI of the 1936 Constitution of the USSR.

Other supporters of the view that the electoral system is an aggregate of legal norms gave an "opposite" definition, seeing electoral law as restricted to that part of the aggregate of legal norms which make up the electoral system.[2] The supporters of this point did not cite a single argument in

---

[1] See *Sovietskoye gosudarstvennoye pravo*, Moscow, 1950, p. 376.

[2] See A. I. Denisov, M. G. Kirichenko, *Sovietskoye gosudarstvennoye pravo*, Moscow, 1957, p. 286.

support of their case. This is understandable, since there is no argument which can be cited in support of such a definition of the relationship between the electoral system and electoral law.

Electoral law is the aggregate of juridical norms which establish and regulate the principles and procedure for the organisation and conduct of elections to representative organs of state power and the relations between deputies and electors.

The electoral system cannot be reduced to an aggregate of legal norms. Rightly criticising the view that the relationship between electoral law and the electoral system was one of differing aggregates of juridical norms, B. A. Strashun expressed the view that the electoral system is the system of social relationships which are regulated by electoral law.[1] The positive feature of this definition is that it rejects the view of the electoral system as an aggregate of juridical norms. It does not, however, constitute a wholly precise definition of the electoral system as the range of social relationships which are regulated by electoral law.

Electoral system should be taken to mean the *operative procedure* for the organisation and conduct of elections to representative organs of state power, and for relationships between deputies and electors. In other words, *the electoral system constitutes the aggregate of legal relationships and non-legal social relationships which take shape during the process of the organisation and holding of elections to representative organs of state power, and of the relationships between deputies and electors.*[2]

Such an aggregate of relationships is by no means confined to the subject of regulation by electoral law. Firstly, the

[1] See B. A. Strashun, *Izbiratelnoye pravo sotsialisticheskikh stran*, IMO Publishers, Moscow, 1963, p. 14. A similar definition is also given by I. P. Ilyinsky, B. V. Shchetinin, *Gosudarstvennoye pravo stran narodnoi demokratii*, Mezhdunarodniye otnosheniya Publishers, Moscow, 1964, p. 222.

[2] A similar defintion is given by A. I. Kim. See A. I. Kim, *Sovietskoye izbiratelnoye pravo*, Moscow, 1965, p. 20.

social relationship which is the subject of regulation by a legal norm is not identical with the legal relationship which is formed as a result of such regulation. Secondly, some of the social relationships which evolve during the organisation and holding of elections to organs of state power are not regulated by law at all and hence are not the subject of regulation by electoral law.[1] In particular, some of the relationships which evolve between political parties and mass organisations and also within mass organisations and which are directly related to the holding of the elections, to the establishment of links between the deputy and the electorate, and to the accountability of the deputy to his electors, are not regulated by legal norms. But a full and correct picture of a country's electoral system cannot be obtained without a consideration of these relationships.

In this way the *correlation* between electoral law and the electoral system is a correlation between a particular *aggregate of legal norms and the corresponding legal relationships, and also other social relationships* which take shape during the organisation and holding of elections and in the relations between deputies and electors.

From this relationship between electoral law and the electoral system it follows that the fundamental principles of electoral law are simultaneasly the *fundamental principles* of the electoral system.

2. THE FUNDAMENTAL PRINCIPLES OF THE ELECTORAL SYSTEMS OF THE SOCIALIST COUNTRIES

The genuinely popular character of the socialist state system and decisive and direct participation of the broadest mass of the working people of these countries in the building of their own state and in the formation of the organs of

---

[1] This is also noted by B. A. Strashun, who thus contradicts his own definition of the electoral system as the subject of regulation by electoral law (see B. A. Strashun, op. cit., p. 14).

state power are clearly manifest in the electoral systems of the socialist countries.

The state law of the socialist countries establishes the following fundamental principles governing their electoral systems: 1) universal suffrage; 2) equal electoral rights; 3) direct elections; 4) secret ballot; 5) the nomination of candidates by political parties, mass organisations and groups of working people; 6) a close contact between deputy and electors, and the electorate's right to recall their deputy.

Since there is no unanimity among socialist jurists regarding the fundamental principles of a socialist electoral system, it is necessary to explain why these six principles are singled out as fundamental.

The first four are generally recognised by socialist experts on state law. But the majority see only these four as fundamental.

It is, however, impossible to accept this point of view. The fact that the right of mass organisations and groups of working people to nominate candidates is set down not in the ordinary laws but in the fundamental laws of a number of socialist countries indicates that the legislator sees this right as a basic institution of the electoral system. There are good reasons for it, when we recall the role of mass organisations in the socialist state, and the significance of nomination not by individuals but by mass organisations and groups of working people from the point of view of the selection of the most suitable candidates for ensuring the popular rule. Therefore the right of mass organisations and meetings of working people's groups to nominate candidates must be considered as one of the fundamental principles of a socialist electoral system.

Many jurists in the socialist countries do not include the establishment of a close link between a deputy and his electors and the latters' right to recall a deputy who has not justified their confidence among the fundamental principles of a socialist electoral system. But one of the most important features distinguishing a socialist from a bourgeois electoral system is the fact that the role of the elector is not confined to the casting of a vote, and that elected representatives are responsible and accountable to their electors throughout their entire term of office. Lenin attached great importance to this principle, declaring that "no elective institution or representative assembly can be regarded as being truly democratic and really representative of the people's will unless the electors' right to recall those elected is accepted and exercised".[1] In the light of Lenin's comments on the significance of the accountability of elected representatives and of the right to recall those who have not justified the confidence of their electors for the democratic character of the electoral system as a whole, this most important institution of electoral law cannot be excluded from the fundamental principles of the electoral system.[2]

The six principles enumerated above represent the *fundamental* principles of a socialist electoral system. Attemps to add other "fundamental" principles have no basis in the law of the socialist countries.

1. *Universal suffrage* is ensured in the socialist countries by the fact that the right to participate in elections to supreme and local organs of state power is enjoyed by all citizens irrespective of sex, race or nationality, religion, education, domicile, social origin, profession or property status. In establishing guarantees for universal suffrage, the constitutions and electoral statutes of the socialist countries lay down that citizens serving in the Armed Forces enjoy electoral rights on equal terms with other citizens, and that women have the right to vote and be elected on equal terms with men.

The principle of universality is becoming firmer established as the socialist state develops and grows stronger. The reduction of the voting age has been a general feature in

---

[1] V. I. Lenin, *Collected Works*, Vol. 26, p. 336.
[2] This is rightly pointed out by R. Klimowiecki. See A. Burda, R. Klimowiecki, *Prawo państwowe*, Warszawa, 1958, pp. 577-78.

a number of socialist countries which have emerged since the Second World War.

In Poland, the first electoral law—the Statute on Elections to the Legislative Seym of September 22, 1946[1]—laid down that all citizens over the age of 21 had the right to vote, while those over the age of 25 had the right to stand for election to the Seym. The Polish Constitution adopted on June 22, 1952 extended the principle of universal suffrage and lowered the voting age for elections to the Seym and National Councils to 18; those at the age of 18 and over also had the right to stand for election to the National Councils, while candidates for the Seym had to be 21 and over.

In Bulgaria, the decree-law of July 8, 1945[2] gave citizens the right to vote in elections to the National Assembly at the age of 19; candidates had to be at the age of 23 and over. The 1947 Bulgarian Constitution reduced the age qualification to 18 for both active and passive electoral right.

In Rumania, in the first parliamentary elections following the overthrow of fascism, which were held in 1946, those at the age of 21 and over had the right to vote, and those at the age of 25 and over, the right to stand as candidates. At the present time the ages are 18 and 23, respectively. The same trends were exhibited in other socialist countries, too.

The age qualification for active fighters for democracy was reduced in a number of countries during the first years after the establishment of popular power.

The subsequent substantial general reduction of the age qualification for both active and passive electoral right meant that hundreds of thousands of young citizens received the right to participate in elections.

At the present time citizens who have reached the age of 18 have the right to vote (active electoral right) in the majority of socialist countries. The lower age qualification

---

[1] See *Dziennik Ustaw RP* No. 48, 1946, Item **274**.
[2] See *Derzhaven Vestnik*, 1945, Item 136.

—17—was established by the 1972 Constitution of the Korean People's Democratic Republic. In the elections held in the Cuban Province of Matanzas in 1974, electoral rights were granted from the age of 16. In Yugoslavia all workers, regardless of age, can participate in elections according to the production principle. In some cases the voting age is established at 18.

The right to be elected (passive electoral right) to all representative bodies of state power is enjoyed by all who have reached the age of 18 in Bulgaria, Hungary, the Mongolian People's Republic, the German Democratic Republic, Yugoslavia and Albania, 17 in the Korean People's Democratic Republic, 16 in Cuba, 21 in Czechoslovakia and the Democratic Republic of Vietnam, and 23 in Rumania. In the USSR and Poland there are differential age qualifications. Citizens who have reached the age of 18 may be elected to local organs of state power. Those who have reached the age of 21 are eligible for election to the Polish Seym and the Supreme Soviets of the Union and Autonomous Soviet Socialist Republics. The qualifying age for election to the Supreme Soviet of the USSR is 23. The 1975 Constitution of the People's Republic of China preserved the age qualification of 18 for both active and passive electoral rights, though elections are in practice replaced, as has been noted, by so-called democratic consultations, i.e. appointment.

The extension of the principle of universal suffrage also finds expression in the repeal of legislation depriving exploiting elements of electoral rights in the USSR and the Mongolian People's Republic and of similar legislation introduced in the majority of socialist countries in the first period of popular rule restricting the electoral rights of certain categories and operating alongside the restriction of individual electoral rights (by verdict of a court).

The first Soviet constitution—the RSFSR Constitution of 1918 (Art. 65) and later the 1925 Constitution of the RSFSR (Art. 69) laid down that the right to elect and be elected was denied not only to those declared insane and to those condemned for grave crimes, but also to those who employed hired labour for profit or lived on unearned income, to private traders and commercial middlemen, monks and professional clergymen of all religions and trends, employees and agents of the former police, the special corps of gendarmerie and the secret political police department, members of the former imperial family, and also to those who had directed the work of the police, gendarmerie and punitive organs. Similar restrictions were imposed by the constitutions of other Soviet republics. After the abolition of all exploiting classes in the USSR, these restrictions were likewise abolished, which found legislative embodiment in the 1936 Constitution of the USSR.

Under the Mongolian Constitutions of 1924 and 1940 (Art. 71) persons exploiting hired labour for profit, money-lenders, former feudal lords, influential shamans and active participants in the White army and counter-revolutionary governments were deprived of electoral rights. On September 28, 1944 the Presidium of the Small Khural restored these rights.

Under Par. 5 of Hungarian Law VIII of 1945 regarding elections to the National Assembly, persons who had held any office in anti-democratic and fascist unions, parties and organisations, former officials of the Hungarian Royal Gendarmerie, persons who had fled from the country when the Soviet Army, the Army of liberation, had approached its frontiers and who had not returned prior to December 31, 1945, and certain others, were deprived of electoral rights. Art. 2 of the Polish Statute on Elections to the Legislative Seym denied, with some exceptions, electoral rights to persons who, being Polish citizens, had between September 1, 1939 and May 9, 1945 declared that they belonged to the German or any other nation placed in a privileged position by the occupation forces, and also to persons who had to the clear disadvantage of the Polish nation derived benefit from economic co-operation with the occupation forces. These restrictions were subsequently repealed.

In Bulgaria, Art. 48 of the 1953 law on elections to the National Assembly and Art. 45 of the 1951 law on elections to the People's Councils deprived those who had voiced fascist or anti-democratic sentiments of passive electoral rights. The 1973 electoral law now in force does not contain these restrictions.

In many socialist countries the limitation of electoral rights is permissible only on the basis of the verdict of a court.

But this sanction was abolished in the USSR by the Law of December 25, 1958 on the Repeal of the Deprivation of Electoral Rights Through the Courts.[1] The 1960 Constitution of the Mongolian People's Republic, the 1963 and 1974 Yugoslav Constitutions and the Bulgarian Constitution of 1971 likewise make no provisions for deprivation of electoral rights through the courts.[2] The view that it is desirable to repeal such limitations is also voiced in other socialist countries which have entered upon the building of a developed socialist society. The repeal of all legal limitations of this kind, as legal commentators in the socialist countries rightly point out, in no way implies that unworthy, undemocratic, anti-social elements may be elected to organs of state power. When the exploiting classes have been abolished, when the social and political unity of the people is constantly growing stronger and the political awareness and activity of the mass of the people is increasing, there are adequate social and political guarantees against the penetration of unworthy elements into the organs of state power.[3]

In no socialist country do the insane have electoral rights. This cannot, however, be considered as a limitation of

---

[1] See *Vedomosti Verkhovnogo Sovieta SSSR* No. 1, 1959, Item 7.

[2] The 1968 Constitution of the German Democratic Republic also makes no reference to the deprivation of electoral rights through the courts. But such a provision is contained in the Electoral Law of 1963, and the 1968 Criminal Code of the German Democratic Republic likewise makes provision for this sanction.

[3] See B. Spasov, *Razvitiye i usovershenstvuvanye na predsavitelnite organi v NR Bulgaria*, pp. 46-47.

universal suffrage. Participation in elections is an act manifesting the conscious will of the citizen, and it is natural that persons not responsible for their actions should not be permitted to participate in elections.

Legislation now in force in the majority of socialist countries has rejected earlier restrictions on passive electoral rights based on "incompatibility". Incompatibility was envisaged, for example, in the Statute on Elections to the Legislative Seym of September 22, 1946. Under Art. 4 officials of general and financial bodies and also of organs of justice and state security could not stand as candidates for the Seym in constituencies where they worked, while under Art. 5 officials of the state administration and organs of self-government on their election to the Seym were granted leave of absence from their place of work for the duration of their term of office. These limitations did not apply to Ministers and their deputies, officials of central administrative bodies, *voivods* and others.

The Bulgarian decree-law on elections to the National Assembly of July 8, 1945 laid down that officials of state, state self-managing and communal establishments might stand for election only if they resigned not later than 10 days since the appointment of elections.

The inclusion of regulations regarding "incompatibility" in electoral laws is partly due to the survival of traditional formal democratic concepts of bourgeois democracy. In the conditions of bourgeois democracy, the concept of the "incompatibility" of parliamentary membership and the holding of some offices in the system of state administration bodies arises from the so-called principle of the separation of powers and is intended to create the impression that members of parliament are independent of the organs of executive power.[1]

---

[1] This is rightly stressed by jurists from the socialist countries. See A. Burda, R. Klimowiecki, *Prawo państwowe*, pp. 590-91; J. Beér, I. Kovács, L. Szamel, *Magyar államjog*, p. 296.

In a socialist state the concept of "incompatibility" has neither a theoretical basis (the acknowledgement and affirmation of the socialist principle of the unity of power in opposition to the bourgeois principle of the alleged "separation of powers") nor practical grounds (in practice the recognition of the principle of "incompatibility" would mean the exclusion of the most active representatives of the working people from either a supreme organ of state power or from administrative bodies). Its rejection implied the further extension of the principle of universal suffrage.

The regulations which exist in some socialist countries regarding the incompatibility of elected office with certain official posts have nothing in common with the bourgeois institution of incompatibility. These regulations are based not on the formal principle of the separation of powers but on the need to ensure the most efficient functioning of the state bodies concerned and the creation of conditions enabling the elected deputy to carry out his duties most effectively. Thus, under the terms of the Constitutional Law on the Czechoslovak Federation and the Yugoslav Constitution, membership of a supreme organ of popular representation is incompatible with the occupation of the office of President[1] or being a member of the Constitutional Court. The Yugoslav Constitution likewise does not permit simultaneous membership of the Skupshina of the SFRY and of the Presidency or the Federal Executive Council. In addition, the Yugoslav Constitution lays down that a member of a particular Skupshina—a representative organ of power—shall not at the same time be high-ranking official of a government body accountable to that Skupshina, and that the functions of judge are incompatible with membership of Skupshina by which he is elected.

The increasingly broad involvement of citizens in the administration of the state and the settlement of its affairs

---

[1] The Constitutions of the Democratic Republic of Vietnam, the Korean People's Democratic Republic and Rumania do not contain such provisions.

is one of the most important laws governing the evolution of the socialist state. This law finds expression, among many other things, in the regular renewal of the membership of representative organs of state power. The Communist and Workers' parties of the socialist countries attach great importance to the renewal principle. In some countries it has been established in law.

According to Art. 140 (i) of the Yugoslav Constitution, "no person having been elected a delegate for four years can be a delegate of one and the same Skupshina for more than two consecutive terms".

The principle of the renewal of the membership of Soviets does not contradict the principle of universal suffrage; on the contrary, it promotes the fullest realisation of the principle of universality because it enables a growing number of citizens to be elected. Like other principles, it must of course be applied wisely. Excessive renewal of representative bodies would harm their work. Persons elected for the first time require a certain time to familiarise themselves with methods of work, with what has already been done and with what remains to be done. Excessive renewal would disrupt the work of representative bodies, and it would be difficult for new members to take advantage of the experience of their predecessors. The principle of renewal must therefore be combined with that of continuity.

In considering the principle of the universality of electoral rights, the suitability of candidates and the proper representation of all social strata and groups must be taken into account. It is not accidental that the Communist and Workers' parties of the socialist countries are paying increasing attention to this question. In order that organs of popular representation should indeed occupy a predominant position in the entire system of state bodies and should really determine the course taken by the work of all other bodies and control that work, it is necessary that, in addition to the appropriate laws, there should be highly qualified people in the representative bodies with great experience in the relevant spheres of public life. If this is not the case, the requirements of the law regarding the supremacy of the representative organs of state power *vis-à-vis* all other state bodies will remain a dead letter. An elected member with no knowledge of affairs can make no serious contribution to the consideration of draft normative acts submitted by executive and administrative organs. Nor can he exercise effective control over the work of administrative bodies or exert any effective influence over the implementation of acts adopted by representative bodies. There are two aspects to the problem of the ability and suitability of deputies elected to the representative organs of state power: firstly, their ability and experience in the relevant sphere, and secondly, ensuring that each representative body should be made up of members with a profound knowledge of all the spheres of public life where the body in question exercises its authority. While the first problem may be resolved within a particular constituency, the second requires the coordinated nomination of candidates in all constituencies. The Report of the Political Bureau of the Central Committee of the Polish United Workers' Party to the March 1965 Plenary Meeting of the Central Committee paid particular attention to the problem of the quality of deputies to the Seym and to National Councils. "As the role of the Seym and the National Councils increases, so do the demands made upon their deputies and members," said the Report.[1] In addition to stressing the political and moral qualities of deputies, the Report also underlined the importance of their knowledge and ability. In Yugoslavia a system of representation of working people engaged in various spheres of activity has been established alongside the general political and territorial representation of all citizens. This is a unique attempt to ensure that representative bodies should contain the necessary number of deputies familiar with all the main spheres of public life controlled by these bodies, and representing the main social strata and groups.

---

[1] *Nowe Drogi* No. 4, 1965, pp. 52-53.

The requirements to the quality and suitability of deputies in the socialist countries have nothing in common with the literacy qualification to be found in bourgeois countries. In the first place, no formal educational criteria are laid down in socialist countries. It is a question of knowledge of substantial matters. Secondly—and most importantly—every citizen in the socialist countries has every opportunity to acquire qualifications in accordance with his ability, inclinations and diligence. The requirement that candidates should be highly efficient is therefore in the interests of the working people, since members who know their business are better able to represent the interests of the working people and to find the most effective means of expressing their will. Thirdly, the question of whether or not a candidate has the necessary qualities is decided by the electors themselves when candidates are nominated.

The great demands made upon a candidate, both politically and as regards his ability, can therefore in no way be seen as a limitation of the principle of the universality of the passive electoral right.

2. In the socialist countries *equal electoral rights* are ensured by the fact that each citizen has *one vote* and participates in elections *on equal terms* with other citizens.

In speaking of equal electoral rights, we have in mind, of course, equality in principle, and not some ideal equality. In the constituencies which return more than one member in Poland, the German Democratic Republic and the Democratic Republic of Vietnam, and which do not have an equal number of electors, equal electoral rights are in principle ensured by the equal basis of representation in the corresponding organ of state power. Constituencies with a large number of electors elect a correspondingly large number of members. But this does not give an ideal equality of electors' votes. In a large constituency each elector decides the fate of a larger number of candidates than an elector in a smaller constituency.

In some circumstances, a certain disparity between the electoral rights of the working class and the peasantry is permitted in a socialist state. This is the case in the Democratic Republic of Vietnam, where deputies to the National Assembly from the countryside are elected on the basis of 1 : 70,000, but in industrial centres and major towns— 1 : 20,000-50,000.

This favourable weighting is due above all to the great preponderance of the peasant population in the Democratic Republic of Vietnam. It is designed to ensure the leading role of the working class. A similar weighting existed during the first period of the development of the Soviet state, during the first years of the Mongolian People's Republic and in the People's Republic of China under the 1953 electoral law. It was in principle a temporary measure and was abandoned as the socialist state became stronger. In discussing this feature of the first Soviet Constitution, Lenin pointed out that "... our Constitution was obliged to introduce this inequality because the cultural level is low and because with us organisation is weak. But we do not make this an ideal; on the contrary, in its programme the Party undertakes to work systematically to abolish this inequality between the better organised proletariat and the peasants".[1] This inequality no longer exists in the Soviet Union or in the Mongolian People's Republic.

3. *Direct elections* mean that members of representative bodies at all levels are elected directly by the electorate. Only direct elections exist in the overwhelming majority of socialist countries.

In Hungary, members of the State Assembly are elected directly; so also are the members of city, ward (in the capital) and rural councils. But the members of the Budapest Council and of regional councils are elected by lower councils—in the capital by the ward councils, and in the regions by town and rural councils.[2]

---

[1] V. I. Lenin, *Collected Works*, Vol. 29, p. 185.

[2] Two-stage elections to the Budapest Council and regional councils

The 1974 Constitution of Yugoslavia established the so-called delegate principle in forming Skupshinas. According to this principle, all members of a particular labour community elect a delegation which must represent all elements of the production process and all social groups of the community. Administrators cannot be elected to the delegation (or to the workers' council, for that matter).

Delegations are also elected by citizens according to their places of residence in local communities which are self-managing components of the communes.

Finally, the elective organs of socio-political organisations such as the Communist League, the Socialist League of the Working People, the Trade Union League, the Youth League and the League of Associations of Fighters in the People's Liberation War, are also considered as delegations.

The delegation's tasks are to discuss questions relating to the Skupshinas' competence, formulate the interests of the appropriate associations of working people and all citizens and to ensure their representation in the Skupshinas. The first two categories of delegation send their own delegates to the communal Skupshinas, with a particular delegate sometimes being sent to the Skupshina not for the whole term of office but to attend one or more meetings. Other delegates may be sent to attend subsequent meetings. Delegates representing social and political organisations in the communal Skupshinas are approved during the citizens' universal ballot.

Accordingly, communal Skupshinas have three chambers: the Chamber of Associated Labour, the Chamber of Local Communities and the Socio-Political Chamber. Republican and provincial Skupshinas have similar chambers, the only difference being that the chamber representing territorial

---

are governed by Law III of 1970 amending Law III of 1966 on the Election of Members of the National Assembly and of Councils (*Magyar Közlöny*, 1970, Item 85).

communities is called the Chamber of Communes. The chambers of communes of republican and provincial Skupshinas are elected by the communal Skupshinas and the other two chambers by corresponding chambers of the communal Skupshinas. The Skupshina of the SFRY consists of two chambers: the Federal Chamber elected by communal Skupshinas and the Chamber of Republics and Provinces elected by republican and provincial Skupshinas. Thus the delegate principle is realised through multi-stage indirect elections.

All other things being equal, direct elections are in principle more democratic than indirect, but the latter may be more democratic in the specific circumstances of a particular country. In the early days of Soviet power Lenin considered direct elections to the lower Soviets and indirect elections to higher organs of state power to be more in accordance with the spirit of proletarian democracy. "Indirect elections to non-local Soviets make it easier to hold congresses of Soviets, they make the *entire* apparatus less costly, more flexible, more accessible to the workers and peasants at a time when life is seething and it is necessary to be able very quickly to recall one's local deputy or to delegate him to a general congress of Soviets,"[1] he wrote.

4. *Secret ballot* means the creation of conditions under which it is impossible to establish how each particular elector voted. Vote by ballot, provided there are genuine guarantees, eliminates the possibility of pressure upon the voter and in this way guarantees him complete freedom to express his wishes during an election.

In guaranteeing the secrecy of the ballot, the electoral legislation of the socialist countries lays down that there must be screened booths at polling stations and makes polling station commissions responsible for checking the booths prior to the start of the voting, while the chairmen of election commissions are responsible for the secrecy of the ballot throughout the period of voting.

---

[1] V. I. Lenin, *Collected Works*, Vol. 28, p. 248.

As an additional guarantee, the regulations of a number of socialist countries lay down that the elector shall be issued with an envelope together with his ballot paper, in which he will insert the latter on completion before placing it in the ballot-box. Such a procedure is laid down in Bulgaria for all elections to the representative organs of state power by the law of November 4, 1958.[1] In Poland envelopes for ballot papers were introduced in local elections by the law of October 31, 1957[2] and for elections to the Seym by the law of December 22, 1960.[3]

5. The legislation of the socialist countries envisages *the nomination of candidates by political parties, mass organisations and groups of working people* to ensure that representative bodies shall be genuinely popular in character. When universal suffrage is introduced while remnants of the exploiting classes have not yet been abolished and the social and political unity of the people is being strengthened, the application of this principle prevents the penetration of exploiters and their accomplices into the organs of state power. When the exploiting classes have been abolished and the social and political unity of the whole of society consolidated, the principle that candidates for election to organs of state power shall be nominated exclusively by mass organisations and groups of working people acquires a new content. It is no longer directed against the exploiting classes, which no longer exist. But it retains its role in ensuring the most comprehensive and businesslike approach to the nomination of worthy candidates who enjoy the respect of groups of working people, and in the enhancement of the role of mass organisations in the life of the state.

In the Democratic Republic of Vietnam the law on the elections to the National Assembly (Art. 24) establishes that, alongside the right of political parties and mass organisa-

---

[1] See *Izvestiya na Prezidiuma na Narodnoto Sobraniye*, 1958, Item 90.
[2] See *Dziennik Ustaw RPL* No. 55, 1957, Item 270.
[3] Ibid. No. 57, 1960, Item 323.

tions to nominate candidates, certain people have the right to nominate themselves. This is due to the fact that in Vietnam some people who come from landowning and other nonworking strata of the population fought against the foreign invaders in the past and are today playing an active part in the struggle for the unification of the country. They are not members of any political party or organisation, but are individual members of the Fatherland Front. The electoral law in this way makes it possible for all the most active fighters for a united and democratic Vietnam to become members of the supreme organ of state power—the National Assembly.[1]

In Hungary, in accordance with Law III of 1966 on the Procedure for the Election of Deputies to the State Assembly and of Members of Councils[2] as amended by Law III of 1970, candidates are nominated by constituency meetings of electors organised by local committees of the Patriotic People's Front with the participation of electoral bodies.

The electoral legislation of Yugoslavia and its constituent republics and autonomous provinces lays down that candidates to the Skupshinas' delegates shall be nominated within the framework of the Socialist Alliance of the Working People of Yugoslavia.

6. The constitutions of the socialist countries declare *close contact between deputy and electors, and the electorate's right to recall their deputy* to be fundamental principles of their electoral systems.

Reference has already been made to the importance of this principle. It should be stressed that Lenin underlined the significance not only of the recognition but also of the implementation of this principle.[3] The electorate's right of

---

[1] See Nguyen Dan Loc, "Izbiratelny zakon Demokraticheskoi Respubliki Vietnam", *Sovietskoye gosudarstvo i pravo* No. 1, 1961, pp. 84-85.
[2] See *Magyar Közlöny*, 1966, Item 71; 1970, Item 85.
[3] V. I. Lenin, *Collected Works*, Vol. 26, p. 336.

recall has always been laid down in the fundamental laws of the socialist countries. But in the past its practical implementation was seriously hampered by the absence of legislation defining the procedure to be followed. Legislation establishing this procedure has been one of the manifestations of the evolution of socialist democracy.[1] This increases the deputy's dependence upon the electors and helps reinforce his contact with his constituents. In the majority of socialist countries the question of the deputy's recall is decided by a poll.

In Hungary the recall of the Councils' members and in Yugoslavia the recall of the Skupshinas' delegates follow the same procedure as the elections.

Under the terms of the Electoral Law of the German Democratic Republic, electors may at meetings convened by the appropriate National Front committees submit proposals regarding the recall of deputies; a decision is taken by the representative body in which the deputy concerned sits. A similar procedure existed in Bulgaria, but the 1971 Constitution and the Law on the Terms and Procedure for the Recall of People's Representatives and Councillors adopted on April 27, 1972[2] on its basis laid down that recall should be direct. The same procedure was established by the Electoral Act of July 10, 1973,[3] which codified the electoral law of Bulgaria.

---

[1] See the USSR Law of October 30, 1959, on the Procedure for the Recall of a Member of the Supreme Soviet of the USSR (*Vedomosti Verkhovnogo Sovieta SSSR* No. 44, 1959, Item 222), and also similar laws adopted by the Union and Autonomous republics regarding the procedure for the recall of members of their Supreme Soviets and of local Soviets, adopted in 1959-61; Arts. 76-81 of the Polish Law of October 31, 1957 entitled "Statute on Elections to the National Councils", as amended in 1973 (*Dziennik Ustaw PRL* No. 38, 1973, Item 226); the law of the Mongolian People's Republic of January 31, 1961 regarding the procedure for the recall of members of the Grand People's Khural (*Unen*, February 1, 1961), etc.

[2] See *Derzhaven vestnik*, 1972, Item 35.

[3] See *Derzhaven vestnik*, 1973, Item 54.

3. THE ORGANISATION AND CONDUCT OF ELECTIONS

The organisation and conduct of elections in the socialist countries, which is governed in detail by their electoral legislation, ensures the practical implementation of the basic principles of electoral law and the decisive participation of the mass of the working people in the formation of the organs of state power. The members of representative bodies are elected by constituencies (electoral units).

These constituencies are at the present time in the main based on the territorial principle. Their formation is, as a rule, determined by the appropriate state bodies and they need not coincide with the country's territorial and administrative divisions.

In some socialist countries, however, the boundaries of administrative and territorial units coincide with those of constituencies of the appropriate level. In elections to the supreme organs of state power in the Democratic Republic of Vietnam, these are provinces, major towns, autonomous regions and large industrial centres.[1]

Small administrative and territorial units constitute electoral units (constituencies) for local elections in the Democratic Republic of Vietnam. Villages or settlements (or hamlets or districts forming part of them) are themselves the constituencies for elections to village and settlement councils.

In the majority of socialist countries *constituencies return single members.*

Constituencies which return more than one member are a distinctive feature of the electoral systems of the Democratic Republic of Vietnam, the German Democratic Republic and Poland, where there are such constituencies for elections to representative bodies at all levels.

The provision for industrial as well as territorial constit-

---

[1] In accordance with Art. 13 of the Law on the Election of Deputies to the National Assembly of the Democratic Republic of Vietnam, if ten or more deputies are elected from one such unit, it may be sub-divided into a number of constituencies.

uencies contained in the 1957 Statute on Elections to National Councils was a distinctive feature of local elections in Poland. They were formed on an industrial basis for the workers of major industrial, construction and transport enterprises, regardless of where they lived. Those who voted in an industrial constituency did not vote in the territorial constituency where they lived. Industrial constituencies were designed to ensure that the workers of large enterprises were properly represented in the National Councils, and to facilitate the establishment of close contact between the workers and the Councils. According to the Statute formation of such constituencies was not mandatory. Such constituencies were formed when elections to the National Councils and the Seym did not coincide. During the elections to the National Councils held on February 2, 1958, 1,025 such constituencies were formed. Since the creation of industrial constituencies during simultaneous elections to the National Councils and the Seym would cause substantial additional difficulties,[1] the Law of December 22, 1960, on Additions and Amendments to certain provisions of the Electoral Law[2] laid down that industrial constituencies should not be established when elections to the Seym and the National Councils coincided. In 1961, 1965 and 1969 elections to the Seym and to the National Councils coincided (in 1963 the term of office of the National Councils was extended to four years). The revised Statute on Elections to National Councils (1973) repealed the provisions on industrial constituencies.

The procedure for the compilation of registers of elections laid down in the socialist countries guarantees universal suffrage.

---

[1] Even in local elections the establishment of industrial constituencies presented substantial problems, because voting to elect Councils at all levels took place simultaneously, while industrial constituencies might be formed only for elections to Councils at certain levels. See S. Rozmaryn, "Nowe instytucje prawa wyborczego do rad narodowych", *Państvo i Prawo* No. 12, 1957.

[2] *Dziennik Ustaw RPL* No. 57, 1960, Item 323.

The registers are drawn up according to place of residence by the local executive and administrative bodies. A separate register is drawn up for each polling station or, if in local elections the station covers more than one constituency, separately for each of the constituencies.

In order that each citizen may verify that his name is on the electoral register, and that no person not entitled to vote has been included, the register is made available for public inspection in good time.

Having inspected the register, any citizen may complain to the body which compiled it regarding any inaccuracy, in particular regarding improper omission or inclusion.

Should no action be taken on a complaint, or should a person be omitted from the register, the person lodging the complaint or omitted may appeal to the court in the area concerned. The decision of the court is final.

The question of voting on the basis of a certificate of authorisation is closely connected with the practical implementation of universal suffrage. In accordance with the electoral laws of the majority of socialist countries, an elector who changes his residence after the compilation of the electoral register is on application placed on the register at his new place of residence and allowed to vote there. The elector exercises this right on the basis of a certificate authorising him to vote issued on his application by the body drawing up the register. In issuing the authorisation, this body deletes his name from the register with the note "removed". In the German Democratic Republic, such certificates are valid in local elections only for voting on the territory of the administrative unit whose governing body is being elected.

Such certificates are clearly desirable in cases when the elector changes his place of permanent residence, or when he changes his address within a particular constituency. Some jurists consider it to be undesirable in other cases, because electoral rights in the socialist countries are not confined simply to the casting of a vote. They also include the principle of close and regular contact between the people's representatives and their electors and the right of recall. But an elector temporarily resident in another constituency has only the right to vote.[1] Others, proceeding from the representative character of the organs of state power, consider voting on the basis of a certificate legitimate in all cases in elections to a supreme organ of state power, and also in any constituency in elections to a local organ of state power for the members of which the elector would vote at his place of permanent residence, since in this case it is a question of ensuring his own representation. Voting for members of a local government body to which the elector is linked neither by residence nor by place of work is considered to contradict the principle of representation upon which local government bodies are based.[2]

The above considerations regarding the limits within which voting on the basis of a certificate of authorisation is permissible are not without foundation. But in practice this form of voting, bearing in mind the small numbers involved, does not in general infringe the representative character of local government bodies. The view that, in voting in an area where he is resident only temporarily, the elector does not make full use of his rights and is unable to play his part in supervising the work of the member and in his possible recall, is correct, but the realisation of his rights would not become any greater if he did not cast his vote. In that case, the elector could subjectively consider himself to be restricted in his rights. It would therefore seem that the rule permitting an elector who changes his address after the compilation of the electoral register to vote if he wishes so at his new address on the basis of a certificate, does not constitute a departure from the democratic principles governing a socialist electoral system.

---

[1] See, for example, A. Burda, R. Klimowiecki, *Prawo państwowe*, pp. 588-89.

[2] See M. Jaroszyński, "Reprezentacyjność rad narodowych", *Państwo i Prawo* No. 7, 1960, pp. 9-10.

The procedure for the nomination of candidates is designed to ensure the genuinely popular character of representative bodies. In practice the political, trade union, co-operative and other mass organisations in the socialist countries exercise their right to nominate candidates jointly, on the basis of the common platform of a communist and non-party block or People's Front.

The working people's organisations nominate candidates both on the initiative of their bodies and on the basis of proposals put forward by the workers at pre-election meetings at factories, offices and state farms, and also at village meetings, etc. At first "candidates to become candidates" are selected and discussed at pre-election meetings. At these meetings, the workers exchange views, object to candidates whom they consider undesirable and make additional nominations. On the basis of these discussions, the appropriate changes are made to the lists of candidates. For example, during the campaign which preceded the elections to the National Councils in Poland in 1965, 6,453 candidates for election to village and settlement National Councils were replaced at some 34,000 pre-election meetings attended by more than 1,500,000 electors.[1]

The procedure for the nomination and discussion of candidates is constantly being improved in order to ensure that the discussion shall be as full, free and effective as possible.

In the German Democratic Republic the decree on elections to the People's Chamber and to local government bodies lays down that candidates nominated by the National Front shall be presented to the electors at constituency conferences of their representatives and also at electors' meetings. The representatives to constituency conferences are elected at meetings of the working people. The conferences (in small populated localities—meetings of electors) discuss and decide upon candidates. If the conference (or meeting)

---

[1] See *Trybuna Ludu*, May 26, 1965.

rejects a candidate, the National Front Committee concerned must nominate another.

In many socialist countries the number of candidates which go forward in each constituency does not exceed the number to be elected.

In Poland, the 1956 Statute on elections to the Seym and the 1957 Statute on elections to the National Councils laid down that the number of candidates going forward in a given constituency should exceed the number of deputies to be elected to the Seym or National Councils. At the same time, in order to avert the excessive dispersion of votes, it was laid down that the number of candidates in a particular constituency should not exceed the number of seats by more than two-thirds in the case of elections to the Seym or by more than a half in the case of elections to National Councils. The elector in this way was able to choose between candidates. The successful candidate was the one who secured the majority of votes.

The Law of the Polish People's Republic of December 22, 1960, On Supplementing and Amending Certain Provisions of the Electoral Law retained the obligatory nomination of a larger number of candidates in elections to the National Councils, but amended the relevant provisions of the 1956 Statute regarding elections to the Seym, laying down that the number of candidates could (and not necessarily had to) exceed the number of seats in the Seym belonging to the given constituency not more than by a half (not two-thirds).[1]

In the German Democratic Republic, the decree of the Council of State of July 2, 1965 regarding changes in the decree on elections to the People's Chamber and to local government bodies (the Statute on Elections)[2] likewise envi-

---

[1] In elections to the Seym in April 1961 and May 1965 460 seats were contested by 616 candidates, on June 1, 1969 by 622 candidates and on March 19, 1972 by 625 candidates.

[2] See *Gesetzblatt der DDR* No. 11, January 1965.

saged the possibility of the inclusion on the voting paper of a number of candidates exceeding the number of seats in the constituency in question. If more candidates than there are seats receive more than 50 per cent of the valid votes cast, then the candidates whose names appear first on the voting paper shall be considered elected, while the remainder shall be considered to have been elected as deputy members.

To ensure the most favourable conditions for voting, electoral regulations lay down that polling shall take place on a non-working day at time suitable for the working people.

In order to be elected it is in the majority of socialist countries necessary to secure an absolute majority (more than a half) of the total valid votes cast, with at least half the electorate voting, and more than other candidates have done, should their number exceed the number of seats. There are some exceptions to this rule. For example, in Poland it is not necessary that more than half the electorate should cast their votes in local elections, nor is it necessary for the successful candidate to obtain an absolute majority of votes cast.

In Yugoslavia the successful candidate must secure a majority vote of all electors included on the electoral register of the constituency in question if the number of candidates does not exceed the number of seats to be filled. If it does the successful candidate must secure a majority.

Seats which become vacant during the term of office of the body in question as a result of the cancellation of a member's mandate are in almost all socialist countries filled by means of by-elections.

At the present time the institution of deputy members, elected at the same time as members and whose number is at present not restricted, exists only in the German Democratic Republic. Should a seat become vacant, it is taken by a deputy member.

The Polish law of April 29, 1969 regarding changes in

the Statute on elections to the Seym[1] laid down that the Seym, having withdrawn a member's mandate, could decide that his seat should be taken by the candidate who had received the second largest number of votes during the election and who had not lost the right to be elected. Thus, although the institution of deputy member is not fully established, a procedure for the filling of vacant seats which is characteristic of that institution is permitted.

The institution of deputy members was in the past much more widespread in the socialist countries. In the USSR prior to the adoption of the 1936 Constitution and of corresponding amendments to existing legislation laying down electoral procedure, candidate-members (in effect deputy members) equal to one-third the total number of members were elected at the same time as members of Soviets. In Hungary, deputy members of local Councils were elected prior to the adoption of a new law on elections to Councils in September 1954, while deputy members of the National Assembly were elected prior to the coming into force in November 1966 of the law governing the election of members of the National Assembly and Councils. In Bulgaria, prior to the adoption on February 10, 1953 of the law on elections to the People's Assembly, deputy members of the Assembly were elected, and deputy members of People's Councils were elected prior to the law of November 2, 1951 relating to elections to these Councils. In Poland, deputy members of the Seym and of Councils (with the exception of village Councils) could be elected under the terms of the 1952 Statute on elections to the Seym and the 1954 Statute on elections to the National Councils.

The rejection of this institution by a number of socialist countries is prompted by the desire to reinforce the links between members and their electorate. The fact that several years may elapse after an election before a deputy member takes his seat and that it is therefore not known whether he

---

[1] See *Dziennik Ustaw RPL* No. 12, 1969, Item 84.

still retains the confidence of the electorate is a serious shortcoming of this institution.

The fact that the organisation and conduct of the elections is carried out by the working people themselves through electoral commissions (committees, boards, presidiums, groups) specially set up for each election is likewise an expression of the socialist democracy characteristic of the electoral systems of the socialist countries. These commissions are made up of representatives of political and mass organisations, leading workers and representatives of all sections of the people with authority among the electors. They are nominated by political parties, mass organisations and workers' meetings and are approved by the appropriate government bodies. In Bulgaria, with a view to enhancing the role of mass organisations, the procedure by which the composition of electoral commissions was approved by government bodies was abolished. The commissions are no longer subject to approval, but simply registered.

By means of the electoral commissions tens of thousands of electors participate directly in the organisation of elections and supervise their proper conduct. For instance, prior to the elections to the Supreme Soviet of the USSR held on June 16, 1974, 172,498 electoral commissions with 1,432,949 members were set up. In the German Democratic Republic 339,000 citizens participated in the work of electoral commissions and boards during the 1974 electoral campaign. In Poland about 18,000 commissions with almost 150,000 members were set up during the 1972 electoral campaign.

Elections to supreme and local representative bodies are held regularly in the socialist countries, in accordance with their constitutions and electoral legislation. In the absence of special circumstances (war, blockade, etc.) regular elections are an essential feature of socialist democracy.

The results of elections are a vivid demonstration of the genuinely democratic character of the electoral system in the socialist countries. The characteristic features of these elections are: firstly, a level of participation (almost 100 per cent) unmatched in bourgeois countries, secondly, the unity of the overwhelming majority of the people on the basis of a programme for the building of socialism and communism. In the elections to the Supreme Soviet of the USSR held on June 16, 1974, 99.98 per cent of the electorate voted, while 99.79 per cent voted for the candidates to the Soviet of the Union and from 99.68 to 99.85 per cent for the candidates to the Soviet of Nationalities. In Rumania, 99.96 per cent of the electorate voted in the elections to the Grand National Assembly on March 9, 1975, while from 99.95 to 99.99 per cent voted in the elections to the People's Councils. The candidates of the Socialist Unity Front secured 96.8 and from 97.72 to 99.01 per cent of the votes, respectively.

In Bulgaria 99.85 per cent of the electorate voted in the elections to the National Assembly on June 27, 1971, and 99.9 per cent of them voted for the candidates of the Fatherland Front. From 99.88 to 99.91 per cent of the electorate participated in the elections to the People's Councils held on January 13, 1974, and from 99.57 to 99.76 per cent voted for the candidates of the Fatherland Front.

In Poland 96.94 per cent of the electorate took part in the elections to the Seym on March 19, 1972, of which 99.53 per cent voted for the candidates of the National Unity Front. From 95.44 to 98.26 per cent of the electorate took part in the elections to the National Councils held on December 9, 1973, with 99.41 or 99.73 per cent of all valid votes cast for the candidates of the National Unity Front.

CHAPTER X

THE SUPREME REPRESENTATIVE ORGANS OF STATE POWER OF THE SOCIALIST COUNTRIES

1. GENERAL DESCRIPTION OF THE STATUS AND ROLE OF SUPREME ORGANS OF STATE POWER

According to the constitutions of the socialist countries, their supreme representative organs of state power are: the Supreme Soviet of the USSR, the Supreme Soviets of the Union and Autonomous Republics in the USSR, the National Assemblies of Bulgaria, Hungary and the Democratic Republic of Vietnam, People's Assembly of Albania, the Federal Assembly and the republican National Councils in Czechoslovakia[1], the People's Chamber in the German Democratic Republic, the Supreme People's Assembly in the Korean People's Democratic Republic, the Great People's Khural in the Mongolian People's Republic, the Seym in Poland, the Grand National Assembly in Rumania and the Skupshina of the SFRY and the Skupshinas of Republics and Provinces in Yugoslavia (in the Socialist Republic of Croatia the *Sobor*, and in the Socialist Republic of Macedonia the *Sobranie*). In the People's Republic of China the All-China Assembly of People's Representatives is considered such an organ.

These bodies differ not only in title, but also in organisation and function. But the general principles governing the organisation and functioning of a supreme organ of state power of a socialist type are the same; this is due to the

---

[1] Prior to 1969 the supreme representative organ of Czechoslovakia bore the title "National Assembly".

role and character of a supreme representative organ of the people in a socialist state.[1]

A supreme representative organ of state power, representing all the people of a state, is the supreme expression of the political will of the people and of its sovereignty. "The National Assembly shall exercise all the powers which flow from the sovereignty of the people," declares Art. 19 (2) of the Hungarian Constitution. "The Seym, as the supreme expression of the will of the working people of town and country, shall exercise the sovereign rights of the people," states Art. 15 (ii) of the Polish Constitution.

Two fundamental requirements must be satisfied if the sovereignty of the people is to be effectively and fully implemented with respect to the organisation and functioning of a supreme organ of state power: firstly, the supreme organ must express the sovereign will of the people, and secondly, it must be able to implement that will in practice.

A supreme organ of state power can express the sovereign will of the people only if its composition is genuinely representative. This is ensured by the genuinely popular, democratic electoral system of the socialist countries.

For example, the 1,517 members of the USSR Supreme Soviet elected on June 16, 1974 included 498 workers (32.8 per cent), 271 collective farmers (17.9 per cent), 77 managers and specialists from all branches of the national economy (4.7 per cent), 215 government officials (14.2 per cent), 241 Party officials (15.9 per cent), 17 trade union and Young Communist League officials (1.1 per cent), 142 people working in the fields of science, culture, the arts, education, health and the press (9.3 per cent) and 56 members of the Armed Forces (3.7 per cent). Among the 352 members of the Hungarian National Assembly elected on April 25, 1971 there are 137 workers, 60 peasants, 131 representatives

---

[1] The above-mentioned undemocratic procedure governing the formation of the All-China Assembly of People's Representatives gives no grounds for describing it as a representative organ.

of the working intelligentsia and 24 representatives of other strata. Of the 349 members of the Rumanian Grand National Assembly elected on March 9, 1975 115 are directly engaged in production, including 70 in industry, building, transport, finances and trade, and 45 in the work on state farms. There are 60 workers in science, education, culture and the arts, researchers and designers, 38 officers, lawyers, doctors, economists and clergymen and 136 leaders of central and local organs of Party, state and mass organisations. Of the 460 members of the Polish Seym elected on March 19, 1972, 90 are workers, 22 engineers and technicians, 15 senior industrial and administrative executives, 62 peasants, 16 agricultural specialists, 16 teachers, 31 scientists, 21 journalists and writers, five doctors, five lawyers, ten craftsmen and members of producer co-operatives and seven members of the Armed Forces; 190 are of working-class origin and 186 of peasant origin, while seven have both a working-class and peasant background; 70 come from intelligentsia and seven from other social groups. Thus, the supreme organs of state power of the socialist countries are representative of all strata of the population. Their varied professional composition and the inclusion of outstanding scholars and experienced officials enable them to solve in a competent manner complex state, social and economic problems.

The party composition of the legislative bodies of the socialist countries demonstrates that the peoples of these countries acknowledge the leading role of the Communist (Workers') parties. For example, 1,096 deputies, i.e. 72.2 per cent of the 1,517 members of the Ninth USSR Supreme Soviet elected on June 16, 1974, were members or candidate members of the CPSU. Of the 460 members of the Fifth Polish Seym elected on March 19, 1972, 255 were members of the Polish United Workers' Party. In countries with a multi-party system, other parties are represented in the supreme organs of popular representation alongside the Communist and Workers' parties in accordance with their role in the country's political life. In the Sixth Seym, 117 deputies were members of the United Peasants' Party, and 39—of the Democratic Party. The Christian Democratic Union, the Liberal Democratic, National Democratic and Democratic Peasants' parties all have their factions in the People's Chamber of the German Democratic Republic, each with 52 members. Members of these parties are also represented in the factions of mass organisations.

A genuinely representative composition of a supreme organ of state power is a necessary prerequisite for, but does not of itself provide any guarantee of, the full and proper expression of the will of the people. To achieve this the legislative body should have a democratic procedure, which enables the popular will to be expressed and fully taken into account. This problem has two basic aspects: (a) ensuring that there is a close link between the member and his constituents, and that the former expresses the will of the latter, and (b) ensuring that the procedure adopted enables each member to express and defend his point of view, and that decisions adopted reflect the collective will of members. From this arises the importance not only of those clauses in the constitutions of these countries which lay down the basic principles governing the organisation and work of legislative bodies, but also of other normative acts which lay down in detail the rights and duties of members, and the procedure, structure and powers of the internal organs of supreme representative bodies.

The supreme representative organs of state power in the socialist countries not only express the will of the people, but also have at their disposal the means necessary to carry it out. Being the supreme political expression of the people's sovereign will, these bodies enjoy the supreme status in the mechanism of the socialist state. All other organs of state are subordinate to them.

This finds expression in the extensive powers of the supreme representative organs set down in the constitutions of the socialist countries.

Only these bodies have the power to amend the fundamental law (constitution), to pass ordinary laws and to approve the national budget. It is these bodies which adopt long-term and, in the majority of socialist countries, also annual national economic plans.

These bodies play a decisive role in forming and changing the composition of other higher organs of state.

In all socialist countries where there are higher permanently functioning collegiate organs of state power (see Chapter XI) these bodies are elected and recalled by the supreme representative body and are accountable to it.[1] In a number of socialist countries there are not only collegiate, but also elected individual Heads of State—Presidents in the case of Czechoslovakia, the Korean People's Democratic Republic, Rumania, the Democratic Republic of Vietnam and Yugoslavia. These Heads of State are also normally accountable to the supreme representative bodies. Only the 1974 Yugoslav Constitution does not establish this principle, while the Constitution of the Democratic Republic of Vietnam lays down that the National Assembly has the right to relieve the President of his office.

In the majority of socialist countries governments are formed directly by the supreme representative organs of state power. The procedure has distinctive features in Czechoslovakia, the Democratic Republic of Vietnam and Yugoslavia.[2] But even in these countries the constitutions lay down that the supreme representative bodies shall play the decisive role. In all socialist countries the governments are accountable to the supreme organs of state power.

In the majority of socialist countries the supreme representative organs of state power directly elect the Supreme Court and appoint the Procurator-General (Chief Procurator).

In the Democratic Republic of Vietnam, Hungary and the

---

[1] The Yugoslav Presidency is an exception. See Chapter XI of this book.

[2] For details see Chapter XII.

Korean People's Democratic Republic, the representative body elects only the chairman of the supreme judicial body, while the other members are appointed by the Hungarian Presidential Council, the Standing Committee of the National Assembly of the Democratic Republic of Vietnam, and the Standing Committee of the Supreme People's Assembly of the Korean People's Democratic Republic, respectively.

In Czechoslovakia, the Procurator-General and the entire State Defence Council are appointed by the President, but are accountable to the Federal Assembly, which may call upon the President to dismiss the Procurator-General or any member of the State Defence Council. The Procurators-General of the socialist republics which make up the Czechoslovak federal state are appointed by the Presidiums of the National Councils, while the republican Defence Councils are nominated by the Chairman of the State Defence Council; all these officials and officers may be dismissed on the demand of the National Councils.

In Poland, the election of the Supreme Court and the appointment of the Procurator-General is a matter for the Council of State. Here too the Seym plays a decisive role, since the Council is elected by the Seym from among its members and is wholly subordinate and accountable to it. Some Polish jurists believe that the election of the Supreme Court and the appointment of the Procurator-General directly by the Seym would strengthen the latter's position as a supreme organ of state power.[1]

The Supreme Court and the Procurator-General (Chief Procurator) are accountable either directly to the supreme representative body or to a supreme collegiate organ of state power which is itself accountable to that body.

From this enumeration of the powers of supreme representative bodies of the socialist countries with respect to the formation of other state bodies which are accountable to them it is clear that these powers differ in different countries,

---

[1] See, for example, T. Stembrowicz, "Uwagi o Radzie Państwa de lege lata i de lege ferenda", *Państwo i Prawo* No. 2, 1957.

depending upon the distinctive features of the system of state organs of the country concerned and the distribution of responsibility between the various state bodies.

The existence in some socialist countries of bodies which are peculiar to those countries gives additional distinctive features to the powers of the supreme representative organs of these countries. The Polish Seym, for example, appoints and dismisses the chairman of the Supreme Chamber of Control. The Skupshina of the SFRY elects higher bodies which are peculiar to Yugoslavia—the Constitutional Court, the Federal Council and the Federal Social Attorney of Self-Management.

Despite these distinctive features, the powers relating to the formation of other state bodies are basically identical in all socialist countries. The essence of this basic identity is that it is the supreme representative bodies which play the decisive role and occupy the dominant place.

The supreme organs of state power also proclaim a state of war in the event of armed attack or when it is necessary to fulfil international treaty obligations for joint defence against aggression.

The supreme organs of state power of the socialist countries derive their powers exclusively from the people and are accountable only to the people. In principle, no state organ may restrict their powers.

The list of the powers of the supreme state organs set down in the constitutions of the socialist countries is not exhaustive. In accordance with their position in the mechanism of the state, these bodies may also deal with other matters, including, if they consider it necessary, those which fall within the competence of bodies accountable to them. For example, the constitutions of the majority of socialist countries place the ratification of international treaties within the competence of the higher collegiate organs of state power accountable to the supreme representative bodies.

But the USSR Supreme Soviet used to ratify international treaties itself. For instance, in view of its great importance, the Warsaw Treaty was ratified directly by the supreme organs of state power of the USSR, Bulgaria, Poland and other socialist countries. The overwhelming majority of experts on state law in the socialist countries rightly share the view that the list of the powers of supreme state organs laid down in the constitutions of these countries does not constitute grounds for any limitation of these organs' supremacy.[1]

During the last few years the Marxist-Leninist parties of the socialist countries have drafted and are carrying out a wide range of measures designed to further enhance the role of the supreme organs of popular representation and to improve their work. To this end, not only *general political conditions, but also concrete legal guarantees* have been established.

The extension of the legal guarantees for the enhancement of the role of the supreme organs of popular representation has been manifest above all in the *extension of the constitutional powers* of these bodies in a number of socialist countries. The powers of the National Assembly were greatly enlarged under the 1960 Czechoslovak Constitution. For the first time the President of the Republic and the Procurator-General became accountable to the Assembly. The rules relating to the government's accountability to the Assembly were also strengthened. The Constitution Law on the Czechoslovak Federation of October 27, 1968 envisaged similar powers for the Federal Assembly.

In Poland, the constitutional provisions inserted into the fundamental law as "Chapter III a" by the law of Decem-

---

[1] See S. I. Lepyoshkin, A. I. Kim, N. G. Mishin, P. I. Romanov, *Kurs sovietskogo gosudarstvennogo prava*, Vol. 2, p. 386; B. N. Topornin, *Vysshiye organy gosudarstvennoi vlasti yevropeiskikh stran narodnoi demokratii*, Gosyurizdat, Moscow, 1962, p. 95; B. Spasov, "Zakonet v pravnata systema na NR Bulgaria", *Godishnik na Sofiiskiya universitet. Yuridicheski fakultet*, Vol. XLVIII, 1955-1956, Sofia, 1957, pp. 176-77; A. Burda, R. Klimowiecki, *Prawo państwowe*, p. 360; T. Beér, I. Kovács, L. Szamel, *Magyar államjog*, p. 225; O. Bihari, *Az államhatalmi-képviseleti szervek elmélete*, Budapest, 1963, pp. 199-200 ff.

ber 13, 1957 and providing for the establishment of a Supreme Chamber of Control gave the Seym substantial new opportunities to exercise its supervisory function.

A comparison of the provisions of the 1965 Rumanian Constitution relating to the powers of the Grand National Assembly with the corresponding provisions of the 1952 Constitution shows that the powers and role of the Assembly were extended. In particular, control of the electoral system[1] and the organisation and work of the People's Councils were placed in the hands of the Grand National Assembly itself.[2] The 1965 Rumanian Constitution contains more precise and concrete formulations relating to the subordination of the Supreme Court and Procurator's Office to the Grand National Assembly. It lays down in particular that the Assembly receives reports on the work of the Supreme Court and supervises the Court's definitive decisions. The Grand National Assembly is empowered to exercise general supervision over the activities of the People's Councils. The Constitution now in force gives a broader definition of the Assembly's powers with respect to foreign policy and foreign relations. This finds expression firstly in the general injunction set down in Art. 43 xx, in accordance with which the Grand National Assembly "shall establish the general line of foreign policy", and secondly in the limitation of the

---

[1] The electoral system had previously been controlled both directly by the Grand National Assembly and by its Presidium. See, for example, the law of September 27, 1952 relating to the election of members of the Grand National Assembly (*Buletinul oficial al RPR*, No. 1, 1952) and the decree of September 26, 1953 of the Presidium of the Grand National Assembly (*Buletinul oficial al Marii Adunări Nationale al RPR* No. 35, 1953).

[2] The organisation and work of the People's Councils could previously be regulated by decrees of the Presidium of the Grand National Assembly. See, for example, the decree of December 28, 1950 regarding the organisation and functioning of the People's Councils (*Buletinul oficial al RPR* No. 122, 1950); subsequently replaced by the law relating to the organisation and functioning of the Councils, adopted by the Grand National Assembly on March 22, 1957, and later the law of December 26, 1968.

powers of the collegiate organ accountable to the Assembly with respect to the ratification and denunciation of international treaties. Under the 1952 Constitution there were no restrictions on the powers of the Presidium of the Grand National Assembly in this respect. The 1965 Constitution makes the ratification and denunciation of international treaties, which requires a change in the country's laws, a matter for the Assembly itself (Art. 43 ix). The 1968 Constitution of the German Democratic Republic contains similar provisions.

According to Art. 289 of the Yugoslav Constitution, the Skupshina of the SFRY shall ratify international treaties regarding political and military co-operation, and international treaties which require the adoption of new laws or the amendment of existing legislation.

Under Art. 36 iii of the Constitutional Law on the Czechoslovak Federation, the prior consent of the Federal Assembly is necessary for the ratification of international political treaties and economic agreements of a general character, and also of treaties which require new legislation.

These constitutional provisions are of great importance from the point of view of ensuring the supremacy of the supreme representative body in the system of state organs. The granting of unlimited powers of ratification to an organ accountable to this body would imply that such an organ could in some cases predetermine the content of laws to be adopted by the supreme representative body.

An analysis of the latest constitutions of the socialist countries shows that the extension of the powers of supreme organs of state power in the main takes two forms. Firstly, the range of the exclusive powers exercised by these bodies is extended and made more specific. Secondly, not confining themselves to an enumeration of these powers, the new constitutions contain general provisions defining the powers of supreme representative bodies in the very broadest terms and emphasising the genuine supremacy of these bodies within the system of organs of the state as a whole. Under

Art. 20 iii of the 1960 Mongolian Constitution, the powers of the Great People's Khural include "the establishment of the basic principles and measures in the sphere of home and foreign policy". The 1974 Yugoslav Constitution lays down that the Federal Assembly discusses and establishes the basic principles of home and foreign policy (Art. 283 ii).

The size of the supreme organs of state power must be determined in a manner which ensures both their representative character and their efficient functioning. On the one hand, they must be large enough to represent all the main social strata and groups in a proper manner. On the other hand, they must not be unwieldy and thus lose their effectiveness. It is appropriate here to recall Lenin's remarks regarding the dangers of the excessive inflation of collegiate bodies.[1] It is therefore not accidental that of nine socialist countries seven (Albania, Bulgaria, Czechoslovakia, the German Democratic Republic, Poland, Rumania and Yugoslavia) have already established the size of their representative bodies.[2] Their membership remains unchanged regardless of population growth.

The new rules governing these bodies, which enable them to fulfil their constitutional role more effectively, are of the greatest importance for the establishment of legal guarantees for the enhancement of the role and effectiveness of the supreme organs of state power.

But, despite the great progress which has been made in enhancing the role and improving the democratic content of the work of these bodies, this process cannot be considered completed. The constant enhancement of the role of the supreme organs of popular representation is not a transient

---

[1] See V. I. Lenin, *Collected Works*, Vol. 29, p. 437.

[2] The National Assembly of Albania consists of 250 members, the Bulgarian National Assembly—400 members, the People's Chamber of the German Democratic Republic—500, the Polish Seym—460, the Rumanian Grand National Assembly—349 (465 before the end of 1974), the Czechoslovak Federal Assembly—350, and the Skupshina of the SFRY consists of 308 delegates.

phenomenon, but a general law governing the development of a socialist state. That is why the Communist (Workers') parties of the socialist countries single out the further enhancement of the role of these bodies and the improvement of their work as one of their most important tasks.

2. THE INTERNAL STRUCTURE OF THE SUPREME REPRESENTATIVE ORGANS OF STATE POWER

The structure, organisational procedure and work of the internal bodies of supreme representative institutions is of great importance for their effective functioning.

In the majority of socialist countries the supreme organs of state power consist of one chamber. The exceptions are the Supreme Soviet of the USSR, the Czechoslovak National Assembly and the Skupshina of the SFRY, which consist of two chambers, and also the republican, provincial and communal Skupshinas in Yugoslavia, which consist of three chambers.[1]

Clearly, in countries where before the revolution there had been two-chamber parliaments[2], in which the second chamber, formed in a specially non-democratic way, had been designed as an additional bulwark of reaction, such a system could not continue after the popular revolution. With the establishment of people's rule, the supreme representative organs of state power became single-chamber. In Poland, the National Council (Krajowa Rada Narodowa) which was formed during the national liberation struggle

---

[1] According to the 1963 Yugoslav Constitution, communal Skupshinas consisted of two chambers, as a rule, and other Skupshinas had four or five chambers.

[2] Under the bourgeois-landowner regime two-chamber parliaments existed in Poland (Seym and Senate), Czechoslovakia and Rumania (Chamber of Deputies and Senate) and in Hungary (Chamber of Deputies and Chamber of Nobility). In Bulgaria reaction many times unsuccessfully attempted to introduce a bicameral structure (see G. Zhelev, "Voprosot za dvukhpalatnata struktura na Narodnoto Sobranie u nas", *Godishnik na Sofiiskiya universitet, Yuridicheski fakultet, 1957*, Sofia, 1958, pp. 465-529).

at the end of 1943 and the beginning of 1944, and which became the country's first provisional parliament after liberation, had only one chamber. In a referendum conducted on June 30, 1946 the Polish people expressed support for a single-chamber system. In Czechoslovakia the Constitutional Decree of August 25, 1945 on the Provisional National Assembly, and later the Constitutional Law of April 11, 1946 on the creation of a Constituent National Assembly established a single-chamber structure. In Hungary the single-chamber structure of the National Assembly was first set down in Law VIII of 1945 on elections to the Assembly. In Rumania a single-chamber structure was established by the decree-law of July 13, 1946 on the organisation of national representation.

A distinctive feature of the development of the supreme representative organ of state power in the German Democratic Republic was the fact that, under the terms of the first variant of the 1949 Constitution, it consisted of two chambers—the People's Chamber and the Chamber of *Landers*. This was because in the specific circumstances of establishing people's democracy in that country, its historical division into *landers* was at that time retained. The republic was divided into a number of *landers*, each of which had its own constitution, its own representative body *(Landtag)* and its own government. The Chamber of *Landers* was elected by the *Landtags* and represented the *landers*. But the building of socialism required the strengthening of democratic centralism, and there was no basis for federation in the national composition of the German Democratic Republic. The *Landtags* and the *lander* governments were therefore abolished by the law of July 23, 1952 on the further democratisation of the structure and work procedure of state organs. The Chamber of *Landers* continued to function, however, though its members were elected by *Bezirke* Assemblies. It was itself abolished by the law of December 8, 1958.

The federal structure of three socialist states—the USSR,

Czechoslovakia and Yugoslavia—determines the distinctive nature of the internal structure of their supreme organs of popular representation, expressed in the existence of a special chamber representing the national state components of the federation. As has already been noted, a socialist federation is a voluntary union of equal national republics, and is a means of achieving a just solution of the national question within the framework of a multi-national state in the spirit of genuine equality and in a manner which takes account of the interests of all the nations and nationalities which inhabit the particular state.

The supreme organ of popular representation of a socialist federal state must therefore be structured in a way which reflects and is able to implement both the will of all strata of the population of the particular country and also the will of all the nations which have in proper legal form united in a federal state.

Therefore the supreme organ of popular representation of a federal socialist state has, in addition to a chamber representing the population of the country as a whole regardless of nationality and citizenship within the union, a second chamber representing the national state formations making up the federation. In the USSR, the first chamber is called the Soviet of the Union, in Czechoslovakia the Chamber of the People and in Yugoslavia the Federal Chamber. In the USSR the second chamber is the Soviet of Nationalities, in Czechoslovakia the Chamber of Nations and in Yugoslavia the Chamber of Republics and Provinces.

The establishment of a special chamber representing the national republics and national regions within the framework of the supreme organs of state power of a federal socialist state was first mooted and substantiated in decisions of the CPSU. The need for such a body was indicated in a resolution of the 12th Congress of the Russian Communist Party (Bolsheviks).[1]

---

[1] See *KPSS v resolyutsiyakh...*, Part 1, 7th edition, Gospolitizdat, Moscow, 1964, p. 716.

In accordance with this, the Central Executive Committee of the USSR which, under the 1924 USSR Constitution, was the supreme state organ of the USSR between Congresses of Soviets of the USSR, had two chambers[1]: a Soviet of the Union and a Soviet of Nationalities. The Soviet of the Union was elected by the Congress of Soviets of the USSR from representatives of the Union republics in proportion to the population of each republic in numbers determined by the Congress. The Soviet of the Union therefore represented the entire population of the USSR on a uniform basis. The Soviet of Nationalities, on the other hand, was formed on the basis of the representation of Union and Autonomous republics (five members from each) and of Autonomous regions (one member from each).

The representatives of the Union and Autonomous republics and also of the Autonomous regions were elected by the congresses of Soviets of the respective republics and regions and were subsequently approved by the Congress of Soviets of the USSR. The Soviet of the Union and the Soviet of Nationalities had equal rights in the CEC of the USSR.

The experience of the Central Executive Committee confirmed the desirability of the organisation, within the framework of the supreme organ of power of a socialist federation, of a special chamber based on the principle of representation from national republics and autonomous administrative units.

Therefore the 1936 Constitution of the USSR, in making provision for a major reorganisation of the supreme organs of the USSR in the direction of their further democratisation, also laid down that the structure of the Supreme Soviet of the USSR should be bicameral.

---

[1] The Central Executive Committee of the USSR elected by the First Congress of Soviets of the USSR in December 1922 was originally single-chamber. Its bicameral structure was first established by the Statute on the Central Executive Committee of the USSR approved in November 1923 (*SU 1923*, No. 106, Item 1030) and by the 1924 USSR Constitution.

One chamber—the Soviet of the Union—is elected by all the citizens of the USSR voting in constituencies formed on a uniform basis of one deputy for every 300,000 of the population.

The other—the Soviet of Nationalities—is elected by citizens of the USSR voting by Union republics, Autonomous republics, Autonomous regions and National areas on the basis of 32 deputies from each Union Republic, 11 from each Autonomous Republic, five from each Autonomous Region and one from each National Area. In accordance with this, 32 constituencies are formed in each Union Republic, 11 in each Autonomous Republic and five in each Autonomous Region for elections to the Soviet of Nationalities. Each National Area is a single constituency. The members of the Soviet of Nationalities are elected by direct election. Representing 15 Union and 20 Autonomous republics, eight Autonomous regions and ten National areas, the Soviet of Nationalities at present has 750 members.

The members of the Chamber of Nations of the Czechoslovak Federal Assembly are likewise elected by direct election in constituencies. The Chamber of Nations has 150 members—75 each from the Czech and Slovak Socialist Republics. The Chamber of the People has 200 members elected by all citizens of Czechoslovakia on an equal basis. What is more, decisions on major issues are taken not by the whole Chamber of Nations but by republican representations separately so as to preclude the supremacy of a particular republic.

It has been mentioned above that the Yugoslav Chamber of Republics and Province is elected by republican and provincial Skupshinas. The Chamber numbers 88 delegates, 12 delegates from each republic and eight delegates from each autonomous province. The Federal Chamber is also formed on a parity basis, 30 delegates from each republic and 20 delegates from each autonomous province. But in the Federal Chamber, the representation of national-state formations is limited to this procedure, whereas in the Chamber of Republics and Provinces a number of major questions are decided not by the general vote, but by voting of republican and provincial delegations pending the receipt of a preliminary consent from the Skupshinas of Republics and Autonomous Provinces.

The existence of a special chamber for the representation of the national republics and national administrative units is therefore a feature common to the internal structure of the supreme organs of popular representation of all the federal socialist states. This principle has, however, been embodied in various ways during the constitutional development of the socialist federal states. The main ways are:

1. The direct election of the members of the chamber in question in the national republics and national administrative units (1936 Constitution of the USSR, the Czechoslovak Constitutional Law of October 27, 1968 on the Czechoslovak Federation).

2. The election of members of the chamber in question by the supreme organs of popular representation of the national republics and national administrative units (USSR Constitution of 1924, the 1963 and 1974 Yugoslav Constitutions). This procedure is explained by the fact that each member of this chamber represents not the electors of a particular constituency but the republic or autonomous unit concerned.

The Soviet of Nationalities of the USSR Supreme Soviet, the Chamber of Nations of the Czechoslovak Federal Assembly and the Chamber of Republics and Provinces of the Yugoslav Skupshina are standing bodies. Experience has shown this to be desirable. The Soviet of Nationalities of the Central Executive Committee of the USSR, the Soviet of Nationalities of the USSR Supreme Soviet and the Chamber of Nations of the Czechoslovak Federal Assembly were from the outset standing bodies, similar to the chambers representing the population as a whole. The status of the organ of representation of republics and provinces in the supreme representative body of Yugoslavia has, however, undergone frequent changes. In this case too, however, the general rule governing the internal structure of the supreme representative organs of socialist federation ultimately became established.

The development of the internal structure of the Yugoslav Skupshina has been marked by substantial distinctive features. According to the 1946 Constitution, the People's Skupshina of the Federal People's Republic of Yugoslavia consisted of two chambers: the Federal Chamber and the Chamber of Nationalities. The Constitutional Law of 1953 relating to the foundations of the social and state structure of Yugoslavia and to the federal organs of power established a special chamber of the Federal Peoples' Skupshina—the Chamber of Producers—alongside the generally representative Federal Chamber. The Chamber of Producers was to represent citizens employed in production, transport and trade. The Federal Chamber had members elected by republican Skupshinas and representative organs of autonomous formations; these members acted as a special chamber—the Chamber of Nationalities—in considering certain questions. The 1963 Constitution went considerably further in organising within the framework of the supreme representative organ a special representation of citizens employed in various spheres of the social division of labour: the Chamber of Producers was replaced by four chambers, each corresponding to a particular sphere of work—Economic, Education and Culture, Social Welfare and Health and Organisational-Political. Thus, whereas only those working in the economic sphere were elected to the former Chamber of Producers, those working in science and culture, health and social security, the mass-political organisations and administration received special representation in the new chambers. As before, the Federal Chamber incorporated the Chamber of Nationalities, the rights of which were expanded by the constitutional amendments of 1967.

The multi-chamber structure of the Yugoslav Federal

Skupshina underwent further change in accordance with the Eighth Amendment to the Constitution adopted in December 1968. The Federal Chamber and the Organisational-Political Chamber were abolished, and a Social and Political Chamber established. The Chamber of Nationalities became not merely a permanent, but also the main chamber. The 1974 Constitution re-established, though on a different basis, the bi-cameral structure of the federal supreme representative organ.

With a multi-chamber structure of the supreme representative body, the question arises of the degree to which each chamber participates in the exercise of this body's powers.

In the USSR and Czechoslovakia, both chambers participate on equal terms. The independent powers of each are confined to matters of internal organisation: the election of internal directing and auxiliary bodies, procedural questions, etc. But in Czechoslovakia the chambers of the Federal Assembly sometimes examine different questions, and no joint decision of the chambers is required, for instance, when the Minister's report is heard.

According to the 1963 Yugoslav Constitution, from the point of view of the participation of the chambers in the exercise of the powers of the Federal Skupshina these powers could be divided into three groups. One group was exercised by all the chambers at joint or separate sessions; the second group was exercised on equal terms by two chambers (of which one had to be the Chamber of Nationalities); the third group was exercised independently by individual chambers.

According to the 1974 Constitution, both chambers of the Skupshina of the SFRY have, as a rule, separate powers. The Federal Chamber adopts decisions on amending the Constitution, approves the basic guidelines on home and foreign policy, adopts the federal budget and the final balance, decides on changes of the frontiers of Yugoslavia and on war and peace, defines the organisational bases of the federal organs and their powers, considers the reports of the supreme government bodies, announces amnesty for crimes provided for by the federal law, etc. The Chamber of Republics and Provinces on some occasions adopts laws on the temporary measures and defines the sources and amount of means for national defence and state security, and exercises other powers. Moreover, on the basis of the consent of republican and provincial Skupshinas, the Chamber of Republics and Provinces approves the Yugoslav social plan, approves the national policy and promulgates laws in finances, foreign trade, price control, etc. It also approves the total expenditure of the federal budget, and so forth.

In the sphere of their competence the chambers issue acts, including laws, on behalf of the Yugoslav Skupshina, approve the manner of their enforcement and give their interpretation. Both chambers participate on equal terms in the formation of the supreme bodies of Yugoslavia and decide other questions.

The republican and provincial Skupshinas have three chambers and their powers, therefore, differ in some respects. Some powers are exercised by each chamber independently on behalf of the Skupshina. For instance, according to Art. 330 of the Constitution of the Socialist Republic of Serbia, the Social and Political Chamber of the Republican Skupshina independently decides the following questions: implementation of the constitutional status and equality of nations and nationalities; internal affairs and public self-defence; legal aid; criminal law, etc. Some powers are exercised by the three chambers on equal terms. These are the election and appointment of judges and certain government officials; implementation, development and protection of self-management; plan and budget, etc. (Art. 332). Some questions are decided by two chambers on the basis of equality. Family law is regulated in Serbia by the Chamber of Communes and the Social and Political Chamber, territorial planning and urban construction by the Chamber of Associated Labour and the Chamber of Communes, and so forth (Arts. 333, 335). Finally, the joint meetings of all chambers decide constitutional questions, form supreme government organs and adopt the Skupshina's Standing Orders (Art. 336).

At their first sessions the supreme representative organs elect their *internal directing bodies*. In the majority of socialist countries these bodies are *collegiate:* a Presidium in Poland, Czechoslovakia, the German Democratic Republic and the Democratic Republic of Vietnam, a Permanent Council in the Korean People's Democratic Republic,[1] and a Bureau in Albania and Rumania.

In Czechoslovakia each chamber of the Federal Assembly elects its own collegiate directing body—a Presidium of the Chamber, made up of 3-6 members.

In the USSR, Bulgaria and Hungary representative bodies elect only individual officers to guide their work: chairmen of the chambers of the USSR Supreme Soviet, chairmen of the Supreme Soviets of the Union and Autonomous republics, the Chairman of the Bulgarian National Assembly and the Chairman of the Hungarian National Assembly.

In accordance with the Yugoslav Constitution, the Skupshina of the SFRY and each of its chambers elect their own chairman and his deputies who carry out certain functions jointly.

The chambers of the Supreme Soviet of the USSR, the Skupshina of the SFRY and its chambers, the Supreme Soviets of the Union republics and the Hungarian and Bulgarian National Assemblies also elect deputy chairmen. Their number varies from two (the Hungarian National Assembly, the Supreme Soviet of the Tajik SSR) to eight (the Supreme Soviet of the RSFSR). The deputy chairmen do not, however, constitute together with the chairman a collegiate directing body with powers distinct from those of the chairman. A deputy chairman individually carries out the functions of the chairman in his absence.

---

[1] The powers of the Presidium of the Federal Assembly in Czechoslovakia and those of the Permanent Council of the Supreme People's Assembly in the Korean People's Democratic Republic are not confined only to those of an internal organ of the Assembly (see Chapter XI).

The individual performance of these functions was in the past more common in the socialist countries. For example, in Poland, in accordance with the 1948 Standing Orders of the Legislative Seym, the Marshal of the Seym exercised on an individual basis the powers subsequently given to the Presidium of the Seym under the 1952 and 1957 Standing Orders. The 1952 Rumanian Constitution made provision for the leadership of the Grand National Assembly by its chairman on an individual basis. The substantial amendments made to the Constitution in March 1961 laid down that the internal directing organ of the Assembly should be its Bureau. This institution was also incorporated into the 1965 Constitution, and the 1974 constitutional amendments further enhanced its role. It is impossible not to agree with those specialists in state law from the socialist countries who rightly stress that the introduction of the collegiate principle in this respect implied a further democratisation of the internal structure of supreme representative bodies.[1]

In almost all the socialist countries these internal directing bodies are elected by the supreme representative institutions for their full term of office. In the Democratic Republic of Vietnam, however, the Presidium is elected by the National Assembly at the beginning of each session and serves for that session only. It is therefore termed "the Presidium of the Session".

In the majority of socialist countries these bodies include the chairman of the representative institution and his deputies (in Poland—the Marshal and three vice-marshals of the Seym[2], in Rumania the Chairman and four vice-chairmen of the Grand National Assembly).

---

[1] See A. Burda, "Niektóre zagadnienia regulamim sejmovego w Polsce Ludowej", *Państwo i Prawo* No. 6, 1957, p. 1043; B. Spasov, *Razvitiye i usovershenstvuvane na predstavitelnite organi v NR Bulgaria*, p. 53.

[2] The number of vice-marshals was increased from two to three (in order that one should represent non-party members of the Seym) by a decision of the Seym on February 13, 1971 (*Monitor Polski* No. 11, 1971, Item 68).

In some socialist countries they are larger. In the German Democratic Republic, the Presidium of the People's Chamber includes other members in addition to the chairman and his deputies. Each group in the Chamber must be represented on its Presidium. In Czechoslovakia, the Presidium of the Federal Assembly has 40 members, half of whom are elected by the Chamber of Nations and the other half by the Chamber of the People. The Chairman and deputy chairmen of the Federal Assembly (it is they who head the Presidium) are elected by the chambers from among their members.

In the Democratic Republic of Vietnam, the Presidium of sessions is differently constituted. Firstly, there is no Chairman or vice-chairmen of the National Assembly elected for its entire period of office. The chairmen of sessions of the Assembly are elected by the Presidiums of Sessions. Secondly, the Presidiums are unique in their composition. They have more than 20 elected members, including members of the Standing Committee of the Assembly, the President and Vice-President of the Republic, the Prime Minister and members of the government.

The terms of reference of internal collegiate directing bodies of supreme representative institutions include initiating the adoption of new standing orders of a supreme representative body or amending them, supervision over the observance of standing orders and their mandatory interpretation; the working out of agenda for sessions or particular plenary meetings of supreme representative bodies; the coordination of the work of standing committees, and the direction of the external relations of the supreme representative institutions. In some socialist countries these bodies also ensure that deputies carry out their duties, and assist them in their work.

The working out of agendas for the supreme organs of people's representation by the supreme collegiate organs of state power (the Presidiums of Supreme Soviets) is a distinctive feature found in the USSR.

In the USSR, Bulgaria and Rumania coordinatory powers with respect to standing committees of supreme representative bodies in periods between sessions are also exercised not by the internal directing organs of these bodies, but by the supreme collegiate organs of state power (the Presidiums of Supreme Soviets, the Council of State and the State Council, respectively).

The coordination of the work of the different chambers and mediation between them in the event of conflict are distinctive features of the powers of the Presidium of the Czechoslovak Federal Assembly and the Chairman of the Skupshina of the SFRY. These arise from the multi-chamber structure of supreme organs of popular representation in these countries. Moreover, the Chairman of the Yugoslav Skupshina exercises these powers jointly with his deputies and the chairmen of the chambers.

The Presidiums of sessions in the Democratic Republic of Vietnam have no functions relating to periods between sessions, since they are elected only for the period of a particular session.

In some socialist countries there are also special *auxiliary and consultative directive bodies*. These are the Councils of Elders in the chambers of the USSR Supreme Soviet, the Supreme Soviets of the Union Republics and in the Polish Seym. These Councils are formed on the territorial and national-territorial principle (the representatives of members elected from Union and Autonomous republics, Autonomous regions and National areas, and from administrative-territorial units). The Council of Elders of the Seym includes the Marshal and vice-marshals, and also the chairmen or vice-chairmen of the party groups (factions) in the Seym. These consultative bodies do not function permanently, but meet only prior to sessions or plenary meetings of a supreme representative body to exchange views and coordinate positions in relation to items on the agenda. They often make proposals regarding the candidates for membership of bodies elected by the supreme representative organ.

The *standing committees (commissions)* play a major role

in enabling the supreme organs of state power to fulfil their main functions successfully.

All questions which lie within the competence of the supreme organs of state power of the socialist countries are decided by these organs themselves.

But a profound analysis and correct solution of complex and important national issues cannot be achieved immediately. Hard, painstaking preparatory work is necessary if plenary meetings are to be fruitful.

Hence the importance of the role of committees (commissions), which function as auxiliary bodies in all spheres of the work of the supreme organ of state power.

In the Political Report of the Central Committee of the RCP(B) to the 11th Congress of the Party, Lenin, discussing the work of the All-Russia Central Executive Committee, the supreme organ of state power in the RSFSR under the 1918 Constitution, stressed the importance of the vigorous work of the sections and sub-committees in improving the CEC performance.[1] The decisions of the Communist (Workers') parties of the socialist countries also point to the great importance of commissions in assisting the supreme organs of state power in the performance of their constitutional tasks.

The measures initiated by the Communist (Workers') parties to extend socialist democracy and in particular to enhance the role of supreme representative organs of state power have led to the development and activisation of the committee system in the majority of socialist countries.

In the first place, the development of the standing committee system has found expression in an increase in the number of these committees. Before 1956, the Supreme Soviets of the majority of Union Republics had only three Standing Committees (Credentials, Legislative Proposals, Budget), and in some cases a Foreign Affairs Committee. The chambers of the USSR Supreme Soviet had only four Standing Committees (Credentials, Legislative Proposals,

---

[1] See V. I. Lenin, *Collected Works*, Vol. 33, pp. 308-09.

Budget, Foreign Affairs). With the formation of new committees dealing in the main with particular spheres of activity the number of such committees in the Union Republics grew from 52 in 1955 to 203 in 1971. The chambers of the USSR Supreme Soviet now have 13 Standing Committees: Credentials; Legislative Proposals; Planning-Budget; Foreign Affairs; Youth Affairs; Industry, Transport and Communications; Building and the Building Materials Industry; Agriculture; Consumer Goods; Health and Social Security; Public Education; Science and Culture; Trade, Communal Services and Municipal Economy, and Conservation of Nature.

Until 1958 the Bulgarian National Assembly had only four Standing Committees: Credentials; Legislation; Budget; Foreign Affairs. Today there are 13: Credentials; Legislation; Uniform Plan and Budget; Conservation of Natural Environment; Industry, Building and Transport; Labour; Health and Social Security; Art and Culture; Science, Education and Technical Progress; Foreign Affairs; Agriculture and the Food Industry; People's Councils and Urban Development; Trade, Services and Tourism; Youth and Sport.

In 1955 the Hungarian National Assembly had only four Standing Committees: Juridical; Economy and Finance; Foreign Affairs; Culture. In accordance with the Standing Orders of the National Assembly adopted in 1956 and subsequently somewhat amended,[1] 10 Standing Committees were set up: Law, Administration and Justice; Foreign Affairs; National Defence; Planning and Budget; Agriculture; Industry; Building and Transport; Trade; Culture; Social Security and Health. Special provision is also made for a committee dealing with deputy immunity and incompatibility.

In the Polish Seym, in accordance with the 1952 Standing Orders, there were only seven Standing Committees: Legislation; Budget; Foreign Affairs; Trade; Education, Science

---

[1] See *Magyar Közlöny*, 1956, Item 69; 1963, Item 21; 1967, Item 25; 1968, Item 29; 1972, Item 82.

and Culture; Municipal Economy and Housing; Labour and Public Health. In accordance with the current (1957) Standing Orders, the Seym establishes 22 Standing Committees: Building and Municipal Economy; Small-Scale Industry, Producer Co-operation and Handicrafts; Maritime Economy and Navigation; Mining, Power and Chemistry; Internal Trade; Foreign Trade; Transport and Communications; Culture and Art; Forestry and Woodworking Industry; Credentials and Regulations; Science and Technical Progress; National Defence; Education; Economic Plan, Budget and Finance; Legislation; Labour and Social Affairs; Heavy and Engineering Industry; Light Industry; Agriculture and Food Industry; Internal Affairs and Justice; Foreign Affairs; Health and Physical Culture.

This enumeration shows that the characteristic trend of the development of the standing committee system is not merely towards an increase in their number, but also towards their organisation in such a way as to ensure that there exists a standing committee for each main sphere or group of related spheres of political, economic and cultural life controlled by central organs of the state. This makes it possible to carry out thorough preparatory work on a systematic basis in all the main spheres of activity of supreme organs of popular representation. Each standing committee, having the appropriate expert membership, is thus competent to draft laws and other acts relating to its sphere and to exercise systematic control over the work of the government bodies concerned. As a result, the supreme organs of popular representation handle the major issues of political, economic and cultural life in a more systematic, thorough and profound fashion.

The increase in the number of standing committees and in their membership also implies a major increase in the activeness of deputies, since a substantially larger number now serve on committees. In 1955 the membership of standing committees of all the Supreme Soviets of the Union Republics totalled 550; in 1971 the corresponding figure was 4,047 or

68.8 per cent of the total number of deputies. The membership of the standing committees of the chambers of the USSR Supreme Soviet has increased from 146 in 1956 to 1,000 at the present time. In the First Seym in March 1955, 130 out of 425 members served on standing committees; in the Fourth Seym, elected in June 1965, their number reached 542 (the Seym itself has 460 members; some serve on two or even three standing committees). In Bulgaria, 377 of the 400 members elected on July 7, 1971—94.25 per cent—serve on standing committees of the National Assembly.

In order that members of standing committees (commissions) shall be able to play an effective part in their work, in a number of socialist countries the Standing Orders of the supreme organs of popular representation lay down that no member may serve on more than two committees simultaneously.[1]

In all the socialist countries the members of the standing committees (commissions) of the supreme representative body are elected from among the members of that body.

There are certain exceptions to this rule in Rumania and Yugoslavia, in the case of the Constitutional Commission of the Rumanian Grand National Assembly and the Legislative Commission of the Skupshina of the SFRY, both of which include experts who are not deputies. The Rumanian Constitution limits the number of experts to one-third of the total membership of the commission, while the Standing Orders of the Yugoslav Skupshina lay down that their number shall not exceed one half.

The inclusion of legal experts who are not deputies arises from the special nature of the work undertaken by these commissions. They assist the supreme representative body in controlling the constitutionality of legislation (that is, they ensure that new laws conform to the Constitution). The

---

[1] See, for example, Art. 24 of the Standing Orders of the Rumanian Grand National Assembly of December 22, 1965, as amended (*Buletinul oficial al RSR*, Part I, No. 22, 1965; No. 31, 1969; No. 45, 1974.)

Standing Orders of the Yugoslav Skupshina give a more extended definition of this task, requiring the Legislative Commission also to ensure that new laws and other acts are in conformity with the legal system and to verify their drafting. Naturally, these commissions must include legal experts to perform this task satisfactorily.

These commissions cannot declare any law or other act unconstitutional. They submit recommendations to the supreme organ of state power (or to its appropriate chamber) in Yugoslavia.

Non-deputies also serve on the Skupshina's Standing Committee on Elections and Appointments. This committee makes recommendations to the Skupshina regarding the election, appointment and dismissal of government officials when this lies within the competence of the Skupshina. In addition to deputies who make up the majority of its members, the committee also includes non-deputies delegated by the Socialist Union of the Working People of Yugoslavia.

The Standing Orders of the Skupshina of the SFRY, while laying down the general rule that members of its standing committees shall be deputies, make provision for the inclusion of a certain number of scholars, experts and public figures who are not deputies to the Skupshina. The chairmen and vice-chairmen of the committees must, however, be deputies, while the number of non-deputies may not exceed the number of deputies.

The normative acts which at present govern the organisation and work of the commissions of the supreme organs of state power in the socialist countries clearly define their purposes and powers. This is of great importance in ensuring that they work effectively.

The functions of the standing committees as laid down in the Standing Orders of the supreme representative organs of state power and in the Statutes on the Standing Committees of the Supreme Soviets of the Union Republics and of the chambers of the USSR Supreme Soviet, include: the preliminary consideration of draft laws and decrees; the consideration of decrees submitted to the approval of the supreme organ of state power; the hearing of reports and communications from Ministers and other heads of supreme organs of state administration, agencies and establishments; the analysis of the state of affairs in particular branches of the administration and the economy; investigations regarding particular state institutions and enterprises. The committees send their conclusions and recommendations to the appropriate government bodies.

An analysis of the legal regulations laying down the main functions of the standing committees shows that they clearly define the status of these committees as auxiliary and initiating bodies which play an important role in the exercise by the representative bodies of their main functions: a) legislation and b) control over the work of other organs of state.

Great importance in improving the committees' work attaches to various means by which the opinion of the electors regarding matters being discussed by the commissions may be brought to light, and to means by which the commissions may familiarise themselves with the state of affairs in the localities, as well as to the involvement in their work of deputies of the supreme organs of state power, who are not members of the commissions, and of representatives of local organs of state power, mass organisations and state institutions, scientists and other experts.

The work of the standing committees (commissions) testifies to their growing links with the electorate. These links take varied forms: the discussion by commission members of draft legislation at local meetings, submission of letters and suggestions from members of the public to the commissions, etc.

The special status of the mass organisations in a socialist state and their increased role in the fulfilment of state functions also determines their growing participation in the work of the standing committees of the supreme organs of state power. This takes the form of the preparation and discussion of draft laws relating to their sphere of activity, the participation of representatives of mass organisations in the work of the committees in a consultative capacity, etc. Representatives of mass organisations also frequently serve on drafting sub-committees and working groups set up by the committees. Some experts on state law in fact suggest that representatives of mass organisations should serve as full members of standing committees.[1] This has however not yet been accepted as a general principle in the socialist countries. There can be no analogy with the standing committees of local organs of state power. The size of the supreme organs of popular representation is quite sufficient for them to include representatives of all the main mass organisations elected at general elections. Such members, by joining the appropriate standing committees, are fully able to represent both their constituents and their mass organisation. The inclusion of additional non-elected representatives of mass organisations with full voting rights could lead to the diminution of the role of elected members. A member of a standing committee who is not deputy would have greater powers than a deputy who is not a member of the committee in question and who therefore has only a consultative voice in its proceedings. It would furthermore be an infringement of the electivity principle, which is of the greatest importance for the development of socialist democracy. The committees, which are extremely important organs of the supreme representative bodies, would be joined by officials of mass organisations elected not by general election but by a particular category of citizens (and in some cases not elected at all).[2] The retention of the existing procedure by which standing

---

[1] See, for example, B. Spasov, "Pryako uchastie na trudeshchite se v zakonodatelna rabota", *Godishnik na Sofiiskiya universitet. Yuridicheski fakultet, 1965*, Sofia, 1966, pp. 102-03.

[2] It is not possible to agree with B. Spasov who writes (op. cit., pp. 102-03) that the inclusion of representatives of mass organisations who are not deputies is a form of the people's direct participation in the work of representative bodies. The inclusion of *individual officials* of mass organisations cannot in any way be considered either as a form or as a manifestation of the people's *direct* participation.

committees or commissions are in principle made up of deputies (with certain well-founded exceptions, to which reference has already been made) would therefore seem to be correct.

The standing committees may in case of need hold joint meetings (when several committees have an interest in matters under discussion), set up standing sub-committees or *ad hoc* (provisional) sub-commissions and form working groups. Standing committee meetings may coincide with the sessions of representative bodies, or they may be held in the intervals between sessions. In a number of countries the committees do a great deal of work. For instance the standing committees of the Fourth Polish Seym (1965-1969) held 801 meetings, set up 54 standing sub-committees and a number of *ad hoc* provisional sub-commissions to study specific problems. These sub-committees and sub-commissions made 336 visits to localities. During two and a half years of the work of the Fifth Seym (1969-1971) its commissions held 517 meetings and approved 542 recommendations to the government and individual Ministers. The frequency of their meetings and the effectiveness of their recommendations particularly increased in 1971. The commissions of the Sixth Seym continue to work with the same vigour.

In addition to standing committees, the supreme organs of popular representation also set up provisional commissions. Unlike the standing committees which are set up for the entire term of the representative body and have permanent functions, provisional commissions are formed to deal with a particular issue and are wound up when their mission is accomplished.

The internal organs of the supreme representative bodies of a number of socialist countries also include *Secretaries*. Secretaries are elected by the Hungarian National Assembly, the Rumanian Grand National Assembly and the Polish Seym. In the majority of socialist countries Secretaries are elected for the entire term of the supreme organ of state power. At the beginning of each meeting the Chairman of the supreme representative body nominates Duty Secretaries from their number who draw up the list of speakers and take a record of the proceedings.

In the Democratic Republic of Vietnam, a Session Secretariat is elected at the commencement of each session. The Secretariat keeps records of all proceedings and carries out other duties as instructed by the Presidium of the Session.

The functions of the Secretary-General of the Skupshina of the SFRY are quite different. He is responsible for the Skupshina's services and also drafts reports, documents and other papers on matters to be examined by the Skupshina's Chairman, supervises the implementation of his decisions and carries out other duties as instructed by the Chairman.

3. THE TERM OF OFFICE AND PROCEDURE OF THE SUPREME ORGANS OF STATE POWER

The term of office and procedure of a supreme organ of state power are not "purely technical" matters. They are of great importance in determining its role, and in the implementation of its functions. In the majority of socialist countries the supreme representative bodies are elected for four-year terms. In Bulgaria, the German Democratic Republic, Czechoslovakia, Rumania, Hungary and the People's Republic of China they are elected for five-year terms.[1]

The constitutions of the socialist countries lay down guarantees which ensure that there shall be no protracted interval between the expiry of the term of office of the supreme representative body of a particular convocation and the induction of its successor. These include the constitutional estab-

---

[1] Until 1971 the supreme organs of popular representation of Bulgaria and Czechoslovakia, until 1972 that of Rumania, until 1974 that of the German Democratic Republic and until 1975 those of Hungary and the People's Republic of China were elected for a four-year term. The theoretical justification for the extension of this term to five years is the need to bring it into line with the main cycles of development of the country's economic life, which are determined by the five-year economic and social development plans.

lishment of *fixed terms* for elections, the determination of polling days and for the convening of the first session of newly-elected governing bodies. This is of great importance for the regular functioning of supreme organs of state power.

The time limits for the appointment and holding of elections laid down by the constitutions are maximal, calculated from the expiry of the term of office of the supreme organ of state power, and therefore great importance attaches to the question of from what precise moment this term is calculated.

Since the constitutions and other normative acts of the majority of socialist countries do not contain any express provisions on this score, there are differing views. Some hold that a supreme representative body of a particular convocation comes into being on *polling day* and that its term of office begins on that day. Others take the view that it comes into being at its *first organisational meeting after the elections*, because the election of members and the formation of a supreme representative body are not one and the same thing; until its first meeting the body has not yet constituted itself, has not elected its internal organs, and has not entered upon the fulfilment of its functions, not to mention the fact that the validity of the elections themselves is finally determined by the supreme representative body.

In line with this point of view, the term of office of the Polish Seym, for example, was calculated from the date of the opening of its first session. But when the terms of office of the supreme representative organ of state power and those of local organs are the same, it is in practice not possible to calculate the term from the day the first session opens, because the dates for the convening of these sessions do not coincide in various representative bodies. Therefore when in Poland the term of office of the local organs of state power—the National Councils—was extended to four years, a change was also made in the method of calculation of the term of office of the Seym, which now dates from polling day.

In the Democratic Republic of Vietnam, there is no specific legislative provision regarding this question. But, since the law lays down that a member's term of office dates from the first session of a newly-elected representative body, it also by the same token establishes that the term of office of the National Assembly shall date from the first session.

In Rumania, according to Art. 45 of the Constitution, the term of office of a new Grand National Assembly originally dated from the expiry of its predecessor's term. The Law of December 20, 1974 amending several articles of the Rumanian Constitution[1] established that the powers of the Grand National Assembly of a former convocation shall cease on the day when elections to a new Assembly are held. Consequently, that day marks the beginning of a new term of office.

Issues lying within the competence of the supreme organs of state power of the socialist countries are decided at *plenary meetings* of these bodies (or of the appropriate chambers). As a rule, plenary meetings take place only during *sessions*.[2] The significance of sessions in the work of these bodies is therefore clear.

The proper *regularity* of the sessions of a supreme organ of state power, and also their *duration* are factors of great importance in the effective and systematic exercise of its functions.

Among measures designed to enhance the role of the supreme representative bodies, the Communist and Workers' parties of the socialist countries are paying great attention to the regularity of their sessions, and to their duration from the point of view of their having adequate time for the serious and businesslike discussion of all the questions placed before them.

The Mongolian Constitution makes provision for the convening of *one* ordinary session of the supreme organ of state

---

[1] See *Buletinul oficial al RSR*, I, No. 161, 1974.

[2] In Yugoslavia Skupshinas are permanently functioning bodies and the institute of a session does not exist.

power per year, and the Constitution of the Korean People's Democratic Republic provides for one or two sessions. The constitutions of the majority of socialist countries however lay down at least *two sessions* a year, and the 1971 Bulgarian Constitution at least three.

Additional sessions may be convened if necessary.

In many socialist countries (the USSR, Rumania, Poland, the Democratic Republic of Vietnam, the Korean People's Democratic Republic and Mongolia) legislation distinguishes between *ordinary* and *extraordinary* sessions. Ordinary sessions are those convened in accordance with the requirements of the Constitution (one or two per year). Others are held to be extraordinary.

In Bulgaria, following the adoption of the law of November 4, 1961 which amended Art. 19 of the 1947 Bulgarian Constitution, the division of sessions into ordinary and extraordinary was abolished. Since the new Art. 19 envisaged the convening not of two but of *at least two* sessions per year, all sessions were held to be ordinary. The 1971 Bulgarian Constitution likewise makes no distinction between ordinary and extraordinary sessions.

The Constitutional Law on the Czechoslovak Federation likewise envisages that sessions of the Federal Assembly shall be convened *at least twice a year*. The formulation regarding the convening of *at least* two (and not merely two) sessions per year, which is also to be found in the Polish, Hungarian and Rumanian Constitutions, could also constitute grounds for considering all sessions to be ordinary. However, the Rumanian Constitution (Art. 54) itself defines the concept of extraordinary sessions. The Standing Orders of the Polish Seym make provision for both ordinary and extraordinary sessions. Unlike its predecessor, the new Hungarian Constitution no longer refers to "ordinary" sessions, but the Standing Orders of the National Assembly (Para. 19 i-iii) retained this concept and in effect divided sessions into "ordinary" and "extraordinary", although the term "extraordinary" is not used.

The enhancement of the role of the representative organs of state power in the majority of socialist countries demands an increase in the number of their sessions. Constitutional provisions which lay down a *minimum number of sessions (at least two)* rather than a definite number of ordinary sessions (one or two) would therefore seem to be more satisfactory.

With such a formulation, the division of sessions into ordinary and extraordinary retain significance only when normative acts establish *dates* for the convening of *ordinary* sessions.

This is of importance as a *guarantee of the regularity* of sessions. Constitutional provisions for the convening of a particular number of sessions per year do not of themselves guarantee their regularity. For example, in 1955 in Poland both sessions of the Seym (the Sixth and Seventh) were convened in March and May. The next, Eighth ordinary session did not take place until April 23, 1956—almost a year later.

The establishment of dates prevents irregularity. Two problems arise, however: 1) in which document (the Constitution or Standing Orders) would these dates be set down, and 2) in what way shall they be defined—by the naming of the *precise date* on which a session must open, or by the naming of a date *by which* a session must begin.

At present, no socialist country except Czechoslovakia lays down dates for the convening of sessions. The 1948 Czechoslovak Constitution and the 1946 Constitution of the Democratic Republic of Vietnam laid down dates for the convening of sessions of the supreme representative organs of state power. Spring and autumn sessions of the Czechoslovak National Assembly had to be held in March and October, while the National Assembly of the Democratic Republic of Vietnam met in May and November. The 1960 and 1959 Constitutions of these countries made no similar provisions. Until November 1961 Art. 19 of the 1947 Bulgarian Constitution laid down dates for the convening of the sessions of the National Assembly. But these provisions proved unsatisfactory because of their great rigidity: ordinary sessions had to be convened strictly on February 1 and November 1. This was unsatisfactory firstly because if it became necessary to consider important issues before these dates an extraordinary session had to be called, followed by an ordinary session perhaps only a day later. Secondly, it is impossible to forecast with such precision whether matters to be placed before the session will be ready for discussion. Therefore the provision regarding dates was deleted from Art. 19 of the Constitution by the law of November 4, 1961.

This, however, does not imply that it is in general undesirable to establish dates for the convening of sessions in any form.

The opponents of the establishment of dates cite as an argument the fact that matters to be placed before the session may not be adequately prepared. There is, however, an example which convincingly refutes this assertion. In the past draft budgets were usually drawn up and submitted to the supreme organs of state power of the socialist countries in February or March. In some instances, they were drafted only by June or even August of the current year. When, however, the rule that these laws had to be adopted before the start of the budget year came into force, it proved quite possible to prepare them in good time. This example clearly shows that the prior establishment of a date not only does not hinder the preparation of a session, but on the contrary enhances the responsibility of the organs and persons dealing with matters to be submitted to sessions and introduces a greater element of planning into the preparatory work. It is desirable that dates should be fixed, not by naming a date on which a session shall open, but *by naming a day (or month) not later than which* a session shall open.[1] This is the

---

[1] The establishment in standing orders of the day or the month not later than which a session shall be convened does not in practice have any significance. For example, the apparently differing formulations in the Standing Orders of the Polish Seym and in the law on the organisation of the National Assembly of the Democratic Republic of Vietnam relating to the convening of an autumn session are in fact the same.

method used by the 1957 Standing Orders of the Polish Seym, the law on the organisation of the National Assembly of the Democratic Republic of Vietnam and the Constitutional Law on the Czechoslovak Federation. Ordinary sessions of the Polish Seym are convened not later that April 1 and October 31, while those of the National Assembly of the Democratic Republic of Vietnam and the Czechoslovak Federal Assembly are convened not later than April and October of each year.

The Standing Orders of the Rumanian Grand National Assembly lay down that one ordinary session shall be convened every six months. However, such provisions cannot of themselves be an adequate guarantee of regularity. Having completed one session on the last day of the first half-year (or semester), it would be possible to call the second on the next day, and then to convene no further sessions for almost a year. Sessions of the Rumanian Grand National Assembly are in practice convened regularly.

The proper *duration* of sessions is ensured by giving the supreme organ of state power itself the right to decide the question of closure. A decision to terminate a session is taken when all the items on the agenda have been considered.

The structure of sessions differs in the various socialist countries.

In the majority of socialist countries the concept of the duration of a session is identical with the number of plenary meetings of a supreme organ of state power. For example, the sixth session of the Sixth National Assembly of Bulgaria lasted three days (March 27-29, 1973). This means that plenary meetings of the National Assembly were held on March 27, 28 and 29, 1973.

In Poland, however, a session of the Seym means the period of time which elapses between the date on which a session is opened and the date on which it is closed, during which a certain number of plenary meetings of the Seym are held, while meetings of the commissions of the Seym are held between these plenary meetings. For example, during the first session of the Sixth Seym which lasted 101 days, there were eight days of plenary meetings.

A similar procedure has evolved in recent years in Rumania. For example, the tenth session of the Fifth Grand National Assembly took place from May 8 to June 24, 1968 and the twelfth from November 11 to December 27, 1968. The third session of the Sixth Grand National Assembly lasted from November 17 to December 29, 1969. During that time there were ten plenary meetings, in the intervals between which there were meetings of commissions and deputies went to localities. The procedure in Czechoslovakia is similar.

In the Democratic Republic of Vietnam, the bulk of sessional time is taken up by meetings of commissions, subcommissions and groups of deputies of the National Assembly.

The duration of sessions and of plenary meetings of supreme representative bodies does not always coincide in other countries too. The second session of the Fourth National Assembly of Bulgaria opened with a plenary meeting on November 19, 1962; this was followed by an interval in plenary meetings, during which commissions continued their work; the session concluded with a two-day plenary meeting on November 27-28, 1962; the sixteenth session of the Fifth National Assembly of Bulgaria also had a prolonged interval between plenary meetings; the meetings of May 7 and 8, 1971 considered and approved the draft of the new Constitution and adopted a law regarding a referendum; the new Constitution, approved by a nation-wide referendum, was proclaimed at a plenary meeting on May 18.

It is therefore incorrect to identify sessions with plenary meetings, as is done by some authors.[1]

In the Democratic Republic of Vietnam, the holding of

---

[1] See, for example, B. N. Topornin, *Vysshiye organy gosudarstvennoi vlasti yevropeiskikh stran narodnoi demokratii*, p. 152; B. I. Kozhokhin, *Vysshiye organy gosudarstvennoi vlasti yevropeiskikh sotsialisticheskikh stran*, LGU Publishers, Leningrad, 1962, p. 47.

preparatory sessions is a distinctive feature of the procedure of the supreme representative organ of state power. They are held prior to the official opening of sessions of the National Assembly. They settle organisational questions and provide a forum for preliminary exchanges of views regarding items on the agenda of the forthcoming session.

The *publicity* of plenary meetings of supreme representative bodies is a democratic principle which enables the electorate to control the work of their representatives. Only when the national interest demands it may a representative body itself decide to meet in secret session. There have as yet been no such instances. Members of the public and the press attend open meetings, occupying places specially set aside for them.

The *discussion* of matters placed before plenary meetings is of great significance, since it is during this discussion that the collective will of the supreme organ of state power representing the entire people of the republic finally evolves. That is why standing orders pay great attention to the establishment of a procedure which ensures the fullest possible expression of this will through guarantees which on the one hand provide for the maximum freedom of discussion and on the other for the constructive nature of contributions.

After a speech by the representative of the body tabling the item in question, or by the reporter of the commission which has been considering the question, the floor is given to members who wish to contribute to the discussion. Members may table amendments to draft laws and decisions. Effective discussion requires not only the speakers' activeness, but also the comprehension of speeches by the necessary majority of members of the representative body, since the fundamental meaning of a speech lies in the consideration of the arguments which it contains by deputies in their adoption of a final decision.

Therefore most satisfactory are the provisions of those constitutions and standing orders of supreme organs of state power which establish *not only the quorum necessary for the adoption of a decision*, but also that necessary for *the validity of the meeting itself*.

Discussion is followed by voting. In accordance with the principle of publicity voting is open as a rule, by show of hands. It may also be by name.

Decisions of supreme representative bodies are held to be valid if adopted by a majority not less than the minimum laid down by the Constitution or Standing Orders.

As a rule, the constitutions and standing orders of the supreme representative bodies of the socialist countries require that a decision shall be approved by a simple majority, with at least half the members present. The Standing Orders of the Supreme Soviets of the Lithuanian and Uzbek SSRs require the presence of at least two-thirds of the members. In Hungary the presence of at least half the members of the National Assembly suffices, and in the Polish Seym at least one-third.

In the Democratic Republic of Vietnam acts of the supreme representative body are adopted by a majority of its members.

In Yugoslavia, two modes of voting are possible if the Skupshina's decision is taken by its two or three chambers. If a decision is taken at a joint meeting of the chambers, it requires the presence of the majority of delegates of each chamber and the majority vote. When a question of the powers of the Skupshina is decided by chambers on equal terms, each chamber usually sits and adopts its decision separately. For such a decision to be valid, the session must be attended by more than half the members of the chamber in question, and the decision must receive a majority of the votes cast. A joint session of two or more chambers may be held by decision of the corresponding chambers. But voting at such a session is conducted separately, by chambers.

In Czechoslovakia, the adoption of a decision by the Federal Assembly requires that it should be approved in identical form by both chambers at meetings attended by more than half their members and with more than half those present voting in favour. Furthermore, more than half the members elected from the Czech Socialist Republic and more than half those elected from the Slovak Socialist Republic must be present in the Chamber of Nations.

The Constitutions of the socialist countries lay down that a qualified majority is necessary for decisions on certain matters of special importance to be valid. A qualified majority is necessary for the adoption, amendment and addenda of constitutions. In the majority of socialist countries this requires a *two-thirds* majority *of all members* (and not just of those present). In some countries the figure is different. In Poland, a *two-thirds* majority with *at least half the members* of the Seym present is required. In Czechoslovakia, the adoption of the Czechoslovak Constitution, its amendments and addenda requires a majority totalling at least *three-fifths* of the members of the House of the People, of the members elected to the House of Nations from the Slovak Socialist Republic and of the members elected to the House of Nations from the Czech Socialist Republic. In Yugoslavia, the adoption of constitutional amendments by the Skupshina requires the consent of all republican and provincial Skupshinas or only republican Skupshinas if amendments affect only them. Consent having been received, the Skupshina's Federal Chamber decides on amendments to the Constitution by a majority of two-thirds of its delegates.

The Constitutions of a number of socialist countries also require a qualified majority for the adoption of decisions relating to other particularly important matters. For instance, the election of the Czechoslovak President requires a majority totalling *three-fifths of all* the members of the Federal Assembly; in the House of Nations, there must be such a majority in each group of deputies—those from the Czech Socialist Republic and those from the Slovak Socialist Republic. The adoption by the Federal Assembly of a decision relating to the declaration of war requires a similar majority.

4. LEGISLATION

In accordance with the constitutions of the socialist countries, the supreme representative bodies are the *sole legislative organs*.[1]

The certain weakening of the role of the supreme representative organs of state power in a number of socialist states in the past found expression in a deterioration in the legislative activity of these bodies. Many matters requiring legislative regulation were regulated by decrees, and sometimes by administrative measures.[2]

Party and state decisions designed to enhance the role of representative bodies indicated the need to eradicate the practice of regulating important matters by sub-juridical measures and re-affirmed the role of the supreme representative organs of state power as *genuinely exclusive* legislative bodies. "All the fundamental issues affecting the life of the working people as a whole," says Resolution No. 1 of the Hungarian National Assembly of 1956, "are subject to regulation by laws. In accordance with this, it is undoubtedly necessary to extend legislative activity in order that the norms affecting the basic rights and the most important duties of the citizen should be laid down in the form of laws."[3]

---

[1] In the USSR the Supreme Soviet is the sole organ exercising all-Union legislative authority, while the Supreme Soviets of Union and Autonomous Republics are the sole bodies exercising the legislative authority of these republics. In Yugoslavia the Skupshina is the sole federal legislative body, while each republican and provincial Skupshina is the sole republican (provincial) legislative body. In Czechoslovakia, federal laws are adoted by the Federal Assembly, while republican laws are adopted by the National Councils of the republics.

[2] See B. Spasov, *Razvitiye i usovershenstvuvane na predstavitelnite organi v NR Bulgaria*, pp. 15-16; A. Kh. Makhnenko, *Predstavitelniye organy gosudarstvennoi vlasti Polskoi Narodnoi Respubliki*, Gosyurizdat, Moscow, 1962, pp. 86-87.

[3] *Magyar Közlöny*, 1956, Item 69.

The September (1956) Plenary Meeting of the Central Committee of the Bulgarian Communist Party resolved that "the practice of settling important issues by decrees of the Presidium of the National Assembly shall not continue in the future",[1] while the October (1956) Plenary Meeting of the Central Committee of the Polish United Workers' Party underlined that "only in exceptional circumstances should matters lying within the competence of the legislative chamber be resolved by decrees of the Council of State".[2]

The practical implementation of these decisions is indicated by the following data. The Third Bulgarian National Assembly (1957-1961) adopted 82 laws—that is, twice as many as the Second National Assembly. Over the same period, the number of normative decrees adopted by the Presidium of the National Assembly decreased 33 per cent.[3] In 1953 the Polish Seym adopted only one law, while the Council of State adopted 44 decrees having the force of law; in 1954 the corresponding figures were five and 40 respectively, and in 1955 two and 43. A radical change took place after 1956. Over the whole period of its term of office (1957-1961) the Second Seym adopted 174 laws and approved only 13 decrees having the force of law. Of these, 11 were promulgated by the Council of State before the Second Seym began its work. Throughout the entire term of office of the Second Seym the Council of State issued only two decrees having the force of law, which furthermore related to matters of comparatively secondary importance. The Third Seym (1961-1965) adopted 93 laws and approved only one decree, the Fourth (1965-1969) 60 laws and one decree while the Fifth (1969-1972) adopted 36 laws but did not approve a single decree, because none were promulgated. The Communist and Workers' parties of the majority of socialist coun-

[1] *Rabotnichesko delo*, September 19, 1956.
[2] *Nowe Drogi* No. 10, 1956, p. 7.
[3] See B. Spasov, "Razvitieto na predstavitelnite organi v NR Bulgaria kato obshchestveni organizatsii (*Novo vreme* No. 4, 1962).

tries continue to see the further improvement of legislative activity as a necessity.[1]

The *legislative process* in the socialist countries is constructed in a way which fosters the fullest expression in law of the will of the people and the drafting of the most suitable and most correct forms for the legislative regulation of social relations.[2]

In all socialist countries *members* of the supreme organs of state power and *government* have the *right to initiate legislation*.[3] The procedure in the case of members varies. In Rumania, a draft law must bear the signatures of at least 35 members and in Poland at least 15. In the USSR, Bulgaria, Albania, Hungary, the German Democratic Republic, Czechoslovakia, Yugoslavia and the Democratic Republic of Vietnam each member has the right to initiate legislation.

In *the majority* of socialist countries the right to initiate legislation is also granted to *the higher collegiate organs of state power* (the Presidiums of Supreme Soviets in the USSR, the Presidium in Hungary, the Councils of State in Poland and the German Democratic Republic, the State Councils in Bulgaria and Rumania, etc.) elected by the supreme representative bodies from among their members, and in *a number of countries also to the standing committees* of supreme representative bodies. There is no doubt that such bodies should exercise the right to initiate legislation. It may, however, be asked whether the granting of this right to these bodies is not superfluous, since they are made up of members who already enjoy the right. But an examination of the pro-

---

[1] See *24th Congress of the CPSU*, p. 94; *Rabotnichesko delo*, April 21, 1971, p. 7 *ff*.

[2] For a detailed analysis of this process in the European countries, see D. A. Kovachev, "Zakonodatelny protsess v yevropeiskikh sotsialisticheskikh gosudarstvakh", *Yuridicheskaya literatura*, 1966.

[3] The right to initiate legislation means the right to table draft laws, to which corresponds the duty of the leading organs of the supreme representative bodies to include the discussion of these drafts in the agenda of these bodies. For a reasoned criticism of other interpretations of this right, see Kovachev, op. cit., pp. 40-74.

cedures laid down by the law shows that this is not the case. The fact that these bodies have this right is of substantial significance. In Bulgaria, for example, the Presidium of the National Assembly did not have the right to initiate legislation. Of course, the Presidium was entirely made up of members of the National Assembly, but if the Presidium was seen as the totality of members, it did not have the right to initiate legislation, because this right could be exercised by groups made up of at least one-fifth of all the members of the National Assembly—a figure substantially larger than the Presidium. Members of the Rumanian Grand National Assembly may, as has been noted, exercise the right to initiate legislation in groups of at least 35; a standing committee of the Assembly may also exercise this right with fewer members. The new 1971 Bulgarian Constitution gives the right to initiate legislation to the State Council which replaces the Presidium of the National Assembly, and also to the standing committees of the National Assembly, thus granting this right to people's representatives (deputies). The 1972 Statute on the work of the National Assembly[1] established that a deputy may exercise this right independently or jointly with other deputies.

In Czechoslovakia, the President of the Republic and the republican National Councils have the right to initiate legislation; in the Democratic Republic of Vietnam, the right is exercised by the Chairman of the Republic and his deputy as well as by the Standing Committee of the Assembly.

The granting of this right to the Supreme Court is a distinctive feature of legislative procedure in the USSR, Mongolia and Bulgaria; in the latter country, the right is also exercised by the Chief Procurator. In the German Democratic Republic the right to initiate legislation is exercised by the Presidium and factions of the People's Chamber.

In the USSR the right to initiate all-union legislation is exercised by the chambers of the USSR Supreme Soviet.

---

[1] See *Derzhaven vestnik*, 1972, Item 36.

The relevant provisions of the 1974 Yugoslav Constitution are very distinctive. Each delegate and working organ of the Skupshina's Federal Chamber enjoys the right to initiate legislation on matters within the Chamber's competence. In the case of the Chamber of Republics and Provinces, the right to initiate legislation on matters within its competence which require the consent of republican and provincial Skupshinas belongs to republican and provincial delegations in this Chamber, its working organs, republican and provincial Skupshinas and the Federal Executive Council.

In a number of socialist countries the mass organisations also have the right to initiate legislation. Under the 1971 Bulgarian Constitution and the Standing Orders of the Supreme Soviets of a number of the Union Republics forming part of the USSR, this right is exercised by the republican-level bodies of the mass organisations, while the 1968 Constitution of the German Democratic Republic and the Fundamentals of Labour Legislation of the USSR and the Union Republics give this right to trade unions.

In a number of other socialist countries it is now proposed that this right be given to the central organs of mass organisations. But the absence of legislation investing these organs with this right does not mean that these organs have not in fact initiated legislation. In Poland the trade unions drafted and submitted Draft Laws on Social Labour Inspection, on the Trade Unions and on Workers' Self-Management adopted by the Seym on February 4, 1949, July 1, 1949 and December 20, 1958, respectively. Thus, to give the central organs of mass organisations the right to initiate legislation is simply to enforce in law a procedure already established in practice.

The *discussion of draft laws* in the socialist countries is conducted in a manner which ensures the active participation not only of all members of the supreme organ of state power, but also of the mass organisations and the broadest mass of the people.

The members of the appropriate standing committees

usually play the most active part in the discussion of draft laws placed before supreme organs of state power. In addition, the Standing Orders of these bodies provide guarantees enabling all members to formulate their views in good time. The Statute on the work of the Bulgarian National Assembly, for example, lays down that a session of the National Assembly shall consider only those draft laws which have been submitted at least 20 days in advance; draft laws relating to the national plan of economic and social development and the state budget must be submitted at least 30 days in advance. The texts of draft laws are distributed among all members at least 10 days before the meeting at which they are to be considered.[1] Reports of the Council of State, the Council of Ministers and its members, of the Chairman of the Supreme Court, the Chief Procurator and local People's Councils must reach the National Assembly at least 15 days before sessions. In order that members should have the time to study the recommendations of standing committees with respect to draft laws, these recommendations are distributed to members or placed in the National Assembly at least one day before they are due to be considered. The Standing Orders of the Hungarian National Assembly simply lay down that its Chairman shall, at the first meeting of the session in question, announce the draft laws, proposals and other matters to be discussed and decided by the session (Par. 22 i).

There are therefore substantial differences in the definition of the legal guarantees providing for the active participation not only of the members of standing committees but of all members in the discussion of draft laws. Regulations which provide for the obligatory distribution of texts to all

---

[1] It is indicative that according to the 1958 Statute on the Internal Procedure of the Bulgarian National Assembly these time limits were 10, 15 and 5 days respectively, and 15, 20 and 7 according to the 1962 Statute. The extension of these time limits is indicative of a tendency to create better conditions enabling members to approach the discussion of draft laws in a more competent fashion.

members several days before their consideration are the most satisfactory. This enables the members to consider drafts more carefully, obtain the views of the electors and to work out their own views and proposals more carefully.

A procedure involving a *series of readings* is a distinctive form of guarantee ensuring the careful consideration of draft laws.

The 1957 Standing Orders of the Polish Seym make provision for two readings. The first reading takes place at least one day after members have received a printed text of the draft. This first reading includes a reasoned presentation of the draft by its proposer and discussion of its general principles.[1] The draft is then referred to the appropriate commission or rejected in its entirety. The second reading follows the consideration of the draft by the commission, and not before at least three days have elapsed following the receipt by members of the commission's report. The second reading includes the presentation of the report of the commission setting out the main principles of the draft and the commission's amendments, if any; discussion and the submission of amendments; the vote. The Seym may, if it is not satisfied with the draft or with the report of the commission, refer it back to the commission and fix a time limit for the presentation of a second report. Under this procedure even those members who do not serve on the appropriate commission may, having received the draft text in advance, express their views on it prior to the start of the commission's work, prepare concrete proposals during its work and submit them either to the commission or to the Seym. Members may take advantage of the interval between the first and second reading to consult their electorate.

The 1971 Bulgarian Constitution also lays down as a general rule that draft laws shall be adopted by two votes at different meetings of the National Assembly. After the

---

[1] In practice there is discussion during the first reading only in the case of the most important draft laws, for example those relating to the state budget.

first vote, the draft is referred to the appropriate commission for further discussion, before being voted on a second time.

The Standing Orders of the Supreme Soviet of the Lithuanian SSR envisage the possibility of two readings, while those of the People's Chamber of the German Democratic Republic make provision for several readings.

Both where provision is made for one reading and where provision is made for two or more, the supreme representative body may when discussing the draft and the report of the commission conclude that the draft is inadequately prepared and refer it back to the commission.

In cases of special urgency the procedure can be accelerated.

In supreme representative bodies with more than one chamber, the legislative procedure is usually complicated by the fact that a law must be approved in identical wording by each chamber.

In the USSR, under Art. 47 of the Constitution in the event of disagreement between the chambers of the Supreme Soviet of the USSR, the matter is referred to a conciliation commission formed by the chambers on a parity basis. If the commission fails to reach agreement, or if its decision does not satisfy one of the chambers, the matter is considered by the chambers for a second time. Should it still prove impossible to reach agreement, the Presidium of the USSR Supreme Soviet dissolves the Supreme Soviet and appoints new elections.

Under the Constitutional Law on the Czechoslovak Federation a law is considered adopted if it has been approved in identical wording by both Houses of the Federal Assembly. If within three months no decision is taken by one House on a draft adopted by the other, the draft is held to have been adopted. If one House rejects a draft adopted by the other, a conciliation committee of the two Houses is formed on a parity basis. If the committee does not reach agreement within five months of the adoption of the first decision, the draft is considered rejected. The draft may be re-considered only after at least a year has elapsed since its rejection. If agreement is not reached between the Houses, the Federal Assembly may be dissolved by the President of the Republic.

In Yugoslavia, the problem of co-ordinating the chambers' will only arises on matters they decide on the equitable basis. In the event of differences between the Skupshina's chambers as regards some normative act (e.g. a law on the ratification of an international treaty, joint Standing Orders of the chambers or decision on the organisation and work of the Skuphsina's services), a debatable act is removed from the chambers' agenda and cannot be submitted during the two subsequent meetings. Unless an agreed decision is reached after that, the approval of the ratification law is postponed for three months and the variant approved by the Federal Chamber is in operation pending the approval of the chambers' joint Standing Orders.

It has been noted that most questions decided by the Skupshina's Chamber of Republics and Provinces require the consent of republican and provincial Skupshinas. Unless this consent has been secured, the Federal Executive Council can in the case of emergency (strained marked situation, threat to the interests of national defence, etc.) enter the Presidency of the SFRY with a proposal to adopt a law on temporary measures. In the event of the Presidency's consent, the Federal Executive Council submits this proposal to the Skupshina of the SFRY. Such a law must be adopted by a majority vote of two-thirds of the delegates to the Chamber of Republics and Provinces. Without this majority, the Presidency of the SFRY can decide that the law in the form approved by the majority of the Chamber's delegates shall apply pending its final approval in conformity with constitutional provisions. Yet the law shall be valid for not more than a year, after which time the procedure relating to the adoption of law on temporary measures is repeated unless agreement has been reached as required. If prior to the day when the federal budget is approved no agreement of republican and provincial Skupshinas has been reached on the amount of federal expenditure, then the federation's needs are financed according to the previous year's budget.

Republics and provinces have their own specific features in the way they overcome differences between the Skupshinas' chambers, the more so because the range of questions decided by the chambers is broader than in the federation. For instance, according to the 1974 Vojvodina Constitution, if no agreement is reached between the Skupshina's chambers after two consecutive discussions of a debatable question joint commission is formed on a parity basis to work out a relevant proposal. If the commission fails to work out such a proposal or if it is not approved by the chambers, the debatable question is moved to the chambers' joint meeting. If no agreement is reached the question is removed from the agenda and unless the authoritative chambers decide otherwise, it can only again be placed on the agenda by one of the chambers after six months. In the event of a failure to reach agreement on the budget, social requirements are financed on the basis of the preceding year's budget. In an emergency, a procedure of adopting temporary measures is applied which is basically similar to the federal procedure, with the sole difference that the decision on temporary measures is taken at the joint meeting of delegates of the authoritative chambers and no qualified majority is required.

The chambers of republican and provincial Skupshinas adopt some decisions on the basis of equality with the Skupshinas of self-managing communities of interest (e.g. in education and public health). These communities unite workers employed in a particular sphere of production and those who use their services. The procedure of settling disputes is the same as that between the chambers of the Skupshina.

The attentive and serious approach of the supreme representative bodies to consideration of draft laws is illustrated by the following data. Of 174 drafts adopted by the Second Seym (1957-1961) only 34 were approved without amendments. These amendments were sometimes so substantial, that the laws finally adopted by the Seym differed greatly in both form and content from the drafts submitted by the government. Of the 93 laws adopted by the Third Seym, 86 were submitted by the government. Only 15 of these were adopted without amendment. Amendments were in the main introduced by the standing committees. For example, the standing committees of the Czechoslovak Federal Assembly proposed more than 200 amendments and addenda to draft laws in 1964-1965 alone.

The genuinely popular character of the laws of the socialist countries is manifest in their content and in the manner of their adoption by genuinely popular, representative bodies. It is also manifest in the most varied forms of direct participation by the broad sections of the working people, their mass organisations, factory and office collectives, etc. in the inception, preparation and discussion of drafts.

Many draft laws are the result of public initiative, public opinion and the opinion of the most varied strata of the working people and their mass organisations. Many are drawn up by mass organisations themselves.

The nation-wide discussion of draft laws prior to their consideration by the supreme organs of state power has become widespread in the socialist countries. Following the Soviet example, it has become a rule that draft fundamental laws—constitutions—shall be the subject of nation-wide discussions. Drafts of many other important laws have been the subject of extensive discussion in recent years.

The mass organisations play an important part in organising such discussion. For example, after the discussion of the draft law on labour relations was completed in the appropriate committees of the Federal Chamber of the Federal Skupshina in December 1964, the Yugoslav Trade Union League was instructed to organise discussion of the draft in all union organisations.

The working people and their mass organisations are in various ways involved in the preparation of draft laws by the commissions of supreme organs of state power.

The direct participation of the working people in the preparation and discussion of draft laws is of great importance not only for the fullest and most correct reflection of the will of the people in the laws which are adopted, but also for the moulding of socialist legal consciousness. The broad mass of the working people, having participated in the drafting and discussion of draft laws, then see the laws as their own creation and carry them out more willingly. The political consciousness of the mass of the people is enhanced, as a result of which the balance between persuasion and compulsion as means of ensuring the observance of the law is changed in favour of the former.

Broad public discussion during the drafting of a law is an important means of mobilising the mass of the people for the achievement of its aims.

Laws approved by supreme organs of state power come into force after their official promulgation.

In several socialist countries the promulgation of laws lies within the competence of the higher collegiate organs of state power elected by the supreme representative bodies (the Presidium of the Supreme Soviet in the USSR, the Council of State in Poland, the State Council in Bulgaria, and the Presidium of the People's Assembly in Albania). Promulgation requires the signatures of the chairman and secretary of the body in question. In Hungary, laws are signed by the Chairman and Secretary of the Presidium; the Chairman of the Presidium is responsible for their promulgation.

In Czechoslovakia federal laws are promulgated by the Presidium of the Federal Assembly. A distinctive feature of Czechoslovak state law is the fact that promulgation requires the signature of the President, the Chairman of the Federal Assembly and the Chairman of the Government. Republican laws are promulgated by Presidiums of the National Councils over the signatures of their chairmen and the chairmen of republican governments.

In the German Democratic Republic laws are promulgated by the Chairman of the Council of State over his signature.

In the Democratic Republic of Vietnam, the Korean People's Democratic Republic and Rumania promulgation is a matter for the President.

In Yugoslavia, laws are promulgated by decrees of the Presidiums over the signature of the Skupshina's Chairman and federal laws are currently promulgated by a decree of the Republic.

The rule that laws must bear the signature of these officials in no way implies any control over the legislative activity of supreme representative bodies by other bodies in the socialist countries, since these officials have no power to withhold signature or promulgation. Prior to 1960 in two socialist countries—Czechoslovakia and the Democratic Republic of Vietnam—the President of the Republic had the constitutional right to refer a law back to the National Assembly together with his observations for further consideration. In the Democratic Republic of Vietnam this power could be exercised within ten days of the adoption of law, and in Czechoslovakia within a month after a law has been passed to the Prime Minister by the National Assembly.

If the Assembly re-affirmed its earlier decision the law had to be promulgated. It should be emphasised that the Presidents of Czechoslovakia and the Democratic Republic of Vietnam did not in fact exercise these powers. The constitutional legislation of Czechoslovakia and the Democratic Republic of Vietnam now in force no longer makes provisions for these powers. This re-emphasises the supremacy of the organ of popular representation in the system of state organs.

No time limits for the signing and promulgation of laws are laid down in the majority of socialist countries. The guarantee of promptitude is the general accountability of those concerned to the supreme representative bodies. But the state law of a growing number of socialist countries, not confining itself to general guarantees, lays down an additional guarantee of prompt signature and promulgation of laws in the form of a time limit. In the USSR laws must be published not later than seven days after adoption; in

Rumania the corresponding figure is ten days, in Czechoslovakia 14 days, in Bulgaria and the Democratic Republic of Vietnam 15 days, and in the German Democratic Republic one month.

In the majority of socialist countries laws come into force on the day of promulgation, unless the law itself states otherwise. The publicising of a law is of great importance in ensuring its observance. Therefore in a number of countries there is a general rule that laws come into force not on the day of promulgation, but some days later (provided, of course, that the law itself does not state otherwise). As a general rule laws come into force three days after promulgation in Bulgaria, ten days after in the USSR, on the 14th day after in the German Democratic Republic, and in Yugoslavia not before the eighth day after promulgation. Bearing in mind the importance of public knowledge of the contents of laws and the fact that the dispatch of official texts to localities requires a certain time, lawyers in those socialist countries where the laws come into force on the day of their promulgation are considering the adoption of another general rule envisaging an interval of time between the promulgation and the coming into force of a law.[1]

5. CONTROL OVER THE WORK OF OTHER STATE BODIES

The exercise of the control function by the supreme organs of popular representation over the work of other state bodies depends upon two basic factors: the *combination of legislative and executive authority* which is characteristic of the socialist representative bodies; the *genuine supremacy* of the supreme representative body in the system of socialist state organs. The combination of legislative and executive authority as applied to the work of a supreme representative organ of state power implies that this organ not only adopts laws

---

[1] See S. Rozmaryn, "Podpisanie i ogloszenie ustaw w Polskiej Rzeczypospolitej Ludowej", *Państwo i Prawo*. No. 1, 1959, pp. 23-24.

and other acts which lay down the main lines of the activity of other state bodies, but also has the powers necessary to secure and verify the implementation of its decisions. This is the purpose of the power given to supreme representative bodies to supervise the work of all other state bodies. The fact that the *limits of the control* exercised by the supreme representative bodies over the entire system of state bodies in the socialist countries *are unrestricted* flows from the genuine supremacy of the representative bodies. These limits are defined by the representative bodies themselves. That is why the Communist and Workers' parties see the strengthening and development of the control functions of the supreme organs of popular representation as being one of the most important tasks in enhancing their role.

To ensure the most effective control, the constitutions and other normative acts of the socialist countries *do not confine themselves to general injunctions regarding the supremacy* of the representative bodies and their control functions, but lay down *a number of concrete guarantees* of such control.

The first guarantee is that *the formation of other supreme organs of the state and the introduction of changes in their membership* is a matter for the supreme representative body, or for the higher collegiate organ of state power accountable to it (see section 1 of the present chapter).

One guarantee of the effectiveness of control by the representative body is *its power to rescind acts* issued by other state bodies. For instance, the Hungarian National Assembly has the right to rescind the acts of state bodies which are at variance with the Constitution or infringe upon the interests of society.

The *mandatory approval* of a number of important measures (both normative and non-normative) of higher state organs by supreme representative bodies is another guarantee of the supervisory function of these bodies written into the constitutions of a number of socialist countries. In particular, major normative decrees issued by collegiate organs of state power between sessions of the supreme representative body and which are akin to laws in their significance and legal force, and also acts relating to individual changes in the composition of the government in the periods between sessions are subject to mandatory approval. The supreme representative body has the power to rescind or amend these acts. In the USSR normative decrees are approved in practice.

The *hearing of reports* from the heads of other higher state bodies is an important means by which the representative body exercises its function of control. Explicit constitutional provisions which list the hearing of such reports among the powers of supreme representative bodies and, secondly, other legal provisions which lay down periodicity of the submission of such reports reinforce this form of control and ensure its regularity. The law on the National Assembly of the Democratic Republic of Vietnam adopted in July 1960 lays down that the government reports on its work to ordinary sessions of the Assembly, while the Supreme Court and the People's Procurator-General's Office are required to submit reports to the National Assembly at least once a year. The Statute on the work of the Bulgarian National Assembly lays down that the State Council, the Supreme Court and the Chief Procurator shall submit reports to the National Assembly at least once during its term of office.[1] The Council of Ministers shall report to the National Assembly annually. The Standing Orders of the Hungarian National Assembly lay down that the Chairman of the Supreme Court and the Procurator-General shall report regularly to the National Assembly. These injunctions are by no means "mere technicalities", but are of great significance. Experience shows that in some countries where the accountability of, for example, the Supreme Court and the Procurator-General to the

---

[1] After 1966 the hearing of reports from the Chief Procurator's Office and the Supreme Court, hitherto the responsibility of the Presidium of the National Assembly, was transferred to the Assembly itself. Reports have to be submitted annually.

supreme representative body is laid down only in general terms and no periodicity is established, representative bodies have in fact never considered such reports. In Czechoslovakia, Hungary and Rumania, however, such reports are considered regularly.

In addition to the mandatory regular reporting of state organs to supreme organs of popular representation provided for by the law, all state organs must submit reports to supreme representative bodies when the latter call for them. This arises from the supremacy of the supreme representative bodies in the system of socialist state organs as a whole.

Control over the work of the higher organs of state administration is a very important aspect of the control function carried out by the supreme organs of popular representation. This is because the implementation of measures arising from the laws and other acts of organs of state power rests primarily upon the organs of state administration.

The *annual discussion and adoption of national economic plans, the plans of social and economic development and state budgets* by supreme representative bodies and also the *approval of reports on their implementation* are a highly important means of control over the work of governments. The budgets of the socialist countries, unlike those of the capitalist states, embrace the entire national economy and all the main spheres of the life of society. Therefore, by adopting appropriate acts the supreme representative bodies control almost every aspect of the government's work.

The policy of enhancing the role of the supreme organs of popular representation being pursued in the socialist countries has also found expression in the strengthening of their control over the organs of state administration. This trend has been clearly manifest during recent years in the majority of socialist countries.

In a number of countries where in the past the approval of annual national economic plans was a matter for governments, these plans are now approved directly by the supreme representative bodies which have always approved the long-term plans (usually in the form of a law).

Laws relating to budgets were in the past usually approved in March or April (and sometimes even later) of the financial year in question, which began on January 1. Laws relating to budgets, which were adopted some three or four months after the budgets had come into operation, constituted mere registration of accomplished facts rather than directives for the future work of governments.

The procedure by which supreme representative bodies as a rule considered budget reports for the last year but one —a procedure followed in the past—likewise diminished the effectiveness of this form of control.

This gives added significance to the transition in the majority of socialist countries to the adoption of plans and budgets on the eve of the budget (plan) year in question, and to the consideration of reports on their fulfilment during the year immediately following, from the point of view of the strengthening of the control function of the supreme representative bodies. Reports on plan and budget fulfilment are usually considered at the end of the year following, at the same time as the budget and plan for the coming year are approved, and sometimes even earlier, in the middle of the year following. For instance, the Ninth Supreme Soviet of the Uzbek SSR usually considers and approves reports on the fulfilment of the state budgets in the summer of the year following.

In Hungary and Czechoslovakia, the supreme representative bodies likewise consider and approve reports on the state budget not at the end but in the middle of the following year, some six months after the actual completion of the budget. This further enhances the effectiveness of the control function of the representative body. So also does the regular consideration by the standing committees of the supreme representative bodies of matters relating to the fulfilment of current plans and budgets by the appropriate organs of state administration—a procedure followed in a number of socialist countries.

In some socialist countries the supreme representative bodies approve only the governments' reports relating to the fulfilment of the state budget. In others they also approve reports on the fulfilment of annual national economic plans. Art. 77(v) of the Rumanian Constitution makes provision for the preparation by the government of a report not only on the budget but also on the single national plan of social and economic development. In view of their close interdependence, it is desirable that reports on budget and plan fulfilment should be considered simultaneously when the supreme representative bodies are empowered to approve both budgets and plans.

Another form of preliminary control which has become widespread in the socialist countries is *hearing and discussion* by the sessions of supreme representative bodies of *government policy statements (declarations)* setting the main tasks facing newly-formed government and outlining measures for their fulfilment. The heads of government of the USSR, Poland, Czechoslovakia, Hungary, Bulgaria, the German Democratic Republic and the Korean People's Democratic Republic have made such statements at sessions of supreme representative bodies. These statements are as a rule the subject of vigorous discussion. Members, guided by the mandates they have received from their constituents, put forward many concrete proposals to implement the government's programme and criticise shortcomings in the work of ministries and departments. The discussion usually culminates in the adoption of an appropriate decision or resolution by the supreme organ of popular representation. In some countries, such as Poland, where the policy statement of the newly-appointed Chairman of the Government coincides with the presentation of the list of proposed new members of the Council of Ministers, no separate decision is taken on the statement. The supreme organ of popular representation expresses its approval of the statement in the form of a decision confirming the composition of the new government.

With a view to reinforcing the control function of the supreme representative bodies, the normative acts of a number of socialist countries (for example, Czechoslovakia) make consideration of a policy statement by a newly formed government at a session of the supreme representative body *juridically mandatory*. In the same way it is the practice of the Czechoslovak Federal Assembly to discuss reports by the government on the fulfilment of its policy statements. The fifth joint session of the two Houses of the Czechoslovak Federal Assembly in December 1972 and the 16th joint session in March 1975 debated the reports of the government on the fulfilment of its policy statement and approved its work.

The *submission by governments of executive provisions based on proposed new laws* together with the drafts of such laws is a new form of preliminary control. So also is the adoption by supreme representative bodies (usually in connection with the adoption of a law or decision) of *resolutions containing mandatory instructions* addressed to the government and relating to particular matters.

Hearing of the reports by the government to representative bodies on specific issues has in recent years become an increasingly frequently used form of retrospective control.

Hearing of the reports to representative bodies by individual Ministers is a new development of the control function. Such reports have become a regular part of the procedure of the Supreme Soviets of many Union republics, the Supreme Soviet of the USSR and the higher representative bodies of other socialist countries. The seventh session of the Sixth National Assembly of Bulgaria in June 1973 heard a report from the Minister of Internal Trade and Services. A detailed co-report was also presented by the Assembly's Standing Committee on Trade, Services and Tourism, containing many observations and proposals designed to improve the work of the ministries. The report and co-report were extensively debated, seven people's representatives participating in the discussion. The Assembly adopted a resolution on the report, indicating concrete measures and making the Minister responsible for the eradication of weaknesses and deficiencies.

The *standing committees (commissions)* of representative bodies play an important part in almost all aspects of the control function performed by these bodies. The committees study and discuss budgets and plans and reports on their fulfilment prior to their submission to the supreme representative body, and usually draft the resolutions and decisions adopted by supreme organs relating to the work of organs of state administration, etc.

The supervisory work of the standing committees (commissions) has greatly increased in recent years. This has been assisted by the increase in their number, and also by the increase in the number of members taking part in their work.

The commissions discuss the work of the various organs of state administration, adopt decisions and recommendations which are referred to Councils of Ministers and the appropriate ministries.

Their decisions and recommendations are not mandatory from the legal point of view and are of a consultative nature, but this does not mean that administrative organs can ignore them. Firstly, it is laid down that the bodies to which commission's proposals are addressed *must consider them within a strictly defined time limit and inform the commission of the results* of such consideration. Secondly, if a commission considers that its recommendations have been rejected without grounds, it may appeal to the supreme representative body or, in periods between sessions, to the higher collegiate organ of state power, submitting an appropriate draft resolution which after approval by these bodies becomes *legally mandatory*. In practice, the overwhelming majority of the recommendations of commissions, being correct and well-founded, are implemented by administrative bodies.

The constitutions of the socialist countries lay down that, as a part of their control function, supreme representative bodies may appoint *investigation and audit commissions* on any matter.

The *right of interpellation* (the deputy's inquiry) is also an important means of exercising control. The new standing orders of the supreme representative bodies, laying down in detail the procedure of submitting and answering inquiries, establish sound guarantees for the effectiveness of this form of control. In a number of socialist countries the range of those to whom inquiries may be addressed has been extended with a view to further enhancing the effectiveness of control. In all socialist countries inquiries may be addressed to the government and its members; additionally, in Hungary members of the National Assembly may address inquiries to the Presidium, State Secretaries, the Chairman of the Supreme Court and the Procurator-General. In Poland and Rumania provision is also made for the deputies' inquiries not only to the government (in Poland to the Chairman of the Council of Ministers) and its members, but also to the Procurator-General and in Rumania also to the Chairman of the Supreme Court.[1] In a number of European socialist countries deputies of supreme organs of popular representation make extensive use of these rights. For instance, deputies of the Fifth and Sixth Hungarian National Assemblies (1967-1971 and 1971-1975) submitted more than 30 inquiries in each Assembly. It is impossible, of course, to judge the effectiveness of the controlling work of a representative body solely on the basis of a mechanical comparison of the number of inquiries. Their small number or even absence is due to the fact that direct forms of contact

---

[1] In Rumania the deputies' inquiries and questions to the Chairman of the Supreme Court and the Procurator-General are subject to supervision by the Grand National Assembly.

between deputies and the government had evolved above all at meetings of the standing committees, at which deputies receive immediate clarifications from members of the government on all matters of concern to them and may include their own proposals in the recommendations of the committees. This, however, in no way diminishes the significance of the right of inquiry, which plays an important part in ensuring that government bodies are subject to the control of supreme representative bodies. Members of the Fifth Seym (1969-1972) submitted 35 interpellations, of which 34 were in 1971—that is, after the work of representative bodies had been re-vitalised on the initiative of the Politbureau of the Central Committee of the Polish United Workers' Party.

The Seym exercises a unique form of *control over the implementation by state organs of the proposals and recommendations of electors*. It held a special meeting to discuss the implementation of the proposals and recommendations in February 1967. Its standing committees also consider proposals and recommendations relevant to their sphere of competence.

Special mention should be made of a feature of Polish state law. In Poland, the establishment of a special organ of state control—the Supreme Chamber of Control—directly subordinate to the Seym, and, within limits laid down by the law, to the Council of State, had great significance as regards the strengthening of the control function of the Seym. Following the establishment of this chamber, the Seym began annually to consider not only the reports of the government on plan and budget fulfilment, but also the Supreme Chamber's comments on these reports and its recommendations regarding the approval of the government's economic policy during the year under review.

The Supreme Chamber of Control presents to the Presidium of the Seym reports on investigations conducted on the instructions of the Seym or having particularly great significance. These reports are considered by the standing committees of the Seym; if necessary, they may be considered by plenary meetings of the Seym. The Chairman of the Supreme Chamber of Control gives the necessary explanations and makes information available at the request of the Seym.

The standing committees of the Seym and the Supreme Chamber of Control co-operate closely. The committees are authorised to instruct the Chamber (through the Presidium of the Seym) to carry out particular assignments. On the basis of proposals from the committees, the Chairman of the Chamber assigns representatives to assist commissions investigating the work of state enterprises, establishments and organisations. On the instructions of the Presidium of the Seym, representatives of the Chamber are also assigned to assist *ad hoc* commissions in investigating any particular matter. Representatives of the Chamber attend meetings of commissions, give explanations and make information available.

CHAPTER XI

HIGHER ORGANS OF STATE POWER ELECTED BY SUPREME REPRESENTATIVE BODIES

In addition to supreme representative bodies, the system of supreme organs of state power of the socialist countries also includes higher organs of state power elected by these bodies.

In a number of socialist countries these are confined to collegiate higher organs of state power. They include the Presidiums of the Supreme Soviets in the USSR, the State Council in Bulgaria, the Councils of State in the German Democratic Republic and Poland, the Presidium in Hungary, the Presidium of the People's Assembly in Albania, the Presidium of the People's Great Khural in Mongolia and the Standing Committee of the All-China Assembly of People's Representatives in the PRC.

Both collegiate and individual organs of state power are set up in other countries: the Standing Committee of the National Assembly and the President in the Democratic Republic of Vietnam; the Standing Council of the Supreme People's Assembly, the Central People's Committee and the President in the Korean People's Democratic Republic; the State Council and the President in Rumania; the Presidium of the Federal Assembly and the President in Czechoslovakia;[1] the Presidency and the President in Yugoslavia.[2] In

---

[1] In the Czech and Slovak SSRs there are only Presidiums of the National Councils.

[2] The office of the President of Yugoslavia has since 1971 been

the Korean People's Democratic Republic, Rumania and Yugoslavia the President heads the supreme collegiate organ of state power (the People's Committee in the case of the Korean People's Democratic Republic).

Unacceptable views regarding the legal nature of higher collegiate organs of state power are expressed in socialist literature. They are described as "organs of the supreme representative body", a "part of the supreme representative organ" or as a "component part of the system of the supreme representative organ".[1]

Such descriptions do not correspond to the real nature of the higher collegiate organs of state power in the socialist countries. The term "organs of the supreme representative body" is usually applied to their internal auxiliary organs. The fact that higher collegiate organs are, as a rule, elected by the supreme representative bodies from among their membership and are usually fully accountable to them does not constitute grounds for describing them as "organs" or a "part of" a supreme representative body. On these grounds it would be possible to describe the government, the Supreme Court and the Procurator-General, which in the majority of socialist countries are elected or appointed by the supreme representative body in the main from among its members and which are accountable to it, as "organs" of the supreme representative body.

Those who see the higher collegiate organs as "organs" or a "part of" the supreme representative body also base their argument upon their title. In a number of socialist

---

regarded as existent only while this office is held by J. Broz Tito. Subsequently the powers exercised by the President will pass on to the Presidency of the SFRY. Only Presidencies function in republics and autonomous provinces.

[1] See *Sovietskoye gosudarstvennoye pravo*, Gosyurizdat, Moscow, 1948, pp. 357-58; B.P. Kravtsov, *Verkhovny Soviet SSSR*, Gosyurizdat, Moscow, 1954, p. 78; A. I. Lepyoshkin, A. I. Kim, N. G. Mishin, P. I. Romanov, *Kurs sovietskogo gosudarstvennogo prava*, Vol. 2, p. 431; B. Spasov, A. Angelov, *Derzhavno pravo na Narodna Republika Bulgaria*, p. 274.

countries they are termed the Presidium of the National Assembly, the Presidium of the Great People's Khural, etc. But it would be more correct to propose more suitable titles than to regard their present titles, which inaccurately reflect their place in the system of state organs, as grounds for a definition of their legal status.

A higher collegiate organ of state power is not a "part of" a supreme representative body, but a *special organ* with extensive *independent powers*.

A more fitting title would be one which excludes the possibility of an incorrect interpretation of their legal status as "organs" or a "part of" a supreme representative body. In the socialist countries such titles as Council of State (Poland, the German Democratic Republic), State Council (Rumania, Bulgaria) are becoming more common. In Hungary, the higher collegiate body of state power is known as the Presidium of the Hungarian People's Republic (not of the National Assembly).

Despite variations in title, composition and powers, the organisation and functions of the higher collegiate bodies are based on common principles. These are: election by the supreme representative bodies; their collegiate character; the absence, as a rule, of powers which would enable them to set themselves against the supreme representative body; accountability in every aspect of their work usually to the supreme representative body.

Under the constitutions of the majority of socialist countries, the collegiate organs are elected at the first meeting of a newly elected supreme representative body from among its members. In the case of the Constitution of the German Democratic Republic election to the Council of State is not confined exclusively to members of the People's Chamber. But in practice the present Council of State is made up only of members of the Chamber. Neither does the Constitution of the Korean People's Democratic Republic provide for the election only of deputies of the Supreme People's Assembly to the Central People's Committee. The formation of

Yugoslav Presidencies also follows a special procedure which will be considered separately owing to several other distinctive features. The genuinely representative, popular character of the supreme organs of state power is also manifest in the genuinely representative, popular composition of the collegiate organs of state power elected by them.

The collegiate organs include a chairman, his deputies, a secretary and members.

Since the higher collegiate organ of state power exercises control over a number of other state bodies this gives rise to the question of whether members may simultaneously hold leading posts in bodies accountable to the higher collegiate organ.

In the majority of socialist countries, members of the government may not serve on higher collegiate organs of state power. In Hungary this is laid down in the Constitution; in the majority of other countries it is a question of practice.

Such a rule is an *additional guarantee* of the effectiveness of the control exercised by the higher collegiate organ over the government. However, there are certain distinctive features in some countries.

In the German Democratic Republic, the Chairman of the Council of Ministers has been elected as a deputy of the Chairman of the State Council ever since this body was established. But in 1973 this practice was discontinued.

The election of the Chairman of the Council of Ministers to the State Council was also permitted under Art. 35 of the 1952 Rumanian Constitution as amended by the law of March 21, 1961.[1] The 1965 Constitution contains no similar provision. The head of the Rumanian Government has not served on the Council since 1969.

In the Korean People's Democratic Republic the Prime-Minister and members of the Administration Council are elected to the Central People's Committee.

---

[1] See *Buletinul oficial al Marii Adunări Naţionale a RPR* No. 9, 1961.

The higher collegiate organs have wide powers. These may be classified as follows:

1. Powers relating to the *organisation and functioning of the supreme representative bodies* form a special group. Higher collegiate organs of several countries call elections, form constituencies, establish the procedure and principles governing the formation of constituency and polling station electoral commissions and sometimes approve standard forms for ballot papers, voting returns of polling station and constituency electoral commissions and certificates of election as a member of a supreme organ of state power. Higher collegiate organs of many countries convene sessions of supreme representative bodies.

These powers should be categorised in a special group because it is a question of powers with respect to the organisation and functioning of a *superior body*. From this arises the *special* character of the exercise of these powers.

This finds expression firstly in the fact that discretionary limits with respect to these questions are reduced to the minimum. For instance, elections must be held and the first session of a newly elected supreme body convened within time-limits laid down by the constitution. A minimum number of sessions must also be convened during a year.

Supreme organs of state power may also influence the decisions of collegiate organs accountable to them on these questions. In some countries standing orders make express provisions for this. Par. 19 (iv) of the Standing Orders of the Hungarian National Assembly lays down that the Assembly itself may determine the date of its next session. In other countries a similar procedure has arisen through custom and practice. On October 24, 1956, because the Polish Seym still had before it a number of important items to discuss and it was therefore necessary to prolong the session and impossible to call new elections while the session was still in progress, the Seym resolved to call upon the Council of State that it amend its resolution of September 24, 1956 calling elections, and call elections on January 20, 1957. The

Council of State carried out this decision and altered the date of the elections.

The 1972 Statute on the work of the Bulgarian National Assembly lays down that the Assembly shall work in accordance with a plan which it itself approves. The provisions of the plan regarding the dates of sessions are mandatory for the State Council.

2. *Powers in the sphere of legislation* are an important category. These include the right to initiate legislation and promulgate normative decrees, resolutions and decisions.

Acts establishing mandatory interpretations of laws are a special aspect of the legislative activity of higher collegiate organs of state power. In our view, these interpretations are a form of legislative activity since, in giving concrete form to a law, they in effect establish new norms.

3. In a number of countries, higher collegiate organs of state power are invested with *powers in respect of the organisation and functioning of the state organs subject to their control and supervision*. In periods between sessions of the supreme representative body they, on the recommendation of the head of government, appoint and dismiss individual members of the government.

In Poland the election of the Supreme Court and the appointment of the Procurator-General is a matter for the Council of State alone. In Hungary all judges are elected by the Presidium. In the Korean People's Democratic Republic the Standing Council of the Supreme People's Assembly elects and recalls the judges and people's assessors of the Central Court.

In Rumania, in the intervals between sessions of the Grand National Assembly the State Council appoints and dismisses the Prime-Minister. In addition, if the Grand National Assembly is unable to meet because of special circumstances, the State Council can appoint and dismiss the entire Council of Ministers and Supreme Court.

The Hungarian Constitution lays down that in the intervals between sessions of the National Assembly the Presidium may exercise all the functions of the National Assembly with the exception of those relating to the amendment of the Constitution. But in practice the work of the Hungarian Presidium does not differ greatly in this respect from that of similar bodies in other socialist countries.

In exercising control over the work of the government, the Supreme Court and the Procurator's Office, higher collegiate organs of state power can usually receive reports from the government, its members, the Chairman of the Supreme Court and from the Procurator-General (Chief Procurator). They usually have this power during the intervals between sessions of the supreme representative bodies. In Poland, since the Supreme Court and the Procurator-General are appointed directly by the Council of State, there is no such limitation with respect to these bodies. In Bulgaria, control over the work of the Council of Ministers and leaders of national organs of state administration is among the permanent powers of the State Council.

The higher collegiate organs of state power also call and supervise local elections, and supervise the activity of local organs of state power.

4. Higher collegiate organs have wide powers in *the sphere of foreign relations and defence*. They usually appoint and recall the republic's diplomatic representatives abroad, receive the letters of credence and recall of foreign diplomatic representatives and ratify and denounce international agreements.

In Bulgaria the acceptance of letters of credence and recall are among the independent powers of the Chairman of the State Council.

The 1971 Bulgarian Constitution also lays down that the National Assembly itself ratifies and denounces treaties, while giving similar power to the State Council.

In the intervals between the sessions of supreme representative bodies higher collegiate organs of state power may declare a state of war in the event of armed attack upon the republic or in fulfilment of international treaties relating to joint defence against aggression. In some countries, when the interests of the defence or security of the state demand it, higher collegiate organs of state power may declare martial law in particular localities or over the whole country. They may also declare general or partial mobilisation.

5. In addition to the powers already enumerated, higher collegiate organs of state power *make civil and military appointments, confer orders, medals and titles of honour, and exercise the right of pardon and other powers* under the legislation of the country concerned. These powers are usually assigned to these organs in the countries where there is no presidential office.

The *subordinate status* of the higher collegiate organs *vis-à-vis* the supreme representative bodies finds its expression *in the powers* with which they are invested.

In the first place, most important powers, such as the adoption and amendment of the fundamental law of the republic—its constitution—and of ordinary laws, and in the majority of countries also the formation of the government as a whole, the Supreme Court as a whole and the appointment of the Procurator-General, lie within the *exclusive competence* of the supreme representative bodies.

In addition, some of the acts taken by higher collegiate organs require *mandatory* subsequent *approval* by the supreme representative body. These include those relating to matters which *during sessions* are decided *solely* by supreme representative bodies and by higher collegiate organs only in the intervals between sessions.

Such acts are of both a normative and non-normative character.

In Albania and the Mongolian People's Republic, all normative acts of the Presidium of the People's Assembly and the Great People's Khural require confirmation by the supreme representative body.

In Poland, Rumania and Hungary, the normative acts of higher collegiate organs for which subsequent approval is mandatory include only those decrees or decisions which have the force of law.[1] The constitution and the standing orders of the higher government organs of these countries, by introducing the term "decree (decision) having the force of law", underline the role and significance of these decrees. They are decrees relating to issues which require legislative regulation. Such decrees may amend laws and must therefore be confirmed by the higher organs of state power, which are the sole legislative bodies. The constitutions of several socialist countries categorically exclude any possibility of constitutional amendment arising from any acts of a higher collegiate organ of state power, including decrees which have the force of law. Art. 64 (i) of the Rumanian Constitution lays down that it cannot under any circumstances be amended even by acts of the State Council which have the force of law. The Hungarian Constitution (Par. 30 v), while making provision for the Presidium to exercise the functions of the National Assembly in intervals between sessions, excludes functions relating to the amendment of the Constitution.

Other less important normative acts of the higher collegiate organs of these countries do not require subsequent approval. The Polish Council of State and the Hungarian Presidium have adopted a number of normative resolutions (decisions) relating to local government bodies, which are not subject to subsequent approval.

This division of the normative acts of higher collegiate bodies into those which are subject to approval and those which are not seems to be legitimate. It is not expedient to approve all the normative acts of a higher collegiate organ, regardless of their significance. A procedure by which the Council of Ministers, Ministers, and local organs of state power and administration subordinate to the higher collegiate

---

[1] In Hungary decisions which have the force of law may also be nonnormative. Approval of decisions of the Presidium which have the force of law is tacit: they must be placed before the next session of the National Assembly and are held to be approved in so far as the Assembly does not reject or amend them.

body may within their terms of reference promulgate normative acts not subject to approval by superior bodies, while the higher collegiate organ has no such power, does not correspond to the status of each organ in the state system. It is another matter when it is a question of normative decrees dealing with matters requiring legislative regulation.

The strengthening of the democratic foundations of the work of the higher organs of state power in the socialist countries is accompanied by a reduction in the number of normative decrees in favour of an increase in the legislative activity of the supreme representative bodies. The Polish Council of State has since 1957 virtually ceased to promulgate decrees having the force of law.

The non-normative acts of higher collegiate bodies which are subject to subsequent approval include decrees relating to changes in the composition of the government.

The higher collegiate organs are in all their work responsible and accountable to the supreme representative bodies, which may at any time recall either individual members or their entire membership.

In those countries in which there is a higher individual organ of power alongside the collegiate organ, the powers which in other socialist countries belong only to the higher collegiate organ are divided between the two higher organs of state power, and in the Korean People's Democratic Republic even three organs.

Features common to these countries[1] are: the election of both the collegiate and individual organ by the supreme representative body; the definition of the powers of both organs in a manner which ensures that both of them together do not have powers which enable them to oppose the supreme representative body; the complete accountability of both the collegiate and the individual organs to the supreme representative body, which may at any time recall both.

---

[1] The features of Yugoslavia are considered below.

The status and powers of the higher (collegiate and individual) organs of state power accountable to the supreme representative body have distinctive features in each country.

In the Democratic Republic of Vietnam, where the Standing Committee of the National Assembly and the President are elected for the entire term of office of the Assembly, the powers of the Standing Committee include:

1. As regards the supreme organ of state power—the appointment and supervision of elections, and the convening of sessions of the supreme representative body.

2. As regards legislation—the right to initiate legislation, promulgate normative decrees and to give mandatory interpretations of laws.

3. As regards the organisation and functioning of state organs accountable to the Standing Committee—the appointment and dismissal of Deputy Prime Ministers and other members of the government during intervals between sessions of the Assembly; the appointment and dismissal of the Chairman's Deputies, members of the Supreme Court, the Procurators-General's Deputies and other senior officials of the Supreme People's Procurator's Office, and control over the work of the government, the Supreme People's Court and the Supreme People's Procurator's Office. As part of its function of control over the work of state organs accountable to it, the Standing Committee may rescind resolutions and decisions of the government which are unconstitutional or contrary to laws and decrees. It may also rescind incorrect decisions of local organs of state power of administrative-territorial units subordinate to the centre.

4. As regards foreign policy and defence—the appointment and recall of plenipotentiaries abroad; the ratification and denunciation of international treaties and agreements; the institution and award of military titles and diplomatic and other ranks; general or partial mobilisation; the proclamation of martial law. In intervals between sessions of the National Assembly the Standing Committee declares a state

of war in the event of an attack upon the republic or in fulfilment of treaty obligations relating to joint defence against aggression.

5. The Standing Committee institutes and confers orders and titles of honour, exercises the right of pardon and other powers bestowed upon it by the Assembly.

The Constitution of the Democratic Republic of Vietnam also gives the Standing Committee authority to conduct a nation-wide referendum.

The President of the Republic occupies a unique position in the system of higher organs of state power in the Democratic Republic of Vietnam. His powers fall into two categories: 1) those which he exercises only on the basis of appropriate decisions of the Assembly or its Standing Committee, and 2) those which he exercises independently.

The first category includes: the promulgation of laws and decrees; the appointment and dismissal of the Prime-Minister and other members of the government; the appointment and dismissal of the Deputy Chairmen and members of the collegiate body responsible for the country's defence (the State Defence Council); the promulgation of decrees proclaiming martial law and mobilisation, and the declaration of a state of war; the ratification of international treaties and agreements; the appointment and dismissal of the republic's plenipotentiary representatives to foreign states; the award of orders and titles of honour; the promulgation of decrees relating to amnesty and pardon.

The second category includes: the representation of the republic in international relations; the reception of the diplomatic representatives of foreign states; the exercise of the functions of Commander-in-Chief of the Armed Forces (the President of the Republic is *ex officio* Commander-in-Chief of the Armed Forces and Chairman of the State Defence Council); the convening of the higher consultative organ of the republic.

The higher consultative organ—the Special Political Conference—for which provision is made in the Constitution, is a distinctive feature of the state law of the Democratic Republic of Vietnam. Such a conference may be convened in case of need by the President of the Republic, who also presides over it. The conference includes: the Deputy President of the Republic, the Chairman of the Standing Committee of the National Assembly, the head of the government and others. Its purpose is to discuss vital national issues and make recommendations which the President of the Republic refers to the supreme representative body, its Standing Committee, and to the government and other bodies for discussion and decision.

In Czechoslovakia, although there are two higher organs of state power subordinate to the supreme representative body, their powers and status differ greatly. This is manifested firstly in the special status of the Presidium of the Federal Assembly *vis-à-vis* the Assembly itself, and secondly in a division of powers between the collegiate and individual organ which differs from that in the Democratic Republic of Vietnam.

The Presidium of the Czechoslovak Federal Assembly, unlike collegiate organs of state power in other socialist countries, has a dual function. On the one hand, it is a higher collegiate organ of state power, and is therefore vested with a number of independent powers as regards the promulgation of normative and other acts. On the other hand, the Presidium fulfils the functions of an *internal directing body* of the Federal Assembly. Hence *in part* its powers are wider than those of higher collegiate organs in other socialist countries. It has a number of functions with respect to the work of the Federal Assembly which in other countries are performed by special internal directing organs. In addition, apart from the customary powers of a collegiate state body, such as those relating to the appointment of elections to the Federal Assembly and local organs of state power, the Constitutional Law on the Czechoslovak Federation defines the Presidium's powers more widely than is the case in the majority of socialist countries. When the

Federal Assembly is not meeting because the session has concluded or because its term of office has expired, the Presidium assumes the powers of the Federal Assembly except those relating to the election of the President, the adoption and amendment of constitutional laws and the state budget, the declaration of war and the adoption of a vote of no confidence in the government. If the Assembly does not meet because of special circumstances, its Presidium assumes all its functions except those relating to the amendment of the Constitution and election of the President of Czechoslovakia. In the intervals between sessions of the Federal Assembly matters which require legislative regulation are regulated by the Presidium by legislative decisions. These must bear the signature of the President, the Chairman of the Federal Assembly and the Chairman of the Government and be promulgated in the same manner as laws. Decisions of the Presidium adopted in these circumstances are subject to approval by the next session of the Assembly. Otherwise they become invalid.

The powers of the Presidium of the Czechoslovak Federal Assembly are therefore in many respects wider than those of the higher collegiate organs of state power of the majority of other socialist countries. But some of the powers exercised by these organs in other socialist countries are exercised in Czechoslovakia by the President, not the Presidium.

The Czechoslovak President represents the state in international relations; concludes and ratifies international treaties; convenes sessions of the Federal Assembly and submits draft measures for its consideration; may require information from the government and individual members; receives and accredits ambassadors; appoints senior government officials and confers the rank of general; confers awards, exercises the right of amnesty, pardon and mitigation of the punishment; declares martial law (on the recommendation of the government). In addition, the President announces the closure of sessions of the Federal Assembly; signs laws adopted by the Federal Assembly and the legislative measures of its Presidium; he may inform the Federal Assembly on the state of the nation and on major political issues; he appoints and dismisses the Chairman and other members of the government and entrusts them with the direction of ministries and other central organs of state administration; he may attend and preside at meetings of the government and also discuss topical matters with the government and its individual members; he is the Commander-in-Chief of the Armed Forces; on the basis of decisions of the Federal Assembly he may declare war in the event of an attack upon the republic or in fulfilment of international obligations relating to joint defence against aggression; he appoints the Chairman and members of the State Defence Council.

The President also exercises other powers with which he is invested under the law.

In the Democratic Republic of Vietnam, the Korean People's Democratic Republic and Rumania the President of the Republic is elected for the term of office of the National Assembly at the first session of each new Assembly. In Czechoslovakia, on the other hand, there is no link between elections to the Federal Assembly and the election of the President, although the term of office of the President (since 1971) is the same as that of the Federal Assembly—five years. Elections to the Federal Assembly were held in November 1971, while the last Presidential election took place in March 1973.

In Cuba, the features of the status and powers of the President are determined by the distinctive features of its present system of higher state organs, and above all by the absence of an elected supreme representative body and the consequent special status and powers of the Cabinet.

The Cuban President has the following powers:

a) *In the sphere of legislation,* he approves and promulgates laws adopted by the Cabinet and ensures their fulfilment; he issues decisions to ensure the fulfilment of laws, and also instructions on administrative matters in strict conformity with the law; he submits draft laws and decisions for Cabinet approval; he submits the draft annual budget to the Cabinet for approval 60 days before it is due to come into force.

b) *In the sphere of relations with other bodies,* the President appoints the Prime Minister and Ministers. With the approval of the Cabinet, he appoints the Chairman of the Supreme Court and a number of other senior officials.

c) *In the sphere of foreign relations and defence,* he conducts diplomatic negotiations and concludes treaties with other states, submitting them for mandatory approval by the Cabinet; appoints members of the diplomatic missions of the Republic in foreign states; receives diplomatic representatives and sanctions the establishment of foreign consulates; commands the armed forces and ensures the defence of the national territory.

In addition, the Cuban President exercises the right of pardon and certain other powers under the Fundamental Law and other legislation.

In the Korean People's Democratic Republic, the 1972 Constitution replaced the former Presidium of the Supreme People's Assembly by three higher state organs which may be considered organs of state power.

There is firstly the Standing Council of the Supreme People's Assembly, which the Constitution defines as the permanent organ of the Assembly. Like the Presidium of the Czechoslovak Federal Assembly, the Standing Council is not merely an internal directing organ of the Assembly; it is also an independent organ of state. It is made up of a Chairman, his deputies, a secretary and members. The Chairman of the Standing Council is simultaneously Chairman of the Supreme People's Assembly; the position of his deputies is similar. In the intervals between sessions of the Supreme People's Assembly the Standing Council may discuss and approve draft laws and amend existing legislation subject to approval by the Assembly. In addition, the powers of the Council include: the interpretation of existing laws, the convening of sessions of the Assembly, the holding of elections to the Supreme People's Assembly, work with members and, in intervals between sessions, with the commissions of the Assembly, the appointment of elections to local People's Assemblies, and the election and recall of judges and People's Assessors of the Central Court. In exercising its powers, the Standing Council adopts ordinances.

The Central People's Committee, defined by the Constitution as a higher directing organ of state power, is a second permanently functioning higher collegiate organ. This body is elected by the Assembly for a term of four years—that is, for the same term as the Assembly itself. It consists of the President of the Korean People's Democratic Republic and (on his recommendation) the vice-presidents, a secretary and members. Its powers include: the determination of home and foreign policy; the direction of the work of the Administration Council (government), local People's Assemblies and people's committees, judicial bodies and of organs of justice and the Procurator's Office; direction of national defence and political security; control over the fulfilment of the Constitution, laws, Presidential acts and of acts taken by the Committee itself and the repeal of acts of government bodies which are at variance with these, the formation and abolition of ministries; the appointment and dismissal of other members of the Administration Council on the recommendation of the Premier of the Council; the appointment and recall of ambassadors and envoys; the appointment and dismissal of the High Command of the Armed Forces and the conferring of the rank of general; the institution of orders and medals, titles of honour, and military and diplomatic ranks; the award of orders and medals and the conferring of titles of honour; the proclamation of amnesties; the establishment and amendment of administrative and territorial divisions; and in extraordinary circumstances the declaration of war and mobilisation. The Central People's Committee forms auxiliary bodies: a Domestic Policy

Committee, a Foreign Policy Committee, a Defence Committee and a Justice and Security Committee. It adopts decrees, ordinances and instructions. It is responsible to the Supreme People's Assembly.

The President of the Korean People's Democratic Republic is seen by the Constitution as a special organ. In accordance with Art. 89, he is the Head of State and represents the state authority of the Korean People's Democratic Republic. In addition to the leadership of the Central People's Committee, his powers include the convening in case of need of meetings of the Administration Council and the guidance of their work; the leadership of the Armed Forces (the President is the Supreme Commander-in-Chief and Chairman of the Defence Committee); the promulgation of laws of the Supreme People's Assembly, decrees of the Central People's Committee and ordinances of the Standing Council of the Supreme People's Assembly; the exercise of the right of pardon; the ratification and denunciation of international treaties; the acceptance of letters of credence and recall of foreign diplomatic representatives. The President issues orders. He is responsible to the Supreme People's Assembly.

The composition of the higher government organs formed on the basis of the new Constitution[1] shows that membership of the Standing Council is incompatible with membership of the Central People's Committee and Administration Council, while the Premier of the Administration Council, his deputies and a number of members of the Council are at the same time members of the Central People's Committee.

In Yugoslavia, the higher organs of state power have developed in a complex way. Originally, the 1946 Yugoslav Constitution instituted the Presidencies of People's Skupshinas as higher, permanently functioning collegiate organs of state power. The 1953 Constitutional Law abolished these

---

[1] *Novaya Koreya* No. 295, 1973, pp. 51-53.

organs and instituted the office of President who simultaneously headed the government—the Federal Executive Council (in republics and the autonomous province[1] some powers exercised by the Federal President belonged to chairmen of Executive Councils). The 1963 Yugoslav Constitution divided the offices of President and the Chairman of the Federal Executive Council, but in republics and autonomous provinces chairmen of Executive Councils continued to exercise certain functions vested in the President in the Federation. The federal higher organs of power were substantially reformed in June 1971 when, in particular, the 36th and 37th constitutional amendments were adopted. The 36th amendment instituted the Presidency of the SFRY and referred to it, among other things, the powers earlier exercised by the President. But the 37th amendment gave the Federal Skupshina the right to elect J. Broz Tito as President of the Republic considering his historical role and granting the recommendation of republican and provincial Skupshinas. So the President headed the Presidency in his own right and, moreover, personally exercised a number of its functions. This system has been retained in principle by the 1974 Constitution which also provided for Presidencies in republics and autonomous provinces.

According to Art. 321 of the 1974 Yugoslav Constitution, the Presidency of the SFRY includes one representative from each republic and autonomous province. These are elected and recalled by secret ballot at the joint sitting of all chambers of a respective Skupshina. Moreover, the chairman of the League of Communists of Yugoslavia is an *ex officio* member of the Yugoslav Presidency. The Presidency members serve for a term of five years and cannot be elected more than two times running. If a Presidency member has been long unable to fulfil his obligations he is replaced by the Chairman of the Presidency of the republic or autonomous province concerned.

---

[1] At the time only Vojvodina had the status of an autonomous province.

The Presidency represents Yugoslavia at home and abroad and co-ordinates the common interests of the republics and provinces concerning their participation in the exercise of the federation's rights and duties; it is the higher organ of leadership and command of the Armed Forces and initiates measures and co-ordinates activities by competent bodies in foreign policy and state security. The Presidency may submit proposals to the Skupshina of the SFRY on approving home and foreign policy, on adopting laws and other acts; it proposes the Skupshina a candidate for the office of the Chairman of the Federal Executive Council and announces the Skupshina's decision on electing this Council; decrees federal laws; nominates members of the Yugoslav Constitutional Court; appoints and recalls ambassadors and envoys of the Socialist Federal Republic of Yugoslavia, receives the letters of credence and recall of foreign diplomatic representatives, promulgates documents on the ratification of international treaties; appoints, promotes and dismisses supreme military leaders, members of military tribunals and military Procurators; submits proposals on the election and dismissal of members of the Federal Council; confers orders; exercises the right of pardon of persons convicted for crimes according to the federal law; approves the basic plans and preparatory measures for national defence and carries out other measures in this field.

If necessary, the Presidency of the SFRY determines the appearance of direct military threat, announces general and partial mobilisation and declares martial law if the Yugoslav Skupshina is unable to meet in session. In time of war or if a direct military danger has arisen, the Presidency on its own initiative or on the recommendation of the Federal Executive Council adopts decisions on matters within the terms of reference of the Yugoslav Skupshina and submits them for the Skupshina's approval as soon as it meets. These decisions can suspend the action of certain constitutional provisions relating to the adoption of normative acts, to the adoption of measures by federal administrative organs on the basis of the consent of authoritative republican and provincial bodies, to certain freedoms, rights and duties of man and citizen, to the rights of self-managing organisations and communities, and to the membership and powers of executive and administrative bodies.

The Presidency informs the Skupshina of the SFRY on the problems of home and foreign policy and can suggest that it adopt decisions on certain matters, while the Skupshina can, in its turn, request the Presidency's opinion on matters within its competence. Unless the Skupshina's authoritative chamber agrees to the Presidency's proposal on the approval of home and foreign policy, on the adoption of a law or another measure or on the delay of its adoption, the chamber and the Presidency jointly define the procedure for discussing the contestable issue and appoint the term for co-ordinating their views, which cannot exceed six months. If an agreement has not been reached by this time the question is removed from the agenda and can again be included on the demand of the Presidency or by a decision of the chamber concerned. If agreement has not been reached in three months after the second discussion of the contestable issue, the Skupshina's chamber is dissolved and the Presidency's powers are annulled. Elections of the chamber are appointed within 15 days after the dissolution and the elections of the Presidency are held not later than 15 days after the formation of a new chamber; the former Presidency sits in office until then.

The Presidency of the SFRY has several powers in relation to the Federal Executive Council. The Presidency may express its opinion on the Council's activity, and can demand that it conduct the policy approved and fulfil the laws and other measures of the Skupshina; it can convene the Council's meetings and place certain questions on their agendas; it can suspend the enforcement of the Council's decisions of general political significance prior to their announcement (in this case they are brought to the discussion and decision by the Skupshina's authoritative chamber); it can place the question of the confidence in the Federal Executive Council before the Skupshina of the SFRY.

The Presidency elects its Chairman and his deputies from among its members for one year and in succession established by its Standing Orders. Should martial law be introduced, the Presidency can prolong the Chairman's powers or elect its other member to President ahead of time. The Presidency works on the basis of the co-ordinated position of its members and is responsible for the observance of the Yugoslav Constitution.

The Presidency's Chairman represents the Socialist Federal Republic of Yugoslavia on behalf of the Presidency, represents the Presidency, convenes its meetings and guides them, signs its acts and takes steps to implement them, promulgates documents on the ratification of international treaties and receives the letters of credence and recall of foreign diplomatic representatives, commands the Armed Forces on behalf of the Presidency and exercises certain rights and duties on behalf of the Presidency when it is unable to meet in session in case of martial law or other extraordinary circumstances. The Chairman heads the National Defence Council formed by the Presidency.

The Presidency may convene the Federal Council elected from among public figures, politicians, scholars and workers in arts to consider general political issues, and may assign certain tasks to its members.

In view of the historical role played by J. Broz Tito, the Yugoslav Constitution granted the Skupshina the right to elect him President of the Republic, without limiting the term of his mandate, on the recommendation of republican and provincial Skupshinas. This was actually done on May 16, 1974. The President represents the Socialist Federal Republic of Yugoslavia; he is the Chairman of the Presidency of the SFRY, the Supreme Commander-in-Chief of the Armed Forces and the Chairman of the National Defence Council. He decrees federal laws, announces the Skupshina's decision on the election of the Federal Executive Council, appoints and recalls ambassadors and envoys, receives the letters of credence and recall of foreign diplomatic representatives, promulgates documents on the ratification of international treaties, confers orders, defines the appearance of direct war danger, announces general or partial mobilisation and introduces martial law if the Yugoslav Skupshina and the Presidency of the SFRY cannot meet in session, and sets up services to help him exercise his powers. In the event of war or direct military danger and if the Presidency cannot meet in session, the President promulgates decisions having the force of law on matters within the Skupshina's terms of reference and submits them for its approval as soon as it meets. The President informs the Skupshina on political problems and can suggest that it settle certain questions. He can convene a meeting of the Federal Executive Council, place questions on its agenda and preside over it; he can convene the Federal Council and assign some task to its member; he can convene a joint meeting of the Presidency of the SFRY and the Federal Executive Council and guide its work. The President can assign certain tasks within his terms of reference to the Deputy Chairman of the Yugoslav Presidency.

The President's functions over, the Presidency of the SFRY exercises all its constitutional rights and duties.

Republican and provincial Presidencies are elected by appropriate Skupshinas on the recommendation of conferences of the Working People's Socialist League. Chairmen of republican and provincial organisations the League of Communists Yugoslavia and, in several republics and in both autonomous provinces, also chairmen of the Skupshinas are *ex officio* members of the Presidency; the Presidency of the Socialist Republic of Serbia also includes, *ex officio,* chairmen of the Presidencies of the autonomous provinces. The powers of republican and provincial Presidencies are similar to those of the Presidency of the SFRY, but republican and provincial constitutions do not provide for the possibility of a dispute between the Presidency and the Skupshina.

The office of the President of the Socialist Republic of Rumania was instituted in March 1974. This involved changes in the terms of reference of the Grand National Assembly and the State Council some powers of which were transferred to the President.

At present the permanent powers of the Rumanian State Council include: establishment of the date of election to representative institutions; organisation of ministries and other central state bodies; ratification and denunciation of international treaties except for those within the competence of the Grand National Assembly; establishment of military ranks; institution of awards and titles of honour. In the period between the sessions of the Grand National Assembly the State Council may establish norms having the force of law, without amending the Constitution. These norms must be presented to the Grand National Assembly at its next session for consideration according to the legislative procedure. The State Council may approve the single national plan of socio-economic development, the state budget and the report on its execution provided the Grand National Assembly cannot meet owing to extraordinary circumstances. Moreover, in the intervals between sessions, the State Council appoints and recalls the Prime Minister, and also the members of the Council of Ministers and the Supreme Court when it is impossible to convene the Grand National Assembly due to extraordinary circumstances. The State Council also exercises the following powers between the Assembly's sessions: mandatory interpretation of laws in force; amnesty; control over the application of the laws and resolutions of the Grand National Assembly, over the work of the Council of Ministers, ministries and other central organs of state administration and the Procurator's Office; hearing of reports made by the Supreme Court and supervision of its guiding decisions; control of decisions of the People's Councils; announcement of general or partial mobilisation in an emergency and announcement of a state of war in the event of aggression against Rumania or of the need for it to fulfil its mutual defence obligations. Unlike Poland, for example, the Rumanian State Council can exercise its powers it normally exercises between sessions, also during a session of the Grand National Assembly when there is a break in the session and when the economic and social situation requires the adoption of urgent measures. The norms which have been adopted, having the force of law, are presented to the Grand National Assembly when it resumes its sessions.

There are several higher Party and state organs under the Central Committee of the Rumanian Communist Party and the State Council: the Defence Council, the Supreme Council of Socio-Economic Development, the Central Council of Workers' Control Over the Social and Economic Activities, etc.

The President of the Socialist Republic of Rumania is elected by the Grand National Assembly at its first session and for its term of powers and remains in office until a new President is elected. He is responsible for his activities to the assembly and periodically submits reports on his work and on the development of the state.

The Constitution characterises the President as the head of the state who represents state power in the Republic's internal and external relations. He is the Commander-in-Chief of the Armed Forces and the Chairman of the Defence Council. He is also the Chairman of the State Council and, if he finds it necessary, can preside in the Council of Ministers. Moreover, the President appoints and recalls deputy Prime Ministers on the Prime Minister's recommendation, and other members of the Council of Ministers who head central organs of state administration; appoints and recalls heads of central state bodies who do not belong to the government, and members of the Supreme Court; in the period between plenary meetings of the Grand National Assembly he appoints and recalls the Chairman of the Supreme Court and the Procurator-General; confers higher military ranks; confers orders and medals, awards titles of honour and permits to bear foreign awards; exercises pardon; grants citizenship, allows the restoration and denunciation of citizenship and permits permanent residence to aliens; grants the right of asylum; establishes the ranks of diplomatic representatives, receives letters of credence and recall of foreign diplomatic representatives; signs international treaties on behalf of the Socialist Republic of Rumania and may authorise a member of the Council of Ministers or a diplomatic representative to exercise this function. In the interests of the national defence and the protection of public law and order or state security, he announces martial law in an emergency in separate localities or in the country as a whole. In pursuance of his powers the President promulgates Presidential decrees and decisions.

CHAPTER XII

THE CONSTITUTIONAL FOUNDATIONS OF THE ORGANISATION AND FUNCTIONING OF THE HIGHER ORGANS OF STATE ADMINISTRATION IN THE SOCIALIST COUNTRIES

1. TITLE AND METHOD OF FORMATION OF GOVERNMENTS

The government is the higher executive and administrative organ of state power in every socialist country.[1]

The official title of the government varies in the different socialist countries: in the USSR (including in the Union and Autonomous republics), Albania, Bulgaria, Cuba, the German Democratic Republic and Hungary it is known as the Government, or Council of Ministers or Cabinet; in the Democratic Republic of Vietnam the term Government Council is used; in the Mongolian People's Republic, Poland and Rumania it is known as the Council of Ministers, in the Korean People's Democratic Republic as the Administration Council, in Yugoslavia as the Federal, Republican or Provincial Executive Council (in the Socialist Republic of Macedonia as the Executive Council), in Czechoslovakia as the Government (both Federal and Republican), and in the People's Republic of China as the State Council. There are

---

[1] In some constitutions the nature of the government is defined differently. Art. 77 of the Rumanian Constitution describes the government as the highest organ of state administration, Art. 71 of the Constitution of the Democratic Republic of Vietnam as the executive organ of state power and the higher organ of state administration, while Art. 107 of the Constitution of the Korean People's Democratic Republic defines it as the executive organ of higher state power. In Art. 346 of the Yugoslav Constitution, the government is defined as the executive organ of the Skupshina of the SFRY, and in Art. 19 of the Constitution of the People's Republic of China it is defined as the central people's government.

likewise differences in the method of forming governments, in their composition and in their powers. It is at the same time possible to single out common fundamental features.

In the first place, despite differences in method, the decisive role played by the supreme representative organ of state power in the formation of governments is a common feature.

In the majority of socialist countries governments are formed directly by the supreme representative body. At one of the first meetings of the first session of a newly elected supreme representative body the Head of Government announces the government's resignation. In accepting this, the representative body in plenary session appoints a new Head of Government and instructs him to submit the names of members of a new government. In the German Democratic Republic, the Chairman of the Council of Ministers is nominated by the most influential faction in the People's Chamber (it is usually the Socialist Unity Party of Germany), and in Rumania by the Central Committee of the Rumanian Communist Party and the National Council of the Front of National Unity. At a subsequent meeting the supreme representative body receives a report from the Head of Government on the composition of the new government and approves it by vote.

In some socialist countries there are important distinctive features, due to the structure of the system of higher organs of the state.

In the Democratic Republic of Vietnam, the Head of Government (Prime Minister) is nominated by the President of the Republic, but the nomination is approved by the supreme representative organ of state power—the National Assembly. This body then approves the composition of the new government recommended by the Head of Government. The President of the Republic may appoint and dismiss the Head and the entire membership of the government only on the basis of decisions of the supreme representative body.

In Czechoslovakia, the Chairman and other members of the Government are appointed by the President, who entrusts them with the direction of ministries and other central bodies of state administration. But before beginning work, the government appointed by the President must appear before the Federal Assembly, present its programme and seek the Assembly's approval. Such approval is mandatory for the appointed government to exercise its powers. The procedure in the republics is similar, except that the function of the President is fulfilled by the Presidiums of the National Councils.

In Yugoslavia, the Presidency of the SFRY nominates the Chairman of the Federal Executive Council to the Skupshina of the SFRY. The election of the Chairman and of other members of the Council on his recommendation is a matter for the Yugoslav Skupshina. The hearing of the views of the Skupshina's commission on elections and appointments is mandatory.

Within the Yugoslav Skupshina, the Chairman and members of the Federal Executive Council are elected by both chambers on the equitable basis. The resolutions on their election are sent to the President, who is responsible for the promulgation of these resolutions. In the republics and autonomous provinces, the duly authorised chambers of the Skupshinas elect the Chairmen of Executive Councils on the recommendation of Presidencies of republics and provinces; members of Executive Councils are elected on the joint recommendation of the Chairmen and of these Presidencies.

Thus, despite the distinctive features, the decisive role in the formation of higher executive and administrative bodies is played by the supreme representative bodies.

In Cuba, the Prime Minister and ministers are appointed by the President.

2. COMPOSITION AND TERM OF OFFICE

The governments of the socialist countries consist of: the Head of Government, known as the Prime Minister or Chairman of the Council of Ministers (in Czechoslovakia as Chairman of the Government, in Yugoslavia as Chairman of the Executive Council), Deputy Heads of Government (in a number of countries there are also First Deputy Heads), and members of the government. Deputy Heads of Government may fulfil only the functions of deputy, or simultaneously head a ministry or other higher organ of state administration. The members of the government as a rule include ministers and the heads of certain other higher organs of state administration dealing with particular spheres of work.

The *ex officio* inclusion of the Chairmen of the Councils of Ministers of the Union Republics in the Council of Ministers of the USSR is a distinctive feature of this body arising from the federal structure of the USSR and prompted by the desire to ensure the fullest representation of the interests of the Union republics forming the USSR. In Czechoslovakia, the Chairmen of the Governments of the Republics are appointed as Deputy Chairmen of the Federal Government. In Yugoslavia, the Federal Executive Council is made up of its Chairman, members who are elected on the basis of equitable representation of the republics and corresponding parity representation of autonomous provinces, federal secretaries and other leaders of federal administration organs and organisations.

In some socialist countries, the governments also include ministers without departmental responsibilities—ministers without portfolio. Under Art. 33 i of the Hungarian Constitution, the Hungarian Council of Ministers includes ministers of state—that is, ministers who are not responsible for particular departments. Art. 66 of the Albanian Constitution states that "the government may include ministers without portfolio". The Rumanian Council of Ministers includes Secretaries of State who are in effect the first deputies of the heads of a number of higher departmental organs of state administration. But in Hungary and in the German Democratic Republic Secretaries of State are not members of the government; some of them head organs directly subordinate to the Council of Ministers.

The following are members of the Rumanian Government with ministerial powers: the Chairman of the Central Council of the General Union of Trade Unions, the Chairman of the National Union of Agricultural Producer Co-operatives, the Chairman of the National Women's Council and the First Secretary of the Central Committee of the Communist Youth League.

In Bulgaria, the Council of Ministers includes, *inter alia*, the Chairmen of state-mass bodies: the Committee on Art and Culture and the Committee on Science, Technological Progress and Higher Education. These committees are elected at periodical congresses of those working in the fields concerned.

In some socialist countries a smaller collegiate body is formed within the government, usually consisting of the Head of Government, his Deputies and some other members. This is the Presidium of the Council of Ministers in the USSR (in Union and Autonomous republics—the Presidium or Bureau of the Council of Ministers) and in the German Democratic Republic, the Standing Committee of the Administration Council in the Korean People's Democratic Republic, the Presidium of the Government in Poland, the Executive Bureau of the Council of Ministers in Rumania, the Presidium of the Czechoslovak Government and the Presidiums of the Governments of the Czech and Slovak Socialist Republics in Czechoslovakia and the Executive Committee of the Cabinet of Ministers in Cuba. These bodies are responsible for the operative consideration and settlement of current issues in the light of the laws, decrees and other acts of the government.

Governments are normally elected for the full term of office of a supreme representative body and exercise their powers until the formation of a new government by a newly elected representative body.

The Communist and Workers' parties of the socialist countries stress the need for the renewal of the membership of leading government bodies, while at the same time maintaining the principle of continuity. The Yugoslav Constitution establishes this principle with respect to members of the Federal Executive Council. In principle the members of the Council may serve only two four-year terms in succession. Only in exceptional circumstances may the Skupshina of the SFRY re-elect members, and then only for one additional term. The Chairman of the Council may on no account be elected more than twice running.

3. POWERS AND PROCEDURE

As a higher executive and administrative organ of state power, a government is a body with *general powers*—that is, it is responsible for general questions of state administration, and not for particular branches. The constitutions of the socialist countries define the powers of governments in accordance with this.

The *basic powers* of the governments of the socialist countries are:

1. To ensure the fulfilment of laws and other acts (including the national economic plan and state budget) adopted by supreme representative bodies, and also of decrees or decisions of higher organs of state power. In stressing the role of governments in this respect, the constitutions of a number of socialist countries (e.g. Yugoslavia and the Democratic Republic of Vietnam) describe the government as the "executive organ" of the supreme representative body.

Under the terms of the responsibility placed upon governments for the fulfilment of the decisions of the supreme representative body, their powers include the preparation of reports regarding the implementation of the most important of these decisions. Governments draw up and submit reports on the fulfilment of the state budget and, in the case of some countries (e.g. Bulgaria and Poland) the national economic plan, to the supreme representative bodies.

2. The co-ordination and general leadership (or guidance) of higher organs of state administration (ministries, com-

mittees, commissions, secretariats); the establishment of central organs of state administration, whose formation does not lie within the terms of reference of the supreme representative body; the approval of measures defining the fundamental principles governing the internal structure of higher organs of state administration responsible for particular fields of work, and the rescission of measures taken by such bodies if they are at variance with the constitutions, laws, decrees and ordinances of the government.

3. The right to initiate legislation. A government which, together with other bodies, has the right to initiate legislation may submit draft laws on any matter to the supreme representative body. The drafting and submission of draft legislation relating to the plan and budget lie within the exclusive competence of the government. This is because the government, exercising general leadership of all fields of state administration, is the only body really able to draw up scientifically based drafts of such acts.

4. The adoption of measures to ensure public order, the defence of the national interest and the protection of the rights of the citizen.

5. General leadership in the field of relations with other states, and the conclusion of international agreements.

6. General leadership of the Armed Forces and the determination of the number of citizens to be called up each year for military service.

7. General leadership and guidance of local bodies of state administration with general powers; the repeal of the measures of such bodies of republican subordination which are at variance with the laws, decrees and ordinances of the government, or inexpedient.[1]

8. The appointment of a number of senior officials in administrative bodies.

9. The suspension of measures of local organs of state

---

[1] The distinctive features of the legal status of local administrative bodies in Yugoslavia are discussed in Chapter XIII (6).

power of republican subordination which are contrary to the law or inexpedient.

The governments of the socialist countries issue ordinances and instructions. These are issued on the basis of, and in fulfilment of, the laws and other acts of the supreme representative bodies, and also of the decrees and decisions of higher collegiate organs of state power.

The governments and Central Committees of the Communist or Workers' parties adopt joint decisions on matters which require particular activity by Party bodies and organisations as well as action by administrative bodies.

In some socialist countries the powers of governments have distinctive features. Without going into detail, some of them should be noted.

In Yugoslavia, the distinctive features of the powers of the Federal Executive Council arise both from the special character of its relationship with higher departmental organs of state administration and from the federal structure of the country.

The most substantial distinctive feature is to be seen in the case of the powers of the Cuban Government, which is not only a higher executive and administrative organ of state power, but also a legislative body. In addition to carrying out the usual tasks of a higher organ of general state administration, it also exercises powers which in other countries lie within the terms of reference of higher organs of state power.

These distinctive powers include the adoption of laws. "Legislative authority," states Art. 119 of the Fundamental Law of the Republic of Cuba, "shall be exercised by the Cabinet." Laws adopted by the Cabinet are passed to the President, who approves and promulgates them within ten days of their adoption by the Cabinet, or refers them back with appropriate observations. If the Cabinet, after discussing for the second time a draft referred back by the President adopts it by a majority of at least two-thirds, the draft becomes law.

The powers of the Cuban Cabinet also include: the approval of international treaties concluded by the President; the approval of heads of permanent diplomatic missions and other officials appointed by the President; the declaration of war and the approval of peace treaties concluded by the President; the right of amnesty.

Powers of direction and control over the work of local representative bodies are a distinctive feature of the terms of reference of the Hungarian Council of Ministers and also of the Governments of the Czech and Slovak Socialist Republics.

The governments of the socialist countries function on a collegiate basis. Decisions are taken by a majority of votes of those present, while meetings are usually considered quorate when more than half the members of the government are present.

The Head of Government directs its work and presides at its meetings.

In socialist countries where the system of higher state organs includes a President (Chairman), the President may convene meetings of the government. If he attends such a meeting, he and not the Head of Government presides.

4. HIGHER DEPARTMENTAL ORGANS OF STATE ADMINISTRATION

In the socialist countries other than the Soviet Union, the higher departmental organs of state administration are ministries and other central bodies (committees, commissions, secretariats) the heads of which are members of the government.

The majority of Soviet authors consider ministries and bodies equated with them to be not higher, but central organs of state administration.

Both a government as a whole and each ministry may be termed central organs of state administration in the sense that their functions are nationwide. But it would seem to be incorrect to consider only a government as a higher organ of state power, while ministries and similar bodies are seen only as central and not higher organs of state administration. Directorates (Chief Directorates and other bodies) attached either to the government or to particular ministries are likewise central departmental organs of state administration. Such bodies have a legal status different from that of ministries and bodies equated with them. Their heads are not members of the government, while the bodies themselves are subordinate not to the government as a whole, but directly to its Chairman or to the appropriate ministries.

The characterisation of ministries as central rather than higher organs of state administration does not reflect the important distinction between the legal status of administrative bodies responsible for particular fields of work whose leaders are members of the government, and other central organs of state administration which are subordinate to them or to the Head of Government.

Therefore, it is more appropriate to describe ministries and other departmental organs of state administration whose leaders are members of the government as *departmental higher organs of state administration*. Such a definition more correctly reflects the real role of these bodies with respect to the administration of particular fields of work. It is here appropriate to recall remarks made by Leonid Brezhnev, General Secretary of the Central Committee of the CPSU, at its September 1965 plenary meeting: "In order to successfully carry out the tasks which have been set, ministries must have *supreme authority in their sphere of work*, and be genuinely governmental bodies." (Italics mine—A.M.)[1] "Higher Organs of State Administration" is how Chapter IV of the Polish Constitution is headed. It refers to the Council of Ministers, ministries and other bodies as "exercising the functions of higher organs of state administration" (Art. 31).

---

[1] *Pravda,* September 30, 1965.

As a rule, higher departmental organs of state administration in the socialist countries take the form of ministries. In the Socialist Federal Republic of Yugoslavia they take the form of Secretariats.

The inclusion in the system of higher organs of state administration of a special planning body, the head of which is a member of the government, is a distinctive feature of a socialist state. This takes the form of a commission or committee responsible for economic planning.

In a number of socialist countries there are other committees and commissions which, like ministries, are higher departmental organs of state administration.

Ministers and the heads of other higher departmental organs of state administration direct their branches and are responsible for the work of their departments. They issue orders, instructions and other measures which may be rescinded by the government.

A Minister is the individual leader of his ministry and is personally responsible for its work. The combination of personal and collegiate responsibility finds expression in the ministry's standing consultative body—its collegium. In addition to the Minister, who is its chairman, this includes his deputies and other senior officials of the ministry and of establishments and organisations under its control. It also includes leading experts appointed by the government or the Head of Government on the recommendation of the Minister. The collegium discusses the fundamental problems of the work of the ministry. Decisions of the collegium approved by the Minister form the basis for his orders and instructions.

The directing bodies acquired a special status in Rumanian ministries under the terms of the decree on the collective leadership of ministries and other central organs of state administration adopted on February 27, 1973.[1] Under Art. 2 of this law, the directing council leads the work of the ministry and has powers to resolve general questions. A special procedure is laid down in the event of disagreement between

---

[1] See *Buletinul oficial al RSR*, I, No. 22, 1973.

the Minister and the majority of members of the directing council. In such a situation the final decision is in the hands of the Executive Bureau of the Council of Ministers. This act does not apply to the Ministries of the Armed Forces and Internal Affairs, and to the Council of State Security.

5. RESPONSIBILITY AND ACCOUNTABILITY TO SUPREME ORGANS OF POPULAR REPRESENTATION

In the socialist countries governments as a whole and individual ministers are responsible and accountable to the supreme representative organs of state power or to the higher collegiate government body (in the case of the Korean People's Democratic Republic, to the Supreme People's Assembly, the President and the Central People's Committee).

The concrete forms of this responsibility and accountability differ in accordance with the distinctive features of the system of higher organs of state power of the particular country.

We have already discussed the varied means by which the supreme organs of popular representation exercise systematic control over the higher organs of state administration.[1]

In the majority of socialist countries the government as a whole or individual members may be dismissed at any time by the supreme representative organ of state power itself.

Under the Constitution of the Democratic Republic of Vietnam, the supreme organ of popular representation (the National Assembly) adopts decisions on the dismissal of the Head of the Government or individual members. The actual dismissal is implemented by the President of the Republic on the basis of such a decision.

In Czechoslovakia, the Federal Assembly in its decisions expresses its attitude to statements and reports by the government, and may call upon the President to dismiss either the government as a whole or individual members.

---

[1] See Chapter X (Section 5).

CHAPTER XIII

THE LOCAL ORGANS OF STATE POWER OF THE SOCIALIST COUNTRIES

1. THE ADMINISTRATIVE-TERRITORIAL DIVISION AND THE SYSTEM OF LOCAL ORGANS OF STATE POWER

The system of local organs of state power is based on the administrative-territorial division, which is determined by the nature of state power and is of great importance in exercising it.

The old administrative-territorial structure bequeathed by the bourgeois-landowner regime could not therefore be retained unchanged.

As new advances were made in the building of socialism, the administrative-territorial division of the socialist countries underwent great changes. Account was taken of the economic and other specific features of each locality in order to ensure the most favourable conditions for its economic, social and cultural development. Particular efforts were made to ensure that the changes made helped to reinforce the links between the local organs of state power and the mass of the working people and between these bodies and production. Changes were therefore usually preceded by an inquiry into the point of view of the local government bodies and population concerned.

In accordance with these principles, territorial-administrative divisions were revised at various stages.

At present, three-tier, two-tier and single-tier systems of territorial-administrative division have evolved in the socialist countries.

A three-tier system exists in several Union republics forming part of the USSR (the RSFSR, the Ukraine, Byelorussia, Uzbekistan, etc.), in the Czech and Slovak Socialist Republics forming the Czechoslovak Federation, in Hungary, the German Democratic Republic, Poland, the Democratic Republic of Vietnam, Cuba and Albania.

In the USSR, Czechoslovakia and Hungary the highest tier is the region, in the German Democratic Republic the district *(Bezirk)*, in Poland the *voivodship*, in the Democratic Republic of Vietnam and Cuba the province and in Albania the district. Capital cities and sometimes other large towns are also usually equated with this tier.

The middle tier is known as districts in the USSR, the German Democratic Republic, Czechoslovakia and Cuba, counties in Poland, Hungary and the Democratic Republic of Vietnam, and as localities and associations of villages in Albania. Medium-sized towns and sometimes wards in major cities are also equated with this level.

In the USSR, the lowest tier is the village Soviet,[1] settlement or town, in the German Democratic Republic and Poland the town or commune,[2] in Hungary, Czechoslovakia and the Democratic Republic of Vietnam the town, village or settlement, in Cuba the municipality and in Albania the village. Urban wards are usually equated to this tier.

In some of the Union republics forming part of the USSR and in the Autonomous republics, as well as in Bulgaria, Albania, Rumania, the Korean People's Democratic Republic and the Mongolian People's Republic there is a two-tier system of administrative-territorial division: the highest link in these Union and Autonomous republics is the district, in Bulgaria the district, in Rumania the county, in the Korean

---

[1] As distinct from the village Soviet as a representative organ of state power, we here refer to the village Soviet as the lowest administrative-territorial unit in a rural area. Such a unit frequently includes several rural populated areas.

[2] In Poland communes may be joined with small towns into single territorial units. In the German Democratic Republic communes may by mutual agreement and with the approval of superior bodies form unions of communes, which may also include small towns.

People's Democratic Republic the province and central town and in the Mongolian People's Republic the *aimak* (district) and town. The lower tier in the USSR is the village Soviet, settlement or town of district subordination, in Bulgaria the commune, in Rumania the commune, town or municipality (large town), in the Korean People's Democratic Republic the district and town and in the Mongolian People's Republic the *somon*. In the socialist republics making up the Yugoslav Federation and in the autonomous provinces there are at present only communes and also large towns which include several communes[1]. Communes in Yugoslavia are in practice divided into so-called local communities.

In this group of countries the larger towns are likewise singled out from the corresponding administrative-territorial units and are directly subordinated to republican bodies. The largest towns (in some cases only the capital cities) are divided into wards (in Yugoslavia—communes, in Rumania—sections and in the Mongolian People's Republic—*khorons*).

A distinctive feature of the state law of the German Democratic Republic, Cuba and Yugoslavia is the fact that the fundamental laws and other normative acts of these countries lay down not only the rights of the local bodies which exercise power and administer the appropriate territorial units, but also the legal status of the territorial units themselves. Furthermore, these units are seen not merely as tiers in the territorial structure, but also as specific elements in the social and political organisation of the country.

In accordance with Art. 41 of the Constitution of the German Democratic Republic, towns, communes and unions of communes[2] are independent collectives within the frame-

---

[1] The regional associations of communes are now in the making.

[2] Lawyers of the German Democratic Republic make the point that the union of communes is a form of all-embracing co-operation of communes and towns rather than a special level of administration which holds an intermediate position between commune and district. See D. Hösel, J. Misselwitz, "Aufgaben, Rechte und Pflichten der Organen der Staatsmacht in Gemeindeverband" (*Staat und Recht*, No. 10, 1974, pp. 1664-65).

work of the system of central direction and planning under the protection of the Constitution. Any intervention in the sphere of their authority is permissible only on the basis of the law.

In accordance with Art. 187 of the Cuban Fundamental Law, "the municipality shall be an organisation of local society created for political purposes on behalf of the legislative authority in a particular area". The Yugoslav Constitution defines a commune as the "basic social-political community" (Art. 116). It also lays down that the rights and duties of the commune are defined by the Constitution and by rules adopted by the commune itself. Commune statutes were adopted after the adoption of the Yugoslav Constitution and the holding of elections. The rules of a commune within the framework of the Constitution define the rights and duties of the commune and the manner in which they are exercised; the procedure of social planning and financing requirements; the procedure of concluding and amending self-managing and social agreements; the status of self-managing associations of interest; the forms of direct democracy; the status of local communities; the protection of self-managing rights and public property; the role of socio-political organisations and associations; the organisation, rights, duties and terms of reference of the commune Skupshina and other organs.

Representative organs of state power function in all the territorial units referred to. In Hungary, representative organs have not been created in the counties; there are instead county administrations which are organs of the regional Executive Committee. The same is the case in the wards of so-called regional towns, where the ward administrations are organs of the Executive Committee of the town Council. Elective organs of self-administration operate in local communities in Yugoslavia.

The constitutions of the socialist countries give different titles to local representative organs of power. In the USSR they are Soviets of Working People's Deputies, in Bulgaria,

Albania, Rumania and the Democratic Republic of Vietnam —People's Councils, in Hungary—Councils, in the Korean People's Democratic Republic—People's Assemblies, in the Mongolian People's Republic—Khurals of People's Deputies, in Poland—National Councils, in Czechoslovakia—National Committees and in Yugoslavia Commune (City) Skupshinas.[1] In the German Democratic Republic they are known as local people's representative bodies, a collective term which includes regional and district, urban and ward assemblies and communal representative bodies. The Constitution of the People's Republic of China provides for the functioning of assemblies of people's representatives in local territorial units.

Despite their distinctive features, representative organs of a socialist type have common basic characteristics.

They combine features of state organs and mass organisations and are organs of public self-administration. As they become more firmly established, the social principles begin to play an increasing role, and their function as organs of public self-administration becomes more pronounced. This is reflected in the new constitutions and legislation of a number of socialist countries. The Czechoslovak Constitution (Art. 86 i) declares that "the National Committees—the broadest organisations of the working people—shall be organisations of state power and administration". Under the new, 1971 Bulgarian Constitution (Art. 110) the People's Councils are local "organs of state power and public self-administration".

Article 132 of the Yugoslav Constitution declares that "the Skupshina shall be the organ of public self-management and the supreme organ of power within the framework of the rights and duties of the socio-political community".

The Communist and Workers' parties of the majority of socialist countries are pursuing a policy of further enhanc-

---

[1] In some socialist republics forming part of the Yugoslav Federation, different titles are used: *Sobors* in Croatia, *Sobranies* in Macedonia, etc.

ing the role of the local organs of popular representation and of the further development of the democratic and social principles in their work.

2. THE REPRESENTATIVE CHARACTER OF LOCAL ORGANS OF STATE POWER AND THE LEGAL STATUS OF THEIR MEMBERS

The representative character of the local organs of state power in the socialist countries is determined by the fact that they are wholly elected by the people on the basis of a genuinely democratic electoral system. Tens and hundreds of thousands of citizens are elected to these bodies. For instance, the Soviets of Working People's Deputies elected in the USSR in June 1973 had 2,193,195 members; the People's Councils elected on March 9, 1975 in Rumania had 51,441 members, while the National Councils elected in Poland on December 9, 1973 had 135,454 members. The democratic method by which they are formed ensures their genuinely popular composition. Their members include workers, working peasants, representatives of the working intelligentsia and other strata of the working people. The figures relating to the proportion of the various groups of the working people in the local representative bodies in each socialist country show that in many countries the peasantry constitute the largest group among the deputies (members, delegates) of these organs. This is because the members of commune (rural) representative bodies constitute the largest single category.

But in the superior local organs of state power representatives of the working class and intelligentsia predominate. The same is true of urban representative bodies.

If account is taken of the guiding role which superior bodies play in relation to lower, it will be seen that this social composition ensures the leading role of the working class in the exercise of state power.

The leading role of the Marxist-Leninist Party finds expression in the party composition of local government bodies. In the USSR, 43.9 per cent of the deputies of local Soviets are members or candidate members of the CPSU, while in Hungary and Poland almost half the deputies of local government bodies are members of the Hungarian Socialist Workers' Party and the Polish United Workers' Party.

The size of the local organs of state power is closely related to their representative character. It is at all levels determined by electoral laws or statutes, or by the laws relating to local organs of state power.

The size of each local government body is determined in accordance with the size of the area and the nature of its economy, the size of its population and the consequent amount of work to be carried out by this body. Legislation usually establishes a maximum and a minimum size for each tier. In Czechoslovakia no maximum is laid down. In the USSR there is no maximum for territorial, regional, or rural district Soviets, or for the Soviets of a number of major cities (Moscow, Leningrad, etc.).

The establishment of a minimum is aimed at ensuring the adequately collective and representative character of local government bodies, while the establishment of a maximum ensures their efficiency. In Poland National Councils of *voivodships* and of non-*voivod* towns have from 100 to 180 members, and county councils from 60 to 80 members. In Hungary, town and Budapest ward councils have 60-150 members, regional councils 70-120 and rural councils 11-100 members. In the German Democratic Republic, the Statute on Elections itself does not at present lay down any size. The limits are laid down by a special decision of the Council of State.

The constitutional establishment of a fixed term of office guarantees the representative character of the local organs of state power. In addition to recalling individual members at any time, the electors may again determine the full membership of the local organs of state power on the expiry of their terms of office as laid down by the law.

The terms of office of local government bodies vary in the different socialist countries.

In the USSR, Bulgaria, Hungary, the German Democratic Republic, the Mongolian People's Republic, Poland, Czechoslovakia, Yugoslavia and Albania uniform terms of office have been established for the local representative bodies of all administrative-territorial units. In the USSR it is two years, Bulgaria 2.5 years,[1] the Mongolian People's Republic and Albania three years, the German Democratic Republic, Poland and Yugoslavia four years and in Czechoslovakia and Hungary five years. In the Korean People's Democratic Republic, the Democratic Republic of Vietnam, Rumania and the People's Republic of China local organs of state power of various levels have different terms of office.

In the Korean People's Democratic Republic members of provincial and central urban representative bodies are elected for four years, while members of other bodies are elected for two years. In the Democratic Republic of Vietnam, the People's Councils of provinces, autonomous regions and central towns are elected for three years; the remainder are elected for two years.

In Rumania, county and municipal (in the capital) People's Councils are elected for five years and all lower councils for 2.5 years. The 1975 Constitution of the People's Republic of China establishes the term of office of Assemblies of people's representatives of provinces and central towns at five years, of regions, towns and districts at three years, and of rural people's communes and settlements at two years.

In all the socialist countries except Yugoslavia the local representative bodies are single-chamber. As is mentioned

---

[1] The 2.5-year term of office of the People's Councils was established by the 1971 Bulgarian Constitution, in order that two such terms should be equal to one term of the National Assembly.

above, in Yugoslavia communal Skupshinas have three chambers: the Chamber of Associated Labour representing labour associations, the Chamber of Local Communities representing territorial associations, and the Socio-Political Chamber representing citizens united in socio-political organisations.

The legal status of the deputies (members, delegates) of the local organs of state power in the socialist countries is determined by their representative character.

The majority of laws relating to local government bodies currently operative in the socialist countries contain special chapters dealing with the rights and duties of deputies. This on the one hand helps to enhance the authority of the representatives of the people, and on the other increases their responsibility for the fulfilment of their obligations.

The legislation of the socialist countries places the following responsibilities upon deputies (members, delegates) of local government bodies:

a) participation in sessions and in the work of commissions to which they are elected, and also the fulfilment of other duties assigned to them by the representative body of which they are members; the maintenance of permanent contacts with their constituents, concern for the highest possible satisfaction of their needs, the reception of their proposals and criticisms and their referral to the appropriate bodies, and control of action taken in relation to them;

b) the explanation to their constituents of the main purposes and policies of people's rule, the involvement of their constituents in the implementation of the decisions of local organs of state power, of their administrative and executive bodies and also of superior bodies;

c) co-operation with local mass working people's organisations;

d) presenting reports to their constituents on their own work, on the work of the representative body of which they are members, and on the work of its executive bodies.

As representatives of the people, the members of local government bodies have extensive rights: they may submit proposals to representative bodies and their executive and administrative organs regarding the consideration of matters arising in the course of their work; they may submit questions to executive and administrative bodies; they may receive time off from their main jobs to be able to perform their duties as members.

The degree of detail in legislation relating to the rights and duties of members of local government bodies varies in different socialist countries. For example, in establishing the member's duty to maintain close contacts with his constituents and to report to them, the legislation of some socialist countries also lays down that they shall regularly be available to receive individual constituents (the USSR, the German Democratic Republic), and lays down a minimum number of annual report-back meetings (at least two per year in the USSR, at least one per year in the German Democratic Republic and Hungary). But despite these differences, the rights and duties of members of local government bodies are in the main similar in the socialist countries.

3. THE POWERS OF LOCAL ORGANS OF STATE POWER

The powers of local government bodies are determined by their status in the system of organs of the socialist state and by the tasks which confront them.

Local government bodies direct state, economic, social and cultural development within their powers and within their own territorial areas. They:

a) participate in the drawing up of the national economic plan and budget, adopt, within their framework, a local plan and budget and ensure that they are carried out;

b) take steps to expand local industry and producer cooperation, paying particular attention to the discovery and development of local reserves and resources;

c) assist the expansion of agricultural output, especially

through the strengthening of producer co-operatives and state farms;

d) develop and strengthen state and co-operative trade;

e) direct urban and rural construction, particularly as regards housing and the laying and maintenance of roads;

f) organise cultural and educational work, build schools, encourage the work of cultural and other bodies and the development of physical culture and sport;

g) ensure the observance of socialist legality, the protection of socialist property and of the rights and lawful interests of the citizens and the maintenance of public order.

Concern for the day-to-day needs of the local population and for the satisfaction of the constantly growing material and cultural requirements of the working people is in the forefront of the attention of local organs of state power.

The role of local organs of state power as regards the control of economic, social and cultural development *has increased substantially* in many socialist countries in recent years.

In the last few years alone, the Central Committee of the CPSU has adopted special decisions designed to enhance the role of the local Soviets at all levels. In March 1967 it adopted a resolution on the improvement of the work of rural and settlement Soviets of Working People's Deputies, and in March 1971 approved measures on the further improvement of the work of district and urban Soviets. In accordance with these decisions, legislation governing the organisation and functioning of the Soviets is being improved. So, too, is the work of these bodies. On April 8, 1968 the Presidium of the Supreme Soviet of the USSR adopted a decree on the fundamental rights and duties of rural and settlement Soviets,[1] and instructed the Presidiums of the Supreme Soviets of the Union Republics to bring their legislation into line with it. Laws on rural and settlement Soviets were adopted in all the Union Republics during the same

---

[1] See *Vedomosti Verkhovnogo Sovieta SSSR* No. 16, 1968, Item 131.

year. On March 19, 1971 the Presidium of the Supreme Soviet of the USSR adopted decrees on the fundamental rights and duties of district Soviets[1] and of urban and ward Soviets[2]. Laws on district, urban and ward Soviets were adopted by the Union Republics during the same year. These measures greatly enhanced the role of rural, urban and ward Soviets with respect to economic, social and cultural development. Many enterprises and organisations were placed under their control. In particular, a number of undertakings hitherto under the control of regional and territorial bodies and which catered mainly for the population of a particular town or district were placed under the control of district and urban Soviets.

Similar processes may be observed in other socialist countries. In Poland in 1956 local budgets accounted for 15.9 per cent of the national budget, while their own revenues accounted for only 14.7 per cent of the total incomes of local budgets. As a result of measures to extend the powers of local government bodies in 1973 the Polish National Councils handled 31.7 per cent of the entire national budget, while their own revenues accounted for more than one-third of the total income of local budgets.

In addition to *the transference of many enterprises and other economic organisations to the direct control* of local government bodies, the *opportunities for these bodies to influence the work of enterprises of central subordination have been increased*. In particular, in the USSR rural and urban Soviets co-ordinate and control the work of all enterprises, establishments and organisations in their areas dealing with housing, construction of communal, social, cultural and services facilities, the production of consumer goods and local building materials, the drawing up and implementation of improvement schemes, trade and public catering, education, health, culture and other spheres providing for the needs of

---

[1] See *Vedomosti Verkhovnogo Sovieta SSSR* No. 12, 1971, Item 132.
[2] Ibid., Item 133.

the public in the district (town); within the limits of their powers, they supervise the activities of factories and economic organisations which are not under their direct control and ensure that they observe the law.

District and urban Soviets receive reports from the heads of these enterprises on these matters and take decisions, submitting their proposals to superior organs in case of need.

The Rumanian law of December 26, 1968 on the organisation and work of the People's Councils[1] gave the Councils powers to supervise the observance by enterprises and economic organisations under central control of the decisions of People's Councils and instructions of Executive Committees issued within their terms of reference.

In Bulgaria, district People's Councils assist and control within their terms of reference the work of establishments, enterprises and organisations under central control which are located in their area, and are authorised to receive reports from their managers, to make recommendations and, in case of need, to raise matters before superior bodies. The district People's Councils have the right to submit recommendations to the State Planning Committee and other central bodies regarding draft plans for the building of centrally-controlled enterprises in their areas.

Under the 1971 Hungarian law on Councils, councils have the right to supervise the observance of educational, health, social security and labour legislation in organisations not subject to their direct control and to call for reports on these matters; they have the right to demand that these organisations submit reports and information regarding their work relating to the satisfaction of the needs of the public, and to supervise this work; they also have the right to call upon these bodies to eradicate shortcomings. The councils co-ordinate work with organisations not subject to their direct control, and the work of organisations existing or being set up in their areas with respect to the development of new

---

[1] See *Buletinul Oficial al RSR*, I, No. 168, 1968.

centres of population and public services. In the event of substantial changes relating to the establishment or work of undertakings and other organisations which serve the public and are not subject to the council's control, such bodies are obliged to seek the opinion of the Council or its Executive Committee.

The *financial basis* of local government bodies has been *greatly extended and reinforced* by making new sources of revenue available to them.

This has been done by transferring to local budgets the incomes from enterprises and other economic organisations hitherto under central control and now placed under the control of the local authorities; by allocations from the incomes of enterprises and organisations which remain under central control; by allocations from certain national taxes; and by the designation of certain taxes as local taxes.

The March 1971 decision of the Council of Ministers of the USSR on measures to strengthen the financial basis of the Executive Committees of district and town Soviets[1] instructed the Councils of Ministers of the Union Republics to resolve questions relating to the additional transference to these Soviets of a number of enterprises and economic organisations, the leaving of additional sums accumulated during the fulfilment of their budgets at the disposal of the Soviets, the transference to the budgets of towns and districts of a part of the profits made by undertakings and economic organisations subject to the control of superior bodies and of a part of the turnover tax on consumer goods manufactured in excess of the plan in these enterprises, etc.

The fact that the expenditure of local budgets is covered mainly from the own incomes of the local government bodies enhances their independence and is an important stimulant for their activities. When most of their expenditure was covered by subsidies from the central budget the local government bodies had neither the conditions for nor an interest

---

[1] See *SP SSSR* No. 5, 1971, Item 37.

in the development of vigorous economic activity. The situation is different today, when the larger portion of the incomes of local budget depends directly upon the results of the work of the local bodies.

With a view to strengthening the initiative and material interest of local government bodies in the achievement of the best possible economic results, new legislation in the socialist countries lays down that if these bodies receive incomes larger than those envisaged in their budgets, they may themselves decide how the surpluses may be used for local needs.

The increased independence of local government bodies with respect to the spending of their own resources is a factor of great importance in encouraging the activity of local organs of state power and administration. The Czechoslovak law of June 29, 1967 gave the National Committees far-reaching powers in this respect. All the resources of the National Committees, except for sums received from the republican budget for major lump-sum investments (for example, for the building of a school or hospital), including receipts as subsidies from the centre, are used at their own discretion. The former procedure by which the centre allocated sums under particular heads has been abolished. The new law also authorised National Committees to use bank credits for terms of up to five years. These credits are used mainly for development of local industries and other undertakings catering for the public needs.

Changes in planning procedure with respect to the enterprises under their control are encouraging the initiative of local government bodies. The number of compulsory plan indices which they receive from the centre has been reduced.

The extension of the powers of local government bodies in the sphere of planning *does not weaken, but on the contrary reinforces single national planning*, because the reduction in the number of mandatory planning indices enables the local government bodies to take account of local conditions and possibilities and in this way organise the fulfilment of the national plan in a more satisfactory manner.

The extension of the powers and functions of the local government bodies in the socialist countries in no way diminishes the economic, organisational, cultural and educational functions of the higher organs of the socialist state, but on the contrary reinforces them, because centralised planning, financing and accounting are harmoniously combined with extensive opportunities for local bodies to work in a manner appropriate to local conditions and specificities.

4. THE ORGANISATIONAL FORMS OF WORK OF LOCAL ORGANS OF STATE POWER

In defining the powers of the local organs of state power in the socialist countries, the relevant laws enumerate not only matters which are decided directly by local representative bodies, but also matters dealt with by administrative bodies subordinate to them. This is legitimate, since all the matters dealt with by administrative bodies subordinate to local representative bodies as a rule lie within the terms of reference of the latter, and not vice versa.

Such a definition of terms of reference underlines the unity of the legislative and executive power in the socialist state. This unity is clearly manifest in the constitutions of a number of socialist countries. According to the Czechoslovak Constitution, the National Committees "shall be organs of state power and administration" (Art. 86).

Sessions of local representative bodies are their most important organisational form of work in the majority of socialist countries.

A session consists of one or more *plenary meetings*. Matters lying exclusively within the terms of reference of the representative body may be decided only during sessions.

Sessions are usually considered quorate when attended by not less (or more) than half their members (deputies or delegates). There has in recent years been a tendency to increase the figure constituting a quorum. Prior to 1958 meetings of Polish National Councils were considered quorate when one-third of the members were present,[1] whereas the January 25, 1958 Law on the National Councils raised this figure to half. The Bulgarian law of June 13, 1964 amending and supplementing the law on People's Councils laid down that in order to be quorate a meeting must be attended by at least two-thirds of the membership (hitherto the figure had been more than half). The laws on rural and settlement Soviets adopted in 1968 by all the republics of the USSR, and the laws adopted in these republics in 1971 relating to district, town and ward Soviets established quorums of at least two-thirds of the membership. Legislation now in force in the USSR, Bulgaria and Czechoslovaka lays down that the decisions of local representative bodies are adopted by a majority vote of all members (and not only of those present).

The enhancement of the role of representative bodies which has become clearly manifest over a number of recent years, found expression both in the increased regularity of their sessions and in the widening of the range of matters which may be resolved only during sessions.

In the majority of socialist countries the legislation relating to local government bodies itself lays down *matters which lie exclusively within the terms of reference* of the representative bodies—that is, the range of questions which can only be resolved during sessions.

These include the adoption of local economic plans and budgets, the approval of reports on their fulfilment, the election and recall of members of standing committees and *ad hoc* commissions and of executive and administrative organs.

The widening of the range of questions which local repre-

---

[1] Exept rural National Councils, for which the Law of September 25, 1954 on the reform of the administrative-territorial divisions in rural areas and the establishment of rural National Councils laid down a quorum of half the membership.

sentative bodies alone are competent to resolve is a characteristic feature of the evolution of the legislation in the socialist countries relating to local government. For instance, the July 29, 1971 RSFSR law on the district Soviet of Working People's Deputies lays down (Art. 36) that sessions of a Soviet may consider and take decisions on any matter lying within its terms of reference. The following matters may be discussed and decided only at sessions of district Soviets: the recognition of members' mandates, the resignation of members at their own request; the election of an Executive Committee and changes in its composition; the formation and election of standing committees and changes in their membership; reports on the work of the Executive Committee and standing committees; the formation of departments and sections of the Executive Committee, the confirmation and dismissal of their heads; approval of the structure and staffing of the Executive Committee and of its sections and departments on the basis of the norms laid down for the RSFSR and the established figures for the Executive Committee's administrative and executive personnel; the formation of the district committee of people's control, the approval of and change in its membership, and the appointment and dismissal of its chairman; the formation of administrative and supervisory commissions and of juvenile commissions of Executive Committees; the confirmation of the chairman of the district People's Court; the approval of summary long-term and annual plans for the district's economy and for social and cultural development; approval of state procurement assignments for collective farms, state farms and other agricultural enterprises; the approval of plans relating to measures to implement the electors' mandates; adoption of decisions on the deputies' inquiries; the approval of the district budget and of reports on its implementation; the approval of decisions of the Executive Committee regarding the utilisation of additional revenues received during the fulfilment of the district budget, and also of the excess of income over expenditure at the end of the year as a result of increased revenues or savings in expenditure; the consideration of district laying-out schemes and projects and their submission to the appropriate superior organs of state administration for aproval.

Par. 39 of the Czechoslovak law on the National Committees adopted on June 29, 1967 lays down that plenary meetings of the National Committees decide all the main questions of economic, cultural, public health and social development in their areas and the main questions of their work. The law places the following matters within the competence of plenary meetings of National Committees: approval of the general principles governing the long-term development of the area in question; the adoption of long-term and current plans (or short-term programmes) in economic spheres subject to the control of National Committees, and the appraisal of their fulfilment; the general appraisal of the plans and budgets of lower National Committees; the adoption of the budget and the approval of a report on its fulfilment; the establishment, winding-up or amalgamation of economic, budgetary and other bodies subject to the control or National Committees and the determination of their sphere of activity; decisions regarding changes in the administrative-territorial division in their area; the establishment of the number of members of National Committees (within limits laid down by the law), and also the determination of the number of constituencies and their boundaries; the establishment and dissolution of commissions, departments and other National Committee organs and the distribution of work between them; the election of the chairman, deputy chairman and secretary of the National Committee, other members of the council, the chairmen, secretaries and other members of National Committee commissions, and also their recall; the appointment and dismissal of heads of departments; the acceptance (or otherwise) of the resignations of members; the adoption of mandatory decisions of the National Committee; the adoption of decisions relating to the acceptance of loans or the granting of credits.

The range of questions considered at sessions is not of course confined to matters which lie within the exclusive competence of representative bodies. The inclusion of a matter within the category of those which lie exclusively within the competence of representative bodies implies that they have both the right and the duty to consider it only during sessions. But this in no way precludes the right to consider other questions during sessions. The Czechoslovak law on National Committees referred to above is characteristic in this respect. Par. 39 iii lays down that a National Committee may at its plenary meetings consider any question lying within the competence of organs of the National Committee, in addition to those enumerated in the article.

Great importance is attached to ensuring that the sessions of local organs of state power should be organised in a businesslike manner, enabling them to discuss matters thoroughly and without haste. Legislation of the socialist countries requires that deputies shall prepare themselves for sessions in good time and find out the wishes and views of the electorate on matters to be considered at meetings.

Local government legislation therefore requires that deputies shall be informed of forthcoming meetings in writing. The notification shall include the date, place and time, and also the agenda. The time, place and agenda are also made known to the general public by the means customary in the district, so that it may take part in the preparatory work. Announcements and notifications of meetings must be made not later than 3-10 days in advance.

Sessions may be either ordinary or extraordinary.

Ordinary sessions are convened within the time-limits provided for by the plan of work adopted by the representative body. Legislation lays down a *mandatory minimum* of the annual number of such sessions for local bodies at all levels.

Extraordinary sessions may be convened in case of need on the initiative of the executive-administrative body or of deputies.

To ensure full publicity, meetings must be public. Closed meetings may be held only when required by the national interest.

The chairman of a meeting may give the floor to persons invited to attend who are not deputies. This enables invited representatives of the public as well as members of the representative organ of state power to participate in the discussion.

Article 27 of the Bulgarian law on the People's Councils as amended in 1964 is characteristic in this respect. It makes reference not only to the right of citizens to attend meetings, but also to their right to take part in the discussion.

In the majority of socialist countries the powers of local representative bodies, except for a number of most important powers, are in intervals between sessions exercised by their executive and administrative organs. Special bodies— the People's Committees—have been set up for this purpose in the Korean People's Democratic Republic.

According to Art. 123 of the Constitution of the Korean People's Democratic Republic, the People's Committees are local organs of power in the intervals between sessions of the appropriate People's Assemblies. The People's Committees are elected by People's Assemblies and consist of a chairman, his deputies, a secretary and members for the term of office of the Assembly. Their powers include: convening sessions of, and conducting elections to, People's Assemblies, working with members of People's Assemblies, taking measures to carry out the decisions of People's Assemblies and superior People's Committees, directing the work of the appropriate Administration Committees, lower People's Committees, state organs, enterprises and mass co-operative organisations in their areas, repealing unwarranted decisions and instructions of Administration Committees and also of lower People's and Administration Committees, suspending the implementation of unwarranted decisions of lower People's Assemblies, and dismissing and appointing the deputy chairmen, managers and members of Administration Committees. The measures of People's Committees take the form of ordinances and instructions. People's Committees are responsible for their work to the appropriate People's Assemblies and to superior People's Committees.

The 1975 Constitution of the People's Republic of China establishes that local revolutionary committees are permanently functioning organs of local Assemblies of People's Representatives. The Constitution does not refer to the right of revolutionary committees to exercise the powers of the Assemblies, but Art. 23 makes no distinction between the powers of both types of state organs. Thus revolutionary committees are legally enabled to decide all questions at a particular level of administration. Assemblies of People's Representatives are actually non-existent and local power is exercised by revolutionary committees formed in a non-democratic way.

The 1958 Polish law on National Councils, as substantially amended in 1972-1973,[1] does not allow for the exercise of the National Councils' powers by executive and administrative organs. Standing internal directing organs—Presidiums—are now being set up in the National Councils to organise the work of these bodies. Standing Presidiums are also being formed in the People's Councils of Albania.

Standing committees play an important part in the work of the local organs of state power in the socialist countries.

In the majority of socialist countries these committees consist only of deputies of local organs of state power. In some socialist countries, however, they also include other citizens as full-fledged members. In the Lithuanian and Latvian SSRs non-deputies may be elected to the standing committees of rural and settlement Soviets. In the Estonian SSR, and also in Poland, Czechoslovakia, Bulgaria and the German Democratic Republic non-deputies may be elected to

---

[1] For the text of the law now in force see *Dziennik Ustaw RPL* No. 38, 1973, Item 226.

the standing committees of local government bodies at all levels. In Poland the number of members of a committee of a National Council who are not members of the Council may not exceed *half* the total of committee members; in Czechoslovakia the *majority* of members of each commission of a National Committee must consist of Committee members. In Bulgaria, *up to one third* of the members of the committees of People's Councils may be non-deputies. Proposals regarding the formation of standing committees in part from non-deputies (non-members) of local government bodies have been put forward in other socialist countries.[1]

The inclusion in standing committees of persons who are not deputies (members) of local representative organs of state power helps to strengthen the links between these organs and the broad mass of the working people and makes it possible to draw a large number of experts, advanced workers and public figures into the work of the committees as their members. In all socialist countries the standing committees are actively assisted by a large number of public helpers.

The standing committees are above all auxiliary bodies of local organs of state power. They are set up to deal with key spheres of activity for the full term of office of the representative body which forms them.

The committees control the work of departmental organs of administration, verify the proper implementation of the decisions and instructions of the bodies that set them up and of superior bodies, draft the most important decisions of the local organs of state power, control the work of establishments and enterprises in their area and receive and consider applications and complaints from members of the public.

The role of the standing committees has steadily increased during recent years. In addition to the power to control the work of enterprises and establishments subordinate to the appropriate representative organ of state power, they have

---

[1] See J. Beér, *A helyi tanácsok kialakulása és fejlödése Magyarozszágon (1945-1960)*, Budapest, 1962, pp. 381-82.

received the power to supervise state bodies, establishments and economic organisations in their area which are not subordinate to the local government body.

In a number of countries, the standing committees of local representative bodies have been empowered to take decisions relating to some matters, which are binding upon appropriate organs.

Many local Soviets in the USSR have authorised their standing committees to take decisions which are mandatory for the heads of departments and sections of Executive Committees, and also of establishments, enterprises and organisations subject to the local Soviets, on all matters arising from the implementation of decisions of the Soviet and its Executive Committee, except amendments to the budget and plan and the allocation of resources. The Soviets of some rural districts and small towns have wound up some departments of the Executive Committees and transferred their functions to standing committees. This experiment is still being studied and discussed.

Great experience has been accumulated by Czechoslovakia in this respect. According to the 1960 law on National Committees, their standing committees became not only initiating and controlling organs of the Committees, but also their executive organs. Practice showed, however, that to overload the committees with a large number of current administrative matters requiring prompt settlement and primarily of an organisational and technical nature, frequently pushed the consideration by them of social and political matters into the background. In resolving narrow administrative matters the committees were often in some measure dependent upon the professional administrative machine, whose officials were better equipped with the knowledge and experience necessary to settle such matters. This made it necessary to enhance the role and responsibility of the departments of National Committees as regards day-to-day administrative matters. The standing committees began to devote their main attention to their work as initiating and controlling bodies contributing to the solution of the most important long-term problems. In the light of the experience which had been accumulated, the 1967 law on National Committees introduced substantial changes in the legal status of the standing committees. They were relieved of the functions of operative administration. While exercising a controlling function, they do not interfere in the day-do-day administration of the organs and organisations concerned. The committees exercise the functions of executive organs (being empowered to issue mandatory instructions to the appropriate organs and organisations) in relation to matters which lie within the independent competence of the National Committees and which are referred to them by plenary meetings of National Committees.

Following the adoption of the law of June 13, 1964 amending and supplementing earlier legislation regarding the People's Councils in Bulgaria, the status of the standing committees of the councils also changed. They are now defined not merely as auxiliary, but as "initiating, executive and controlling organs of the People's Council". Their earlier powers were supplemented by a number of additional powers, including: the convening of conferences and meetings to discuss particular matters and the submission of appropriate proposals to the Council and its Executive Committee; the issuing within their terms of reference of mandatory instructions to the heads of departments and sections of Executive Committees, and also to the heads of enterprises, establishments and other organisations subordinate to the People's Council should the committee disclose a gross violation or failure to implement normative acts or decisions of the People's Council, its Executive Committee or superior organs of state power and administration; the submission of proposals to the People's Council regarding the repeal of unlawful and incorrect decisions and instructions of the Executive Committee, and reporting to superior organs as regards unlawful and wrong decisions and instructions of the People's Council. People's Councils may authorise their standing committees to adopt mandatory decisions regarding the work of enterprises and establishments subordinate to the People's Councils, except for questions which lie within the exclusive competence of the Councils and their Executive Committees. Councils give standing committees these rights where the necessary conditions for doing so exist, and where the committee membership is suitably competent.

The importance of the question of whether standing committees should be authorised to adopt mandatory decisions on certain matters is stressed in the legal literature of other socialist countries.[1]

In accordance with the constitutions of the socialist countries, the *collegiate executive bodies* of local representative organs are: Executive Committees in the USSR, Bulgaria, Albania, Hungary and Rumania; the Councils of the National Committees in Czechoslovakia; Councils in the German Democratic Republic; Administration Committees in the Democratic Republic of Vietnam and the Korean People's Democratic Republic; Executive Directorates in the Mongolian People's Republic; Revolutionary Committees in the People's Republic of China, and Executive Councils in Yugoslavia.

In Poland there are no longer collegiate executive and administrative bodies; their functions are performed by the commune (commune and town) and county heads, by city presidents (in major cities) and *voivods* who are appointed by superior organs of state administration, have their terms of reference, and who are executive and administrative organs of National Councils.

These bodies are executive and administrative agencies with general powers. They ensure and organise the performance of the following functions:

—drafting and implementation of the economic plan and budget;

—general leadership and co-ordination of the work of the local organs of administration—departments and director-

---

[1] See J. Beér, op. cit., pp. 381-82.

ates—and of enterprises, establishments and other organisations subject to the control of the local government body;

—co-ordination of the work of enterprises and organisations which are subject to local control with the work of those which are subject to central control;

—drawing up of measures to implement the decisions of the local representative bodies which elected them and of superior organs of state power and administration;

—discussion of proposals made by committees, deputies, departments (directorates) of lower organs of state power and administration, and adoption of appropriate measures;

—assistance to the committees of the local representative body which elected them and co-ordination of the committees' work (except Poland and Yugoslavia);

—direction and supervision of lower executive organs.[1]

The executive organs of local representative bodies are as a rule responsible and accountable to the latter and also to superior administrative organs.

The legislation of the socialist countries establishes a number of *legal guarantees* of the subordinate status of executive bodies *vis-à-vis* the local representative bodies which elect them.

These include:

1. The establishment in laws relating to local organs of state power of the exclusive competence of representative bodies regarding the most important questions of these organs' work.

2. Executive organs are required to implement the decisions (ordinances) of the representative body which elects them.

3. Executive organs are accountable to sessions of the representative bodies, in particular with respect to the implementation of the local plan and budget.

4 The deputies (members) of representative bodies have

---

[1] For the peculiarities of the relations between local organs of state administration in particular socialist countries, see Section 6 below.

the right to address inquiries to executive organs; the latter must reply within a time-limit laid down by the law.

5. The representative body has the right at any time to recall the entire membership or individual members of the executive organ elected by it.

The Executive Committees (Councils, etc.) are, as has already been noted, executive bodies with *general powers.*

Departments (directorates) are formed under the Executive Committees as local *departmental* and functional organs of state administration. These departments function on the basis of decisions (ordinances) of the corresponding local representative body and also of the Executive Committees under which they are set up.

A local representative body, and also its executive and administrative organ with general powers may rescind incorrect decisions taken by sections or departments.

In Czechoslovakia, departments are set up not under executive organs, but under the representative bodies themselves —the National Committees. Their heads are appointed and dismissed by the Committees. The work of the departments is directed by the Committees and their Councils, to which the departments are fully accountable. The status of departments, directorates and services in Bulgaria is similar.

Departments (sections, directorates, etc.) are not set up in the small, lower administrative-territorial units in the socialist countries.

5. POPULAR PARTICIPATION IN THE WORK OF LOCAL ORGANS OF POWER

The local organs of popular representation, their committees and executive-administrative organs in the socialist countries carry out their work with the active participation of the working people.

There are extremely varied forms of strengthening the links between the local organs of state and administration on the one hand and the broad mass of the working people on the other, and the means by which the working people of the socialist countries are drawn into direct participation in the work of these bodies.

In the first instance, the *ascertainment, recording and implementation of the wishes and demands of the electors* by the local organs of state power and administration are of great importance.

At the first sessions of many newly-elected local representative bodies reports are made regarding wishes and comments expressed by electors during the electoral campaign and measures are planned with a view to implementing them.

The recording and classification of electors' proposals, and also the supervision of their implementation are of great importance in this respect. This supervision is carried out both with the aid of the standing committees and also by periodic consideration at sessions of the practical implementation of electors' suggestions. In some socialist countries, legislation requires that local government bodies shall consider these matters at their sessions. The Polish law on National Councils lays down that the Councils shall at their sessions periodically consider the progress being made in implementing the proposals and satisfying the demands of electors.

In some socialist countries (e.g. Bulgaria) the law requires that local government bodies shall periodically report to the electorate on their work.

During recent years socialist legislation has made increasing provision for the direct participation of electors in the accomplishment of tasks facing local government bodies and the population of the apropriate territorial units. The Polish law of February 25, 1964 on the promulgation of legal regulations by National Councils lays down that draft regulations which are of fundamental importance may be submitted for public discussion. In accordance with the Bulgarian law of June 13, 1964 amending and supplementing the law on the People's Councils, communal People's Councils, when taking decisions on major local matters, must first submit them for discussion by the electorate. Under Art. 117 of the Bulgarian Constitution, People's Councils, when deciding important questions lying within their terms of reference which affect the interests of the population of the appropriate administrative-territorial unit or inhabited area, may hold a referendum.

Field sessions or meetings of representative organs of state power held in factories, agricultural producer co-operatives and communities whose affairs are under discussion are an important direct link between local government bodies and the working people in the socialist countries.

Local executive and administrative organs also hold meetings in factories and communities to decide matters relating to the particular enterprise or area.

The examination and settlement of applications and complaints from members of the public is an important means of maintaining a close link between local organs of state power and administration and the public. It is also an important means of protecting the rights and lawful interests of the citizen, and of bringing to light and eradicating shortcomings both in the work of local government bodies and of enterprises, establishments and organisations under their control. The socialist countries pay great attention to this matter. Special normative acts have been adopted envisaging the improvement of procedures for the consideration of applications, complaints and letters, and also for the reception of visitors. The executive organs of local representative bodies must establish definite days and times when members of the public will be received personally by the chairman, deputy chairmen, secretary and members of the Executive Committee in order to ensure the most convenient access for members of the public, especially the working people. In addition, the Executive Committees organise the daily reception of applications and complaints from the public. Applications and complaints are also received by committees and members of local representative bodies.

A constant growth in the number of statements and letters in which working people voice their concern regarding matters of general, national interest is a characteristic development in the socialist countries.

The *standing committees,* to which reference has already been made, are particularly important means by which local representative organs maintain contact with the working people and draw them into direct participation in their activities.

Citizens', block, village, street and house committees are a widespread organisational form of contact. They are elected at public meetings and their purpose is to help local government bodies improve everyday services and cultural facilities. To do so they rely in the first instance upon the initiative and participation of members of the public. The committees work under the leadership of the executive organs of the local representative bodies and are accountable to their electors in all aspects of their work.

Village meetings are important links between commune (rural) organs of state power and administration and the public.

They are convened to consider matters of concern to particular villages: the improvement of economic, cultural and other aspects of village life; the improvement of farm output; health services and other village amenities; proposals from villagers. Village meetings may be convened to explain government aims and policy decisions, or to organise the improvement of economic, social and other amenities by mass voluntary work and contributions.

Village meetings are also convened to hear reports on the work of commune (rural) organs of state power and of their members, and on the work of executive and administrative organs.

In Rumania, meetings of inhabitants, termed popular assemblies, are held not only in villages but also in towns. They are convened by the Executive Committees of People's Councils on a block and residential area basis.

In Yugoslavia, the inhabitants of rural and urban areas making up a commune play a direct part in self-management within the framework of the local community. A general meeting of all the electors of a particular area is the organ of the local community. This meeting decides matters bearing on the satisfaction of the cultural and everyday life requirements of the working people. The powers of the local community are defined in detail by the rules of the commune.

Mass voluntary work is a means by which the working people are drawn into the fulfilment of the tasks confronting the local organs of state power and administration with respect to the satisfaction of the economic, cultural and everyday life requirements of the public. Members of the public, on their own initiative and without payment, work to improve amenities, build schools, clubs, medical centres, roads, bridges etc., in the area where they live. The state helps with material, plant, design work, etc. The working people themselves frequently raise money to cover part of the cost of amenities for their area.

Mainly local building materials are used, which leads to substantial economies, enabling the local authority to do much more work for the same expenditure.

New forms of closer contact with the public are developing in the course of such practical activity.

The social principles have in recent years become more widespread. In many Executive Committees of local representative bodies in lower administrative-territorial units the members, and in some cases the chairmen, work on a social basis. The role of the standing committees, as has already been noted, is increasing. Other forms of public participation in the work of local government bodies and their executive and administrative organs are also developing. In the USSR and Bulgaria, for example, there are many non-staff departments of Executive Committees, social councils attached to the Committees' departments and directorates, and groups of workers and inspectors who are not on the staff numbering tens of thousands.

6. THE DIRECTION, CONTROL AND SUPERVISION OF THE WORK OF LOCAL ORGANS OF POWER AND ADMINISTRATION

Each local representative organ of state power not only represents the population of the area which elected it, but is also a *link in the integrated system* of representative organs of state power of the republic in question. Each local administrative organ is not only the executive organ of a particular representative body, but is similarly also a *link in the integrated system* of organs of state administration.

Superior organs of state power and administration in the socialist countries are therefore invested with certain powers with respect to the direction, co-ordination, control and supervision of the work of lower organs.

In line with the status of local representative bodies and their executive and administrative organs in the system of organs of the socialist state, the legislation of the socialist countries clearly defines the system of control over their work.

Control over local representative organs of state power is in principle exercised only by superior organs of state power.

Control over collegiate executive and administrative organs is exercised by superior collegiate executive and administrative organs.

Control over departmental and functional organs of state administration is exercised by superior departmental and functional organs of state administration.

There are some exceptions to these general principles, which will be considered below.

Higher control over local representative bodies is exercised in the main by the higher collegiate organ of state power of the republic—by the Presidium of the Supreme Soviet in the USSR, the Council of State in Bulgaria, the German Democratic Republic, Poland, Rumania, etc.

The higher collegiate organ of state power among other things considers reports from regional representative organs of state power and organs equated with them and from some lower representative bodies regarding their work and also issues appropriate instructions; it takes steps to publicise experience gained by local government bodies; it rescinds decisions of regional and similar local bodies if they are at variance with the law or national policies, and may on the same grounds rescind decisions of lower local organs of state power. In addition, the constitutions and legislation of several socialist countries (the Democratic Republic of Vietnam, Hungary, Poland) give higher collegiate organs of state power the authority to dissolve a local government body which systematically violates the law, departs from the main lines of national policy, or causes serious harm to the national interest.

Supreme representative bodies also exercise direct leadership of the work of local representative bodies within certain limits.

The formation of special standing committees by supreme representative bodies is a manifestation of the increased attention being paid to this question. These include the Committee on People's Councils of the Bulgarian National Assembly, the Committee on People's Councils and State Administration of the Rumanian Grand National Assembly, the Committee on National Committees, State Administration and Nationalities of the Slovak National Council and the Committee on National Committees and Nationalities of the Czech National Council.

In controlling lower organs of state power, superior local organs exercise powers similar to those of higher collegiate organs. But they do not have the right to dissolve lower organs, except in the Democratic Republic of Vietnam, where the Constitution makes provision for such action.

The government co-ordinates the work of local organs of state administration with general powers and lays down the main lines of their activity.

Superior executive and administrative organs co-ordinate the work of lower executive and administrative organs, and also lay down the main lines of their activity.

Ministers and heads of central institutions, in exercising the function of directing particular spheres of state administration, issue instructions to the corresponding local departments; they assist these departments and ensure that they are briefed to carry out their tasks, and take steps to publicise experience; they exercise control over the work of departments, and also assess their work to ensure that it accords with the law and the main lines of national policy; they rescind or amend the decisions of departments in accordance with legislative requirements.

The heads of superior departments have similar powers in relation to lower departments.

In some socialist countries the organisation of supervision over the work of local organs of state power and administration has important distinctive features.

In the Czech and Slovak Socialist Republics which form the Czechoslovak Republic, and also in Hungary the government has the right of supervision and control over the work not only of executive and administrative organs, but also of the local representative bodies themselves.

In Yugoslavia, the departmental organs of administration of the local Skupshinas are accountable only to their Skupshinas and their executive councils. Superior organs of administration exercise supervision over lower local administrative organs only in relation to matters which lie within the exclusive competence of the Federation or within the sphere of interest of the Federation and a socialist republic or province. Republican and provincial organs of power and administration retain certain powers of control in relation to local Skupshinas and their organs, within the extremely wide limits of decentralisation and independence of local organs of power and administration, in Yugoslavia. In exercising their functions of control, the organs of state power of socialist republics and provinces may rescind or annul general measures of local Skupshinas. Republican administrative organs may suspend relevant measures of local Skupshinas and transfer cases for settlement by organs of power of socialist republics. Another distinctive feature of the Yugoslav state system is the constitutional courts' control designed to ensure that all acts adopted by Skupshinas are in line with the Yugoslav Constitution, republican and provincial constitutions and legislation. This is a specific form assumed by a measure of centralisation in conditions of the far-reaching local self-management in Yugoslavia.

Hence, while there are certain distinctive features, which are at times very important, as regards the structure of the system of local representative organs of power and their executive and administrative bodies in the various socialist countries, there is a measure of uniformity in all these countries. On the one hand, the degree of independence necessary for the development of local activity and initiative, and for the consideration of local circumstances is guaranteed by the constitution and legislation of each country and is assured in practice; on the other hand, the centralisation necessary for the uniformity of the economic and state organisation of each country is likewise assured.

REQUEST TO READERS

Progress Publishers would be glad to have your opinion of this book, its translation and design, and any suggestions you may have for future publications.

Please send your comments to 21, Zubovsky Boulevard, Moscow, USSR.